Vitality and Change in Warlpiri Songs

Juju-ngaliyarlu karnalu-jana pina-pina-mani kurdu-warnu-patu jujuku

Indigenous Music, Language and Performing Arts

Associate Professor Myfany Turpin, Series Editor

The many forms of Australia's Indigenous music and temporal arts have ancient roots, huge diversity and global reach. The Indigenous Music, Language and Performing Arts series aims to stimulate discussion and development of the fields of Aboriginal and Torres Strait Islander music, language and performing arts, in both subject matter and approach, as well as looking beyond Australia to First Nations cultures around the world. Proposals are welcomed for studies of traditional and contemporary performing arts (including dance), popular music, art music, experimental and new media, and the importance of First Nations languages for culture and empowerment, as well as theoretical, analytical, interdisciplinary and practice-based research. Where relevant, print and ebook publications may be supplemented by online or audiovisual media.

Archival Returns: Central Australia and Beyond
Edited by Linda Barwick, Jennifer Green and Petronella Vaarzon-Morel

For the Sake of a Song: Wangga Songmen and Their Repertories
Allan Marett, Linda Barwick and Lysbeth Ford

Music, Dance and the Archive
Edited by Amanda Harris, Linda Barwick and Jakelin Troy

Recording Kastom: Alfred Haddon's Journals from the Torres Strait and New Guinea, 1888 and 1898
Edited by Anita Herle and Jude Philp

Reflections and Voices: Exploring the Music of Yothu Yindi with Mandawuy Yunupingu
Aaron Corn

Singing Bones: Ancestral Creativity and Collaboration
Samuel Curkpatrick

Songs from the Stations: Wajarra as Sung by Ronnie Wavehill Wirrpnga, Topsy Dodd Ngarnjal and Dandy Danbayarri at Kalkaringi
Myfany Turpin and Felicity Meakins

The Old Songs are Always New: Singing Traditions of the Tiwi Islands
Genevieve Campbell with Tiwi Elders and knowledge holders

Wurrurrumi Kun-Borrk: Songs from Western Arnhem Land
Kevin Djimar

Vitality and Change in Warlpiri Songs
Edited by Georgia Curran, Linda Barwick, Valerie Napaljarri Martin, Simon Japangardi Fisher and Nicolas Peterson

Vitality and Change in Warlpiri Songs

Juju-ngaliyarlu karnalu-jana pina-pina-mani kurdu-warnu-patu jujuku

Edited by Georgia Curran, Linda Barwick,
Valerie Napaljarri Martin, Simon Japangardi Fisher
and Nicolas Peterson

With Warlpiri transcriptions and English
translations by Theresa Napurrurla Ross and
Mary Laughren

SYDNEY UNIVERSITY PRESS

This book contains the cultural and intellectual property of Warlpiri people and has been presented and published with the consent of knowledge custodians. Dealing with any part of the knowledge for any purpose that has not been authorised may breach the customary laws of the Warlpiri people and may also breach copyright and moral rights under the *Copyright Act 1968* (Australian Government). Please contact the publisher for further details.

First published by Sydney University Press 2024
© Warlpiri Media Aboriginal Corporation trading as PAW Media and Communications 2024
© Sydney University Press 2024

Reproduction and Communication for other purposes
Except as permitted under the Australian *Copyright Act 1968*, no part of this edition may be reproduced, stored in a retrieval system, or communicated in any form or by any means without prior written permission. All requests for reproduction or communication should be made to Sydney University Press at the address below:

Sydney University Press
Fisher Library F03
Gadigal Country
University of Sydney NSW 2006
AUSTRALIA
sup.info@sydney.edu.au
sydneyuniversitypress.com.au

 A catalogue record for this book is available from the National Library of Australia.

This book's Warlpiri title "Juju-ngaliyarlu karnalu-jana pina-pina-mani kurdu-warnu-patu jujuku" translates as "Elders passing on ceremonial knowledge to the young people". This was a collaborative decision made by Warlpiri contributors and reflects the sentiment of the English title.

We acknowledge that this book was produced on the unceded lands of Warlpiri, Arrernte, Gadigal, Gundangurra, Kaurna, Ngambri and Ngunnawal people.

We acknowledge all First Nations Australian people who have passed on their culture through generations and continue to do so into the future.

This publication was supported by the Australian Academy of the Humanities Publication Subsidy Scheme.

ISBN 9781743329061 paperback
ISBN 9781743329559 epub
ISBN 9781743329535 pdf

Cover artwork and design: Jason Japaljarri Woods, based on his award-winning photograph "Napaljarri passing knowledge to Nampijinpa" (Best photograph, First Nations Media Awards 2023).

We acknowledge the traditional owners of the lands on which Sydney University Press is located, the Gadigal people of the Eora Nation, and we pay our respects to the knowledge embedded forever within the Aboriginal Custodianship of Country.

The names and images of Warlpiri people who have passed away are included in this book with permission from families.

Contents

List of tables	xi
List of figures	xiii
Foreword	xix
Editors' preface	xxi
Juju-ngaliya-patu	xxix
List of contributors	xxxi
Glossary of Warlpiri words	xli

Chapter 1
 Vitality and change in Warlpiri songs and ceremonies
 Georgia Curran, Linda Barwick, Valerie Napaljarri Martin, Simon Japangardi Fisher and Nicolas Peterson 1

Rex Japanangka Granites 26
Harry Jakamarra Nelson 27
Otto Jungarrayi Sims 29

Chapter 2
 Archiving documentation of Warlpiri songs and ceremonies on-Country at the Warlpiri Media Archive
 Georgia Curran, Valerie Napaljarri Martin, Simon Japangardi Fisher, Elizabeth Napaljarri Katakarinja and Linda Barwick 31

Alice Nampijinpa Henwood 54
Paddy Japaljarri Sims 56

Chapter 3
 A Warlpiri winter solstice ceremony: Performance, succession and the jural public
 Nicolas Peterson 59

Tommy Jangala Watson	81
Thomas Jangala Rice	83
Barbara Gibson Nakamarra	84

Chapter 4
Dreaming to sing: Learning and dream creation in the Australian desert
Barbara Glowczewski and Barbara Gibson Nakamarra (translated by Georgia Curran and Nicolas Peterson from the original French) — 85

Ruth Napaljarri Oldfield	101
Coral Napangardi Gallagher	103
Peggy Nampijinpa Brown	104

Chapter 5
Minamina *yawulyu*: Musical change from the 1970s through to the 2010s
Georgia Curran, Barbara Napanangka Martin and Linda Barwick — 107

Fanny Walker Napurrurla — 142

Chapter 6
Expert domains of knowledge in Ngurlu *yawulyu* songs from Jipiranpa
Fanny Walker Napurrurla, Linda Barwick and Mary Laughren, with contributions from Sarah Holmes Napangardi, Jessie Simpson Napangardi, Judith Robertson Napangardi and Theresa Napurrurla Ross — 145

Nellie Nangala Wayne	199
Maisie Napurrurla Wayne	201
Peggy Nampijinpa Martin	203
Lucy Nampijinpa Martin	205

Chapter 7
Warnajarra: Innovation and continuity in design and lyrics in a Warlpiri women's song set
Myfany Turpin, Megan Morais, Mary Laughren, Peggy Nampijinpa Martin and Helen Napurrurla Morton — 207

Lorraine Nungarrayi Granites	252
George (Cowboy) Jungarrayi Ryder	254

Chapter 8
   Reanimating Ngajakula: Lander Warlpiri songs of connection and transformation
   Petronella Vaarzon-Morel, George Jungarrayi Ryder†, Teddy Jupurrurla Long, Jim Wafer and Luke Kelly   257

Dolly Nampijinpa (Daniels) Granites   283
Judy Nampijinpa Granites   284
Lynette Nampijinpa Granites   285

Chapter 9
   To perform or not to perform the Ancestral Fire Dreaming from the Warlukurlangu ranges (Central Australia)
   Françoise Dussart   287

Jerry Jangala Patrick   307

Chapter 10
   Milpirri: A revitalisation movement, a *purlapa* or a festival?
   Stephen Wild, Steven Wanta Jampijinpa Patrick and Yukihiro Doi   309

Index   329

List of tables

Table 0.1. Warlpiri skin names and their groupings into patricouples and patrimoieties. — xxiv

Table 1.1. Features of Warlpiri song genres and ceremonies based on contemporary attitudes (which may shift over time). — 9

Table 1.2. Assessment of the vitality of Warlpiri song genres against the 12 factors of Grant's "Music Vitality and Endangerment Framework" (2014). — 12

Table 3.1. The songs sung on the final day of the ceremony with exegeses provided by a senior man. — 74

Table 5.1. Comparison of features of the six recorded performance instances. — 118

Table 6.1 Four performances of Ngurlu *yawulyu* recorded at Alekarenge by Linda Barwick and David Nash in 1996 and 1997. — 152

Table 6.2 Distribution of song items and verses from Jipiranpa and Pawurrinji across the corpus. — 153

Table 6.3. Standard and non-standard forms of five rhythmic text features and their distribution across the corpus of 48 rhythmic texts. — 161

Table 6.4. Distribution of standard text-rhythm features according to thematic groups. — 164

Table 7.1. The 1981/1982 recordings by Megan Morais. — 210

Table 7.2. The 2016–2019 recordings in which Warnajarra was performed or translated. — 211

List of figures

Figure 1.1. The Warlpiri regions.   4

Figure 2.1. Paddy Sims, Paddy Stewart and Paddy Nelson watching television in the mid-1980s.   36

Figure 2.2. Simon Japangardi Fisher and Elizabeth Napaljarri Katakarinja visit the Sydney University Archive, 2019.   43

Figure 2.3. Warlpiri men and women visit the Australian Institute of Aboriginal and Torres Strait Islander Studies in 2018 to review materials to return to the Warlpiri Media Archive.   44

Figure 2.4. Warlpiri women viewing videos made during Women's Law and Culture meetings in the 1990s at a dance camp at Bean Tree outstation in August 2019.   46

Figure 2.5. Trish Lechleitner and Ruth Napaljarri Oldfield view old photographs on an iPad at a dance camp at Bean Tree outstation in 2019.   47

Figure 3.1. The three leading *kirda*, Jimmy Jungarrayi, Paddy Japaljarri Sims and Banjo, dancing on one of the first days, with women visible in the background but not yet dancing.   64

Figure 3.2. *Kirda* men moving to the ground for the daily dance.   65

Figure 3.3. (Left) Body painting on Joe Jampijinpa, a *kurdungurlu,* with the black pigment from burnt Hakea bark outlined in ground white ochre (*ngunjungunju*) mixed with plant down and laid onto a greased back; (right) a shield with another version of the Munga image.   66

Figure 3.4. *Kirda* dancing in front of the Milky Way earth mound with a *kurdungurlu* standing on the right.   67

Figure 3.5. *Kirda* bringing the Wulpararri emblem onto the ceremonial ground on the final afternoon.   68

Figure 3.6. The ground at the end of the ceremony showing the Milky Way as an earth mound covered in the ashes from the overnight fires of people sleeping at the ground, with four of the *kukulypa* still upright on the mound and the emblems placed on it. The group of *kirda* and *kurdungurlu* men is settling up after the ceremony.   69

Figure 4.1. Barbara Gibson Nakamarra leading the Yawakiyi *yawulyu* dance. 89

Figure 4.2. Sketch of the Emu designs on the wooden dish. 92

Figure 4.3. Barbara Gibson, Yakiriya, Beryl Gibson and Barbara Glowczewski with the male and female wooden emu eggs. 95

Figure 5.1. Barbara Napanangka Martin leads the Minamina *yawulyu* dances for the film. 114

Figure 5.2. Two sisters, Alice Napanangka Granites and Elsie Napanangka Granites, dance as two ancestors from Minamina, who meet up with their age-brother from Mount Theo, danced by Audrey Napanangka Williams. 116

Figure 5.3. Barbara Napanangka Martin and Alice Napanangka Granites dance as the Two Age-Brothers from Minamina with Jean Napanangka Brown as the Age-Brother from Mount Theo. 117

Figure 5.4. Minamina and the Country to the east are dominated by desert oak trees, symbolically representing the ancestral women as they travel and the digging sticks that they carry. 122

Figure 5.5. Barbara Napanangka Martin and Joyce Napangardi Brown painted up with Minamina designs in 2016. 130

Figure 6.1. The general location of Warlpiri and Anmatyerr "Edible Seed" *yawulyu*, including (in the north) Jipiranpa and Pawurrinji. 148

Figure 6.2. Fanny Walker Napurrurla discusses her *yawulyu* Jipiranpa songs with Mary Laughren and Linda Barwick, witnessed by her daughters and other family members, Alekarenge, 19 July 2010. 150

Figure 7.1. Map of the Warlpiri region. 209

Figure 7.2. Women's Warnajarra body design that represents Majardi (hairstring waistbelt, see Figure 7.4), 26 April 1982. 212

Figure 7.3. The Warnajarra verse from 1982 (Verse 33, DJ_M02-021714, song items 1–3) that inspired Peggy's new design, which was drawn after Peggy sang this verse on 25 November 2019 (audio recording 20191125_6). 213

Figure 7.4. The 2019 *yawulyu* design created by Peggy Nampijinpa Martin after singing the Warnajarra verse in Figure 7.3 (Verse 33). 214

Figure 7.5. Warnajarra yawulyu body design from Pawu. 215

Figure 7.6. A verse of Warnajarra where the dance represents the Two Snakes ancestors looking around (Verse 6). 216

Figure 7.7. Ambiguity in the words of a Warnajarra verse (Verse 13). 217

Figure 7.8. A Warnajarra verse with speech equivalents from neighbouring language varieties, here showing Arandic words on which the song text is likely based (Verse 18). 219

Figure 7.9. A Warnajarra verse with Arandic vocabulary and final consonant "l" transferred to the beginning of the next word and "m" to the beginning of the next line (Verse 30). 221

Figure 7.10. A Warnajarra verse in the fast meter, with 153 clap beats per minute (Verse 3). It is based on the words *kana*, *ingkatyel* and a form of either *jurtampi* or *jutapi*. 222

Figure 7.11. A Warnajarra verse in the slow meter, with 50 clap beats per minute (Verse 2). Note that it is based on the same words as the verse in the fast meter in Figure 7.10 above. 222

Figure 7.12. An example of lexical reduplication, *munga-munga* "darkness", forming an entire line (Line B) in Warnajarra (Verse 22). 224

Figure 7.13. A lexical reduplication *jarna-jarna* in the second half of the lines (A and B) in Warnajarra (Verse 1). 224

Figure 7.14. Grammatical reduplication marking distributive action (Verse 4). 225

Figure 7.15. Grammatical reduplication marking plurality (Lines A and B, Verse 19) in the slow meter (Verse 19). 226

Figure 7.16. Partial reduplication from the left edge – *warnaja* – with identical rhythm, base preceding reduplicant. Line B is in three Warnajarra verses: Verse 8 (shown here), 12 and 14. 228

Figure 7.17. Base that has a vocable as its final (fourth) syllable. Reduplication from left edge of word, base followed by reduplicant. Fast meter (Verse 23). 229

Figure 7.18. Partial reduplication from the left edge – *ninjapa* – with identical rhythm, base followed by reduplicant. Line B, fast meter (Verse 15). 230

Figure 7.19. Base after reduplicant in both lines of the verse. Partial reduplication from the left edge base after reduplicant. Fast meter (Verse 6). 230

Figure 7.20. Partial reduplication from right edge: Arandic base *atywerrk* reduplicated and consonant added to beginning (Verse 17). 231

Figure 7.21. Partial reduplication from the right edge: Line B consists of syllables that repeat in a triplication pattern of 123 23 123 (Verse 3). 232

Figure 7.22. Triplication with partial reduplication from the right edge. Fast meter (Verse 15, Line A). 233

Figure 7.23. Triplication with partial reduplication from the right edge. Contrasting rhythm in Line A; identical rhythm in line B. Fast meter, Verse 26. 234

Figure 7.24. Triplication with partial reduplication from the right edge and additional syllable. Fast meter (Verse 8). 235

Figure 7.25. Right-edge triplication: 123 23 123. Fast meter (Verse 7, one line only). 236

Figure 7.26. Partial reduplication *lardi-lardila*. Slow meter (Verse 27). 237

Figure 8.1. Ngajakula sites along the Lander River, north of Willowra. 258

Figure 8.2. *Kurdungurlu* Teddy Jupurrurla Long instructing younger people about *jukurrpa* places (Willowra, 2018). To the left is Dwayne Ross. 260

Figure 8.3. Preparing to record Ngajakula song cycle (Willowra, 2018). 261

Figure 9.1. Judy (left) as the older brother, Dolly as the younger brother, both getting ready to perform. Lucy Napaljarri Kennedy as a manager getting ready to join the singers. 290

Figure 9.2. (Top) Judy and Dolly going hunting while their father (represented here by Judy-Peggy Nangala) starts singing the magical fire. (Bottom) Judy and Dolly hunting for kangaroos. 292

Figure 9.3. (Top) While they hunt, the father redoubles his effort to send the magical fire to destroy his sons. (Middle) The brothers are hunting and finding many kangaroos. (Bottom) The father sees his sons in the distance and can see that the fire is closing in on them. 293

Figure 9.4. (Top) The father relentlessly sings the magical fire. (Bottom) The brothers see black smoke coming from the area where they live and worry about their father and try to run back to him. 294

Figure 9.5. (Top) Soon, the fire is enveloping them and forces them to travel a long way south to Kaltukatjara. (Bottom) They try to push the fire away unsuccessfully and they worry for their father under the watchful eye of a manager Emma Nungarrayi, a sister of Dolly's mother. 295

Figure 9.6. (Top) The fire burns their hair, their ears, their skin off – it burns them inside out. Now they are very worried about their father. (Bottom) They managed to return towards their home camp while the Ancestral fire burns them. 296

Figure 9.7. (Top) They can barely walk, continuously pursued by the magical Ancestral Fire Being. (Middle) The older brother is helping his younger brother. (Bottom) Exhausted and charred, they both enter a men's secret cave. 297

Figure 10.1. Warlpiri patricouples and the four colour groups for Milpirri. 316

Figure 10.2. *Mangulpa* by male Red dancers. 320

Figure 10.3. *Witi* by Yellow female dancers. . 320

Figure 10.4. *Karli* and *wirlki* by male Green dancers. 321

Figure 10.5. Junior boys dancing with DJ Bacon Mix. 321

Figure 10.6. *Karnanganja* by Yellow and Green dancers. 322

Figure 10.7. Sky Lantern being flown by *kardiya* people with "Yungkaju Kurdari". 322

Figure 10.8. Blanket exchange after *Milpirri 2009*, community area near basketball court. 323

Foreword

The Board of Directors
Warlpiri Media Aboriginal Corporation trading as
PAW Media and Communications

Pintupi Anmatyerr Warlpiri Media and Communications (PAW Media) began life as Warlpiri Media Association in 1984. We are based at Yuendumu, a remote but important Aboriginal community on the edge of the Northern Territory's Tanami Desert. The organisation was established by *yapa* (Warlpiri people) in 1984 to research, record, protect and share our culture through media and technology. As a result of that work, we have built the most prominent audiovisual cultural archive on-Country in Central Australia. The substantial records of Warlpiri cultural heritage are deeply meaningful for our communities. The songs, stories, activities and people who feature in those collections are core to our cultural identity.

This book was made possible by the Australian Research Council–funded Linkage project, in which PAW Media's Warlpiri researchers and community members partnered with researchers from the University of Sydney and Australian National University. It is the first co-publication we have produced with Sydney University Press, and we hope there will be more in the future.

This project has involved two Partner Investigators: our Directors Simon Japangardi Fisher and Valerie Napaljarri Martin. Japangardi and Napaljarri were co-editors of the book and co-authors of the first two chapters. They also oversaw important interviews with Elders, in which they shared their aspirations for younger generations to engage with our cultural collections as a way they can learn about their culture into the future. Many other staff have also been involved in the project activities, including our graphic designer Jason Japaljarrri Woods, who contributed to the book's cover design.

The chapters in this publication have all been written by Warlpiri people from our communities in Yuendumu, Nyirrpi, Lajamanu, Willowra and Alekarenge in collaboration with researchers with whom we have enjoyed rich relationships going back decades. The chapters highlight the challenges we face in passing on our songs and stories to younger generations. For that work, the Directors are deeply grateful to Dr Georgia Curran and her colleagues, who worked with us to record a priceless collection of traditional Warlpiri songs.

It is really important for us to document those songs and ceremonies. Too many of our Warlpiri Elders are passing away without the opportunity to share this core knowledge with younger generations.

The work that underpins this book will help keep our culture strong into the future.

Directors: Simon Japangardi Fisher, Valerie Napaljarri Martin, Elizabeth Napaljarri Katakarinja, Ned Jampijinpa Hargraves, Wilfred Jupurrurla Nelson, Robert Jampijinpa Robertson, Adam Japaljarri Gibbs, Francis Jupurrurla Kelly and Karl Japaljarri Hampton

Editors' preface

Nyampuju milya-pinjaku kuruwarri-kirli warlalja-kurlu. Purda-nyangka manu nyangka nyuntu-nyangu warlalja. Jaja-nyanu-kurlangu, jamirdi-nyanu-kurlangu, kirda-nyanu-kurlangu, ngati-nyanu-kurlangu, ngamirni-nyanu-kurlangu, pimirdi-nyanu-kurlangu. Manu warlalja warringiyi-kirlangu.

This [book] is so we can know our families' *kuruwarri* [our *jukurrpa* and our stories]. Listen and look at your family! [Those] belonging to our grandmothers (mother's mothers), our grandfathers (mother's fathers), our fathers, our mothers, our uncles (mother's brothers) and our aunts (father's sisters). And belonging to our paternal grandfathers (our father's fathers).

Milya-pinjaku kuruwarriki warlaljaku – jaja-nyanu-kurlanguku, jamirdi-nyanu-kurlanguku, kirda-nyanu-kurlanguku, ngati-nyanu-kurlanguku, ngamirni-nyanu-kurlanguku, pimirdi-nyanu-kurlanguku manu warlaljaku warringiyi-kirlanguku. Manu yungulu-nyanu manngu-nyanyi nganakurlangu. Nyarrpara jukurrpa nganakurlangu? Kujalku.

So we can remember and learn the knowledge for our *kuruwarri*. To know our stories that belong to us – that belong to our grandfathers, our grandfathers on our mother's side, our fathers, our mothers, our uncles and our aunties. Belonging to our great-great-grandfathers and grandfathers on our father's side. So that we can keep our culture strong. How can we know our *jukurrpa*? This is how.

Valerie Napaljarri Martin

"Vitality and Change in Warlpiri Songs" project (2016–2021)

This book has grown out of an Australian Research Council Linkage project (LP160100743) that arose from concern about the vitality and future of Warlpiri ceremonial song performance, especially in light of changes over the last 90 years. In response to widely expressed concerns over a decline in knowledge of ceremonial songs, the project aimed to develop targeted strategies to enhance intergenerational transmission of and community engagement with these song traditions. The chapters in this book address these themes and illustrate the ways in which previously recorded materials can be of use for maintaining and rejuvenating the knowledges and practices core to Warlpiri cultural heritage. Pintubi Anmatjere Warlpiri Media and Communications, which maintains an archive of video, photographic and written materials made over the last 50 years, partnered with the University of Sydney and the Australian National University to undertake this research.

Warlpiri people, language, Country and communities

Warlpiri people who have connections to the Country across a broad area of the Tanami Desert of Central Australia are united in that they speak one language. Warlpiri does, however, have a number of dialects that reflect the regions in which people live and have historical ties. These dialects are mutually comprehensible but have some differing words and accents. Warlpiri people identify with these dialect names such that they mark social differentiation in this area. The seven dialects of Warlpiri are Warrmala (western Warlpiri), Ngardilypa (north-western Warlpiri), Wawulya (south-western Warlpiri), Warnayaka (central-northern Warlpiri), Ngaliya (southern Warlpiri), Yarlpiri (Lander River Warlpiri) and Wakirti (Hansen River Warlpiri). Nowadays, people living in Lajamanu identify with Warnayaka, people living in Yuendumu and Nyirrpi with Ngaliya, people in Willowra with Yarlpiri and those living in Tennant Creek and Alekarenge with Wakirti. Ngardilypa, Wawulya and Warrmala have been merged into the predominant dialect spoken in Lajamanu, although some older individuals still identify with these terms as a marker of their social identity.

Prior to the 1930s, Warlpiri people lived in small family groups across the Tanami Desert, many coming in for seasonal work at cattle stations that were established on the eastern fringes of this region in the early decades of the 20th century. The community of Willowra began as a cattle station in 1940, and Yuendumu and Lajamanu were established as government reserves in the years following World War II. Many outstations were established around Warlpiri

Country in the 1980s, some becoming thriving communities in themselves during this time. Nyirrpi was one of these and has a population of around 300 today. There are four main Warlpiri communities – Yuendumu, Lajamanu, Willowra and Nyirrpi – but Warlpiri families have also long lived in other communities, including Tennant Creek, Alekarenge, Wirrimanu (Balgo) and in the town of Mparntwe (Alice Springs). Nowadays, there are also diasporic Warlpiri groups living in Darwin, Adelaide and Port Augusta, Warlpiri school children attending boarding schools, and various other individuals and families live in other locations across Australia and beyond (see Burke 2018).

Yuendumu is the largest Warlpiri community, with a population of 800, and is the epicentre of the project through which this book has been developed. Because of this, the book contains a large representation of the Southern Ngaliya region of Warlpiri Country. However, we have also ensured the inclusion of contributions from Elders, cultural leaders and researchers from each of the other Warlpiri regions.

Warlpiri "skin" names

In everyday Warlpiri worlds, all people are categorised into one of the eight subsections colloquially known as "skin" groups, which are referred to often throughout this book. Warlpiri people are born with a skin name (or sometimes more than one if their parents did not have an ideal relationship match), and all non-Warlpiri people who engage with Warlpiri people for any length of time are given a skin name to facilitate their involvement in community life. Each skin name has a male term starting with "J" and a female term starting with "N". These "skins" are grouped into patricouples (represented by cells in Table 0.1) consisting of father–son/daughter pairs or aunt (father's sister)–nephew/niece (brother's children) pairs, who share ownership for the same *jukurrpa*, songs, ceremonies and Country. These patricouples are further grouped into two patrimoieties, represented by the two columns in Table 0.1.

Table 0.1. Warlpiri skin names and their groupings into patricouples (represented by cells in the table) and patrimoieties (represented by columns).

Ngurra-kurlarniyarra (lit: home in the south	Ngurra-yatujumparra (lit: home in the north
Jangala/Nangala	Jungarrayi/Nungarrayi
Jampijinpa/Nampijinpa	Japaljarri/Napaljarri
Jakamarra/Nakamarra	Japanangka/Napanangka
Jupurrurla/Napurrurla	Japangardi/Napangardi

Kirda and *kurdungurlu*

All Warlpiri songs and ceremonies are connected to *jukurrpa* and Country and are owned by different *kirda* groups. These rights are inherited from a person's fathers and fathers' fathers, so all people, songs and ceremonies are identified with one patrimoiety or the other. The role of people in the opposite patrimoiety, *kurdungurlu*, in relation to ceremonies and songs is to organise and oversee the performance. In general, the people in this role in any ceremony are close relatives of the *kirda*, the younger ones being the people who do the organising – such as clearing the ground, getting ochres and other materials, and decorating the *kirda* – and the senior people ensuring the correct performance of the ceremony (see Curran 2020; Dussart 2000; Nash 1982). The relationship between *kirda* and *kurdungurlu* is complex; where these close relatives are not available, others may step in to attend to their duties because no ceremony can occur without people of both categories being present.

In smaller, land-based ceremonies, the patrimoieties of Warlpiri society are less prominent. However, they are still crucial for the larger ceremonies, including Ngajakula (discussed in Chapter 8), Jardiwanpa and the annual initiation ceremonies known as Kurdiji, which are incorporative as they include large numbers of participants from across both patrimoieties: Ngurra-yatujumparra (home in the north), and Ngurra-kurlarniyarra (home in the south). Although these terms are not widely used nowadays, this ideology is nonetheless still prevalent among most Warlpiri people across generations as they are required to operate within these groups for the larger-scale Kurdiji ceremonies held each summer.

Editors' preface

Warlpiri orthography and other terminology

Warlpiri words are used throughout this book to maintain the particular meanings associated with their Warlpiri use and are listed in the Glossary. For the spellings of all Warlpiri words, we have followed the conventions set out in the *Warlpiri Encyclopaedic Dictionary* (Laughren et al. 2022), based on the orthography established by Lothar Jagst and Maurice Jupurrurla Luther in Lajamanu in 1974 (2022: 4–6).

There are several other terms we have used throughout the book in specific ways. We have used the word "Aboriginal" to refer generally to Indigenous peoples from across mainland Australia and Tasmania (but not including the Torres Strait Islands). We have used "Indigenous" when referring to First Nations peoples from across the Australian mainland, the Torres Strait Islands and overseas. We have also used words that have specific meanings in Aboriginal English. The word "Elder" has been used to refer to senior Aboriginal people who are widely respected for their views and knowledge. The word "Country" has been used as it is in Aboriginal English to refer to the particular tracts of land that connect to *jukurrpa* and are owned by specific Warlpiri families. The word "song" is used generally throughout the book to refer to the interconnected packages of music (including rhythmic, melodic and textual aspects), designs, dances and accompanying ritual actions. The following specific terms for the components of songs are used throughout this book (based on those set out by Barwick 1989; Ellis 1964, 1967, 1969, 1983, 1992; Moyle 1974; Turpin 2007b). Despite divergence within other literature, we have tried to use these terms systematically throughout this book with the following meanings:

Songline	the theoretical concept of a series of song verses, which all relate to the journey of a particular ancestor and which bring to mind the Country and stories associated with this ancestor as they travelled in a timeless creational moment
Song set	a collection of related song verses, which are sung together in one performance instance
Verse	a two-line (or sometimes three) unit of rhythmic text, which is often associated with a particular place or ancestral action
Rhythmic text	the association of a fixed song text with a particular syllabic rhythm so that the same lines of a particular verse are always performed with the same rhythm
Song item	uninterrupted verse sung repeatedly for a short duration of 30 seconds to one to two minutes

Acknowledgements

We are grateful to all the authors and contributors included in this book. We especially acknowledge the long-term relationships and commitments in Warlpiri communities that have allowed the teams of authors to contribute to the rich quality of each of the chapters. We thank Mary Laughren and Theresa Napurrurla Ross for their work on the transcriptions and translations and checking of Warlpiri texts. We thank Jason Japaljarri Woods for creating the cover artwork and design and Brenda Thornley for the two maps. We also thank Jeff Bruer for his assistance in finding photographs and interview recordings in the Warlpiri Media Archives and Cecilia Alfonso for her generous access to the Warlukurlangu Artists database of profile photographs. We thank PAW staff, especially Tess Foxworthy, Grace Marshall and Tegan Rogers, who have been very helpful during the production stage. Individual photographers are credited within each of the chapters.

Research for and production of this book have been supported by the Australian Research Council Linkage project (LP160100743) with Chief Investigators Barwick, Peterson and Turpin, Partner Investigators Martin and Fisher, and Research Associate Curran. This project has been a partnership between the University of Sydney, the Australian National University, PAW Media and Kurra Aboriginal Corporation, who provided significant funding. We have also benefited from the support of the Indigenous Languages and Arts program. A grant from the Australian Academy for the Humanities has supported the publication of colour photographs in this book.

We thank the board of PAW Media for their role in supporting the co-publication of this book with Sydney University Press. This book has been peer-reviewed, and we are grateful to the anonymous reviewers for their insightful and constructive feedback. Thanks must also go to the editorial staff at Sydney University Press.

> Georgia Curran, Linda Barwick, Valerie Napaljarri Martin, Simon Japangardi Fisher and Nicolas Peterson

References

Barwick, Linda. 1989. "Creative (Ir)regularities: The Intermeshing of Text and Melody in Performance of Central Australian Song". *Australian Aboriginal Studies* 1: 12–28.

Burke, Paul. 2018. *An Australian Indigenous Diaspora: Warlpiri Matriarchs and the Refashioning of Tradition*. New York: Berghahn Books.

Curran, Georgia. 2020. *Sustaining Indigenous Songs: Contemporary Warlpiri Ceremonial Life in Yuendumu, Central Australia*. New York: Berghahn Books.

Dussart, Françoise. 2000. *The Politics of Ritual in an Aboriginal Settlement: Kinship, Gender, and the Currency of Knowledge*. Washington, DC; London: Smithsonian Institution Press.

Ellis, Catherine. 1964. *Aboriginal Music Making: A Study of Central Australian Music*. Adelaide: Libraries Board of South Australia.

Ellis, Catherine. 1967. "Folk Song Migration in Aboriginal South Australia". *Journal of the International Folk Music Council* 19: 11–16.

Ellis, Catherine. 1969. "Structure and Significance in Aboriginal Song". *Mankind* 7(1): 3–14.

Ellis, Catherine. 1983. "When is a Song Not a Song? A Study from Northern South Australia". *Bikmaus* 4(3): 136–44.

Ellis, Catherine. 1992. "Connection and disconnection of elements of the rhythmic hierarchy in an Aranda song". *Musicology Australia* 15(1): 44–66.

Hoogenraad, Robert, Mary Laughren with Warlpiri people from Yuendumu, Lajamanu, Willowra and Nyirrpi. 2012. *Warlpiri Picture Dictionary*. Alice Springs: IAD Press.

Laughren, Mary, Kenneth Hale, Jeannie Egan Nungarrayi, Marlurrku Paddy Patrick Jangala, Robert Hoogenraad, David Nash and Jane Simpson. 2022. *Warlpiri Encyclopaedic Dictionary*. Canberra: Aboriginal Studies Press.

Moyle, Alice. 1974. North Australian Music: Taxonomic Approach to the Study of Aboriginal Song Performances. PhD thesis, Monash University, Melbourne.

Nash, David. 1982. "An Etymological Note of Warlpiri Kurdungurlu". In *Languages of Kinship in Aboriginal Australia* (Oceania Linguistic Monographs (24), edited by Jeffrey Heath, Francesca Merlan and Alan Rumsey, pp.141–59. Sydney: University of Sydney.

Turpin, Myfany. 2007. "The Poetics of Central Australian Song". *Australian Aboriginal Studies* 2(1): 100–15.

Juju-ngaliya-patu

This is a list of senior singers and ceremonial leaders who have been involved in the research for various aspects of this book, some over many decades. Many of these people have now passed away (marked by †), and their names have been included with permission from families to honour their contributions and knowledge.

Lajamanu

†Henry Jakamarra Cooke

†Lily Nungarrayi Hargreaves

Jerry Jangala Patrick

Rosie Napurrurla Tasman

Willowra

Lillian Nakamarra

Lily Napaljarri Kitson

Maisie Napaljarri Kitson

Marlene Nampijinpa Martin

May Napurrurla Presley

†Molly Napurrurla Presley

Peggy Nampijinpa Martin

Lucy Nampijinpa Martin

Yuendumu/Nyirrpi

Alice Nampijinpa Henwood
†Coral Napangardi Gallagher
†Connie Nakamarra White
†Dolly Nampijinpa Daniels
†Harry Jakamarra Nelson
†Jeannie Nungarrayi Egan
†Judy Nampijinpa Granites
†Long Paddy Jakamarra White
Lorraine Nungarrayi Granites
†Lucy Napaljarri Kennedy
Lynette Nampijinpa Granites
Maisie Napurrurla Wayne
Nellie Nangala Wayne
†Paddy Japaljarri Sims
Peggy Nampijinpa Brown
Ruth Napaljarri Oldfield
Thomas Jangala Rice
Thomas Jangala Watson

Tennant Creek/Alekarenge

†Ada Dickenson Napurrurla
†Edna Brown Nungarrayi
†Engineer Jack Japaljarri
†Fanny Walker Napurrurla
Gwen Brown Napurrurla
†Joe Bird Jangala
†Irene Driver Nungarrayi
†Mary Small O'Keeffe Napurrurla
†Tommy Driver Jupurrurla

List of contributors

Linda Barwick is a musicologist specialising in the study of Australian First Nations musics, immigrant musics and the digital humanities (particularly archiving and repatriating ethnographic field recordings as a site of interaction between researchers and cultural heritage communities). She has studied community music practices through fieldwork in Australia, Italy and the Philippines. She has collaborated with Warlpiri performers since 1996 when she first visited Alekarenge. Recently, she has collaborated with Central Australian organisations, including the Central Land Council and Pintubi Anmatjere Warlpiri Media and Communications (PAW Media), on various projects concerning cultural archiving and supporting community performance traditions. Linda's co-edited book *Archival Returns: Central Australia and Beyond* (Sydney University Press, 2020; co-edited by Jennifer Green and Petronella Vaarzon-Morel) won the Australasian Society of Archivists Mander Jones Award. She is an Emeritus Professor at the University of Sydney, Sydney Conservatorium of Music and a Fellow of the Australian Academy of the Humanities.

Georgia Curran is currently an Australian Research Council Discovery Early Career Researcher Award postdoctoral fellow at the Sydney Conservatorium of Music, working on a project titled "Rethinking the Dynamics of Place in Warlpiri Song" (2020–2023). She received her PhD from the Australian National University for a thesis on "Contemporary Ritual Practice in an Aboriginal Settlement: The Warlpiri Kurdiji Ceremony" (2010). Her interests include Indigenous music and languages, performance ethnography, and cultural continuity and change, and the revitalisation of endangered song traditions. Since 2005, she has undertaken research with Warlpiri people in Yuendumu and other Central Australian communities, including collaborative research projects with PAW Media. Georgia is the author of *Sustaining Indigenous Songs: Contemporary Warlpiri Ceremonial Life in Central Australia* (2020, Berghahn Books, with Foreword by Otto Jungarrayi Sims), as well as numerous journal articles and book chapters. Georgia has collaborated with senior Warlpiri women to produce two song books, *Jardiwanpa Yawulyu* (2014) and *Yurntumu-Wardingki-Juju-Ngaliya-Kurlangu Yawulyu: Warlpiri Women's Songs from Yuendumu* (2017), both published by Batchelor Institute Press.

Yukihiro Doi completed a bachelor's degree in International Culture Studies at Tenri University (Nara Prefecture, Japan) in 2000. In 2004, he completed a master's equivalent-level course at the Tenri Graduate Seminary. In 2016, he was awarded a PhD by the Australian National University for his research on *Milpirri* at Lajamanu. He was a researcher at Oyasato Institute for the Study of Religion at Tenri University from 2013 to 2015. He performed at 95 concerts, workshops and TV appearances with gagaku composer and musician Hideki Togi from 2000 to 2015. He was accredited by Australia's vocational education and training assessment provider, VETASSESS, as a Music Professional Not Elsewhere Classified in 2016 and Musician (Instrumental) in 2017. Currently, he is a tutor at CIT Solutions of the Canberra Institute of Technology and the Canberra Japanese Supplementary School.

Françoise Dussart is a Professor in the Department of Anthropology and Women's, Gender and Sexuality Studies at the University of Connecticut. Her specialties in social anthropology include Australian Aboriginal visual systems; Indigenous rights; various expressions of gender, ritual and performance; and Indigenous ontologies, entanglements, health and citizenship. In 2015–2016, she curated a major presentation of contemporary Australian Aboriginal and Torres Strait Islander arts at the Musée de la civilisation in Quebec City, Canada. She is the author of *La Peinture des Aborigènes d'Australie* (*Australian Aboriginal Painting*, 1993, Parenthèses) and *The Politics of Ritual in an Aboriginal Settlement: Kinship, Gender and the Currency of Knowledge* (2000, Smithsonian Institution Scholarly Press). She is the author of many articles and chapters as well as edited volumes on media and ontology, *Media Matters: Representations of the Social in Aboriginal Australia* (2006, VAR, 2006), Engaging Christianity in Aboriginal Australia (2021, *The Australian Journal of Anthropology*, with Carolyn Schwarz), *Entangled Territorialities* (2017, University of Toronto Press, with Sylvie Poirier) and *Contemporary Indigenous Cosmologies and Pragmatics* (2021, University of Alberta Press, with Sylvie Poirier).

Simon Japangardi Fisher is a Director and Archives Researcher at PAW Media and Communications in Yuendumu. He is the owner for Pikilyi region to the north-west of Yuendumu and has a Master of Arts (Indigenous Studies) from Charles Darwin University, Sydney, for a thesis titled Pikilyi Water Rights –

Human Rights. Simon has been a Partner Investigator on the "Vitality and Change in Warlpiri Songs" project (2016–2020); in this role, he has presented his archiving work at various conferences, including at the Foundation for Endangered Languages conferences in Alcanena, Portugal, in 2017 and in Sydney, Australia, in 2019. These presentations have resulted in papers in published conference proceedings. Simon has also held an Indigenous Remote Archival Fellowship to work at the National Film and Sound Archive of Australia in Canberra (2015). He has conducted archival research for many documentary films created at PAW Media, particularly those on Warlpiri history, including *So They Can Carry On – Jack Cook's Story* (2014), *Coniston* (2012) and a recent documentary on Olive Pink (2022). He is currently also researching the story of his great-grandfather, Warlpiri man Gwoya Tjungurrayi, 'One Pound Jimmy', who was sketched by Ainslie Roberts and whose portrait features on the Australian $2 coin.

Barbara Gibson Nakamarra was born in 1938 in the Tanami Desert. She settled at Yuendumu as a young girl and was married, along with her sister Beryl, to Tony Japaljarri Gibson. She worked at the clinic in Yuendumu and then moved to Lajamanu, where she became a leading authority in rituals. In the 1980s, the family spent much time at the Kurlurrngalinypa outstation, where they were asked to re-enact their hunter–gatherer life for a Japanese museum crew. She helped B. Glowczewski with many translations for the *Dream Trackers: Yapa Art and Knowledge of the Australian Desert* CD-ROM (United Nations Educational, Scientific and Cultural Organization 2000) and started to paint in 1986, exhibiting in many galleries. One of her paintings was presented in a touring exhibition in France (1991, B. Glowczewski, *Yapa: peintres aborigènes de Balgo et Lajamanu* (*Yapa: Painters from Balgo and Lajamanu Catalog*), edited by Baudoin Lebon) and the Lenz Culture Institute, in Austria (2000, Zeit: Mythos Phantom Realität, Springer: https://www.amazon.com/Zeit-Mythos-Phantom-Realit%C3%A4t-German/dp/3211834176). After her husband's death, she went to live in Tennant Creek and Kununurra, where she continued to paint. She passed away in the mid-1990s.

Barbara Glowczewski is a high-distinction professorial researcher at the French National Centre for Scientific Research (CNRS), a member of the Laboratory of Social Anthropology at the Collège de France and teaching at the School of Advanced Studies in the Social Sciences (EHESS) in Paris. She has undertaken regular fieldwork with the Warlpiri people from Lajamanu (since 1979), with the Djugun and Yawuru people from Broome (where she lived in the 1990s), and with Palm Islanders (adjunct professor at James Cook

University 2004–2017). She is an anthropologist specialising in Australian Indigenous issues, strategies of recognition and networks shared with other Indigenous peoples, and alternative collectives for social and environmental justice against ecocide. She is the author of many publications and multimedia productions in collaboration with Warlpiri artists from Lajamanu (www.odsas.net) and Djugun/Yawuru/Jabirr Jabirr filmmaker Wayne Barker, *The Spirit of Anchor* (https://images.cnrs.fr/en/video/980). Her latest books are *Indigenising Anthropology with Guattari and Deleuze* (2020, Edinburgh University Press) and *Réveiller les esprits de la terre* (2021, Dehors).

Elizabeth Napaljarri Katakarinja is a Western Arrernte woman who was born in 1963 in Ntaria (Hermannsburg). After her schooling at Yirara College in Alice Springs and Early Childhood Studies at Batchelor College, she moved to Yuendumu when she married Simon Japangardi Fisher. She has worked for the Yuendumu Social Club, the Yuendumu Old People's Program and the Mount Theo Program, the Yuendumu Night Patrol and, most recently, at PAW Media. Elizabeth has a Warlpiri connection through her grandfather. She has been involved in numerous video productions with PAW Media as well as research projects, including the Whole of Community Engagement Initiative with Charles Darwin University and the "Vitality and Change in Warlpiri Songs" Australian Research Council Linkage project with the University of Sydney.

Luke Kelly is a consultant applied anthropologist based in Istanbul, Turkey, specialising in land tenure, cultural mapping and survey work. He worked in the Tanami Desert, Central Australia, as a regional anthropologist for the Central Land Council between 2009 and 2016. At the invitation of the Warlpiri Education and Training Trust (WETT) and the Granites Mines Affected Area Aboriginal Corporation (GMAAAC) Willowra committees, Luke helped Elders organise and conduct field trips for the Willowra cultural mapping project. This work was undertaken during various periods between 2013 and 2020; in 2018, he assisted Elders with the *Ngajakula* recording sessions. He has a Master of Arts in Social Anthropology and Sociology from the Central European University, Budapest.

Mary Laughren has researched and documented Warlpiri language since 1975. From 1975 to 1993, she was employed by the Northern Territory Department of Education to conduct linguistic research to support bilingual education programs, mainly in the Warlpiri community schools in Central Australia. In 1993, she joined the linguistics program at the University of Queensland and has continued researching Warlpiri and supporting language and culture programs in those communities. She is the chief compiler of the *Warlpiri Encyclopaedic Dictionary* (Laughren et al. 2022). Between 2000 and 2008, she undertook fieldwork to record and document the Waanyi language and engaged in a series of language renewal workshops with Waanyi people from Doomadgee (Queensland). In collaboration with anthropologists, linguists, musicologists and Warlpiri Elders, Laughren has recorded and documented traditional Warlpiri *yawulyu* songs, building on her extensive photographic collection of performances at Yuendumu and Willowra in the 1970s and 1980s.

Teddy Jupurrurla Long was born on Coniston Station on his Country, Yarruku, and grew up at Willowra. He is Anmatyerr and also speaks Warlpiri. When he was young, Teddy worked as a stockman at Willowra and on neighbouring stations. During holidays, he lived with the old people in bush camps, where he continued learning Lander Warlpiri Anmatyerr Law. Reflecting on earlier *Ngajakula* performances, Jupurrurla commented, "that business was holding a lot of young people really safely, a safe life without people hurting each other; it was really very good times". Now, as the last surviving male Elder at Willowra, Jupurrurla takes seriously his responsibility to teach younger generations about their *jukurrpa* and Countries. It was Jupurrurla's vision to undertake the Willowra cultural mapping project. As senior *kurdungurlu* for *Ngajakula*, he led the singing and recording of the songline with *kirda* George Jungarrayi Ryder and shared his deep knowledge of the ceremony for this chapter.

Barbara Napanangka Martin has dedicated her life to working as a teacher at the Yuendumu School. She is now retired but still assists the school's Bilingual Resource Development Unity, as well as working on other community-based cultural projects. She is a skilled Warlpiri to English transcriber and translator and is interested in engaging senior women to figure out ways of representing oral stories and songs in written forms from which younger Warlpiri people can learn. Barbara has inherited *kirda* rights for Minamina, a region in the far west of Warlpiri Country. She was involved in the production of two Warlpiri women's songbooks (*Jardiwanpa Yawulyu*, 2014, Batchelor Institute Press; *Yurntumu-Wardingki Juju-Ngaliya-Kurlangu Yawulyu*: *Warlpiri Women's Songs from Yuendumu*, 2017, Batchelor Institute Press) and has also collaboratively published numerous other research articles and educational resources.

Valerie Napaljarri Martin is a Director at PAW Media and Communications and Partner Investigator on the "Vitality and Change in Warlpiri Songs" project (2016–2021). She is *kirda* for Yarungkanyi (Mount Doreen), which is important Country to the north-west of Alice Springs, and has inherited these ties from her father, Jimija Jungarrayi. Valerie has worked in areas of cultural liaison, interpreting services (especially for the Yuendumu court), video and production work, and archive management. Valerie is also politically active and has spoken out about issues of the Northern Territory Intervention and involved in more localised mediation work for the Yuendumu Council. She was a founding member of the Warlpiri Media Association board and has sat on the board continuously since the 1980s. Some of Valerie's early work on the Warlpiri Media radio features in the documentary film *Fight Fire with Fire – 30 Years of PAW History* (2014).

Megan Morais (aka Jones and Dail-Jones) has studied dance since 1961 and Indigenous Australian dance since 1974. She trained in movement analysis and notation at the Benesh Institute of Choreology (London, UK) and went on to teach choreology at the United States International University, Sussex. Later, she received degrees in Anthropology (San Francisco State University) and Dance Ethnology (University of Hawai'i). Her first experience in ethnochoreology began with notating dances from film, recorded during the Groote Eylandt Project in 1969. Via various grants, Megan has documented dances of several Indigenous Australian groups, including Nunggubuyu, Wanindilyaugwa, Anindjilana, Yanyuwa and Warlpiri. She has been Visiting Researcher with the University of New England and with the University of Sydney, and has published articles in various journals and encyclopedias. Currently, she is the lead author for *Yawulyu: Warlpiri Women's Ceremonies* (in press); co-authors include Peggy Nampijinpa Martin, Helen Napurrurla Morton and Myfany Turpin.

Helen Napurrurla Morton is the daughter of the late Dick Jakamarra Morton from eastern Warlpiri Country and Lady Napaljarri Morton from Willowra on the Lander River. Helen was raised at Yuendumu, where her father worked as a stockman, and attended Yuendumu primary school. She received her secondary education at Yirrara College in Alice Springs. On leaving school in 1979, Helen returned to Yuendumu, where she was employed as a literacy worker composing texts in Warlpiri and English for use in the bilingual education programs in Warlpiri community schools. Upon her marriage, Helen moved to Willowra, where she was employed in the school. Helen has successfully completed a number of linguistics and pedagogy courses run by the Batchelor Institute. Some of the children's books written by Helen can be viewed on Charles Darwin University's Living Archive of Aboriginal Languages (https://territorystories.nt.gov.au/). Helen has worked alongside many researchers at Willowra and Yuendumu and, over the past 20 years, has been closely associated with efforts to document traditional Warlpiri songs.

Steven (Wanta) Jampijinpa Patrick was born in Lajamanu, northern Tanami Desert, Northern Territory. He is *kirda* for Pawu (also known as Mount Barkly). Kurlpurlunu, a rain *jukurrpa* site, is also his and his grandfather's homeland. Jampijinpa has worked as a teacher in the Lajamanu School for roughly 18 years. He has stated:

> Milpirri is an event held every two years. It is something that supports my cultural teaching at the school. Teaching Warlpiri language is not enough, I need to show what being Warlpiri means to the younger generation. In addition, I have taught Warlpiri culture to students at the Australian National University. Over the four years I met lots of new people. I have two sons, one is 30 and the other is 19, and an adopted daughter who is four years old. My wife's name is Likitiya Meika Napangardi.

Nicolas Peterson is Emeritus Professor of Anthropology in the School of Archaeology and Anthropology at the Australian National University. For his PhD research in the late 1960s, he lived for eight months on the edge of the Arafura swamp with two groups of Aboriginal people who still supported themselves from the bush. Subsequently, he spent 13 months at Yuendumu working with Warlpiri people, learning about their ceremonial life and relationships to land. This led to working as the research officer for the Royal Commission on Aboriginal Land Rights (the Woodward Commission) and to the preparation, with others, of four land and native title claims for Warlpiri people, including the Warlpiri and Kartangarurru–Kurintji claim. His research interests include economic anthropology, social change, land and marine tenure, fourth-world people and the state, and the anthropology of photography. He has a strong interest in applied anthropology. From 2010 to 2021, he was the Director of the Centre for Native Title Anthropology at ANU.

Theresa Napurrurla Ross is a skilled Warlpiri translator and interpreter who has worked for decades in Warlpiri schools as well as for organisations including the Aboriginal Interpreter Services, Summer Institute for Linguistics, Institute for Aboriginal Development, PAW Media and the University of Sydney. She is a National Accreditation Authority for Translators and Interpreters–certified translator and interpreter. She has worked as a translator on many documentary films produced by PAW Media. Theresa lives with her family in Yuendumu, where she is heavily involved in caring for her grandchildren. She is currently writing a book in collaboration with Tess Napaljarri Ross on 'Mothers and babies' in which she documents traditional Warlpiri ways that mothers cared for their babies.

†George Jungarrayi Ryder was known to many as Cowboy. Jungarrayi sadly passed away in 2020. As a senior Warlpiri man and *kirda* for Ngunulurru and Yinapaka in the Lander region, Jungarrayi led the Willowra *Ngajakula* revitalisation project. Jungarrayi's deep knowledge was gained through a life lived on the land. He was born "in the bush before Welfare time", near Mungakurlangu on the Lander. Jungarrayi recalled that his father, Fred Japaljarri Karlarlukarri, and mother, Beryl Nakamarra, took him around the Country and "taught me everything. They told me, 'Don't do the wrong thing, you've got to follow your grandfathers'. The *kurdungurlu* and old people taught me the stories about country way, Jukurrpa, the law". From a young age, Jungarrayi worked as a stockman on Willowra and nearby stations and maintained an intimate relationship with the land. He was given the name "Ryder" because he was "among horses all the time". As an Elder, Jungarrayi shared his knowledge generously, teaching his family as well as other Lander families about their Countries. He also taught *kardiya* (non-Aboriginal people) while working tirelessly for his people on numerous projects including with Warlpiri rangers, on the Willowra cultural mapping project, and on native title claims. Jungarrayi was a wonderful, caring family man. He was happy to have recorded *Ngajakula* and to share the story.

Myfany Turpin is an Associate Professor at the Sydney Conservatorium of Music, University of Sydney, and an affiliate of the Department of Linguistics, University of Sydney. She has been involved in language and music documentation with Aboriginal communities since 1994. Her research focuses on Aboriginal song-poetry, Arandic languages, the relationship between language and music, and ethnobiology. Her research on the Kaytetye language resulted in a co-authored encyclopaedic dictionary, picture dictionary and collection of stories with the late Kaytetye speaker Alison Nangala Ross. She has written scholarly articles in the areas of music, linguistics and ethnobiology, and produced multimedia resources on language learning and Aboriginal songs. She supports remote school language and culture programs in Central Australia and works with local organisations to produce resources and provide opportunities for Aboriginal people to assist in their struggle for cultural and linguistic survival.

Petronella Vaarzon-Morel is an anthropologist who has worked with Warlpiri people for over 40 years. In 1976 and 1977, she taught with Jim Wafer at Willowra School and helped initiate the Warlpiri bilingual program. She subsequently co-authored four land claims and a native title claim involving Lander Warlpiri and Anmatyerr people. At the invitation of Willowra community, in 1987–1989 she undertook PhD research and collaborated on an oral history project that resulted in the book *Warlpiri Women's Voices* (1995, Institute for Aboriginal Development). More recently, she was engaged by the Warlpiri Education and Training Trust and Willowra committees for the GMAAAC to work with Elders on and help organise the Willowra cultural mapping project. In 2018–2019, as part of an archival project, she returned photos and recordings made with Willowra people over the years and co-edited (with Linda Barwick and Jennifer Green) *Archival Returns: Central Australia and Beyond* (2019, University of Hawai'i Press and Sydney University Press). She is Global Lecturer in Anthropology at New York University Sydney (since 2013) and an Honorary Research Associate at the University of Sydney.

Jim Wafer is a conjoint senior lecturer in anthropology at the University of Newcastle and has worked with Aboriginal languages since 1976. That year, he and Petronella Vaarzon-Morel were appointed as teachers to the two-teacher school at Willowra, where they helped to initiate a bilingual program in Warlpiri. He subsequently studied anthropology at Indiana University's Bloomington campus, where he received his PhD, based on fieldwork in Brazil, in 1989. He has also worked for the Institute for Aboriginal Development (Alice Springs) and the Northern Land Council (Darwin). He is the co-author of numerous land claim reports for the Central Land Council and co-editor of *Recirculating Songs: Revitalising the Singing Practices of Indigenous Australia* (2017, Pacific Linguistics & Hunter Press). He is currently collaborating with Wonnarua and Guringai people on language revitalisation, under the auspices of Muurrbay Aboriginal Language and Culture Co-operative.

†**Fanny Walker Napurrurla** was a traditional Warlpiri woman who maintained a very strong connection to her father's Country of Jipiranpa, its stories and rituals. She was born in the Pawurrinji area near a rockhole called Karlampi, from which her personal name Karlampingali derived. Napurrurla lived at the Phillip Creek Native Settlement before being moved with two of her daughters to the Warrabri Aboriginal Reserve, now known as Alekarenge, established by the government in 1956. Napurrurla had a great love and knowledge of Warlpiri *yawulyu* and was an active performer until her death in 2019. In 2009, she and her sisters collaborated with their son Brian Murphy and his Ali Curung group, Band Nomadic, to create innovative performances combining her traditional *yawulyu* singing with western-style country rock music, including a song about Jipiranpa. In 1996–1997, Napurrurla was among a large group of Alekarenge women recorded by Linda Barwick singing two series of *Ngurlu* songs associated with Jipiranpa and Pawurrinji. In 2010, she collaborated with Barwick and Laughren in their documentation of the Jipiranpa song series

by again singing the verses, speaking them in Warlpiri and explaining their meaning and geographic context.

Stephen Wild received his Master of Arts in Musicology in 1967 from the University of Western Australia and his PhD in Anthropology in 1975 from Indiana University. He has taught at Monash University (1969–1972), City University of New York (1973–1978) and the Australian National University (1990–2011). He was a Research Fellow (1978–1998) and Research Director (1998–2000) at the Australian Institute of Aboriginal and Torres Strait Islander Studies. He has carried out field work in Lajamanu (1969–1980, 2007–2009), Maningrida (1980–1990) and elsewhere in Australia. Stephen has published articles and chapters in many journals, books and encyclopedias and has edited several books and scholarly journals. He was elected a Fellow of the Australian Academy of the Humanities, was twice President of the Musicological Society of Australia and Vice President of the International Council for Traditional Music (ICTM), and was Secretary General of ICTM 2006–2011. He was elected as an Honorary Member of ICTM in 2019. He is currently serving as a member of the Advisory Board of the Music and Minorities Research Center based in Vienna.

Glossary of Warlpiri words

Jardiwanpa	a large-scale and popular ceremony held for conflict resolution (owned by J/Nakamarra-J/Napurrurla and J/Nangala-J/Nampijinpa patrimoiety)
jilkaja	travels of a big group with a young male initiate to gather relations for initiation ceremonies
juju-ngaliya	Elders who have deep knowledge of Dreamings, songs and Country
jukurrpa	a timeless moment in which the world was and continues to be created (often translated as Dreaming)
Kankarlu	a secondary phase of initiation rites held in the past
kardiya	non-Indigenous people
kirda	owners for Dreamings, songs and Country through inheritance from father and father's father
Kirrirdikirrawanu	the second night of initiation rites held after Kurdiji (nowadays often replaced with Warawata)
Kurdiji	the public first day and night of initiation ceremonies
kurdungurlu	people who hold management rights for Dreamings, songs and Country through inheritance from their mother and mother's father
kuruwarri	the painted designs associated with Dreamings, songs and Country
Milpirri	a festival-like gathering in Lajamanu incorporating men's *purlapa*, women's *yawulyu* and choreographed hip-hop by Warlpiri youth

Ngajakula	a large-scale ceremony owned by J/Napaljarri-J/Nungarrayi and J/Napanangka-J/Napangardi
parnpa	men's songs and ceremonies
purlapa	public ceremonies involving men and women as singers and dancers
Warawata	a short ceremony held in the late afternoon of the day following Kurdiji ceremonies, held directly prior to the circumcision of initiates
watirirririrri	ceremonial boss, leader for Kurdiji ceremonies
yapa	Indigenous people (including those from outside Australia)
yawulyu	public women's ceremonies
yilpinji	men's and women's songs that make people fall in love

Chapter 1

Vitality and change in Warlpiri songs and ceremonies

By Georgia Curran, Linda Barwick, Valerie Napaljarri Martin, Simon Japangardi Fisher and Nicolas Peterson

Milya-pinjaku warlaljaku kuruwarriki manu jukurrpaku ngulaju yangka yaninjaku juju (ceremonies)-kurra jukurrpaku nyanjaku manu milya-pinjaku. Yungurlupa mardarni jukurrpa tarnngangku-juku. Juju, yangka nganakurlangu warlalja (families)-ku. Yalumpu ngulakanpa nyina, kajikanpa kanginy-karri, yangka jujungka manu jukurrparla ngulakalu yirrarni.

To know our own *kuruwarri* and stories we must go to the ceremonies so we can learn about them. We must look after them and remember them. We can keep them for ourselves, for our own knowledge. How can we know who they belong to, to which families? You might not know who a design or a ceremony belongs to. But by attending these [ceremonies] you will know these *jukurrpa*.

Nganaku purda-nyanjaku, nganangkulpangku ngarrikarla? Yungunpa pina-pina-jarrimi kuruwarriki. Nyarrpara-wana-jangka nguru-jangka manu nyarrpara-wana-jangka jukurrpa parnka manu ngurukari-kirralku ka yanirra. Nyarrpa karlipa kanginy-karri, nganangku kapu-ngalpa pina-pina-mani kurdu-kurduju … (our generations today). Yangka warlalja (family) nganakurlangu family kujarra generations murnma kaji yanirni. Yungulu milya-pinyi kurdukurdurlu (our generations) jalangu-warnu-paturlu. Nyarrpa kalu-jana rdanparni jukurrpa-kurraju nganakurlangu? Nganangkulku kapu-jana pina-pina-mani nyampurra kajilpalu walku-jarrimi? Nganangkulku? Yungurlupa ngalipa-nyangu juju milya-pinyi junga-nyayirnirli jukurrpa-wati manu kuruwarri-wati. Nganangkulku kapi-jana pina-pina-mani yalumpurraju jukurrpaku manu kuruwarriki? Nganangkulku kapu-ngalpa pina-mani kurdu-kurdu ngalipa-nyangu?

How can you know about your *jukurrpa* and stories? Who is going to tell you or teach you about which country you are from and what you should know? Which country does the *jukurrpa* travel from and where does it go to? We worry a lot about how we can learn! Who is going to teach us and our kids now, today? Our own family that belongs to that [Dreaming] should keep passing on this one, so that our kids today will know how our *jukurrpa* and stories are connected. How will they know that? Who will teach them? Who? Who will teach us our own *jukurrpa* and stories the right way. Who is going to teach them that strong knowledge about *jukurrpa* and *kuruwarri*? Who is going to teach them those *jukurrpa* stories? Who is going to keep teaching our kids in the near future?

Jalangurluju, jalangurlu-juku yungunkulu milya-pinyi jukurrpaju nyurrurla-nyangu warlalja-kurlangu, nyarrpara-wana kajinpa yani. Ngana-kurlangu yungunpa milya-pinyi manu yungunpa-nyanu milya-pinyi nyuntu-nyangu warlalja-nyayirni nguru-jangka nyarrpara-jangka kuruwarriji nyarrpara-jangka jukurrpaju. Nyarrpara-wana-jangka yanurnu, nyarrpara ka yani? Kujarra. Yangka milya-pinja-nyayirniki yungulu ngalipa-nyangurlu kurdu-kurdurlu jalangu-warnu-paturlu milya-pinyi, manu mardarni yungulu, kajili wiri-jarrilki yungulu-jana yinkijirni nyampurra kuruwarriji yinyakarilki yinyakarilki yinyakarilki kurdukarilki nyanungurra-nyangu. Kujaku karna wangkami.

Now, today you should know and acknowledge our own family connections, so that our kids will know their cultural heritage. How can you know for sure your own *jukurrpa* and stories from your country, where it comes from? Where is it going? Like that. So that our kids today will really know and acknowledge their own stories and *jukurrpa*, and keep them. When they grow up and come to know their *jukurrpa* and stories and to pass them on to the next generation, to their kids, to their kids and so on, generation to generation.

Nyiya-jangka karnalu warrki-jarrimi? Nyiya-jangka? Jalangu-warnupaturlu kamparru-warnurlu yungulu milya-pinyi-nyayirni ngingingingirli. Nyanungurra-nyangu warlalja-nyanu jukurrpa. Nyarrpara-jangka nguru-jangka yanurnu? Yungulu-nyanu mardarni nyanungurra-nyangu, warlalja-kurlangu juju. Yungulu-jana pina-pina-mani nyanungurra-nyanulku kurdukur-

1 Vitality and change in Warlpiri songs and ceremonies

dulku. Kamparru-warnupaturlu ngulaju … yungulu yani nyanjaku warlalja nyanungurra-nyangu jukurrpa.

Why are we doing this work? What for today? So that our generations today can know for sure and keep their own stories and *jukurrpa* and their knowledge, their cultural heritage. Where did [that *jukurrpa*] come from? Where did it go? How far? They are their own stories and *jukurrpa*. So that from generation to generation they can teach their kids, our future generations, even the ones here can teach our future generations.

Ngaliparlu yungurlupa-jana manngu-nyanyi wiyarrpa ngalipa-nyangu family yungurlupa-jana kujanya proud nyina. Yungurlupa-jana kujarlu manngu-nyanyi tarnngangku-juku. Jukurrpa, kuruwarri kalalu milyapinjarla nyurruwiyi-nyurruwiyi langangku mardarnu. Mardarnu kalalunyanu jujuju kujapiyarlu. Family connection kalalu-nyanu mardarnu junga-nyayirnirli. Yirriyirrirli kalalu kuruwarriji milya-pungu manu jukurrpaju. Nganalpa yukayarla yangka kujarra-piya kala-nyanu milyapinjarla ngarrurnu … jungarngirli right way. Ngana-kurlangu jukurrpa? Kalalu-jana yinyapatu kujarra-piya langa-kurra mardarnu jukurrpakungarduyurlu? Kalalu-jana wiyarrparlu mardarnu ngulalpalu nyurruwiyi-nyurruwiyi jujungka nyinaja. Nyinanjarla kalalu-nyanu purda-nyangu tarruku-nyayirni nyurru-warnu-paturlu.

All of us now we can think back and remember and be proud of our families and keep remembering forever. How they used to be strong and had knowledge and kept it in their minds from way back a long time ago for their *jukurrpa* and stories. Like that. They used to know their connections and were really careful with their *kuruwarri* and their *jukurrpa*. They were careful of who could join in and who could not – they did it the right way. They used to wonder and ask who the *jukurrpa* belongs to, like that, they would hear/see it and know who it belongs to. The poor things, they used to keep ceremonies and the knowledge from a long time ago. They would sit and listen to one another about the really sacred things from way back.

(Statement and translation by Valerie Napaljarri Martin)

Ceremonies are vital to the cultural identity of Warlpiri people living in communities across the Tanami Desert region of Central Australia (see Figure 1.1). At the heart of ceremonies are the songs that make ceremonies effective; that celebrate people's relationships to the land; and that encode detailed information about Warlpiri Country, cosmology and kinship.

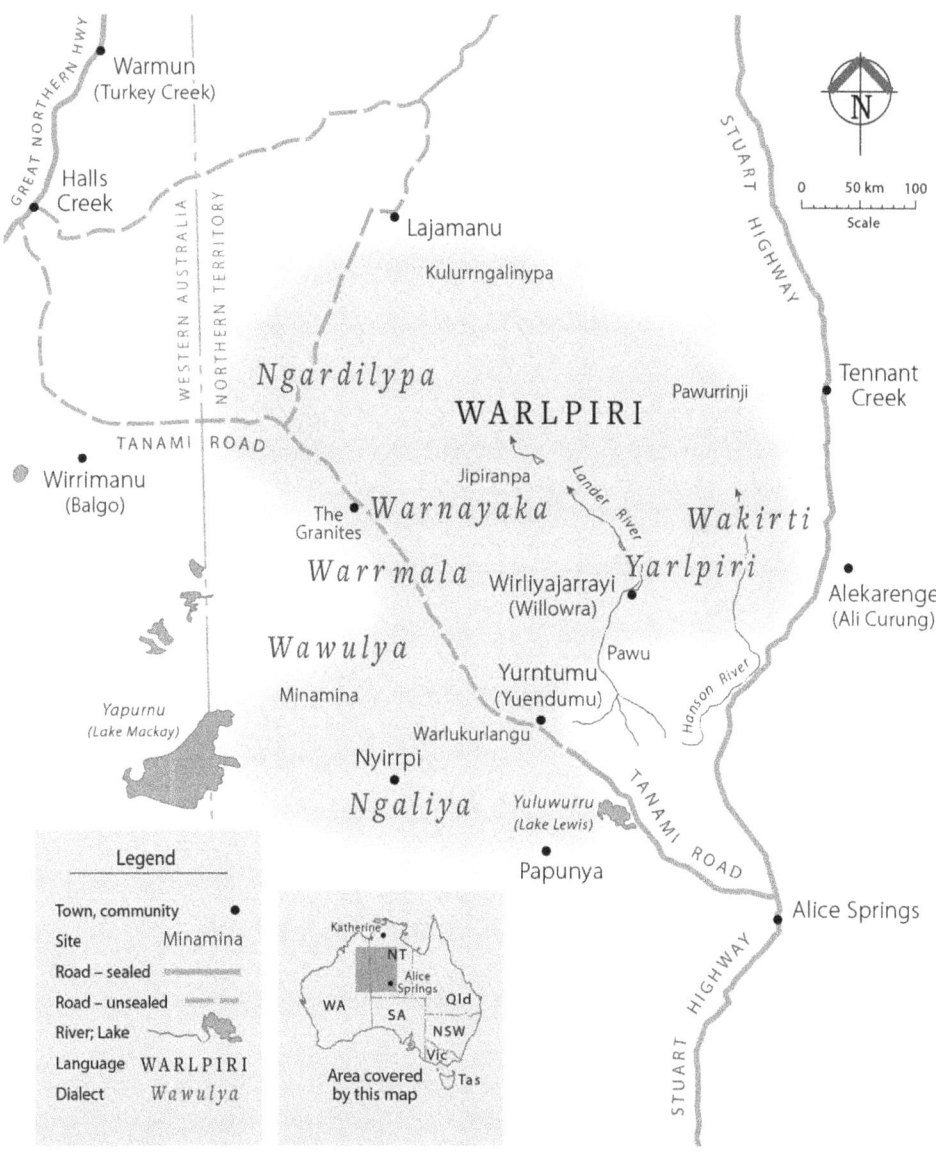

Figure 1.1. The Warlpiri regions. (Map by Brenda Thornley)

Warlpiri ceremonies are organised into named genres and repertories comprised of defined songs whose textual, musical and dance characteristics mark them as belonging to particular groups of people who also own the associated Country and cultural knowledge. Today, however, the ceremonies in which the songs are sung are in decline, and only a small group of the eldest generation has full knowledge of the songs and their associated meanings. For many Warlpiri people, as Valerie Napaljarri Martin emphasised above, this raises a level of uncertainty about how these important aspects of their cultural life will be carried forward into the future. Can the songs continue to have meaning without the ceremonial contexts?

In 2018 Warlpiri Elder Rex Japanangka Granites (c. 1949–2019) replied to questions on whether he was concerned about a decline in knowledge and practice of songs among younger generations of Warlpiri people in the following way:

> Well with our old songs, they should be taught, because that's the songline. We can't change it because it's there all the time, you know the country never changes. *Kuruwarri* tracks are always there. I mean, the songs don't change, it's there because we still sing the tracks of how it is. Like if it's trees or rocks, it never changes, you never pull it down. It's there all the time in the tracks. (R. Granites 2018)

In this way, he compared his Warlpiri Country to a living archival repository; because Warlpiri cultural heritage is held to be within Country eternally, he expressed his assured faith and optimism around its safety, continuity and future. As is the case for many Aboriginal peoples across Central Australia whose worldviews centre around a timeless creational epoch known in Warlpiri as *jukurrpa*, historical time merges with the present and the future (Myers 1986, 48–54), accounting for this affirmation of the ever-presence of Ancestral Beings and their songs and stories. Other Warlpiri Elders also share this view. For example, senior *yawulyu* singer Lorraine Nungarrayi Granites stated that:

> *Nyampuju tarnnga-juku ka nguna, jukurrpaju ka nguna tarnnga-juku. Nuulpa change-jarriyarla-rlangu lawa. Tarnnga-juku ka nguna jukurrpaju, kajili kamparru-warnu-paturlu wajawaja-maninjayani, kapu yinyakarirlilki mardarni jujuju.*
>
> [Songs are] always here forever. There will be no change. *Jukurrpa* is here forever. If the older generations pass on, then the younger generations can carry on with the ceremonies. (Granites and Brown 2017)

While these assertions pervade the thinking of older generations of Warlpiri people, there is also deep reflection on the past vibrancy of ceremonial life and its decline in recent decades. When listening to recordings of Warlpiri women's ceremony made in the 1970s, senior female singer Lynette Nampijinpa Granites nostalgically reflected:

> Back then there were so many women dancing. Listen to their feet – there are so many of them. We used to do business every day back then. Now we only do it sometimes. (Granites and Brown 2017)

The same Elders also reiterate the importance of making sure that younger generations have the means to reactivate and access the songs and ceremonies in the future. Another Elder and prominent *yawulyu* singer, Peggy Nampijinpa Brown, explained that:

> *Kuruwarriji tarnngangku-juku, kurdu karnalu-jana pina-pina-mani yangka, yungulu kurdungku mardarni tarnngangku-juku ngula karnalu-jana pina-mani. Nyampunya karlipa-janarla yirrarnilki.*

> *Kuruwarri* are here forever, we teach the young generations so they can learn and keep the culture with them. That's why we teach them. That is why we are doing this work [documenting songs]. (Granites and Brown 2017)

Nyirrpi-based *yawulyu* singer Alice Nampijinpa Henwood (2018) explained how she addresses this concern by proactively teaching younger generations about songs and ceremonies and continually reiterating the importance of the stories for their family history and cultural heritage:

> *Wangkami karna-jana yangka "Nyuntu-nyangu warringiyi-kirlangu-nyanu yunpaka waja, nyampukari yangka warringiyikari-kirlangu yunparni". Wangkami karna-jana yangka kalu nyinami, nyinami yangka kalu. Nyuyumani karna-jana, wali wangka karnalu, wangka karna-jana ngajulu yungulu yangka jungangku yangka warringiyi-nyanu-kurlangu might be yapirliyi-nyanu-kurlangu yunparni. Warringiyi-nyanu-kurlangu-juku-jala, ngula-kurlangu yungulu yangka yunparniyi nyanungurrarlulku kajili yangka lawarra jarrilki ngularlanguku yangka.*

> I say to them "This is your grandfather's Country and Dreaming – you sing it". I get them together and they listen to me when I tell them the stories about their grandfathers' and grandmothers' Dreamings. So later on when we pass away they can carry on with the singing. (Henwood 2017)

Responding to these concerns about the passing on of knowledge of ceremonies and their associated songs, this chapter addresses the tension between the continuity of tradition and the inevitability of change. Although Warlpiri people are often adamant that *jukurrpa* ancestors created traditional songs in the exact forms in which they are sung today, changes to and inventions within Warlpiri song forms are common and easily incorporated into this Warlpiri understanding of song transmission. Françoise Dussart (2000) has detailed the Warlpiri process of dreaming "new" songs – a phenomenon also addressed by Stephen Wild (1987) and illustrated in Chapter 4 of this book by Glowczewski and Gibson. Both Ken Hale (1984) and Peter Sutton (1987) have discussed processes by which songs are sung with slight but deliberate differences so

1 Vitality and change in Warlpiri songs and ceremonies

that knowledgeable Elders have avenues for control of the dissemination of knowledge and creativity while maintaining the powerful essence at the core of the ceremonial manifestations of *jukurrpa* (see also Marett 1994; Merlan 1987; Sutton 1987). The renowned ethnomusicologist Bruno Nettl explained this relationship of the past to the present as "the idea that something that a society maintains and shares can change in character and detail and yet remain essentially the same" (Nettl 1996: np).

This conceptual framework allows for change in different ways and at different rates, while also recognising the ever-presence of a life-force or essence that is referred to by Warlpiri people as *jukurrpa* or *kuruwarri*.[1] This essence is held consubstantially within places on Warlpiri Country, within Warlpiri people with inherited ties to it, and within songs and ceremonies. In Chapters 3–10, the authors present case studies of different aspects of Warlpiri songs and ceremonies as they relate to continuity and change. Each of these is historically contextualised, some are based on ethnographies of past decades (e.g., Chapters 3, 4 and 9), some on more contemporary initiatives (e.g., Chapters 8 and 10), and others have as their focus the analytical aspects of musical details in recordings (e.g., Chapters 5, 6 and 7). In this chapter, we address some of the major themes that arise through this concern with continuity and change, particularly through an assessment of the present-day vitality of Warlpiri songs and ceremonies, barriers to intergenerational transmission and considerations for potential revitalisation. We begin, however, by setting out the social and musical context against which to consider these issues.

The Warlpiri social and musical context

The Warlpiri region of Central Australia dominates the expansive Tanami Desert covering a broad region north-west of the major town of Alice Springs, flanked by Lake Mackay on the western side and Anmatyerr communities, including Yuelamu, Laramba and Ti-Tree, on the eastern side. Willowra lies on Warlpiri land, but many people residing there also have Kaytetye, Anmatyerr or Alyawarr links. The most northern Warlpiri community, Lajamanu, is located on Gurindji Country, but close by to the south is Warlpiri land with its associated *jukurrpa*, songs and ceremonies. The southern part of Warlpiri Country borders Luritja and Pintupi lands and the communities of Papunya, Haasts Bluff and Mount Liebig.

---

1 In some Aboriginal languages in Central Australia, the word for "taste" or "scent" is used to refer to this essence (Ellis 1985: 86).

In Alice Moyle's 1974 classification of musical regions of Australia, Warlpiri groups are within the region described as "'C' Central and South Central (interior Northern Territory to Bight)" (1974, xiv), encompassing a large section of the western half of South Australia and all the Central Australian region of the Northern Territory. Moyle described songs in this region (as well as many others in Australia) as "Continuous" in that they have "*similar* strings of syllables and melodic divisions marked by descents. The sound instruments used in accompaniment … belong to the idiophone class [percussion instruments]" [emphasis in original] (1974, 352). According to Moyle, other shared features across this region are the use of sound instruments to mark a finish to singing, song items of comparatively short duration (one minute or less) and several vocal descents within the one song item (Moyle 1974, 352). She also noted similarities with the region to the west, an influence recognised more recently by Treloyn (2017) despite Moyle's categorisation of the Kimberley as a different "musical region".

Aboriginal groups across this desert region and beyond engaged in significant trade and exchange of songs and ceremonies well before Europeans arrived. Some Elders today reflect on these histories to time-depths well beyond their own memories. A recent example of ceremonial borrowing is evident in the present-day Kurdiji ceremonies held each summer for the initiation of young boys into adulthood, in which the original Warlpiri Kirrirdikirrawarnu ceremony has been replaced by the simpler and less time-intensive ceremony Warawata, borrowed from Pintupi groups in the south (Curran 2020; Myers 1986). Despite the complexity of the interrelationships between different Aboriginal groups and the fluidity of ceremonial authority in contexts of trade and exchange, Warlpiri people are quite clear about the lines of authority with regards to being "boss" for ceremonies, so much so that there are bitter disputes on the rare occasions when this is questioned. Ceremonies, and their role in fostering social connections between groups, have been a primary reason for extensive travel across this region. Widespread travel continues to this day, with most Warlpiri people undertaking long-distance journeys to participate in initiation ceremonies in various locations across the desert, a practice only enhanced as more Warlpiri people have come to own cars since the 1970s (Peterson 2000).

Since the establishment of settlements across Warlpiri Country in the years following World War II, there has been a tendency for larger-scale ceremonies that are inclusive of more community members to predominate (Kolig 1981; for descriptions of the sweeping "Balgo business" in the 1980s, see also Laughren 1981; Wild 1981; Young 1981). By far and away, the most common of these today are the regional variations of the Kurdiji (for initiation), which has expanded significantly in scale in the last five decades, now often involving hundreds of people from numerous family groups. Smaller-scale site-based ceremonies are nowadays only held in connection with Kurdiji ceremonies. However, senior Warlpiri singers hold in their minds a score or more of different *jukurrpa*, each including many unique songs.

Table 1.1 lists the main Warlpiri song genres, named according to the ceremonies in which they are sung.[2] The table distinguishes these different genres based on performative restrictions, the gender of the performers and the ceremonial contexts in which they are performed. These are the genres of Warlpiri songs and ceremonies currently known by singers living in Warlpiri communities today.

Table 1.1. Features of Warlpiri song genres and ceremonies based on contemporary attitudes (which may shift over time).

Song genre / ceremony name	Performance restrictions (restricted, private, public)	Gender of performers	Ceremonial contexts in which they are sung
Kurdiji (songline chosen from community)	Public	Male singers, female dancers	Kurdiji (initiation ceremonies) held in public community contexts
Jardiwanpa/ Ngajakula	Public	Male singers, female dancers	Conflict resolution ceremonies (see Chapter 8) held in public community contexts
Parnpa	Restricted to men	Male singers and dancers	Components of Kurdiji, private men's contexts
Purlapa	Public	Male and female singers, male dancers	Public community events

---

2 Meggitt (1962, 209) and Dussart (2000) have also defined Warlpiri song genres and ceremonies with some slight differences to these categories. Curran (2020) also included a genre of men's singing *juyurdu* "sorcery songs", but these have been excluded here as they are no longer sung.

Song genre / ceremony name	Performance restrictions (restricted, private, public)	Gender of performers	Ceremonial contexts in which they are sung
Yilpinji (men's and women's)	Restricted to men or women only, some men's songs are sung in public contexts	Male singers and dancers, or female singers and dancers	Gender-restricted contexts
Yawulyu	Private and public (depending on performance context)	Female singers and dancers	Private women's contexts and public community events
Jilkaja-ku	Women only	Female only (boys and men are asleep)	While accompanying boys on *jilkaja* (initiatory) journeys

While some of these genres share names and basic forms with neighbouring Aboriginal groups (e.g., *yawulyu*, or *awely* in Arandic languages, are sung by women across Central Australia; Gurindji *wajarra* have similar entertaining purposes to *purlapa*), others are distinctly Warlpiri. Warlpiri songlines relating to sites on Warlpiri Country are also incorporated into imported ceremonial forms traded from other regions. For example, the Jardiwanpa/Ngajakula ceremonial complex, held high by people in Warlpiri communities, has historical links to the north-east from where it was brought south-west to Warlpiri Country in the early 20th century. A version of this ceremony was described by Spencer and Gillen (1901) as it was held among Warumungu people near Tennant Creek. Despite its origin, the Warlpiri Jardiwanpa does not relate to Warumungu Country but rather is centred around a songline beginning at Wirnparrku (west of Haasts Bluff) and travelling northwards through owned Warlpiri sites (see Chapter 8 for a discussion of a counterpart and similarly performed ceremony: Ngajakula). The larger-scale ceremonies held by Warlpiri people today, like Kurdiji, may include sections of different genres, with men and women separately performing *parnpa* and *yawulyu* in the earlier stages and later joining to sing Kurdiji songs in the all-night section of the ceremony.

Musical vitality of Warlpiri song genres

Internationally, there are some standard measures of musical vitality, including trends in the number of proficient musicians, the age range of participants and the performance frequency and contexts. Catherine Grant's "Musical Vitality Endangerment Framework" (2014) is a 12-factor assessment tool to systematically measure the vitality or endangerment of music genres worldwide. Both a quantitative and qualitative measurement is given against each of the factors. Schippers and Grant further argue that this systematic way of measuring musical vitality is important for at least three reasons:

> 1) To enable diagnosis of situations of music endangerment and determine the urgency to implement initiatives towards sustainability; 2) to ensure the right remedial action is taken, as assessing the factors causing endangerment will help establish focus and priorities for action, and 3) to enable methodical evaluation of the efficacy of any efforts to maintain or revitalise the music genre. (Schippers & Grant 2016, 106)

Such a tool provides one way to measure the vitality of Warlpiri songs against a broader international context. Additional measures specifically developed for Aboriginal Australian song include the average number of unique songs performed per occasion, changes in the relative frequency of performance of different songs and the musical diversity of song repertoires (e.g., how many different tempi, melodies and rhythmic types are performed per repertory over time; Treloyn and Charles 2021; Treloyn, Martin and Charles 2016). In Warlpiri contexts, the number and complexity of specific dances performed and *kuruwarri* designs painted are also important measures of ceremonial vitality.

While presenting points for comparison with the transmission of oral traditions on a broader international scale, such data must be set against broader understandings of transmission and vitality of ceremonial song in Aboriginal Australia developed by and with practitioners, including practitioner understandings of the contemporary decline in the holding of ceremonies and collaborative development of practical ways by which song transmission can be revitalised.

The assessment presented in Table 1.2 has taken "Warlpiri song" as a general category, encompassing all genres outlined in Table 1.1. We acknowledge that some Warlpiri genres, and certain repertories within these genres, have relative strength compared to others and have included more specific comments to this effect in italics in the "Assessment of Warlpiri songs" column. We have followed the guide as set out by Grant in undertaking this assessment (2014, 111–24). For further consideration of how the Warlpiri context compares to other international contexts on this scale, Grant's guide is a useful reference. Grant's assessment requires placement of the music genre on a scale from 0 to 5, representing increasing vitality.

Table 1.2. Assessment of the vitality of Warlpiri song genres against the 12 factors of Grant's "Music Vitality and Endangerment Framework" (2014).

Grant's 12 factors	Degree of vitality (0–5)	Assessment of Warlpiri songs (using Grant's assessment rubrics and with Warlpiri specific comments in italics)
Factor 1: Intergenerational transmission *A key indicator of strength	2 Severely endangered: the music genre is performed mostly by older generations.	*Some younger people attend ceremonies and participate in dancing and are painted with designs but are not learning how to sing.*
Factor 2: Change in number of proficient musicians in the past 5–10 years	1 Significant decrease in proficient musicians.	*Songs are only known by a small group of Elders, and many have passed away in the last 5–10 years.*
Factor 3: Change in number of people engaged with the genre in the past 5–10 years	2 Moderate decrease in people engaged with the genre.	*Many older singers are passing away with an overall decrease in engagement. Nevertheless, there is some recent interest in revitalisation projects from middle and younger generations.*
Factor 4: Pace and direction of change in music and music practices in the past 5–10 years	1 Pace and direction of change reflect significantly decreased strength.	*For most songs, there is a rapid rate of change in a negative direction (harmful for the music genre). For public genres, particularly yawulyu but also purlapa to a lesser degree, new contexts for performance are being taken up and the rate of change is slower (more people retaining) and more positive (is useful for maintenance of the music genre).*

Grant's 12 factors	Degree of vitality (0–5)	Assessment of Warlpiri songs (using Grant's assessment rubrics and with Warlpiri specific comments in italics)
Factor 5: Change in performance context(s) and function(s) in the past 5–10 years	2 The music genre is performed only in irregular formulaic contexts and functions.	*Warlpiri songs are mostly performed in ceremonial contexts, so their social function has changed, but this does not apply to Kurdiji in the summer ceremonial season.*
Factor 6: Response to mass media and the music industry	2 Weak – The genre shows reluctance in its engagement with and response to mass media and the music industry.	*Senior singers are not interested in engagement, and younger people feel a lack of authority to drive engagement with mass media.*
Factor 7: Accessibility of infrastructure and resources	4 All infrastructure and resources required for creating, performing, rehearsing and transmitting the music genre are accessible, but not necessarily easily.	*Minimal infrastructure and resources are required and are mostly available (e.g., ochres, feathers, materials), although there can be some difficulty in accessing these.*
Factor 8: Accessibility of knowledge and skills for music practices	1 The community holds only some of the required knowledge and skills.	*Warlpiri songs are embedded in complex multimodal ceremonial forms, which only a small number of people have the learned skills and knowledge required to perform.*
Factor 9: Official attitudes towards the genre	4 The genre is supported through overarching policies supporting cultural expressions, without differentiation and without consultation with culture bearers.	*Australian governments provide theoretical and funding support for "maintenance of endangered songs" but do not consult with Warlpiri singers about their specific context.*

Grant's 12 factors	Degree of vitality (0–5)	Assessment of Warlpiri songs (using Grant's assessment rubrics and with Warlpiri specific comments in italics)
Factor 10: Community members' attitudes towards the genre	3 Community support for the maintenance of the music genres is moderate.	*Warlpiri Elders and middle-aged generations are proud of these traditions and see them as core to their cultural identity, whereas younger generations see them as old-fashioned.*
Factor 11: Relevant outsiders' attitudes towards the genre	4 Support for the music genres by relevant outsiders is strong.	*Staff of community organisations and researchers provide support for activities that promote and set up regular performance contexts. There is also interest in the music genres from a broader intercultural audience outside Warlpiri communities.*
Factor 12: Documentation of the genre	2 Limited documentation exists in varying quality.	*Warlpiri women's* yawulyu *have been better documented than other genres of Warlpiri song, but many repertories remain undocumented, and only a small number have been documented in an accessible and usable way, although current work is adding to this.*

Eight of the 12 factors (1–6, 8, 12) firmly place Warlpiri song in a category of endangerment, which is a red flag, as many senior and middle-age generations of Warlpiri people recognise, as do outsiders who understand these kinds of song traditions to be unique and valuable expressions of humanity (United Nations Educational, Scientific and Cultural Organization 2021). As expressed by Fisher:

1 Vitality and change in Warlpiri songs and ceremonies

> [Support for ceremonial vitality] is dear to my heart as a Warlpiri man. Within my lifetime I have witnessed the decline in traditional modes of transferring knowledge that is core to Warlpiri identity. This project will initiate new ways for our community to ensure the passing on of this knowledge to younger generations.

Despite their clear endangered status, the ceremonies and their related songs remain key to Warlpiri life and cultural heritage; Warlpiri people, young and old, express a deep desire for their continuation even if they are unable to muster the support to hold the ceremonies. It is significant to note from the above assessment of musical vitality that, despite the challenges to intergenerational transmission and struggles to pass on the knowledge required to sing songs, there is community interest in supporting the maintenance of Warlpiri song (Factors 9 and 10), and the relevant infrastructure continues to be available (Factor 7), as well as relatively good levels of support from outsiders including researchers and non-Warlpiri staff who work at community organisations (Factor 11). Although considerable efforts to document the songs have been made (Factor 12), existing documentation is patchy (especially indexing of older material, which affects searchability). Community-led efforts to improve documentation of certain genres (e.g., *yawulyu*) have served to highlight the urgency and complexity of undertaking this time-consuming work with other genres. This work is dependent on strong collaborative relationships between Warlpiri Elders, Warlpiri linguists and language workers; younger participants; and support from researchers and community organisations (Curran 2020; Curran, Fisher and Barwick 2018).

Barriers to intergenerational transmission

Despite all this interest and concern, loss of song knowledge is unavoidably continuing apace. This is because it is an effect of modernisation. For older Warlpiri people, songs and the ceremonial contexts of their singing have been instrumental in achieving a wide range of practical ends ranging from affecting the weather, affecting people's affections, curing sickness, making people fall sick, causing plants and animal species to flourish, making boys into men and resolving disputes, to mention the most important. The loss of song knowledge is driven by a complex of factors, including declining acceptance of the instrumental effectiveness of some of the ceremonies and, therefore, the motivation to hold them. Other important factors are changing world views and loss of detailed knowledge of Country (Barwick, Laughren and Turpin 2013). These key factors also reflect changing demographics within the Warlpiri communities, marked by an expanding young population and an older population with disproportionate levels of chronic illness. Although increased mobility has extended the range of social networks across the desert (Peterson 2000), leading to initiation ceremonies becoming larger than ever, this is putting disproportionate pressure on the few senior men who possess the knowledge and fitness required to sing the songs for them, and fewer individuals seem to be actually mastering the related songlines (Curran 2011; Peterson 2008).

While Grant's music vitality assessment emphasises that a key indicator of the strength of a musical genre is the level of intergenerational transmission, the loss of song knowledge is not about musical tradition, as such, but rather the loss of the significance of the ceremonies and, therefore, the motivation of the younger generations to invest the necessary discipline and time required to learn the songs. The songs cannot just be picked up through rote learning or copying what is heard on a recording because their significance is embedded in ceremonial purpose and is highly multimodal, joining singing with dancing, body decoration and ceremonial constructions. Musically, these songs come together in complex ways, with the words and rhythms to which verses are set needing to be matched to melodic forms that are not the same each time the song is performed (Curran and Yeoh 2021). To be able to pick up these musical skills, extensive background experience participating in ceremonial contexts is essential; however, the issue of belief is also fundamental.

For songs to have a life independent of their traditional ceremonial context, there must be a repurposing that provides people with a meaningful motivation to learn and perform them. Warlpiri women have successfully achieved this in relation to the *yawulyu* genre that was in the past particularly linked to women's health maintenance and conflict resolution but which has now found a role in the intercultural domain of cultural exchange such as exhibition openings (see Curran and Dussart 2023; Dussart 2004).

Some ideas for community-led revitalisation

Strategies for supporting the survival of the important cultural knowledge held in song, especially as it relates to place, are necessary if future generations are to have a way of accessing this. These must recognise that the old motivations for holding ceremonies are fading fast (with the exception of the *Kurdiji* ceremonies) and that new and rewarding forums need to be created if interest in songs is to be revitalised. Targeted projects across Australia, including the Top End (Marett et al. 2006), Kimberley regions (Treloyn and Charles 2015, 2021) and Noongar region (Bracknell and Scott 2019), have shown some success in revitalisation efforts. Here, we suggest several strategies for community-led revitalisation and engagement with vulnerable musical traditions. These suggestions have been developed from discussions within our project (detailed in Chapter 2), as well as noted successes in other similar projects.

1. Supporting existing ceremonial contexts

The late senior Elder H. Nelson highlighted that one of the main ways in which songs and ceremonial knowledge are passed on today is in the Kurdiji ceremonies held each summer, sometimes several times in individual Warlpiri communities (as well as other communities across Central Australia). Warlpiri people also travel widely across the desert to participate in these ceremonies in other communities with which they share social and ceremonial relationships. In these contexts, adult men often learn for the first time how to paint the designs of their patrilineally inherited *jukurrpa*, as well as how to dance to the *parnpa*. Women may also participate in *yawulyu*, and large numbers of people participate in dancing in the all-night component (Curran 2020). It is evident, however, that only a small group of senior men know how to sing the songs to pull this ceremony together. Providing practical and logistical support for these ceremonies, which are still being held annually, is perhaps one of the most crucial areas where revitalisation can occur.

2. Setting up and supporting performance spaces and occasions in communities

In many Warlpiri communities, there are initiatives to set up new spaces for the performance of these vulnerable song traditions. For example, Warlpiri women from across the Tanami Desert communities participate biannually in the Southern Ngaliya dance camps in which community organisations support a camp-out in an outstation near a Warlpiri community, including transport, food and payments for participation. The Women's Law and Culture meeting led by the Central Land Council is another example of this kind of support for a set-up context.

Men have generally not sought the same level of support, but there have been grassroots efforts to revitalise *purlapa* in southern Warlpiri communities with Elders singing while instructing young men on how to dance (Curran and Sims 2021). This is empowering for Warlpiri men but lacks frequency as it does not occur to a schedule or have external support. By contrast, the biennial Lajamanu-based Milpirri festival (designed, in Wanta Steven Jampijinpa Patrick's words, to "make *jukurrpa* relevant to the 21st century"; Biddle 2019) is carried out with external funding and in partnership with Tracks Dance Company (discussed in

Chapter 10). Chapter 8 of this volume describes a song documentation project that aspired to the revitalisation of song knowledge of Ngajakula in Willowra. Warlpiri women from Yuendumu have also become involved in many projects to support *yawulyu* events, including setting up dance camp events and staged performances in larger cities and towns (Curran and Dussart 2023).

3. Documentation of song and ceremony

Song documentation, a recognised factor in Grant's framework, has been undertaken for a number of decades in Yuendumu, with a recent surge in the last 10 years. While these documentary projects produce valuable resources that can be used by communities, it is the process of working on these materials that is one of the biggest factors contributing to revitalisation. Recent documentation work (Gallagher et al. 2014; Laughren and Turpin 2013; Warlpiri Women from Yuendumu and Curran 2017; many of the chapters in this book) has contributed to a better understanding of Warlpiri songs but has made it obvious that the substantial recorded legacy of this important element of Warlpiri cultural heritage is still inadequately documented and thus of limited usefulness as a basis for revitalisation. It is urgent to bring older and younger generations of Warlpiri people together to document further details of the language, music and other associated cultural information for these legacy recordings – not only to pass down the cultural knowledge embedded in them but also to plan how to sustain their traditions into the future.

4. Engagement with archival materials

While we devote more attention to this in Chapter 2, it must be mentioned that engagement with archival resources contributes significantly to song knowledge. In reviewing and managing collections of audio, visual and audiovisual materials that have been made in Warlpiri communities, Warlpiri people can gain significant understanding and knowledge of vulnerable traditions (Curran, Fisher and Barwick 2018). In Chapter 2, we address this further.

5. Promoting performance to a broader audience

Aboriginal Australian arts, culture and languages represent and are recognised as crucial and highly visible components of Australia's national identity; this high level of outside recognition can contribute to slowing if not reversing progress towards further endangerment. Opportunities for Warlpiri people to perform in broader public contexts engender support from outsiders who recognise the value of this unique song tradition and its encoding of biocultural knowledge and practices (Curran et al. 2019). Community engagement with research also

1 Vitality and change in Warlpiri songs and ceremonies

enables Warlpiri voices to participate in national and international debates on Indigenous cultural heritage and to contribute to current assessments of music vitality. This unique and innovative Indigenous perspective has a bearing on questions of song repatriation and revitalisation and, ultimately, to understandings of song change. By sharing information with other communities affected by similar issues and the broader community, new collaborations can emerge across Australia and internationally. The impacts of globalisation in Warlpiri communities have been pronounced, with all younger people having easy and frequent access to social media, which dominates a large part of their lives. While this connectivity provides greater access to entertainment from outside (with the consequent withdrawal of attention from local contexts), it also enhances sharing of cultural information via digital means with families and the broader Warlpiri diaspora, as well as the general public (Vaarzon-Morel, Barwick and Green 2021).

Outline of book structure

This book includes profiles of a number of Warlpiri people who were involved in interviews conducted at Pintubi Anmatjere Warlpiri Media and Communications (PAW Media) in 2017–2019. Valerie Napaljarri Martin and Simon Japangardi Fisher led these interviews, which were conducted in Warlpiri, transcribed and then translated by Theresa Napurrurla Ross into English. In these interviews, some with respected Elders and some with emerging cultural leaders, individuals reflected on the changes to songs and ceremonies across their lifetimes and the value of access to written, audio, video and photographic documentation of these ceremonies through the Warlpiri Media Archive held at PAW Media. Perspectives from these interviews have been included in individual profiles and incorporated into the ideas presented in Chapters 1 and 2.

The chapters gathered in this book relate directly to the issues raised in this chapter addressing the central tensions for Warlpiri people who see songs as forever held in Country and fundamental to their cultural identity but struggle to maintain and foresee their relevance in the current and future Warlpiri lives in which ceremonies are becoming increasingly less important for social functioning.

Chapter 2, written collaboratively by a team of researchers who have been working in Yuendumu at PAW Media, focuses on archiving and the value of on-Country archiving in Warlpiri communities. The perspectives of Elders who were interviewed on this topic are central to this chapter; their voices articulate the ways in which archival resources can be utilised by future generations to connect to their cultural heritage. This chapter also outlines, through the history of Warlpiri Media Association, how many of these issues have been at the forefront of Warlpiri minds since the beginnings in the mid-1980s. It details documentary efforts reaching back to early expedition-style recordings to present-day Warlpiri-led efforts.

The remaining chapters all focus on particular songlines or ceremonial contexts. Chapters 3 and 4, both based on ethnography from the 1970s and 1980s, illustrate the ways in which change is inherent in Warlpiri ceremonies, with negotiation and adaptability being central features. Chapter 3 provides a case study of how the motivation to hold a certain class of ceremony is unintentionally destroyed by factors external to the Warlpiri community. It follows the specific negotiations required of Paddy Japaljarri Sims to hold a winter solstice ceremony that would form public community recognition of his succession to and control of an important area of Warlpiri Country. However, this traditional mode of proving links to land was made irrelevant by the passing of the *Aboriginal Land Rights (Northern Territory) Act 1976*; the 1979 success of the Warlpiri land claim meant that being on lists and genealogies held by the Central Land Council was the key to recognition of rights.

Chapter 4 documents the main way in which a songline can be changed not by loss but by addition. Gibson recounts and reflects on the process of dreaming a "new" song and the ways this was incorporated into established Ngapa "Rain" and Yankirri "Emu" *jukurrpa* collectively held by Warlpiri women. The authors also reflect on how this song responded to particular contemporary circumstances and was a necessary addition to the repertory as it renewed spiritual links to land by incorporating this song into those that had been passed down through generations.

Chapters 5, 6 and 7 all focus on analyses of the songs sung during particular recorded performance instances, all dealing with technical aspects of the musical, linguistic and performative complexity of classical women's songs. Chapter 5 turns to the changes that have taken place in the Minamina *yawulyu* songline between 1972 and the 2010s. This chapter reveals that there have been significant changes in the extent and modes of performance, including song selection and explanation, musical setting and body designs; however, nevertheless, key themes expressed in song verses, music and body designs persist across the generations. In particular, those linked to connection to Country are emphasised, ensuring that a strong female cultural identity continues to be passed on to younger Warlpiri women.

1 Vitality and change in Warlpiri songs and ceremonies

Chapter 6 underlines the discipline and time that must be put into acquiring the old levels of performance, gives details of the rhythmic texts and reflects on the difficulty of working on the hard language of Warlpiri song in relation to two "edible seed" songlines. These are associated with Country around Jipiranpa and Pawurrinji, in the north-west of the Warlpiri region, as they were performed and explained by Fanny Walker Napurrurla. The analysis of the musical conventions of these songs as they are broken into verses uncovers thematic links to a trickster, Jakamarra, central to the *jukurrpa* storyline at Jipiranpa.

Chapter 7 unpacks the details of reduplication in a song set sung by Warlpiri women in Willowra, a Warlpiri region with many Kaytetye language influences. Through detailed examples of the Warnajarra verses recorded by Morais over 40 years ago, and more recently documented by the authors in 2019, they illustrate how the use of reduplication is associated with a particular faster syncopated meter, which relates to particular Warnajarra sites. In contrast, a slower rubato meter in which other verses are sung seems to relate more to other *jukurrpa*. This case study elegantly illustrates how rhythm and tempo encode the essence of the ancestors, furthering Catherine Ellis's observations of the representation of particular Ancestral Beings in melodies.

Chapters 8, 9 and 10 turn to Warlpiri efforts to ensure that ceremonial songs maintain their purpose and function against shifting social contexts. Chapter 8 addresses the attempt to reanimate the songs associated with the Ngajakula ceremony by involving the community in mapping the long songline to give the songline new relevance. The past role of the Ngajakula and related Jardiwanpa revolved around the resolution of conflict, but current emphasis is on it reinforcing connections to particular Warlpiri *jukurrpa* and sites and the shared Law of all Warlpiri across a broad region. This gives the songs significance without the ceremony, which may or may not be revived with a new focus of celebrating interconnectedness between Countries.

Chapter 9 concerns the most successful repurposing of both songs and ceremony. It is a classic study of how one group of Warlpiri women, among the first in the early 1980s, took their *yawulyu* songs and dance to southern Australia for the opening of exhibitions and meetings. It follows the travels of a group of Warlpiri people from Yuendumu to Adelaide to perform the Warlukurlangu *yawulyu*. Importantly, it presents the motivation of the ritual leaders, Dolly Nampijinpa Daniels/Granites and Judy Nampijinpa Granites, via discussion of their negotiations around the choices of performances, and recognises the rewards of travel and compensation.

The final chapter addresses the radical transformation of ceremony into theatre. It describes an entirely new musical performance of the Milpirri at Lajamanu, examining whether this follows a traditional form and can, therefore, be called a *purlapa* – or whether it is a quite new form and a festival. Milpirri is an emergent event that has been held biannually in Lajamanu since 2005 and which is intended to provide a platform for the rejuvenation of specific forms of song and dance, including from men's *purlapa* and women's *yawulyu*, joining these with choreographed hip-hop primarily performed by children from the school. The authors show the influences from Ancestral ritual genres, from the church and from the emergence of popular reggae and rock bands, and how these have been integrated with the assistance of Tracks Dance Company from Darwin working closely with Artistic Director Wanta Jampijinpa Patrick and other community members. This event marks the complete transformation from ceremonies motivated by traditional purposes, replacing them with a theatrical event with contemporary motivations and purposes.

References

Barwick, Linda, Mary Laughren and Myfany Turpin. 2013. "Sustaining Women's Yawulyu/Awelye: Some Practitioners' and Learners' Perspectives". *Musicology Australia* 35(2): 191–220. https://doi.org/10.1080/08145857.2013.844491

Biddle, Jennifer. 2019. "Milpirri: Activating the At-Risk". In *Energies in the Arts*, edited by Douglas Kahn, 351–371. Cambridge: MIT Press.

Bracknell, Clint and Kim Scott. 2019. "Ever-Widening Circles: Consolidating and Enhancing Wirlomin Noongar Archival Material in the Community". In *Archival Returns: Central Australia and Beyond*, edited by Linda Barwick, Jennifer Green and Petronella Vaarzon-Morel, 325–38. Honolulu; Sydney: University of Hawai'i Press and Sydney University Press.

Curran, Georgia. 2011. "The 'expanding domain' of Warlpiri initiation rituals". In *Ethnography and the Production of Anthropological Knowledge: Essays in Honour of Nicolas Peterson*, edited by Yasmine Musharbash and Marcus Barber, 39–50. Canberra: ANU E Press.

Curran, Georgia. 2020. *Sustaining Indigenous Songs*. New York: Berghahn.

Curran, Georgia and Françoise Dussart. 2023. "'We Don't Show our Women's Breasts for Nothing': Shifting Purposes for Warlpiri Women's Public Rituals –Yawulyu – Central Australia – 1980s–2010s". *Studies in Religion/Sciences Religieuses*. https://doi.org/10.1177/00084298231154430

Curran, Georgia and Otto Sims. 2021. "Performing *Purlapa*: Project Warlpiri Identity in a Globalised World". *The Asia Pacific Journal of Anthropology* 22(2-3): 203–19.

Curran, Georgia and Calista Yeoh. 2021. "'That is Why I Am Telling This Story': Musical Analysis as Insight into the Transmission of Knowledge and Performance Practice of a Wapurtarli Song by Warlpiri Women from Yuendumu, Central Australia". *Yearbook for Traditional Music* 53: 45–70. https://doi.org/10.1017/ytm.2021.4

Curran, Georgia, Simon Japangardi Fisher and Linda Barwick. 2018. "Engaging with Archived Warlpiri Songs". In *Communities in Control: Learning Tools and Strategies for Multilingual Endangered Language Communities – Proceedings of FEL XXI Alcanena 2017*, edited by Nicholas Ostler, Vera Ferreira and Chris Moseley, 167–74. Hungerford: Foundation for Endangered Languages. http://hdl.handle.net/2123/20389

Curran, Georgia, Linda Barwick, Myfany Turpin, Fiona Walsh and Mary Laughren. 2019. "Central Australian Aboriginal Songs and Biocultural Knowledge: Evidence from Women's Ceremonies Relating to Edible Seeds". *Journal of Ethnobiology* 39(3): 354–70. https://doi.org/10.2993/0278-0771-39.3.354

Dussart, Françoise. 2000. *The Politics of Ritual in an Aboriginal Settlement: Kinship, Gender and the Currency of Knowledge.* Washington: Smithsonian Institution Press.

Dussart, Françoise. 2004. "Shown but Not Shared, Presented but Not Proferred". *The Australian Journal of Anthropology* 15(3): 253–66.

Ellis, Catherine. 1985. *Aboriginal Music, Education for Living: Cross-cultural Experiences from South Australia.* Brisbane: University of Queensland Press.

Grant, Catherine. 2014. *Music Endangerment: How Language Maintenance Can Help.* New York: Oxford University Press.

Hale, Kenneth. 1984. "Remarks on Creativity in Aboriginal Verse". In *Problems and Solutions: Occasional Essays in Musicology Presented to Alice M. Moyle*, edited by Jamie C. Kassler and Jill Stubington, 254–62. Sydney: Hale & Iremonger.

Kolig, Erich. 1981. *The Silent Revolution: The Effects of Modernisation on Australian Aboriginal Religion.* Philadelphia: The Institute for the Study of Human Issues.

Laughren, Mary. 1981. *Religious Movements at Yuendumu 1975–1981.* Canberra: Australian Institute for Aboriginal Studies.

Marett, Allan. 1994. "*Wangga*: Socially Powerful Songs?" *The World of Music* 36: 67–81.

Marett, Allan, Mandawuy Yunupiŋu, Marcia Langton, Neparrnga Gumbula, Linda Barwick and Aaron Corn. 2006. "The National Recording Project for Indigenous Performance in Australia: Year One in Review." In *Backing Our Creativity: The National Education and the Arts Symposium, 12–14 September*

2005, 84–90. Surry Hills: Australia Council for the Arts. http://hdl.handle.net/2123/1337

Meggitt, Mervyn. 1962. *Desert People*. Sydney: Angus & Robertson.

Merlan, Francesca. 1987. "Catfish and Alligator: Totemic Songs of the Western Roper River, Northern Territory". In *Songs of Aboriginal Australia* (Oceania Monograph 32), edited by Margaret Clunies Ross, Tamsin Donaldson and Stephen Wild, 142–67. Sydney: University of Sydney.

Moyle, Alice. 1974. North Australian Music: A Taxonomic Approach to the Study of Aboriginal Song Performances. PhD thesis, Monash University, Melbourne.

Myers, Fred. 1986. *Pintupi Country, Pintupi Self: Sentiment, Place, and Politics Among Western Desert Aborigines*. Los Angeles: University of California Press.

Nettl, Bruno. 2013. "Relating the Present to the Past: Thoughts on the Study of Musical Change in Ethnomusicology". https://api.semanticscholar.org/CorpusID:221935861

Peterson, Nicolas. 2000. "An Expanding Aboriginal Domain: Mobility and the Initiation Journey". *Oceania* 70(3): 205–18.

Peterson, Nicolas. 2008. "Just Humming: The Consequences of the Decline of Learning Contexts among the Warlpiri". In *Cultural Styles of Knowledge Transmission: Essays in Honour of Ad Borsboom*, edited by J. Kommers and Eric Venbrux, 114–18. Amsterdam: Askant.

Schippers, Huib and Catherine Grant. 2016. *Sustainable Futures for Music Cultures: An Ecological Perspective*. New York: Oxford University Press.

Sutton, Peter. 1987. "Mystery and Change". In *Songs of Aboriginal Australia*, edited by Margaret Clunies Ross, Tamsin Donaldson and Stephen Wild, 177–96. Sydney: University of Sydney.

Treloyn, Sally. 2017. "Singing with a Distinctive Voice: Comparative Musical Analysis and the Central Australia Musical Style in the Kimberley". In *A Distinctive Voice in the Antipodes*, edited by Kristy Gillespie, Sally Treloyn and Don Niles, 147–69. Canberra: ANU Press.

Treloyn, Sally and Rona Googninda Charles. 2015. "Repatriation and Innovation: The Impact of Archival Recordings on Endangered Dance-Song Traditions and Ethnomusicological Research". In *Research, Records and Responsibility: Ten Years of PARADISEC*, edited by Linda Barwick, Nicholas Thieberger and Amanda Harris, 187–205. Sydney: Sydney University Press.

Treloyn, Sally and Rona Goonginda Charles. 2021. "Music Endangerment, Repatriation, and Intercultural Collaboration in an Australian Discomfort Zone". In *Transforming Ethnomusicology Volume II*, edited by Beverley Diamond and Salwa El Castelo Branco, 133–147. New York: Oxford University Press. https://doi.org/10.1093/oso/9780197517550.003.0009

Treloyn, Sally, Matthew Dembal Martin and Rona Googninda Charles. 2016. "Cultural Precedents for the Repatriation of Legacy Song Records to Communities of Origin". *Australian Aboriginal Studies* 2: 94–103.

Turpin, Myfany and Mary Laughren. 2013. "Edge Effects in Warlpiri *Yawulyu* Songs: Resyllabification, Epenthesis, Final Vowel Modification". *Australia Journal of Linguistics* 33(4): 399–425.

United Nations Educational, Scientific and Cultural Organization. 2021. "What is Intangible Cultural Heritage?" https://ich.unesco.org/en/what-is-intangible-heritage-00003

Vaarzon-Morel, Petronella, Linda Barwick and Jennifer Green. 2021. "Sharing and Storing Digital Cultural Records in Central Australia". *New Media & Society* 23(4): 692–714. https://doi.org/10.1177/1461444820954201

Warlpiri Women from Yuendumu and Georgia Curran. 2017. *Yurntumu-Wardingki Juju-Ngaliya-Kurlangu Yawulyu: Warlpiri Women's Songs from Yuendumu* [including DVD]. Batchelor: Batchelor Institute Press.

Wild, Stephen. 1981. *Contemporary Aboriginal Religious Movements of the Western Desert (Lajamanu)*. Canberra: Australian Institute for Aboriginal Studies.

Wild, Stephen. 1987. "Recreating the *Jukurrpa*: Adaptation and Innovation of Songs and Ceremonies in Warlpiri Society". In *Songs of Aboriginal Australia* (Oceania Monograph 32), edited by Margaret Clunies Ross, Tamsin Donaldson and Stephen A. Wild, 97–120. Sydney: University of Sydney.

Young, Elspeth. 1981. *Balgo Business in Yuendumu*. Canberra: Australian Institute for Aboriginal Studies.

Interviews

Granites, Lorraine Nungarrayi and Peggy Nampijinpa Brown. 2017. Interview by Valerie Napaljarri Martin, recorded by Georgia Curran, 8 April 2017. Yuendumu: Pintubi Anmatjere Warlpiri Media and Communications.

Granites, Rex Japanangka. 2017. Interviewed by Simon Japangardi Fisher, recorded by Georgia Curran and Linda Barwick, 25 May 2017. Yuendumu: Pintubi Anmatjere Warlpiri Media and Communications.

Henwood, Alice Nampijinpa. 2018. Interviewed by Valerie Napaljarri Martin, recorded by Georgia Curran and Linda Barwick, 15 May 2018. Yuendumu: Pintubi Anmatjere Warlpiri Media and Communications.

Nelson, Harry Jakamarra and Otto Jungarrayi Sims. 2018. Interviewed by Valerie Napaljarri Martin, recorded by Georgia Curran and Linda Barwick, 10 May 2018. Yuendumu: PAW Media and Communications.

Rex Japanangka Granites (c.1948–2019)

Japanangka was born around 1949 and grew up in many different areas, including Yuendumu, the Granites and Lajamanu. He did his early schooling in Lajamanu and then moved to Yuendumu. He was one of the first groups of young blokes to go back to school after going through the Law. He remembers that in the mid-1960s, he would stay in the Munga business camp at night and then go to school in the morning. He also went through Kankarlu in the 1970s. He became a bilingual teacher at Yuendumu School in the 1970s, was Chairman of the Central Land Council in the 1990s and worked as an artist and in mediation and pastoring in his later years (see Granites 2009). Japanangka was *kirda* for Minamina *jukurrpa*.

> We have a lot of our old people and old ladies who are always there in those communities. When we growing up they'd look at us and see if we were suitable for ceremonies. And the fathers would look at them and then say "Yes, we're ready for our young people to go through the Law." Some of us, we are part of it. When we were teenagers we were frightened but that's our Law and we go through it. We still do this today. Not just in one place, but in places where they originated from west to east following the Dreaming patterns.

> We still sing and teach it. Not in a classroom but outside here. Outside where it's open. The country is there. We sing about the country. Some of my family here are part of that country and we are *kurdungurlu*. *Kurdungurlu* is what we call the custodians – our mothers, our grandfathers – it's the father's side [*kirda*] that we look after.

Reference

Granites, Rex. 2009. *What I am Part of* [unpublished autobiography].

Harry Jakamarra Nelson (c.1944–2021)

Jakamarra was born at Mount Doreen Station as one of 12 children. He was *kirda* for the Country around Wapurtarli, close to the station area. When he was a child, his family moved into Yuendumu so that the children could attend school, and they became close to the Fleming family, who served as missionaries over many decades. He had a key role as an educator in the early years of the Yuendumu School's bilingual education program. From a young age, Jakamarra acted as a cultural broker for his community's engagements with visitors. He famously spoke at the National Aborigines Day in Martin Place in 1963 at the young age of 19. He was a passionate advocate for Warlpiri land rights and self-determination over many decades, including as a spokesperson against the Northern Territory (NT) Intervention and the prior amalgamation of councils in the NT. Jakamarra was the driving force in the establishment of the Yuendumu Men's Museum built in the 1960s and its reopening as a refurbished museum in 2015. He was a leader (*watirirririrri*) for the annual ceremonies held over summer in Yuendumu and regularly travelled across a broad region of the Central Desert to assist other communities with their ceremonial activity. Jakamarra was involved in the production of *Yarripiri's Journey* (Pintubi Anmatjere Warlpiri Media and Communications), which documented the Jardiwanpa songline for which he was responsible. Jakamarra sadly passed away in February 2021.

Ngajuju karna nyinami ngulaju ngampurrpa-nyayirni yungulu juju-mani kajili nyanyi ngakalku kajirlipa ngalipa lawa-jarrimirra. Ngaju kajirna lawa-jarrimirra, yungulu palka nyanyi ngaju-kurlu kujajulu record-manu nyampu jukurrpa like jardiwanpa-kurlu might be kurdiji-kirli-rlangu kujarra, ngakalku yungulu nyanyi, that's ngurrju no tikirliyi.

I want them [young people] to learn, to see and listen, when we all pass away. When I pass away I want people to still see my photos, and Jardiwanpa and Kurdiji, all those kind of things – I want them to see them later on. That's good, not to be restricted.

Warlpiri-patu nyurrurlarlu, yungunpalu-jana purda-nyanyi warringiyi-puraji-patu ngamirni-puraji-patu manu wantirri-puraji-patu, jamirdi-puraji-patu kujarralku. Aunty-nyanu too, mardukuja-paturlu, pimirdi-nyanu purda-nyangka, yaparla-nyanu kujarra walirra, yunkulu-jana purda-nyanyi yunparninja-karra law ngalipa-nyangu jukurrpa Warlpiri-kirlangu.

You Warlpiri young people, I am talking to you today, so you can listen to your grandfathers and your uncles singing. Women can listen to their aunties' and their grandmothers' songs. This is our law, Warlpiri law.

Otto Jungarrayi Sims (c.1960)

Jungarrayi was born and grew up in Yuendumu and Nyirrpi. He is *kurdungurlu* for the Country around Wapurtarli (Mount Singleton, see profile photo). Following in the footsteps of both his father, Paddy Japaljarri Sims, and his mother, Bessie Nakamarra Sims, Jungarrayi is an internationally acclaimed artist. He works tirelessly as an advocate for Warlpiri culture to ensure that his cultural traditions remain strong into the future. Jungarrayi is the chairperson for Warlukurlangu Artists Aboriginal Corporation.

Yuwayi jalangu karna wangkami jalangu-warnu-patuku. Japikalu-jana jarlu-patu yungulu-nyarra pina-yirrarni, manu yantalu PAW-kurra, nyangkalu yardiwajirla nyarrpalpalu nyinaja jarlupatu ngulalpalu yunparnu, jukurrpa ngulalpalu mardarnu, parnpa juju ngulalpalu mardarnu wirijarlu. Yungunkulu nyurrurlarlulku mardarni pirrjirdirli, tarnngangku-juku yungunkulu mardarni rdukurdukurla, pirlirrpa yungu-nyarra pirrjirdi mardarni. Ngulalpalu jarlu-patu nyinaja pirrjirdi, yungunkulu nyurrurlarlulku mardarni, yuwayi.

Yes, I am speaking today to the young generations, ask your elders to teach you or go to PAW to watch videos. This is how people in the olden days used to live and participate in corroborees – they had big *jukurrpa*. So that you can keep it and carry it on in your hearts and spirits and to keep you strong, the way our ancestors were, they were strong, it's your turn to keep it and to carry on.

Ngulangku kapungku mardarni, nyuntu-nyangu jukurrparlu kapungku mardarni pirrjirdi, yijardu-nyayirni kapunpa nyinami junga, nyiya-kujaku kajikanpa warntarlakari yani, jukurrpa ngula kajika warntarlakari yani kajikanpa wapakarra wapami. But jukurrpa nyuntu-nyangu kajinpa manngu-nyanyi, mardarni kirda-nyanu-kurlangu manu jamirdi-nyanu-kurlangu manu warringiyi-nyanu-kurlangu, kapunpa nyinami nyanungu-nyayirni pirrjirdi. Yuwayi, mardaninjaku palkarni, yungurlipa-jana, yungunkulu-jana nyurrurlarlulku pina-yirrarni yungulu mardarni nyampu, manulu yanta PAW kurra. Japikalu-jana warrkini-patu: "Yungurna nyanyi nyampu waja, nyarrpalpalu yunparnu jarlu-paturlu".

That will keep you strong, your jukurrpa will keep you strong, keep it, that way you won't lose it, as you won't know what to do when you lose it. But if you keep your father and grandfather's jukurrpa it will keep you really strong. Yes let's look after our precious knowledge, so that you can keep on teaching and also go to PAW and ask the workers, "I want to see this, how the old people sang in their time."

Chapter 2

Archiving documentation of Warlpiri songs and ceremonies on-Country at the Warlpiri Media Archive

By Georgia Curran, Valerie Napaljarri Martin, Simon Japangardi Fisher, Elizabeth Napaljarri Katakarinja and Linda Barwick

Archival materials are increasingly becoming a reference point for specialised cultural knowledge of Warlpiri songs and ceremonies. Many Warlpiri Elders are also keen to make further recordings and utilise those made in the past to ensure that there is a way for future generations to connect to and understand these highly valued aspects of their cultural heritage. In some instances, archival materials are being drawn upon to inform contemporary ceremonial spaces (Curran 2020b, 102–105; Curran and Yeoh 2021), and Warlpiri Elders, in particular, are developing an insatiable hunger for access to archival documentation to trigger their memories and reactivate the knowledge required to maintain songs. The late Harry Jakamarra Nelson, a widely respected Warlpiri Elder who was a prominent cultural broker from a young age, explained:

Nyurrurla-patuku young-pala-patuku karna-nyarra wangkamirra, nyampu yangka yardiwajikari-yardiwajikari nyangkayili, recording-li purda-nyangka jarlu-paturlu kajili yunparni, nyurruwiyi, kujalpalu yunparnu nyurruwiyi, recording-manulpalu. Yalili-jana payika. Kardiya-patulu-jana payika ngayi nyampurlaju PAW Warlpiri media. Warlpiri-patu nyurrurlarlu, yungunpalu-jana purda-nyanyi warringiyi-puraji-patu ngamirni-puraji-patu manu wantirri-puraji-patu, jamirdi-puraji-patu — kujarralku. Pimirdi-nyanu too, mardukuja-patu, pimirdi-nyanu purda-nyangka, yaparla-nyanu kujarra walirra. Yunkulu-jana purda-nyanyi yunparninja-karra law ngalipa-nyangu jukurrpa Warlpiri-kirlangu. Palka-jala ka ngunami kujalu-jana record-manu yawulyu-kurlu, parnpa-kurlu. Parnpa-wangu-kurlu yawulyu-wangu-kurlu different kujarra side ka karrimi. Mardukuja-kurlangu, wati-kirlangu kujaju ka karri, karna-nyarra warnkiri-mani.

I am telling the young people to sometimes go to watch the old videos and listen to the old recordings from the early days. Go and ask the workers there at PAW Media. You young Warlpiri people, I'm telling you now, so you can go and listen to your grandfathers and your uncles singing. Women can listen to their aunties' (father's sisters) and their grandmothers' (father's mothers) songs. This is our Warlpiri law. There is so much recorded from long ago, on both women's and men's sides. (Nelson and Sims 2018)

In the same ways that Warlpiri Elders facilitate access to deep knowledge of the Country and *jukurrpa* through their leadership roles in ceremonies and through telling songs and associated stories, they are increasingly using archival recordings to tap into this powerful knowledge of their ancestors from generations before them. Documentation through audiovisual recordings and photographs can ensure that these important and valued aspects of Warlpiri cultural heritage are available for future generations. Otto Jungarrayi Sims stated:

Ngurrparlipa jukurrpakuju but ngulangku nawu kangalpa mardarni ngula kalu yunparni, ngulangku kangalpa pirrjirdiji mardarni yungulu kurdu-warnu-paturlu mani ngukunyparla, nyampurla kajikalu mani marda kurdu-warnu-paturlu.

We [middle-aged generations] don't know about the *jukurrpa* but those recordings on which old people sing can keep us strong and we need to learn from them and the young generations need to learn from them. (Nelson and Sims 2018)

With consideration of the cultural value of and increasing community interest in archival material, this chapter illustrates the importance of supporting community-based archiving practices and access to archival materials in Warlpiri communities. We begin with a historical overview of the many documentation projects conducted around Warlpiri song and ceremonial material, reaching back to the 1930s expeditions into Central Australia by the South Australian Board for Anthropological Research through to present-day efforts led by Warlpiri people to preserve, maintain and revitalise these valued components of Warlpiri cultural heritage. We then go on to discuss PAW Media (formerly Warlpiri Media Association), which has held a pivotal role since the early 1980s

2 Archiving documentation of Warlpiri songs and ceremonies on-Country at the Warlpiri Media Archive

in producing Warlpiri-owned and Warlpiri-produced media of various forms, including significant ceremonial content that Warlpiri people have filmed over the last five decades. For Warlpiri people, having the Warlpiri Media Archive (WMA) located in Yuendumu is imperative for two reasons: this is the Country where songs and ceremonies come from and belong, and this is where the large majority of Warlpiri people live and they need to be able to access these repositories of cultural heritage materials. We conclude this chapter with an overview of several contemporary initiatives, including digital platforms, to make audiovisual media of songs and ceremonies more accessible for current generations of Warlpiri people.

Documentary history of Warlpiri songs and ceremonies

In the Indigenous Australian context, Warlpiri culture has received significant ethnographic attention and is one of the best documented desert cultures, being the focus of 15 books on various topics (Curran 2020a; Dussart 2000; Gallagher et al. 2014; Glowczewski 1991; Hinkson 2014; Kendon 1988; Meggitt 1962, 1966; Mountford 1968; Munn 1973; Musharbash 2008; Napaljarri and Cataldi 1994; Saethre 2013; Vaarzon-Morel 1995; Warlpiri Women from Yuendumu and Curran 2017a;). There is also a large body of linguistic work, including an extensive encyclopaedic dictionary (Laughren et al. 2022) and a number of unpublished theses (Elias 2001; Wild 1975). Significant numbers of recordings have also been made of Warlpiri songs and ceremonies over the last 90 years, beginning with those made by Norman Tindale as far back as 1931 with Warlpiri men at Cockatoo Creek (just 30km to the north of present-day Yuendumu), well before the establishment of the government reserve in 1946.[1] The Australian Institute for Aboriginal and Torres Strait Islander Studies (AIATSIS) library catalogue lists collections of mostly audio but also some audiovisual materials deposited by 31 people (Barry Alpher, Murray Barrett, Linda Barwick, H. Basedow, Jennifer Biddle, L. Bursill, J. Capp, Lee Cataldi, Georgia Curran, Megan Dail-Jones, Yukihiro Doi, R. Edwards, A.P. Elkin, Barbara Glowczewski, M.K. Hansen, M.C. Hartwig, Sandra Brun Holmes, J. Horne, Mary Laughren, M.J. Murray, Laurie Reece, Kenneth Hale, R. Larson, Alice Moyle, Richard Moyle, David Nash, Nicolas Peterson, K. Pounsett, Les Sprague, Gertrude Stolz and Stephen Wild). AIATSIS also has copies of Warlpiri women's *yawulyu* recorded at the Central Australia Aboriginal Media Association (CAAMA) in Alice Springs. Many independent scholars also hold

---

1 Kramer was sent out to bring Warlpiri people in to meet the members of the Board for Anthropological Research, who were set up at Cockatoo Creek.

significant collections of Warlpiri songs that they have recorded over many decades (significantly Françoise Dussart, Diane Bell, Jennifer Biddle and Myfany Turpin). More recently, Carmel O'Shannessy has recorded several Warlpiri song genres in Lajamanu, Myfany Turpin at Willowra and Jennifer Green at Ti-Tree (these are all archived in the Endangered Languages Archive).[2]

Despite the extent of these recordings, documentation on the details of songs and their associated content is minimal, and relatively little is written about this important component of Warlpiri cultural heritage. Françoise Dussart's (2000) book sets out the social context for Warlpiri ceremonial life in Yuendumu in the 1980s, mentioning the kinds of song genres and performance contexts. Wild's unpublished thesis (1975) and Curran's book *Sustaining Indigenous Songs* (2020a), as well as two Warlpiri songbooks (Gallagher et al. 2014; Warlpiri Women from Yuendumu and Curran 2017a), give details of Warlpiri song genres and performance contexts, alongside a number of journal articles and book chapters (Barwick and Turpin 2016; Barwick, Laughren and Turpin 2013; Curran 2010, 2011, 2013, 2017, 2018; Curran et al. 2019; Laughren et al. 2016; Turpin and Laughren 2013) and an audiovisual DVD (Laughren et al. 2010) and four-CD pack (Warlpiri Women from Yuendumu and Curran 2017b). This more recent work has produced detailed linguistic and musical transcriptions of these songs, bringing awareness to the value of the knowledge that they contain. However, the majority of the recordings of songs and ceremonies have little contextual documentation. The chapters in this book significantly add to their understanding, increasing the accessibility of these records for future generations by engaging present-day Warlpiri Elders and custodians in providing commentary and exegesis.

Beginnings of Warlpiri-led media production in Yuendumu: Warlpiri Media Association

PAW Media was formed in Yuendumu in 1983 as Warlpiri Media Association in response to advances in new media and communication technologies. Of particular importance was the announcement of the impending launch of the AUSSAT satellite in 1985, which would bring national television and radio

---

2 David Nash has an online bibliography of Warlpiri song materials (http://www.anu.edu.au/linguistics/nash/aust/wlp/wlp-song-ref.html) that lists approximately 60 items.

programs to remote areas of Australia for the first time.[3] A concern rose in Yuendumu, particularly among Elders, regarding the effects that imported television would have on their culture. Founding member Francis Jupurrurla Kelly remembered that:

> [The old people] were worried about losing their culture and language and how they were going to teach young people with the satellite and everything pulling away the systems from their culture. In those times there weren't even telephones for communications and all that. There was nothing and finally this satellite came along and people were talking about it. (Kelly 2013)

Another Warlpiri Media Association founder, the late Kurt Japanangka Granites, described the Warlpiri response to these technological advances:

> When we started Warlpiri Media, we started taking our cameras and doing videos of the old people dancing and doing their culture. They were really happy and they wanted to show the world about our culture … From what we thought was the only way to get our message across … The media was coming in from outside and taking our stories outside which was not what we wanted. We wanted our stories to be told from our point of view, what we thought and were doing … And old people said, "Why can't we have our own television in our language?" And without telling the government we went and did it ourselves – pirate television. We just did it for the community. (Granites 2013)

Kelly described this pirate television in more detail:

> We were just putting VHS [tapes] in a little camera to take around to the communities because in that time they were all frightened of it. The television would go there, and they were shy. The people were shy to be on the television – they weren't used to telling stories and all that and people were worried because they weren't used to it. We were just sending out the signals to all the little communities – it only goes about 5–6 km around the communities just to watch it in black and white first. We did that and then the government found out that we were doing this for our

---

3   See the documentary *Fight Fire with Fire* (1995), by Pitjantjatjara Yangkunytjatjara Media and Warlpiri Media Association, for an overview of the establishment of remote media organisations in Yuendumu and Ernabella in the 1980s. In 2016, the documentary *Satellite Dreaming*, produced by Ivo Burum and Tony Dowmunt, gives an overview of the introduction of media communications into remote Australia, featuring Yuendumu and Warlpiri Media Association's history.

Figure 2.1. Paddy Sims, Paddy Stewart and Paddy Nelson watching television in the mid-1980s. Photo still from *Satellite Dreaming* (2016), courtesy of PAW Media.

> communities and they decided to give us BRACS[4] … Finally, we got this thing going and we made a formal committee and made Warlpiri Media as a representative of the communities. (Kelly 2013)

A core group of senior men formed the Warlpiri Media Committee and drove the use of television and engagement with media in the early days (see Figure 2.1). Kelly explained that:

> There were a couple of old people like Murray Wood. He was the first chairperson for Warlpiri Media. And we had Long Paddy Jakamarra and Jack Jakamarra Ross, Darby [Jampijinpa Ross], Paddy Stewart, Paddy Nelson and Paddy Sims – they were the strong people in that time … The money [for the televisions] came from the community themselves. On Friday, every pay day, [those] old men would sit at the shop and they

---

4   The Broadcasting for Remote Aboriginal Communities Scheme (BRACS) was introduced by the Australian federal government in 1985 and allowed for local broadcast of radio and video services via being beamed from the new AUSSAT satellite, including locally produced video and radio programs.

used to talk "Chuck in for [a] television" and [people] used to chuck in $10, $20 of donations for the television so that people could see more. They were strong old people sitting there – they were the Elders in that group. (Kelly 2013)

Aboriginal activist and anthropologist Marcia Langton AO summarised the Warlpiri response to the new media in Yuendumu, highlighting that there was concern that:

> a daily stream of imported programming would undervalue and limit local cultural traditions and control, whereas video production projects and exchange in the community reinforced certain cultural traditions. (1994, xxx)

During this time, when Warlpiri Media Association was being set up, the anthropologist Eric Michaels had been employed by the Australian Institute for Aboriginal Studies (now AIATSIS) to conduct research on Warlpiri people's engagement with new media (Michaels 1986, 1987). Michaels saw his research as an opportunity to support a shift in filmed representations of Warlpiri people; on his own accord rather than as part of his government job, he brought with him to Yuendumu video equipment for community use. This formed significant background for the beginnings of Warlpiri Media Association and its focus on Aboriginal-owned and Aboriginal-made productions for broadcast on radio and television.[5] Langton explained that Michaels' work "can be located in the middle of a local revolution: the empowerment of Aboriginal people in representations of them and by them" (Langton 1994, xxvii) and that it shows how "image production is another example of how Western technology and artefacts have been incorporated as part of Aboriginal customary law" (Langton 1994, xxxii). David Batty, who established the TV production unit at CAAMA and co-directed with Francis Jupurrurla Kelly the award-winning series *Bush Mechanics*, emphatically stated that:

> The instrument [BRACS] we have in our hands is I think *the* most powerful instrument that Aboriginal people have ever been handed in

---

5   Hinkson criticised Michaels' approach in the 1980s, arguing that he pushed for Warlpiri engagement with a particular version of self-determination that was focused on "cultural maintenance" or "cultural reproduction" and allowed Warlpiri people only "one way of engaging with new media" (2002, 205). In the 1990s, the Tanami Network rose as the first publicly accessible and Aboriginal-owned videoconferencing facility in the Northern Territory, and the use of new technology was incorporated into ever-developing intercultural social relations and engagements (Hinkson 2002, 209–212).

terms of maintaining Aboriginal culture and languages. Ever. [emphasis in original] (Burum and Dowmunt 2016)

The Warlpiri Media Archive

Despite not being formally established until 2005, the WMA housed at PAW Media is one of the oldest and most extensive local archives in Aboriginal Australia, having operated as a keeping place for valuable audio and audiovisual materials since the beginnings of the organisation in the early-mid-1980s. Today it is well established, and further WMA productions and other donated materials are stored on hard drives in a climate-controlled room for conservation purposes and backed up on the PAW server. This archive holds collections of analogue video productions made by Warlpiri Media between 1983 and 2001, from which time their productions were shot digitally and were stored on their redundant array of independent disks (RAID) storage system. There are also over 1,000 tapes comprising Warlpiri Media Associations' News presented by Warlpiri speakers, recorded ceremonies and films of Yuendumu School Country visits and Yuendumu Sports' Weekends, as well as 13 episodes of the Warlpiri-language children's *Manyu Wana*. The 400 most significant items in this archive are also duplicated at AIATSIS and the National Film and Sound Archive of Australia, both in Canberra. For Warlpiri communities, this archive has immense social significance because it provides documentation of Warlpiri culture and history; it is particularly valued as it is on-Country, mediated by Warlpiri people and part of their living culture. Hinkson (2015), however, has told of the fragility of this system, emphasising the impact of inter-institutional and political pressures on Indigenous archiving projects. PAW Media has seen disaster in recent years with the collapse of their RAID server. Significant records were lost because there was no backup for the materials on this server and many of the originals were covered in dust. Due to the impediments to providing high-quality preservation in a remote, hot and dusty location, PAW Media is working through an ongoing digitisation process for its archive to strengthen its longevity and enable better cataloguing and user access.

Simon Japangardi Fisher, the senior archive manager at PAW Media, is responsible for ensuring that cultural protocols regarding deceased people and sensitive and restricted materials are adhered to, with Valerie Napaljarri Martin and Elizabeth Napaljarri Katakarinja overseeing the women's materials. They all have an overview of materials in the archive and work with this collection, listening through the audio recordings, particularly to screen for content and produce a better cataloguing system. Fisher described his role as follows:

I am a Warlpiri researcher. I do a lot of archiving work, researching all my families. I've looked at a lot of collections at the libraries, at the museums and I work with various universities. The old people tell me what to do – the person that they trust is me. I'm [a] Warlpiri person who's an Elder who has the two systems of knowledge – the *kardiya* philosophy and the *yapa* knowledge – I can be in both cultures.

My partner [Katakarinja] is also researcher and my boy [is interested] too. It was interesting last night, we were looking at old footage and he said to me "How can I do research?" This was the first time he asked me a question like this. He said how can I do research? I want to learn more about this knowledge. And I told him about how his grandfather was a tour guide for Norman Tindale in 1931 and 1932 onwards, when they went to Cockatoo Creek. But mostly that is all sensitive.

We have a Keeping Place in the other building. It's more important because mostly this has been taken away by western anthropologists and we want it returned so we can start doing research. A lot of old people used to come along and say, "My father has been recorded by this anthropologist". It is a bit sad [when we can't find it] but some are returned. A lot of young people want to come with their USBs for recordings of their grandfather and grandmother. Even older people, they [sometimes] want to look at the sensitive stuff. Jampijinpa, Nic Peterson has done a lot of research around the Tanami with men. (Fisher and Curran 2021)

As put forth by Linda Barwick, the advent of digital archiving has meant that the traditional archives, which had previously dealt only with "collectors who typically travelled to remote places", can now be replaced to "put the user/owner, not the institution, at the top of the model, and explore ways in which reciprocal relationships can, indeed must, be acknowledged and implemented" (Barwick 2004, 254). She explained that:

When there are effective and rapid communications between individuals and their community cultural centres on the one hand, and between the cultural centres and the digital archives on the other, it becomes practical to reassert the cultural authority of the home communities and individuals. The archive can then take on its most effective role in providing a service of managing, backing up, and providing access to data rather than having to assume the additional burden of administering the data it "owns" at arms' length from the communities involved. (Barwick 2004, 256)

As a community organisation, PAW Media also plays an essential role in mediating and providing space for working through the inevitable dilemmas that arise from the reincorporation of old cultural materials back into present-day social worlds. Gibson has commented more broadly that "Indigenous peoples are increasingly making use of archival records to answer questions about cultural heritage" (Gibson 2020). It must also be noted that this can be an uncomfortable space as there may be questions around restricted or sensitive materials, questions around authority or gendered access to particular cultural knowledge, and uncertainty about the rapid shifts that are occurring around listening and viewing materials with images and voices of deceased people. Additionally, the form of knowledge management within archives with emphases on documentation, metadata, provenance and controls over access requires shifts to traditional Warlpiri forms of knowledge management, which emphasises strategic ambiguity as a way of managing access (see Michaels 1991).

PAW Media is supported by First Nations Media (formerly the Indigenous Remote Communications Association), who promote cultural management of the collections and provide training opportunities for local media workers, including around access platforms such as Keeping Culture, which is installed on the computers in the Warlpiri Research Space room at PAW Media. In 2020, PAW Media was also chosen as a pilot organisation to trial Mukurtu, another access platform to cultural materials. Their review concluded that "no single platform [is] able to meet the diverse archive needs in the First Nations community media sector" (First Nations Media 2020). Long-term and ongoing efforts by PAW Media workers to continue collaborating with archives and researchers aim to ensure the proper preservation, digitisation and documentation of cultural materials within an era of rapid technological advances. Fisher described some of his experiences:

> I work with people at Sydney University and I've done a lot of research with Charles Darwin University. I did work with Ara Irititja, at the Strehlow Centre, NT Archives and Alice Springs library – I do a lot of research at these places. I've done repatriation too with the State Library and the Museum. I look at the protocols and intellectual property – I look through old photos, old slides, documents … all from various communities [across the western part of Central Australia]. I went to Portugal, to a conference on the other side of the world. This inspires me – collaborating with everybody like that. (Fisher and Curran 2021)[6]

---

6   Fisher is refering to the Ara Irititja Archival Project at the Strehlow Research Centre and NT Library. PAW Media purchased a licence for the archival access point Keeping Culture based on this platform.

"Vitality and Change in Warlpiri Songs" project (2016–2020)

In recent years, an Australian Research Council–funded Linkage project collaboration between the University of Sydney, Australian National University and PAW Media (of which this book is a product) has also seen the return of many large collections of song and ceremonial recordings that have previously only been held at AIATSIS or by individuals to the WMA, Warlpiri individuals and other community organisations. While many researchers, filmmakers and other people who have undertaken audiovisual recordings of Warlpiri songs and ceremonies have supplied community copies and regularly provide individuals with CDs, DVDs and USB sticks of these materials, the hot and dusty conditions and outdoor lifestyles of most Warlpiri people mean that these do not last long. Systematic organisation of these materials at a local repository like PAW Media is essential if Warlpiri people are to have long-term access to these legacy recordings.[7] Further, we have shown that for proper repatriation of these cultural materials, support must be provided for activities that is led by knowledgeable Warlpiri people to appropriately engage relevant community members (see Curran 2020b). Some of the initiatives undertaken as part of the project are discussed below.

Murray Barrett's recordings (1950s): Australian Institute of Aboriginal and Torres Strait Islander Studies

In March 2017, Simon Japangardi Fisher travelled to Canberra to visit AIATSIS and facilitated the return of digital versions of recordings made in the 1950s by Murray Barrett with people in Yuendumu. Barrett had regularly visited Yuendumu to provide dental care to residents throughout the 1950s and 1960s. Barrett recorded many hours of songs and stories, mostly with senior Warlpiri men, including Fisher's grandfather, but also with some women and men who had only recently passed away.[8] Engagement with these recordings has been led by Fisher, with Curran assisting with the women's content (for further details, see Curran, Fisher and Barwick 2018). Many of the recordings captured "older"

---

7   In addition to the collections outlined in this chapter, this project has also seen additional digitisation and organisation of other collections of recordings of Warlpiri songs, including those made by Jennifer Biddle in Lajamanu and Françoise Dussart in Yuendumu in the early 1980s.

8   The late Harry Jakamarra Nelson, who passed away in February 2021, was a cultural broker for Barrett and older Warlpiri men that he recorded. Many older Warlpiri people also remember Barrett's visits to their communities, with Francis Jupurrurla Kelly even being trained as a dental assistant to Barrett.

styles of song and dance, which contemporary Warlpiri people remember but no longer perform today.⁹

1953 Collections from Phillip Creek: University of Sydney Archives

In December 2019, Fisher and Katakarinja visited the University of Sydney Archives (see Figure 2.2); they now have community copies of many photographs and sound recordings taken by anthropologist A.P. Elkin in 1953 when visiting the settlement at Phillip Creek near Tennant Creek.¹⁰ Fisher has spent time separating those photos and recordings that are for men's-only viewing. There is also some women's content associated with Wakirti Warlpiri women from Alekarenge and Tennant Creek.¹¹

Collections from the 1970s and 1980s: Australian Institute of Aboriginal and Torres Strait Islander Studies

In March 2018, a group of 16 Warlpiri people travelled to AIATSIS and spent several days in male and female groups reviewing materials (see Figure 2.3). The listening rooms were filled with nostalgia and emotion as the groups reviewed recordings from many decades ago. This group delegation took back a hard drive of many large collections of audio recordings to WMA; this is now available for Warlpiri people, who have begun listening through these recordings and annotating their contents. Martin explained:

Ngularna yanu Canberra-kurra, maninjunurna hard-drives AIATSIS-jangka. Ngulajangkarna kangurnu PAW-kurra, yalumpu-juku ka nguna yardayarda-kurlu. Rdujupaturlu ngulalpalu nyurruwiyi-nyurruwiyi yunparnu, mardarnulpalu-nyanu. Ngulajangkaju kalalu-jana pina-pina-manu nyurruwiyiji yijardu-nyayirnirli. Jalanguluju yungulu generations to generation jalangu-warnu-paturlu pina-pina-mani nyanungurra-nyangu kurdu-kurdulku yungulu yani PAW-kurra-nyayirni, yungulu-nyanu milya-

---

9 For example, when Nancy Napurrurla Oldfield heard these recordings, she reminisced about the *purlapa* that used to be held in Yuendumu's south camp when she was a young girl. She described how men used to dance around in a circle beating their fists alternately on their chests in keeping with the rhythm of the song (Curran, Fisher and Barwick 2018; Curran and Sims 2021).

10 In this community, Warlpiri people identify with Wakirti Warlpiri language, also spoken in the communities of Alekarenge and Willowra (see O'Keeffe et al., in press).

11 Linda Barwick has organised and documented this collection to be accessed easily by appropriate Warlpiri women.

2 Archiving documentation of Warlpiri songs and ceremonies on-Country at the Warlpiri Media Archive

Figure 2.2. Simon Japangardi Fisher and Elizabeth Napaljarri Katakarinja visit the Sydney University Archive, 2019. Photo by Georgia Curran.

Figure 2.3. Warlpiri men and women visit the Australian Institute of Aboriginal and Torres Strait Islander Studies in 2018 to review materials to return to the Warlpiri Media Archive. (Photo courtesy of Georgia Curran)

pinjarla mardarnilki warlaja nyanungu-nyangu kuruwarri manu jukurrpa manu nguru-nyanu. Nyarrpara-ngurlu yanurnu, nyarrpara-kurra yanu?

When I came back from Canberra, I brought hard drives from AIATSIS to PAW and it's there. That's sensitive materials for older women to see as well, and that was from a long time ago the old ladies used to sing and dance. In the hard drives there's sensitive material, only the older women can have access to it. Our kids today can go to PAW and have access to the public material (not the forbidden ones). And they can see and keep it to themselves. Those stories and *jukurrpa*. Where did it come from, where did it go to? (Martin 2021)

Most of these song recordings are accompanied by sparse notes containing little more than a song genre, *jukurrpa* and the names of the singers. Song custodians have become more aware of these recordings and are now able to collectively maintain them. In bringing these recordings into the awareness of the contemporary generation of song custodians, an overview of their contents has begun to be maintained collectively. There are many songs that were long forgotten and many that linked closely to the identities of particular Warlpiri people and families. This documentation process has made it possible to extract clips from these recordings for family use; for example, the kanta ("bush coconut") *yawulyu* songs sung on a recording by Stephen Wild in 1973 were listened to by Lynette Nampijinpa Granites and other female singers in 2021 prior to the initiation ceremonies of related boys.

Carrumbo: Film by Victor Carell

During this same trip to AIATSIS, music historian Amanda Harris facilitated a viewing session for senior Warlpiri men Harry Jakamarra Nelson, Rex Japanangka Granites and Otto Jungarrayi Sims of the film *Carrumbo*, made by Victor Carell in the 1950s and including footage of a restricted men's ceremony. These men identified the restricted parts of this film and those that were open for public viewing. In collaboration with Fisher, Harris then produced an edited (unrestricted) version of the film and deposited both restricted and unrestricted versions with PAW Media in Yuendumu for use and viewing by relevant community (see Harris 2020, 180). This remains some of the oldest video footage of Warlpiri people in existence.[12]

Warlpiri Women's Law and Culture meetings (1990s): Anne Mosey's collection

While the group from Yuendumu was visiting AIATSIS in March 2018, former Yuendumu Women's Centre coordinator Anne Mosey also joined the group for several days. Mosey had a collection of video materials that she had filmed during the 1990s alongside Lorraine Nungarrayi Granites (now a senior *yawulyu* singer in Yuendumu, but then a young woman) when she worked in Yuendumu. At the time, led by powerful female singers, in particular Dolly Nampijinpa (Daniels) Granites (see Chapter 9), the Yuendumu Women's Centre's main purpose was to raise funds to support travel for a group of women to attend business meetings across the western side of the Tanami Desert and beyond into the Kimberley. The videos made during these trips capture many of the *yawulyu*, which women from Yuendumu shared during these large ceremonial gatherings. Edited versions of these videos have now been created and are regularly played during screening

---

12 Extensive black and white cinefilm footage was also taken during the Board for Anthropological Research missions at Cockatoo Creek (1931, 1936, 1951), but this has remained only available in archives (South Australian Museum and AIATSIS) and contains restricted material that Warlpiri men have not wished to make publicly available.

Figure 2.4. Warlpiri women viewing videos made during Women's Law and Culture meetings in the 1990s at a dance camp at Bean Tree outstation in August 2019. Photo by Georgia Curran.

evenings at women's dance camps (see Figure 2.4), as well as being in popular demand at the Yuendumu Women's Centre and Old People's Program.[13]

Digital spaces for Warlpiri songs and cultural continuity

In response to the increasing desire of people in Yuendumu and other Warlpiri communities to have better access to archival materials, a 2018–2020 project has seen the development of a password-protected website space through which archival audio and audiovisual materials, as well as photograph collections, can be viewed (see Figure 2.5). This website space is devoted specifically to materials on Warlpiri songs and ceremonies that are open for public viewing; at the time of writing, it contains only Warlpiri women's materials. The website also hosts additional educational resources, including lyric videos designed for learning women's *yawulyu*, created through collaborations with Warlpiri transcribers

---

13 Thanks to Lauren Booker who assisted with the reviewing and editing of these films, working closely with senior Warlpiri women and Anne Mosey in Yuendumu in 2019.

Figure 2.5. Trish Lechleitner and Ruth Napaljarri Oldfield view old photographs on an iPad at a dance camp at Bean Tree outstation in 2019. Photo by Georgia Curran.

and senior owners and managers of the songs.[14] Offline accessibility of the website is important, and the use of a Raspberry Pi server is being developed so that Warlpiri families who do not have internet access in Yuendumu can access the website materials and resources.[15] This will also mean that people can access these archival materials during family camp-out events, including the Yuendumu School's "Country visits" and the biannual dance camps held by Warlpiri women in outstations across the Tanami Desert.[16] Enid Nangala Gallagher, who has been central to the co-design of the website, commented:

---

14 Pacific and Regional Archive for Digital Sources in Endangered Cultures (PARADISEC) staff member Jodie Kell and honours student Grace Barr have adopted a key role in developing these lyric videos in collaboration with Warlpiri singers and younger, literate learners.

15 For more information on the Raspberry Pi server, which provides remote offline access to a website, see https://language-archives.services/about/data-loader/.

16 Yuendumu school has "Country visits" each term to various outstations around Yuendumu. Family groups go together to these sites and spend the week focused on learning about the places, *jukurrpa*, songs and dances from Elders. The Southern Ngaliya dance camps are held biannually and involve women from Warlpiri communities gathering for three or four days to sing and dance *yawulyu*. Incite Arts and Warlpiri Youth Development Aboriginal Corporation have collaborated with Warlpiri women to organise these since 2010.

> This is more than a space to store old recordings and photographs, it is a way for past and present generations to engage together in teaching and learning of songs, dances and designs into the future.

Singers and dancers produce and maintain digital technology from this community base in Yuendumu to continue to pass on their cultural knowledge to future generations and share elements with a broader world.

Fisher commented on the digital literacy of younger generations of Warlpiri people:

> These younger generations … they know how digital things work. A lot of young people want to record in language, their music – reggae, gospel, making radio documentaries – young people are really interested, they've got facebook, instagram, twitter, they get carried away. They are recording new things and some want [to access] sensitive stuff which is not shown in public but is used to teach younger generations. I take them to the archives into the special room and look at it. A lot of people come, even older people, and they say, "Can you record [give me copies of] me?" We get a hard drive and record [copy] their stuff. (Fisher and Curran 2021)

For the future: "They can listen to the voices of the old people"

The role of archives and cultural organisations in this space is complicated, and access to archival materials is certainly not without dilemmas. However, Warlpiri interest in accessing, managing and learning from archival materials is continuously increasing. In Martin's words:

> *Nyampu ngulakarlipa mardarni PAW-rla kuruwarri-kirli manu jukurrpa-kurlu. Marda kuurlu-jangka yungulu yanirra yinya-kurraju. Ngurrju-nyayirni karlipa mardarni PAW-rla (archiving). It's really important ngalipa-nyanguku kurdu-kurduku jalangu-warnu-patuku. Yungulu-jana pina-pina-mani nganungurra-nyangu kurdu-kurdulku yangka kamparrurlu.*

> It's good that here at PAW we got our own archives with stories and Dreamings, so the kids from the school will have access to it. And it's really important that our kids today get to know this so that they can teach their own kids in the future.

Martin continues:

> *Yinyarla PAW-rlaju, archive-rlaju nyanungurra-nyangu warlalja. Yungulu milya-pinyi, ngana-kurlangu? Nyarrpara-jangka, which family-jangka? Kuja.*

2 Archiving documentation of Warlpiri songs and ceremonies on-Country at the Warlpiri Media Archive

Ngana-kurlangu family ngajuju? Kuja. Kujarraku yungulu nyanyi PAW-rlaju, archive-rlaju. Yungulu yinjani jalangu-warnu-paturlu (generations to generations). Yungulu-nyanu milya-pinyi, nyarrpara-jangka family-jangka? Yungulu mardarni junga-nyayirnirli warlalja.

So that at PAW they can see and learn at the archive their own stories and Dreamings. Who does it belong to, which family? That one. Which family, that one. So they can see for themselves at PAW, at the archive, who it belongs to. So that they can know, generation to generation. To know for themselves which family they are from. So they can keep knowing their own stories and Dreamings. (Martin 2021)

Nelson reflected in 2018 on the values of archival recordings for future generations and the kinds of ways in which Elders can facilitate engagement with younger generations, who may not have learned about these songs and ceremonies in the traditional ways. In the following statement, he gives a kind of permission to future generations, encouraging them to access archives, engage with them and recognise that these legacy materials are part of their identity that is passed down to them as Warlpiri people:[17]

Kurdu-kurduku kajili-jana jiily-ngarrirni, kajilpalu-jana yirrakarla video picture-rlangu marda, kurdu-kurdu kajikalu nyina and purlka-patu there jirrama marda three-pala marda, four-pala marda. Ngulangku kajika-jana ngarrirni jukurrpa-wati nyampu waja yirdi nyampu waja, nyampuju jukurrpa so and so. Ngajuju karna nyinami ngulaju ngampurrpa-nyayirni yungulu juju mani kajili nyanyi ngakalku kajirlipa ngalipa lawa-jarrimirra. Ngaju kajirna lawa-jarrimirra, yungulu palka nyanyi ngaju-kurlu kujajulu record-manu nyampu jukurrpa like jardiwanpa-kurlu, might be kurdiji-kirli-rlangu, kujarra, ngakalku yungulu nyanyi, that's ngurrju no tikirliyi. Linpa nyampu purda-nyanjaku, purda-nyanjaku.

The Elders, maybe two, three or four of them, might sit with the young generations and look through the videos and the photos. They will then tell them the names of the *jukurrpa* and who it belongs to. I am keen for them to learn, to see and listen. By the time when we all pass away, when I pass away I want people to still see my photos, and the Jardiwanpa and

---

17 Because this statement may sit at odds with some traditionalist understandings of taboos around viewing images and listening to the voices of deceased Aboriginal people, Nelson made this statement explicitly to ensure that future generations would recognise the value of engagement with these media and the shifts that had occurred within his lifetime around these cultural protocols.

the Kurdiji,[18] all those kind of things, they can see later on, that's good. They can listen to the voices of the old people. (Nelson and Sims 2018)[19]

References

Barwick, Linda. 2004. "Turning it All Upside Down? Imagining a Distributed Digital Audiovisual Archive". *Literary & Linguistic Computing* 19(3): 253–63.

Barwick, Linda and Myfany Turpin. 2016. "Central Australian Women's Traditional Songs: Keeping *Yawulyu/Awelye* Strong". In *Sustainable Futures for Music Cultures: An Ecological Perspective*, edited by Huib Shippers and Catherine Grant, 111–44. New York: Oxford University Press.

Barwick, Linda, Mary Laughren and Myfany Turpin. 2013. "Sustaining Women's *Yawulyu/Awelye*: Some Practitioners' and Learners' Perspectives". *Musicology Australia* 35(2): 1–30.

Burum, Ivo, dir, prod, and Tony Dowmunt, prod. 2016. *Satellite Dreaming: The History of Indigenous Television Production and Broadcasting* [The CAAMA Collection]. Ronin Films.

Curran, Georgia. 2010. "Linguistic Imagery in Warlpiri Songs: Some Examples from Minamina *Yawulyu*". *The Australian Journal of Linguistics* 30(1): 105–15.

Curran, Georgia. 2011. "The 'Expanding Domain' of Warlpiri Initiation Ceremonies. In *Ethnography and the Production of Anthropological Knowledge: Essays in Honour of Nicolas Peterson*, edited by Yasmine Musharbash and Marcus Barber, 39–50. Canberra: ANU E Press.

Curran, Georgia. 2013. "The Dynamics of Collaborative Research Relationships: Examples from the Warlpiri Songlines Project". *Collaborative Anthropologies* 6: 353–72.

Curran, Georgia. 2017. "Warlpiri Ritual Contexts as Imaginative Spaces for Exploring Traditional Gender Roles". In *A Distinctive Voice in the Antipodes*, edited by Kirsty Gillespie, Sally Treloyn and Don Niles, 73–88. Canberra: ANU Press.

Curran, Georgia. 2018. "On the Poetic Imagery of Smoke in Warlpiri Songs". *Anthropological Forum* 28(2): 183–96.

Curran, Georgia. 2020a. *Sustaining Indigenous Australian Songs*. New York: Berghahn Books.

Curran, Georgia. 2020b. "Incorporating Archival Cultural Heritage Materials into Contemporary Warlpiri Women's *Yawulyu* Spaces". In *Archival Returns:*

---

18 Jardiwanpa and Kurdiji are the names of two ceremonies in which men sing and women dance (see Curran 2020 for further descriptions).

19 Harry Jakamarra Nelson and Otto Sims, interview with Simon Japangardi Fisher, 2017.

Central Australia and Beyond, edited by Linda Barwick, Jennifer Green and Petronella Vaarzon-Morel, 91–110. Sydney: Sydney University Press.

Curran, Georgia and Otto Sims. 2021. "Performing *Purlapa*: Projecting Warlpiri Identity in a Globalised World". *The Asia Pacific Journal of Anthropology* 22(2): 203–19.

Curran, Georgia and Calista Yeoh. 2021. "'That Is Why I Am Telling This Story': Musical Analysis as Insights into the Transmission of Knowledge and Performance Practice of a Wapurtarli Song by Warlpiri Women from Yuendumu, Central Australia". *Yearbook for Traditional Music* 53: 45–70.

Curran, Georgia, Simon Japangardi Fisher and Linda Barwick. 2018. "Engaging with Archived Warlpiri Songs". In *Communities in Control, FEL XXI Alcanena 2017*, edited by Nicholas Ostler, Vera Ferreira and Chris Moseley, 167–74. Hungerford: Foundation for Endangered Languages.

Curran, Georgia, Barbara Napanangka Martin and Margaret Carew. 2019. "Representations of Indigenous Cultural Property in Collaborative Publishing Projects: The Warlpiri Women's Yawulyu Songbooks". *Journal of Intercultural Studies* 40(1): 68–84.

Dussart, Françoise. 2000. *The Politics of Ritual in an Aboriginal Settlement.* Washington: Smithsonian Institution Press.

Elias, Derek. 2001. Golden Dreams: Place and Mining in the Tanami Desert, PhD thesis, Australian National University, Canberra.

First Nations Media. 2020. "Archive Platform Project 2019–2020". Accessed 1 July 2021. https://firstnationsmedia.org.au/projects/archiving-project/archive-platform-project-2019-20

Fisher, Simon Japangardi and Georgia Curran. 2021. "Country Doesn't Change". Presentation at *PARADISEC@100* conference, 17–19 February 2021. Sydney: University of Sydney. https://youtu.be/cQCGFipzJbQ?list=PLP7ZXIu_hereTOj-lRBF7frTUT-v2PbX6

Gallagher, Coral, Peggy Brown, Georgia Curran and Barbara Martin. 2014. *Jardiwanpa Yawulyu*. Batchelor: Batchelor Institute Press.

Gibson, Jason. 2020. *Ceremony Men: Making Ethnography and the Return of the Strehlow Collection.* New York: State University of New York Press.

Glowczewski, Barbara. 1991. *Du rêve à la loi chez les Aborigènes.* Paris: Presses Universitaires de France.

Harris, Amanda. 2020. *Representing Australian Aboriginal Music and Dance 1930–1970.* New York: Bloomsbury Academic.

Hinkson, Melinda. 2002. "New Media Projects at Yuendumu: Inter-Cultural Engagement and Self-Determination in an Era of Accelerated Globalization". *Continuum: Journal of Media and Cultural Studies* 16(2): 201–20.

Hinkson, Melinda. 2014. *Remembering the Future*. Canberra: Aboriginal Studies Press.

Hinkson, Melinda. 2015. "Pictures that move: Two tales from the Warlpiri archives". Paper presented at the *Image, Music, Text* symposium, University of Sydney, 20 March 2015.

Kendon, Adam. 1988. *Sign Languages of Aboriginal Australia*. Cambridge: Cambridge University Press.

Langton, Marcia. 1994. "Introduction". In *Bad Aboriginal Art*, edited by Eric Michaels, xvii–xliii. Minneapolis: University of Minnesota Press.

Laughren, Mary, Myfany Turpin and Helen Morton. 2010. *Yawulyu Wirliyajarrayi-wardingki: ngatijirri, ngapa. (Willowra songlines: Budgerigar and rain)* [DVD]. Willowra: Willowra community.

Laughren, Mary, Georgia Curran, Myfany Turpin and Nicholas Peterson. 2016. "Women's *Yawulyu* Songs as Evidence of Connections to and Knowledge of Land: The Jardiwanpa". In *Language, Land and Song: Studies in Honour of Luise Hercus*, edited by Peter K. Austin, Harold Koch and Jane Simpson, 425–55. London: EL Publishing.

Laughren, Mary, Kenneth Hale, Jeannie Egan Nungarrayi, Marlurrku Paddy Patrick Jangala, Robert Hoogenraad, David Nash and Jane Simpson. 2022. *Warlpiri Encyclopaedic Dictionary*. Canberra: Aboriginal Studies Press.

Meggitt, Mervyn. 1962. *Desert People*. Sydney: Angus & Robertson.

Meggitt, Mervyn. 1966. *The Gadjari Among the Warlpiri Aborigines of Central Australia* (Oceania Monograph 14). Sydney: University of Sydney.

Michaels, Eric. 1986. *The Aboriginal Invention of Television: Central Australia 1982–86*. Canberra: Australian Institute of Aboriginal Studies.

Michaels, Eric. 1987. *For a Cultural Future: Francis Jupurrurla Makes TV at Yuendumu*. Sydney: Art & Text.

Michaels, Eric (ed.). 1991. *Bad Aboriginal Art*. Minneapolis: University of Minnesota Press.

Mountford, Charles P. 1968. *Winbaraku and the Myth of Jarapiri*. Adelaide: Rigby.

Munn, Nancy. 1973. *Warlbiri Iconography*. Ithaca: Cornell University Press.

Musharbash, Yasmine. 2008. *Yuendumu Everyday*. Canberra: Aboriginal Studies Press.

Napaljarri, Peggy Rockman and Lee Cataldi. 1994. *Yimikirli: Warlpiri Dreamings and Histories*. San Francisco: Harper Collins.

O'Keeffe, Isabel, Georgia Curran, Jodie Kell, Linda Barwick, Ruth Singer, Simon Japangardi Fisher, Elizabeth Napaljarri Katakarinja, Jenny Manmurulu and Sandra Makurlngu. Forthcoming 2023. "Endangered Languages or Endangered Multilingual Ecologies? Intercultural and Interdisciplinary

Perspectives from communities in Arnhem Land and Central Australia". In *Teaching and Learning Resources for Endangered Languages,* edited by Jakelin Troy, Mujahid Torwali and Nicholas Olster. Leiden: Brill.

Pitjantjatjara Yankunytjatjara Media and Warlpiri Media Association. 1995. *Fight Fire with Fire*. Ernabella and Yuendumu: Pitjantjatjara Yankunytjatjara Media and Warlpiri Media Association.

Saethre, Eirik. 2013. *Illness is a Weapon: Indigenous Identity and Enduring Afflictions*. Nashville: Vanderbilt University Press.

Turpin, Myfany and Mary Laughren. 2013. "Edge Effects in Warlpiri Yawulyu Songs: Resyllabification, Epenthesis and Final Vowel Modification". *Australian Journal of Linguistics* 33(4): 399–425.

Warlpiri Women from Yuendumu and Georgia Curran (eds). 2017a. *Yurntumu-Wardingki Juju-Ngaliya-Kurlangu Yawulyu*: Warlpiri Women's Songs from Yuendumu [including DVD]. Batchelor: Batchelor Institute Press.

Warlpiri Women from Yuendumu and Georgia Curran (eds). 2017b. *Yurntumu-Wardingki Juju-Ngaliya-Kurlangu Yawulyu*: Warlpiri Women's Songs from Yuendumu [4-CD set]. Batchelor: Batchelor Institute Press.

Wild, Stephen. 1975. Warlbiri Music and Dance. PhD thesis, University of Indiana, Bloomington.

Vaarzon-Morel, Petronella (ed.). 1995. *Warlpiri Women's Voices*. Alice Springs: Institute for Aboriginal Development.

Venner, Mary. 1988. "Broadcasting for Remote Aboriginal Communities Scheme". *Media Information Australia* 47(1): 37–43.

Interviews

Granites, Kurt Japanangka. 2013. Interviewed by Denis Charles. Yuendumu: Pintubi Anmatjere Warlpiri Media and Communications.

Kelly, Francis. 2013. Interviewed on 23 September 2013 for the "30 Year Anniversary of Warlpiri Media Association". Yuendumu: Pintubi Anmatjere Warlpiri Media and Communications.

Martin, Valerie Napaljarri. 2021. Interviewed by Georgia Curran, 21 May 2021. Yuendumu: Pintubi Anmatjere Warlpiri Media and Communications.

Nelson, Harry Jakamarra and Otto Jungarrayi Sims. 2018. Interviewed by Valerie Napaljarri Martin, recorded by Georgia Curran and Linda Barwick, 10 May 2018. Yuendumu: Pintubi Anmatjere Warlpiri Media and Communications.

Alice Nampijinpa Henwood (c.1945)

Nampijinpa was born at Mount Doreen Station, a cattle station to the west of Yuendumu, where her father worked as a stockman. During her early childhood, she learned to find food in the surrounding bush. When her family was moved to Yuendumu after World War II, Nampijinpa spent her childhood attending missionary school. When she was married to her promised husband, she moved southwards to Haasts Bluff, where she had her first child. She then returned to Yuendumu and had three more children. In 1983, following the *Aboriginal Land Rights (Northern Territory) Act* of 1976, she moved back to traditional lands in Nyirrpi and Emu Bore, where she has lived ever since. Nampijinpa is a senior singer and *kirda* for the Ngapa (Rain) *jukurrpa*, which travels along the south side of Yuendumu. She currently works for the Southern Tanami Rangers and is involved in species rehabilitation and teaching biocultural knowledge to younger generations.

> *Ngajuju kalarna-jana nyangu wirntinja-kurraju panu-jarlu and jalangu-jalanguju ngulaju wirntimi kiyini karnalu. Yuwayi ngajurna learn-jarrija-jala that's why karna yunparni yangka jalpi-rlangurlu yuwayi. Yunparninjarla yangka wirntimi karna, panu-jarlu yangka karna-jana teachji-mani you know wirntinjaku even wiri-wiri-rlangu yangka.*

I saw lots of dancing in the old days, and still today we dance. I learned all these a long time ago, that's why I can sing all the songs today – like on my own. I sing and dance, I teach a lot of girls to dance. I even teach the older women to dance.

Kalalu wirntija panujarlu-jala, wali yangka jalangu-jalanguju yangka karlipa marnkurrpa-karrikarrilki wirntimi. Yuwayi, kalalu yirrarnu, puul-yirrarnu yangka panungku-wiyi yangkaju jalangu-jalangu lil bit-lki yangka yukanti-yukantilki, yukanti-karrikarrilki yangka.

In the olden days, lots of people joined in for the dancing and the singing, but now only a few people participate in dances. Yes, they sang together, they were big mobs, and today only a few songs are sung.

Paddy Japaljarri Sims (c.1931–2010)

Japaljarri was born at Kunajarrayi (Mount Nick). Japaljarri was *kirda* for Yiwarra (Milky Way), Ngarlkirdi/Warna (witchetty grub/snake), Warlu Kukurrpa (fire) and Yanjirlpirri (star). He grew up on his traditional lands until he was a young man. All his life, he hunted for goannas, kangaroos, emus and other bush tucker; he passed this knowledge on to other young men. As a young man, he worked sawing mulga trees for firewood and later became a gardener in the Yuendumu area near Four Mile Bore, where he was involved in growing watermelons, cucumbers, carrots, tomatoes and other vegetables. He worked at the Yuendumu School teaching *jukurrpa*, painting, hunting, traditional dancing and bush tucker, and helping out with excursions "out bush", as well as to Alice Springs and Darwin.

For a long time, Japaljarri painted at the Warlukurlangu Artists Aboriginal Corporation, an Aboriginal-owned and -governed art centre, and exhibited regularly with Warlukurlangu Artists both nationally and internationally from 1985. In 1988, Japaljarri was selected by the Power Gallery, University of Sydney, to travel to Paris with five other Warlpiri men from Yuendumu to create a ground painting installation at the exhibition *Magiciens de la terre* at the Centre Georges Pompidou. The trip took place in May 1989, and the painting received worldwide acclaim.

Japaljarri was also one of the five senior male artists who painted the original Yuendumu Doors – groundbreaking in pioneering two-way learning at the Yuendumu School and beginning the Warlpiri art movement. In 2000,

Paddy Japaljarri Stewart, his good friend, undertook to produce 30 etchings of the original Yuendumu Doors in collaboration with Japaljarri and under the guidance of Basil Hall, Northern Editions Printmaker (Northern Territory University). The first print of the etchings was all on one page and had its debut alongside the Yuendumu Doors when they were exhibited in Alice Springs. As a set, the etchings were launched in 2001 to great acclaim, winning the 16th Telstra National Aboriginal and Torres Strait Islander Art Award for works on paper.

Japaljarri's work has been included in numerous general exhibitions of Aboriginal art including *Dreaming: The Art of Aboriginal Australia* (The Asia Society Galleries, New York, 1988), *The Continuing Tradition* (National Gallery of Australia, Canberra, 1989), *Mythscapes: Aboriginal Art of the Desert* (National Gallery of Victoria, Melbourne, 1989) and *L'été Austràlien a Montpellier* (Musée Fabre, France, 1990).

Japaljarri sadly passed away in 2010.

Chapter 3

A Warlpiri winter solstice ceremony: Performance, succession and the jural public

By Nicolas Peterson

Warlpiri people heartily dislike the bitter cold of midwinter nights when the temperatures can drop to freezing, and the daytime temperatures are kept cool by the winds from the south-east that blow into Central Australia, bringing cold air from the aptly named Snowy Mountains. In 1972, I witnessed a publicly held winter solstice ceremony at Yuendumu, the explicitly articulated purpose of which was to shorten the night and hasten the warmth that comes with daylight.[1] I imagined that such a ceremony would be a regular event – but, to my surprise, I learned that it had last been held probably between 1947 and 1949[2] and a performance before that had been held when many Warlpiri were living at Mount Doreen Station, immediately to the west, probably in the

---

1   Nancy Munn (1973, 196, 200–3) mentioned a night ceremony she recorded, but this was a restricted men's ceremony (*parnpa*), combined with a berry dreaming and events unrelated to anything mentioned to me in connection with the ceremony described here, although the *kirda* were of the same patricouple.
2   Long Paddy Jakamarra saw the ceremony during the period that Wally Langdon was superintendent (several people mentioned this). It was held near the Kirrirdi Creek turn-off beside the Alice Springs–Vaughan Springs Road. Long Paddy said he had also seen it at Mount Doreen Station after the war, when it was organised by BulBul and Wally Japaljarri, but maybe I misheard this and it was before the war; otherwise, this would mean it was held very close to the early Yuendumu one.

late 1930s. Nor has the ceremony been held again since 1972.[3] Thus, despite the obvious avowed purpose, the ceremony had been held only three times in roughly 70 years, suggesting there were additional reasons for holding it. These emerged gradually.

The ceremony was held over 12 days, from 4 to 15 July 1972. Shortly after it finished, an Aboriginal friend of mine, Sammy Japangardi, who had worked closely with linguist Ken Hale but who had not been at much of the ceremony, came across to where I was living in the south-east of Yuendumu and said he wanted to record a letter for his friend Ken Hale (Japanangka) about the ceremony. This is what he said, as translated by Hale:[4]

Jampijinparlu ka mardani panulku marda. Jintakarirlangu wulpararri-yangka ngularra. Pinalku ka nyina Jampijinpaju. Wulpararri yangka nyampu kankarlumparra kujaka nguna; ngulaju ka Jampijinpaju pinalku nyina. Kulakalu yanga pinyi purlapapiya kala ngula-kalu wirnti Ngarrkapatuju kalu yangka wirnti, wati. Yarlu ka wiri karrimi. Ngunamika yangka walya, yarlu wiriyijala. Ngulakalu wirnti; karnta, ngarrka. Wulpararri, ngula kalu manyulunyangu(?) jukurrpawarnu, nguru ka rdangkarlmani munga, mungajala wulpararriji. Ngulakalu wirnti yunparni kalu parrangkarlu, mungangkarlu. Kurdungurlu, kurdungurlu kalurla mungalyurrulku kalu wirnti. Mungalyururlangu. Kurdungurluju. Kirda, kirda ngulaju Jungarrayi, Japaljarri, Japanangka, Japangardi kirdaju. Wulpararriji [and] Jakamarra, Jupurrurla ngula kurdungurlu. Jangala, Jampijinpa kurdungurluyijala kalu nyina [That's' right and]… Napaljarri, Nungarrayi, ngula kirdayijala. Yangka ngarrkapiyanyijala kalu nyina kirda. Nungarrayi, Napaljarri. Napanangka, Napangardi. Ngulaji kirdayijala. Ngarrkangku kalunyanu kijini yangka purlapapiya, mardukuru, kirdangku, Jungarrayirli Japaljarrirli; karntangku, ngulakalunyanu kijini yawulyu. Yawulyuyijala kalunyanu kijirni karntangkuju yangka Napaljarrirli, Napanangkarlu, Napangardirli Nungarrayirli. Ngulakalunyarnu kijini yawulyu. Wirntinjakungarntirliyijala. Ngarrkaku kalujana kurdungurlurlu kijini madukurru. Nguyungku kalujana maparni maru. Maru yangka jukurrpa yangka nguyu, ngula munga. Wulpararri maruju. Ngulaju. Wanjilypiri. Kujaka yangka wulpararrirla nyinanjarra yani wanjilypiri, ngulaji

---

3   In an online video, Otto Sims, the son of Paddy Sims (the promoter of this ceremony), who was 12 at the time this ceremony was held, commented that "we don't perform that ceremony any more but we do tell stories to our young people" (Sims 2017).

4   The Warlpiri orthography has changed since Ken Hale transcribed the tape; with the help of Georgia Curran and David Nash, the transcript has been converted into the current orthography.

3 A Warlpiri winter solstice ceremony: Performance, succession and the jural public

jukurpayijala kalu purami nyanungu munga. Kulalparna(ngku) ngaka nyampu nyurruwiyirlangu ngarrurnu Japanangka nyuntuku.

Jampijinpa [NP] has a lot now evidently. Including among others the Wulpararri [the Milky Way ceremony]. He is knowledgeable about that. About the Wulpararri which lies above (i.e., classed as *kankurlumparra*, open, public [?]); with that, Jampijinpa is now familiar. It is not performed like a *purlapa* [a secular camp ceremony], but they dance. The men dance, the men. A large clearing is there, the land lies there, a big clearing. And they dance; men and women. They perform the Wulpararri of the *jukurrpa*. They shorten the sky, I mean the night. The Wulpararri is of the night. They dance and sing, in day time and night time. The *kurdungurlu* dance if in the morning (?) for example, in the morning. The *kirda*, that is jungarrayi, japaljarri ... That's the *kirda* of the Wulpararri. The *kurdungurlu*, that's jakamarra, jupurrurla, jangala and jampijinpa – those are the *kurdungurlu* [that's right, and] napaljarri, nungarrayi, they are also kirda. Just like men they are *kirda*. Nungarrayi, napaljarri, napanangka and napangardi. They are also *kirda*. The men decorate as for *purlapa*, with *mardukuru* [plant down], i.e., the *kirda* – Jungarrayi and Japaljarri. The women, they decorate *yawulyu*; they decorate *yawulyu*, those women – Napanangka, Napaljarri, Napangardi, Nungarrayi. They decorate *yawulyu*. They decorate *yawulyu* in preparation for dancing. The *kurdungurlu* men put the *mardukuru* on the men they rub them with charcoal. Black. Black is the *jukurrpa*, charcoal, that is the night. The Wulpararri is black. That's stars. That lie along the Wulpararri, you know. Thus, they follow the night *jukurrpa*. I never told you about this before Japanangka.

Ngaka karnangku nyampuju jalangurlu yilyamirra. Yangka munga jukurrpa nyanungu, Wulpararri. Yarrungkanyi, manu kumpu. Ngulaji kulkurrujarra ngulakula yangka nyanunguju munga jukurrpa. Ngulajangkalpa yanulku yangka wirlinyilpa yanu, ngulalparla yalikarilki mungajarrija. Wulpararri yanurnu Yarrungkanyi ngula karlarralku yanu. Mungaju parrangkawiyilpa yangka yanu. Nyampu karnarla Jampijinparlanguku milki-wangka, karnangku yilyamirra Jampijinpawana, jaru, yimi nyampu karnarla ngarrini munga, wirlinyilpa yanu yangka munga, parrangkawiyilpa yanu. Ngulalparla mungajarrijalku Wulpararri; jintajukujala. Ngulajangka, purlapapiyalku kalu yangka pinyi. Wirntimilki yikalu kulakalu pinyirlangu, kala wirntimilki kalu. Karnta kalu wirntimi pirdangirli, ngarrka kalu kamparru wirnti. Yangka kanardijarra. Kanardiyijala, ngarrka, watiji kanardijikijala kalu wirnti. Ngarrka manu wati jintajukujala; karnta kalu pirdangirli wirnti, watingka purdangirliyijala. Ngarrkangka yangka purdangirliyijala. Kanarliyijala. Ngarrka kamparru. Kamparrukura kalu wirnti. Kakarrarapurda. Karnta, kakarrarapurdayijala purdangirli, ngarrkangka purturlurla. Wulpararri nyanungu yarlungkaju kalu wirntimi. Kujakalu wirnti, ngula kalu munga rdangkarlmani. Nyiyaku kalu yangka rdangkarlmani yunparni kujakalu wulpararri. Wulpararri kalu rdangkarlmanilki. Yinga yaruju rdangkarrkanyi. Rdangkarrkurluku yangka, kajipanpa ngunakarla, jarda, ngula kajikanpa kapanku nyanyi, mungalyurrulku. "Hey!! Nyurru rdangkarrkangu". Ngulalku kalu yangka rdangkarlmani. Yunparninyjarluju. Mungangkarlu kalu yunpani. Mungangkarlu tarnnga kalu yunpani. Nyina kalu parrangka … mungangkarlu kalu yunparniyijala, mungalyurru-mungalyurrulku yangka. Kujaka rdangkarrkanyjani, wurnturuwiyi, wanyjiljpiri ka yangka wiri jinta yarnkamirni, kujakalu ngarrini "daylight star", ngulapiya, ngula kalu ngarrini "yarnkamirni ka" wurnturu yangka kujaka rdangkarrkanyjani. Yunpani kalu, nyiyaku wulpararri ngula kalu rdangkarlmani. Yangka kujaka, yinga yarujulku rangkarrkanyi. Rdangkarrkanyi yinga rdangkalpalku. Nyiyaku, kujakalu ngarrini rdangkarlpa, ngula yangka, short while kujaka yanirni ngulapiya. Kujakalu yangka panukari ngunamirra ngurrangka, ngula kulalpa kapankurnu rdangkarrkangkarla. Kirda yangka kujakalu ngunamirra ngurrangka. Kirda kalu panukari nyina, ngampurrpa, ngampurrpa kalu yangka yanirni panukari, ngulajuku ngurrju. Panukari kulakalu marda yangka ngurrju nyina ngampurrpa yaninyjarniki, manyukurra, wulpararrikirra yangka mungaku nyanunguku yunparninyjaku rdankarlmaninyjaku, mungaku yangka rdangkarlmaninyjaku yinga yaruju rangkarrkanyi. Kala panukari kujakalu yangka ngunamirra kirda, kulalpa ngulangkaji yaruju rangkarrkangkarla mungaju. Mungaju. Munga ka nyina, yangka tarnnga, kujaka, rangkarrkanyi, wurra, ngaka, ngulaji, yangka yaliki kajana, ngampurrpayijala mungaji nyina, kulakalurla panu yanini turnujarrimi. Kirda. Ngulangkaji kulalpa yantarlarni yangka munga yaruju rangkarrkangkarla. Pulyayijala ka yanirni mungaju. Rangkarrkanjarni yani. Kala kajilpalu panu nyinakarla, kirda, wulpararriki, yangka yarlukurra yantarlarni, ngurrangka ngunanyjaku ngulangka, ngulaju ngurrju. Japaljarri, Jungarrayi, Japangardi, Japanangka. Panujuku yangkalpalu yantarlarni. Kurdungurluju ngulajukujala ngurrjujala kurdungurluju, Jakamarra, Jupurrula, Jampijinpa, Jangala yangka kalu yanirni panujala, ngurrju, ngulanya.

Only now am I sending you this. About the night *jukurrpa*, you know, Wulpararri. Yarrungkanyi and Kumpu [two places associated with the

3 A Warlpiri winter solstice ceremony: Performance, succession and the jural public

night Dreaming]. Between them, that's this night *jukurrpa*. From there he went hunting and at some point darkness fell on him. The Wulpararri came (from) Yarrungkanyi and went west then. The night. First, he went in daylight. This I am speaking for Nic's instruction as well; I'm sending you this talk, I'm speaking this word about night, he went hunting, the night; first he went in daylight. Then night fell on him. It's the very same Wulpararri. Now they perform it like a *purlapa*, you know, they dance but do not *pinji* [contrast *wirnti-* with *pu-*] They do not *pu-* but rather *wirnti*. The women dance behind, the men dance in front. You know, in two lines. The man, or men dance in a line. *Ngarrka* and *wati* mean the same [mature male]; the women dance behind, at the backs of the men, at the backs of the men, in a line also. The men are in front. They dance toward the front eastward. The women also dance eastward but behind; at the backs of the men. That Wulpararri is danced on a clearing. When they dance they shorten the night. (? …) they shorten something while singing the Wulpararri. They shorten the Wulpararri. In order that it will quickly dawn. The dawn, you know, if you sleep then you suddenly see the morning. "Hey, it has already dawned." So they shorten it, by singing. They sing at night. All night they sing. They sit during the day and they sing at night, till early morning. When it dawns, in the distance at first, the big star appears, that they call the "daylight star", like that, they say "it's appearing" in the distance when it begins to dawn. They sing to thereby shorten the night. You know … in order for the dawn to come quickly. So it dawns short. What they say short, that you know, "short while" coming, like that. When some sleep in camp, it won't dawn quickly. If the *kirda* sleep in camp. But [when] some of the *kirda* are desirous and come, that is good. Some might not want to come to the performance, to the Wulpararri to sing the night and shorten it so that it dawns quickly. But when some *kirda* stay away, in that event the dawn cannot come quickly. The night. The night stays long, only eventually will it dawn, after a long while. If they don't all gather for it. The *kirda*. In that event, the night can't come quickly and dawn. The night passes slowly and the dawn is slow. But if all the *kirda* attend the Wulpararri, at the clearing and if they camp there, then it is good Japaljarri, Japangardi, Japanangka all should come. The *kurdungurlu* likewise, Jakamarra, Jupurrurla, Jampijinpa, Jangala they all come. Good. That's all.

Figure 3.1. The three leading *kirda*, Jimmy Jungarrayi, Paddy Japaljarri Sims and Banjo, dancing on one of the first days, with women visible in the background but not yet dancing. Photo by Nicolas Peterson, 1972.

Pattern of daily activity

The general pattern of activity on each of those days was for men and women to gather, in two separate spaces, 50 or so metres apart, during the course of the afternoon (see Figure 3.1). By most late afternoons, between 20 and 50 men had come to the ground at some stage, with most staying. The numbers of women were similar but sometimes higher. Up to 12 men of the *kirda*'s (owner's) patrimoiety would be decorated with black on their bodies outlined in white plant down (*mardaguru*) and with wood shavings (*rilyi*)[5] in their headbands

---

[5] The *Warlpiri Encyclopaedic Dictionary* (Laughren et al. 2022) defines *rilyi* as the shavings made when a man scrapes smooth a boomerang, leaving the bark and wood in small pieces. *Rilyi* must be differentiated from *kukulypa* headband decorations that are used in circumcision ceremonies. *Kukulypa* decorations keep the shavings attached to the stick. The *Warlpiri Encyclopaedic Dictionary* gives several meanings for *kukulypa*. The first is multiple individuals of a kind in close proximity to each other, thus forming a unit. It is also used to refer to when men go together in an armed group. "*Kukulypa* is when they pile together sticks, like those short small ones – like of Whitewood or Witchetty – that they gather together. Then they put the bundle on their heads, and then they go off – that is how the armed men travel – with bundles. Many of them." This is slightly ambiguous but probably means that people embarking on revenge parties put these shaved sticks into their headbands.

3 A Warlpiri winter solstice ceremony: Performance, succession and the jural public

Figure 3.2. *Kirda* men moving to the ground for the daily dance. Photo by Nicolas Peterson, 1972.

at first and in later days *kukulypa* (shavings still attached to the stick). In the case of the men, this would take place 30 metres or so to the south-east of the main ground (see Figure 3.2). Several oblong objects 68 centimetres long and 25 centimetres wide were made that represented uncircumcised boys, and some small oval objects 25–30 centimetres in diameter, representing stars. Like the two shields used, all the objects were painted in black, outlined in white (see Figure 3.3).

The women painted up each day with a range of *yawulyu* designs over the 12 days for the important places of Janyingki, Minamina and Kunajarrayi, as well as for the route of the initiated men or *Munga* (night or darkness) *jukurrpa*. As with the men, some of the *kurdungurlu* were also painted up, the women often sitting in two separate *kirda* patricouple groups, the Napapangka-Napangardi group being decorated with Minamina or Janyinki designs. These two places relate to the travels of an ancestral group of women going east, taking young boys for circumcision in Anmatyerr Country, which contrasts with the route of the initiated men taking boys to the west. At the conclusion of the singing, most of the women returned to their camp, and only a few older women stayed behind.

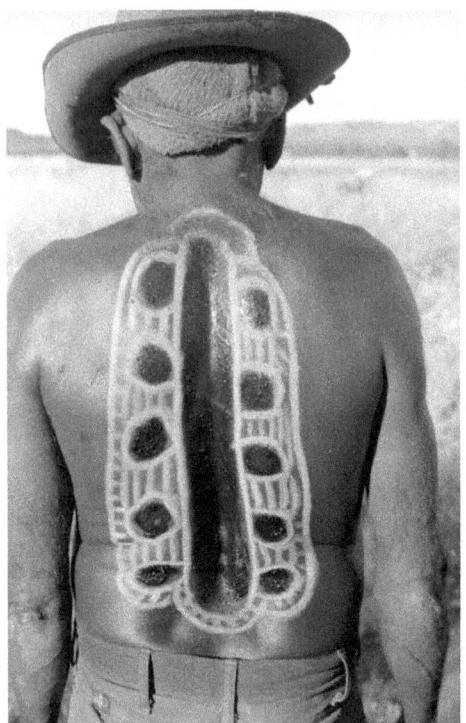 

Figure 3.3. (Left) Body painting on Joe Jampijinpa, a *kurdungurlu*, with the black pigment from burnt Hakea bark outlined in ground white ochre (*ngunjungunju*) mixed with plant down and laid onto a greased back; (right) a shield with another version of the Munga image. A few black lines can be seen attached to some of the stars. This is night emerging at sunset. Photo by Nicolas Peterson, 1972.

In the initial days, the oblong objects used by the men were mainly held horizontally while dancing in a sideways hopping way, north–south and facing east.[6] At the end of the dance, the objects were thrown over the heads of the men and caught by the women dancing behind (see Figure 3.4). Those not holding objects danced with their arms bent at the elbows, palms face up, moving their arms up and down towards their shoulders as if throwing something over them, a movement in common with the women dancers. This was explicitly to encourage the Milky Way to move across the sky more quickly so that daylight would arrive sooner. The dancing took place between 5.00 pm and 6.30 pm each evening for three to five minutes, as it started to get dark, to the

---

6   During the first days of the ceremony, these objects represented boys as babies; the horizontal orientation of the objects reflected them at the stage when they were carried by their mothers in coolamons. Later, the objects were held vertically, marking the growth of the babies into young boys – all this in the care of the men.

3 A Warlpiri winter solstice ceremony: Performance, succession and the jural public

Figure 3.4. *Kirda* dancing in front of the Milky Way earth mound with a *kurdungurlu* standing on the right. Their body decoration is made with plant down (*mardukuru*) coloured from the same sources as the *kurdungurlu's* decoration. Photo by Nicolas Peterson, 1972.

accompaniment of singing. The managers danced briefly after the owners each night. Some few people, less than half a dozen, were sleeping on the ceremony ground.

On the first day, as the dancing began, there was a brief period of wailing in memory of Wally Japaljarri, the previous holder of the ceremony. That night, a small group of men may have sung all night or at least late into the night. On day three, the ground was modified with a long, raised mound of earth 19 metres long, 76 centimetres wide and 23 centimetres high, stretching north–south, on which the ashes and charcoal from the night fires were scattered each morning (see Figure 3.4). On day four, a trip was made to Jiri, a site associated with the travels of the ancestral initiated men, to collect natural stones that were manifestations of these ancestral men. These stones were incorporated into the headdresses of the senior male dancers in subsequent days.

On days 10–11, much time was spent by the *kurdungurlu* making an object 7.6 metres long and approximately 20 centimetres in diameter of grass and cloth wrapped around two sturdy saplings, which in turn were wrapped around

Figure 3.5. *Kirda* bringing the Wulpararri emblem onto the ceremonial ground on the final afternoon. This image appears in the David Betz film *Singing the Milky Way* (2006). Photo by Nicolas Peterson, 1972.

with hairstring, near the preparation area, to the south-east.[7] When completed, this would represent the Milky Way. On the evening of the penultimate day, there was talk of singing all night, but it was bitterly cold, and we all went to sleep after a couple of hours. In the middle of the night, there was a brief period of singing; however, due to the cold, we were soon asleep again. One of the oblong objects had a cross piece added to the top and was explicitly identified as a *marlulu* (male novice prior to circumcision).

Throughout the ceremony, a series of payments was made between the *kirda* and *kurdungurlu*. When food was involved, it was brought by the *kirda* for the *kurdungurlu*. Most of these payments happened very informally; I witnessed only one group of them on the penultimate day. A *kirda* brought a large billy can full of boiled eggs and chicken for the *kurdungurlu*. Earlier, the senior *kurdungurlu* had received about $40 from the *kirda*. He kept $12 and put the $28 down on the ground where a group of *kurdungurlu* was sitting; most took $2, but one senior *kurdungurlu* gave $10 to one man. The *kurdungurlu* then

---

7 There was a lot of hair string at the ceremonial ground, one ball made from the hair of the two domesticated camels at Yuendumu owned by Thomas Rice.

3 A Warlpiri winter solstice ceremony: Performance, succession and the jural public

Figure 3.6. The ground at the end of the ceremony showing the Milky Way as an earth mound covered in the ashes from the overnight fires of people sleeping at the ground, with four of the *kukulypa* still upright on the mound and the emblems placed on it. The group of *kirda* and *kurdungurlu* men is settling up after the ceremony. Photo by Nicolas Peterson, 1972.

collected $26 for the *kirda*, four of whom got $5 apiece and one $6, with $10 coming from the senior *kurdurngurlu*, who had kept $12 of the original payment, and the rest contributed by other *kurdungurlu*, who had not shared in the distribution of the $40.

On the final afternoon at 4.00 pm, the *kurdungurlu* brought the *kirda* over to see the emblem of the Milky Way they had been working on for the last few days to the south of the dancing space. When the organiser of the ceremony, Paddy Sims, whose name was Wulpurrari, arrived at the ground, his face was painted red, and he wore a feather through his nose; but, by sunset, his face was black and white like the rest. At sunset, 11 *kirda* men carried the long object representing the Milky Way onto the ground and danced facing east, moving it up and down.[8] The women danced behind them. They danced for three verses

---

8   It had originally been planned to finish the ceremony on Sunday but because some men had driven to Alice Springs for alcohol, it was decided to finish the ceremony before they returned as it was feared the people involved might disrupt the ceremony.

and then put the object down on the mound, thus concluding the ceremony (see Figure 3.5).

The ceremony raised a number of questions, but no answers were forthcoming at the time: Why was it held so sporadically? How did people remember what to do and keep the right songs in mind with such infrequent performances? What precipitated the holding of the ceremony in 1972? And what was the connection between night and initiated boys?

Travels of initiated men *jukurrpa*

Upon inquiring as to whom the appropriate person was to ask about the travels of the initiated men connected to the Munga *jukurrpa*, I was directed to Karlijangka, Peter Japaljarri, a ceremonial leader in the north camp. I asked him about the travels of the men, and this is what he told me:[9]

> A group of initiated men emerged out of the ground at Bilinara north of the Tanami in Mudburra/Gurindji country. They travelled south to Dunmarra where they held a Kankarlu ceremony making the youths travelling with them into men, travelling further south they arrived in Warnayaka country and at Mirirrinyungu held an initiation ceremony with young boys brought to the place by a Nangala from the southwest. Further on they arrived at Kurlurrngalinypa holding both circumcision and subincision ceremonies before moving on. At a certain point the group took to the sky and landed north of Kiriwaringi. An old man sleeping some way away saw the travellers, picked up his boomerang and pretended to be asleep. The leading traveller was attacked by this man, Pirilpungu, and killed. The skin and bone of the dead man were scattered but when the head fell to the ground the skin and bones gathered around it and the man reconstituted himself. He then killed Pirilpungu and the same thing happened to him. The two men became friends. From Kiriwaringi the party split into four groups all travelling south, at least two of the parties travelled through Lungkardajarra where there was a big rainbow snake. At Ngiji one of the groups lit firesticks from a soakage and before meeting up with the other three groups at Kaljukarrka, north of Jila well rockhole. They flew away from here and landed at Pakarlipanta where there are three soakages, before going on to Manajarrayi where they made more young men. At Jalayanpiri, a large claypan, they used vines to make *witi* poles for a circumcision ceremony before flying away

---

9   Peter Japaljarri (pers. comm. 1972) to Nicolas Peterson.

3 A Warlpiri winter solstice ceremony: Performance, succession and the jural public

to Yanjilypiri. Here Pirilpungu was killed as they were short of fat. They removed the fat from his kidneys and kept it in small parcels behind their ears like tobacco. The man he had fought with in the north looked around for him but could not find him. He made a sacred object in memory of his dead friend, brought it around in the darkness to where the men were sitting on the ceremonial ground, and sat down feeling sorry. He then painted a cross on his chest and moved closer to the men. They asked him what songs he wanted to hear. He was not fooled by their friendliness knowing they had killed his friend. When they started singing *Walupurrkupurrku jipijipi* he gathered everybody up in a whirlwind and pushed them deep into a hole in the ground, putting them to death for ever. The skin and bones of the dead friend went back to Mirirrinyungu and there the dead man reconstituted himself.

This account brought together partial information given to me by numerous people about the travels of the initiated men over the days of the ceremony. I also spoke to Banjo Jungarrayi, a close Countryman of Paddy Sims, who would have been more actively involved in the ceremony had he not been unwell. He listed the places the men travelled to after Yanjilypiri as they went west: Jiri, Manjagururri, Yaljawariji/Paryilpilpa, Ngalpi (the Munga emblem was dropped here and unravelled), *Kurijiydulpa, Kunjari* (the head of the Munga ancestor fell down here and the travels ended).[10]

Mervyn Meggitt has an account of the travels of the initiated men (1966, 106–113); however, other than a few commonalities regarding where the travels started from, the account is quite different from that of Karlijangka – only the places of Kurlurrngalinypa and Yanjilypiri are in common. Indeed, the two accounts could hardly be more different. Further, while Meggitt's account includes references to night and the Milky Way, Karlijangka's account does not. This is because, in Karlijangka's account, the circumcision ceremony is the Munga ceremony.

---

10 On another day, Banjo mentioned that there was a "big *wulpararri* hail stone" (i.e., "Milky Way manifestation as a stone") at Pirilyi near the Western Australian border, which is broken in half. After this happened, the ancestral man travelled on to Ngarrkakurlungu.

The right to hold the ceremony

The 1947–1949 performance of the ceremony was associated with Wally Japaljarri, the senior owner of the ceremony, having speared a Jupurrurla man in the foot.[11] The ceremony was held by way of compensation, although exactly how this acted as compensation is still unclear. It was also the occasion when Paddy Sims, the organiser of the ceremony I witnessed, learned about the ceremony, but he did not make it clear to me why he decided to put the ceremony on when he did. It was not until many years later, when I was talking with a man in his forties, that I got an answer, even if only obliquely: "Wulpurarri [Paddy Sims] held the ceremony because he could."

Wally was the former senior owner of the ceremony and of the unrelated site of Kunajarrayi, as well as a formidable man with a reputation as a fighter, who had died around 1968.[12] Paddy had acknowledged rights in Country 30 kilometres to the north-west of Kunajarrayi at Nyinyirripalangu and Panma, where his father was buried. He was of the same patricouple as Wally and as the ancestral travelling men with boys who had come from Kurlurrngalinypa in the northern Tanami to Yarrungkanyi (Mount Doreen) in almost all accounts I heard, except that from Karlijangka, and then on to Yanjilypiri before travelling west. Although Paddy was named after the Milky Way, he could not hold the ceremony while Wally was alive, as Wally was the senior man in the area and would not let him. Once Wally had passed away, he could hold the ceremony himself and appeared to be motivated to do so by two factors: he intended to have his son circumcised the following year and, by using this reason for putting on the ceremony, Paddy was able to demonstrate that he was now in control of the ceremony and the associated sites. Further, he was also keen to assert that he was the appropriate person to control the important nearby site of Kunajarrayi, as Wally had not left any heirs. This recognition was provided by the willingness of the senior men in the neighbouring estates at Yarripilangu to the south-east and Janyinki to the north to participate in the ceremony as their acceptance of the legitimacy of holding it was essential to its widespread acceptance.

---

11 See Meggitt (1962, plate opposite page 44, 122) for reference to Wally.

12 In August 1967, myself as anthropologist and Roger Sandall as filmmaker working for the Australian Institute of Aboriginal Studies (now the Australian Institute of Aboriginal and Torres Strait Islander Studies) filmed several men's rites at Kunajarrayi. The most important rite was Wally's celebration for the site. It had particular significance for all present because of his great age, which made it clear that it was the last time he would do this. The resulting film, *Walbiri Ritual at Gunadjari* (1969), is not for public viewing but is archived at the Australian Institute for Aboriginal and Torres Strait Islander Studies.

3 A Warlpiri winter solstice ceremony: Performance, succession and the jural public

Their support is shown by the list of men who were present on most days the ceremony was held and, particularly, on the final day when the key men of the *kirda* moiety joined together to carry the main Milky Way emblem onto the ceremonial ground (see Figure 3.5). These were the men in order, with their Country indicated in brackets:

Jimmy Jungarrayi (Yarripilangu)
Mick Jungarrayi (Yarripilangu)
Dinny Japaljarri (Kunajarrayi)
Paddy Sims Japaljarri (Panma)
George Japangardi (Country unknown)
Andy Japangardi (Janyinki)
Pompey Japanangka (Janyinki)
Paddy Lewis Japanangka (Pintupi from the west)
George Japangardi (Pintupi from the west)[13]
Arthur Japanangka (Pintupi from the west)
Jack Japanangka (Pikilyi)

It was essential to involve the two brothers Jimmy and Mick, as the senior men in the area to the south, which is why they were up the front. Both men were fathers-in-law to Paddy Sims' wife's siblings, one to a brother and the other to a sister. Next was Dinny Japaljarri, a recognised *kirda* for Kunajarrayi; although knowledgeable about ritual matters, he did not seem to have any ambition to be a leader in ceremonial affairs, as is indicated here in his endorsement of Paddy's actions. I am unable to place George Japangardi, but Andy and Pompey were the two senior men from the Country to the north, with Andy married to Paddy's mother's brother's daughter. The Pintupi men were close Countrymen of Paddy's from further west. Jack Japanangka was the senior man for the important area around Pikilyi to the east, which is also close to both Kunajarrayi and Yanjilypiri. The senior manager was the father of Paddy's wife, and three of the most active *kurdungurlu* were his mother's brother's sons.

---

13 Although my notes have this man at ninth position, it is quite clear from the photograph that he was in eighth position given his size relative to Arthur Japanangka.

The songs

Twenty-two distinct songs were sung over the days of the ceremony. The singing was typical of such ceremonies. From time to time, while people were getting decorated and preparing ceremonial objects, they would sing one or two verses. Then, in the late afternoon, as the sun set, they would dance and sing a sequence of songs. I did not record the songs each day, so I am unclear how much variation there was, but my impression was that there was little if any. Table 3.1 lists exegeses for the songs recorded on the final day, based on commentary by Long Paddy Jakamarra with permission from Paddy Sims.

Table 3.1. The songs sung on the final day of the ceremony with exegeses provided by a senior man.

	English exegesis of verse
1[14]	The men are walking along carrying the Milky Way on their shoulders. Their backs are getting sore. The managers threaten to spit in disapproval because of the behaviour of the owners in putting down the Milky Way on the plain.
3	In the very distant east, the second light is appearing.
4	In the distant east, as the women dance, daylight starts to come quickly.
5	I was running quickly, daylight in the distance, I with my child's legs running.
9	As the sun sets, the sky is red and black with patches of darkness as the sun goes behind the mulga windbreak.[15]
13	Evening stars emerging in the east, all the other stars emerging in the east.[16]
21	The legs of all the Jungarrayis are shining.
22	The legs of all the Japaljarris are shining.
30	Coming close, coming quickly from Yaruju, the children are playing.
33	All the stars of the Milky Way are falling down in the south.

---

14 The numbers in this column refer to the actual place in the sequence of verses sung when this verse was sung for the first time. The actual sequence of songs sung is listed at the bottom of this table. While 143 verses were sung, there were only 22 different verses. Most verses were sung a number of times at different places in the overall sequence.

15 Several men commented to me that at sunset, one could see night coming out of the ground in the east. This black band is the shadow of the earth with the pinkish Belt of Venus immediately above it. Thanks to David Nash for drawing my attention to the Belt of Venus.

16 David Betz's film *Singing the Milky Way* (2006) is an introduction to Aboriginal art and the Dreaming via a biographical essay on Paddy Sims. The film was made in the early 2000s. and includes Figure 3.5. At the end of the film, Paddy says that he wants the video/DVD to keep being shown after he has died to keep the knowledge of the Munga ceremony alive.

3 A Warlpiri winter solstice ceremony: Performance, succession and the jural public

	English exegesis of verse
39	I, Yijingapi, am running quickly like the flight of the moth.
42	The moth hangs in the wurrkali tree opposite the sitting singer.
48	Holding a ceremonial object that looks white like the butterfly that appears in the daylight hours.
51	Holding the white ceremonial object that looks like the Morning Star coming out.
55	Over there in the distant east, black streaks appear between the first rays of the sun.
92	Morning Star, stands out as the shining one among many stars.
97	I straighten out the file of people as they walk along.
118	(obscure – may refer to rubbing ochre and fat over the boys to be initiated each day).
122	I am going to make plant down for my relatives.
132	Stars slipping away (i.e., nearly morning).
135	Look to the west and see the sacred object.
136	They walk along in a spread-out line.

The actual sequence of songs sung is listed below.

1(1); 2(1): 3(3); 4(4); 5(5); 6(5); 7(1); 8(1); 9(9);10(9); 11(5); 12(5); 13(13); 14(1); 15(1); 16(13); 17(1); 18(1); 19(1); 20(9); 21(21); 22(22); 23(22); 24(22); 25(4); 26(5); 27(5); 28(4); 29(4); 30(30); 31(30); 32(9); 33(33); 34(33); 35(9); 36(9); 37(33); 38(33); 39(39); 40(39); 41(39); 42(42); 43(39); 44(33); 45(33); 46(33); 47(33); 48(48); 49(48); 50(48); 51(51); 52(51); 53(51); 55(55); 56(55); 57(55); 58(55); 59(55); 60(51); 61(51); 62(51); 63(51); 64(51); 65–72(1); 73–76(30); 77–82(28); 83–87(48); 88–91(51); 92(92); 93–96(92); 97(97); 98–106(97); 107–111(33); 112–117(1); 118(118); 119–121(118); 122(122); 124–127(48); 128–131(51); 132(132); 133–134(132); 135(135); 136–137(135); 138–140(92); 141(141); 142–143(141); 144–145(21); 146–147(22) (it's not clear at the end of the tape that the ceremony is finished, but it is very close if not).

In the songs, there is no direct mention of night, only of the Milky Way, daylight, the setting sun and the Morning Star. The orientation is to the east, but the reference of the rest of the songs is to carrying the Milky Way on the shoulders going west. The reference to carrying the Milky Way on the shoulders is to the initiates who are being taken to a circumcision ceremony, alluded to as a Munga ceremony here. The other references in the songs are obscure, and no interpretation was offered by the men I spoke with. Most of the songs are shared with other rituals, including those held at the last Kankarlu ceremony under Karlijangka's direction two or three years before this ceremony, and the Ngarrka or initiated men's *jukurrpa* songs that can be part of the annual initiation ceremonies.

While discussing this ceremony with a colleague, David Nash, he asked whether the conjunction of the Morning Star with the winter solstice was a significant part of the ceremony. I do not know; however, on the basis of our conversation, I think it possible, given that this ceremony (and the previous one) appear to have a relationship with it. This is because the Morning Star would only be around at the time of the winter solstice every eight years, when the star reaches its maximum elongation – that is, rising with the greatest time gap before sunrise.[17] In 1972, this was on 27 August. Going on this calculation, the previous performance of the ceremony, which I had estimated to be between 1947 and 1949, would have been in 1948, when the maximum elongation was on 3 September. Unfortunately, I have not been able to verify this link with any knowledgeable Warlpiri person at this stage. It makes a great deal of sense to me that the ceremony was not performed every year, as I originally assumed, and this is an object lesson in taking anything to do with Warlpiri ritual and religious life too literally.

---

17   David Nash (pers. comm 2021) has pointed out that Venus, usually identified as the Evening Star, would be in the west so it is not entirely clear which star Long Paddy Jakamarra had in mind. Nash provided the following table of the dates on which Venus becomes most clearly visible ordered by month so the approximate link with the winter solstice is evident. David Nash provided the following table of the dates on which Venus becomes most clearly visible ordered by month so the approximate link with the winter solstice is evident.

Morning	1961	Jun	20	Evening	1967	Jun	20
Morning	1953	Jun	22	Evening	1959	Jun	23
Morning	1945	Jun	24	Evening	1951	Jun	25
Morning	1980	Aug	24	Evening	1943	Jun	28
Morning	1972	Aug	27	Evening	1978	Aug	29
Morning	1964	Aug	29	Evening	1970	Sep	1
Morning	1956	Aug	31	Evening	1962	Sep	3
Morning	1948	Sep	3	Evening	1954	Sep	6
Morning	1940	Sep	5	Evening	1946	Sep	8
Morning	1975	Nov	7	Evening	1981	Nov	11
Morning	1967	Nov	9	Evening	1973	Nov	13
Morning	1959	Nov	11	Evening	1965	Nov	15
Morning	1951	Nov	14	Evening	1957	Nov	18
Morning	1943	Nov	16	Evening	1941	Nov	23

Performance, succession and the jural public

While the tendency today is for outsiders to see ceremonies such as this one as cultural performances that can be revived if the proper details exist in the ethnographic record, the word "performance" is misleading (e.g., see Michaels 1989). While the performative approach to the Munga ceremony would usually emphasise the enactment, staging and aesthetics of the dancing, singing, fabrication and decoration – which fits with the idea of revival and restaging of such ceremonies – this is to approach the ceremony from the point of view of an audience member. However, there is no audience at such a ceremony, even if some people are apparently just watching. The importance of the performance is that it is doing something, bringing something about and changing things; consequently, it is integral to the social relations between all the people present.

Sims had to secure agreement from a range of parties with different interests to hold the ceremony. A group of regional kin had to agree that he could legitimately take control of the ceremony despite his inability to hold it earlier. By holding the ceremony, he consolidated his claim as Wally's heir and to a wide area of Country east of Panma, including the important site of Kunajarrayi. Although there must have been verbal discussion of this, only by holding the ceremony could this be publicly ratified. By holding the ceremony, he could demonstrate that he had not only the ritual knowledge but also, and more importantly, the support of the senior men in the area. This required their active physical participation in the ceremony for all to see. The important people in this event were the *kirda*, senior men in the same patrimoiety from neighbouring Countries. This was not a situation in which the *kurdungurlu* were custodians of knowledge in a regency context but one in which a *kirda* man could succeed to an adjacent Country and the high status associated with it, due to the important site it encompassed, only by getting other senior Countrymen to acknowledge his claim through their participation.

This gathering was a manifestation of what is now frequently referred to as the jural public, which must, in effect, ratify the succession. What is striking is how small the effective core of such a public can be. The average daily male presence at the ground was 36, and not one of those who attended more than four times came from the north or east sections of the Yuendumu community. The highest number of men at the ground was on the second day, when several people clearly came just to see what was happening. Of the total of 89 men who appeared over the 12 days, 35 came on only one or two days. A number of younger men appear to have come due to kinship obligations, three men because they were actual brothers-in-law to Paddy Sims, and at least four others because they were sons of key participants. One key Janyinki *kirda* and his son came three times between them when it might have been expected that the father, at least, would have been there most days. Thus, the participation was virtually entirely from the west camp, underlining that the ceremony was very much about social relations within that group of Countrymen, and the participating women being the wives, sisters and other close female kin of these men. The core people were the 10 people with Paddy Sims bringing the Milky Way emblem onto the ceremonial ground and dancing with it, but the presence of others as witnesses to the event was essential.

Conclusion

The emphasis on munga (night) with initiation reflects a cultural association between darkness, the west and women, contrasting with light, the east and men. The ritual death of circumcision takes place at night; the next morning, the boy wakes up as a young man. The more common tradition associated with the initiation of Warlpiri boys is the songline associated with the travels of a party of women from Minamina, near the Western Australia–Northern Territory border, taking young boys east to be made into men (see Curran 2020). In this Munga ceremony, revived after more than 20 years of it not being held, the songs sung were associated with a separate but well-known songline, so it was not a case of the men having had to remember songs they had not sung for a long time. Regarding the Munga emblem and ground plan, the situation was different – as far as I am aware, they had not been created since the last time the ceremony was held.

From a historical perspective, the holding of this ceremony is impressive evidence of the radically different world Warlpiri people inhabited up to the early 1970s. The senior generations clearly believed the underlying title to the land was theirs to be managed in transactions between themselves. They were, of course, aware of the pastoralists' rights, which were understood just as usage rights; however, as Coniston Johnny, the head Aboriginal stockman for Coniston station, put it so eloquently in 1972, the shade and the kangaroos belong to the Aboriginal people (see Bryson 2002, 46; Mortimer 2019, 162). It is sobering to realise that this ceremony was probably one of the last times that such a claim and ratification to Country took this traditional form at Yuendumu because, by 1979, the *Aboriginal Land Rights (Northern Territory) Act 1976* had been passed, and the Warlpiri land claim had been successful. With those events, Warlpiri people, as had other Aboriginal people in the Territory, quickly understood that their claims to land must be recognised by their being on genealogies and lists held by the Central or Northern Land Council, expanding the politics of recognition beyond their own relatives into the intercultural field.

Acknowledgements

I thank Paddy Sims and the other senior people involved in the ceremony for allowing me to attend, take photographs and record the singing. My greatest debt is to Long Paddy Jakamarra for his year-long tutoring of me about the Warlpiri world. In respect to the Munga ceremony, he helped me transcribe the songs and provided a detailed exegesis. My thanks are also due to Karlijangka for his account of the travels of the initiated men from the north. I am grateful to Ken Hale for transcribing and translating the recording I made of Sammy Johnson's account of the ceremony for him, to Rosalind Peterson for her notes on the women's activities and to Georgia Curran for helpful advice. I have benefited enormously from David Nash's enthusiastic interest in the topic of this chapter, knowledge of Warlpiri culture and our many invaluable conversations.

References

Betz, David. 2006. *Singing the Milky Way: A Journey into the Dreaming* [film]. San Francisco: Song Lines Aboriginal Art.

Bryson, Ian. 2002. *Bringing to Light: A History of Ethnographic Filmmaking at the Australian Institute of Aboriginal and Torres Strait Islander Studies*. Canberra: Aboriginal Studies Press.

Curran, Georgia. 2020. *Sustaining Indigenous Songs: Contemporary Warlpiri Ceremonial Life in Central Australia*. New York: Berghahn.

Laughren, Mary, Kenneth Hale, Jeannie Egan Nungarrayi, Marlurrku Paddy Patrick Jangala, Robert Hoogenraad, David Nash and Jane Simpson. 2022. *Warlpiri Encyclopaedic Dictionary*. Canberra: Aboriginal Studies Press.

Meggitt, Mervyn. 1962. *Desert People*. Sydney: Angus and Robertson.

Meggitt, Mervyn. 1966. *Gadjari Among the Walbiri Aborigines of Central Australia* (Oceania Monograph 14). Sydney: University of Sydney.

Michaels, Eric. 1989. *For a Cultural Future: Francis Jupurrurla Makes TV at Yuendumu*. Melbourne: Art and Text Publications.

Mortimer, Lorraine. 2019. *Roger Sandall's Films and Contemporary Anthropology: Explorations in the Aesthetic, the Existential and the Possible*. Bloomington: Indiana University Press.

Munn, Nancy. 1973. *Walbiri Iconography: Graphic Representation and Cultural Symbolism in a Central Australian Society*. Ithaca: Cornell University Press.

Sims, Otto Jungarrayi. 2017. "Otto Jungarrayi Sims, Yanyilpirri Jukurrpa (Milky Way Dreaming)". Uploaded 9 May 2017. Facebook video, https://www.facebook.com/watch/?v=1192303170892978

Tommy Jangala Watson (1948–)

Jangala was born at Mount Doreen Station, where he grew up walking around and eating bush foods. Jangala is *kirda* for the Ngapa "Rain" *jukurrpa* that travels through Puyurru. In the 1960s, he worked as a drover, then as a fruit picker and later for the Department of Aboriginal Affairs, fixing fences and building houses. He lived with his family at his outstation on his Country in the 1980s. He has worked at the Yuendumu School for a long time teaching kids about Warlpiri culture. He is an important senior man in Yuendumu and has recently been involved in the repatriation of cultural objects from the South Australia Museum.

Culture way, learn jarrijarna, still karna nyinami yangka pirrjirdi karna mardani, milya pinyi nguruju ngaju nyanguju. Karna jana yangka puta puta nganayi mani yangka pina mani nyampuju kurdukurdu-pinki. Wali yantarnirli nyinakalu ngaju nyangurla yirna nyarra pina pina mani yirna nyarra nguru kurrarlangu kanyi, warru kanyi nguru yinya ngalipa nyangu big one ka karrimi, ngulaku.

I know about culture, and I am still strong today. I know everything about my Country. I'm trying to teach my younger generations. Come to me so I can teach you and take you back to country to learn about it, our country is big.

Parnpa waja pinjaku karnalu jana yirrarni young people warrki jarrinjaku. Karnalu jana ngarrirni "ungunpa mardani nyuntu nyangu kurlangu warringiyi kirlangu, ngaju nyangu warringiyi kirlangu whole lot yangka". Carry on warringiyi nyanu kurlangu tarnnga juku.

We help the young men prepare for the *parnpa* (where the father of the son in bush camp does the dancing). We say to them, "So you can keep your grandfather's (father's father's) and my grandfather's [culture] and so on." They can carry on their grandfather's culture.

Tarnngajuku karnalu mardani pirrjirdi jiki, karnalu yangka start mani marnakurrawarnu every Christmas time still karnalu mardani palka juku kurdijiji. We also join in Anmatjerre people. Wariyiwariyi-rla and Ti-tree-rla and Willowra-rla, Lajamanu and Nyirrpi kuja nawu.

We still have our culture strongly, we start every Christmas time and we still have our Kurdiji. Anmatyerr people join with us when there's ceremony going on. People come from Mount Allan, Ti-Tree, Willowra, Lajamanu and Nyirrpi.

Junga waja learn jarrija we bin learn that way, we are living strong jalangurlu but like young people they don't come and ask em yangka nganimpa Nuu kalu nganpa payirni yangka nganimpa "Like pina manta nganpa yungurnalu pina jarri" nuwu kalu nganpa yanirni yangka japirni nganimpa.

True we learned proper in them days, and we are strong but nowadays young people don't come to us and ask us, "Teach us so that we can know." They don't come and ask us, nothing.

Thomas Jangala Rice (c.1938–)

Thomas Jangala Rice was born in 1938 and grew up around the region of Mount Doreen Station to the west of present-day Yuendumu. He learned traditional hunting skills during this time and worked as a drover for the cattle station as a young man. He is *kirda* for the Country around Mikanji and the *Ngapa jukurrpa*, which is important to this region. As a young adult, he moved into Yuendumu with his two promised wives and has had an important role in his community ever since. Later in his life, he married Jeannie Nungarrayi Egan; together, they had an important role in the Warlpiri Youth Development Aboriginal Corporation's *Jaru-pirrjirdi* bush trips. Jangala and Egan worked closely with Georgia Curran on the Warlpiri Songlines project between 2005 and 2008, shortly before Egan's untimely death in 2009. Jangala has worked as a police aid and tracker with the Yuendumu Men's Night Patrol and at the school, teaching traditional culture. He has had roles on the Yuendumu Council, Central Land Council and the Warlukurlangu Art Centre, through which he was central to the refurbishment of the Yuendumu Men's Museum in 2010.

Barbara Gibson Nakamarra (1938–c.1995)

Barbara Gibson Nakamarra, born in 1938 in the Tanami Desert, was settled at Yuendumu as a young girl and married with her sister Beryl to Tony Japaljarri Gibson. She worked at the clinic and was moved again to Lajamanu, where she became a leading authority on rituals. In the 1980s, the family spent much time at the Kurlurrngalinypa outstation, where they were asked to re-enact their hunting–gathering life for a Japanese Museum crew. She helped B. Glowczewski with many translations for the *Dream Trackers* CD-ROM (United Nations Educational, Scientific and Cultural Organization 2000) and started to paint in 1986, exhibiting in many galleries. One of her paintings was presented in a touring exhibition in France (Glowczewski, *Yapa. Painters from Balgo and Lajamanu* catalogue, edited by Baudoin Lebon, 1991) and the Lenz Culture Institute in Austria (*Zeit: Mythos Phantom Realität*, Springer, 2000). After her husband's death, she went to live in Tennant Creek and Kununurra, where she continued to paint. She passed away in the mid-1990s.

Chapter 4

Dreaming to sing: Learning and dream creation in the Australian desert

By Barbara Glowczewski and Barbara Gibson Nakamarra
Translated by Georgia Curran and Nicolas Peterson from the original French (Glowczewski and Gibson 2002)

Barbara Nakamarra Gibson was born in the early 1930s in the Tanami Desert on the Warlpiri lands of her father. Her mother was a Mudburra speaker from the north-east. At the time, Aboriginal people of the region were still maintaining their semi-nomadic way of life, travelling in small families from water point to water point and gathering in large numbers on certain sites for initiations, funeral rites and land-based ceremonies celebrating the *jukurrpa*, totemic ancestors who presided over the formation of landscape features and their renewal. Her father had inherited from his own father a spiritual connection with the Janganpa (Possum), Yarripiri (giant Taipan snake) and Wampana (Wallaby ancestors associated with several sacred sites in the Granites region and for which he was the ritual leader). Barbara Gibson had inherited from him and her paternal aunts the role of ritual owner, *kirda*, for the Yawakiyi (Black Plums) and Ngurlu (Edible Seed) *jukurrpa*, the names of the ancestral beings who had accompanied the Possum and Wallaby heroes, respectively, on their epic journeys.

B. Gibson[1] said that her lips and those of her sisters became blackened when the plums became ripe, a sign of their spiritual connection as *kirda* to Black Plum *jukurrpa* totems. All the *jukurrpa* watched over the people at the sites that had formed during their own *jukurrpa* journeys. To maintain the reproduction of the species and their proper balance, men and women had to follow the Law: hunting rules, promised marriages and the totemic rites on associated sacred sites. Like all other Warlpiri people, Barbara was said to embody a spirit-child (*kurruwalpa*) left in the earth by the *jukurrpa* and who had passed on her first name, Nakakut, given to her by the *Yawakiyi* (Plum) at Rirrinjarra, a water source in the rock formed by the tears of the Yawakiyi Plums, who had lost some of their companions in a battle with the black sugar-leaf corkwood tree (Parrawuju).

The spirit-children *kurruwalpa* reveal their future birth, their identity and their place of conception in a dream that the mother, father or another loved one has before the birth of the child; sometimes, the child embodies a *jukurrpa* different to that inherited from his or her father because the spirit-children are said to "catch" their parents when they move on other people's territories. Nakakut's childhood was full of these stories of a desert of infinite forms, matters and spirits. As soon as she learned to walk, Nakakut began to read the ground for all the signs that allow her to orientate herself: bird tracks indicating the proximity of hidden water sources, lines of ants piling up the grains of acacia seeds that the women then collect to make seedcakes, cracks in the soil revealing the underground presence of yams or other tubers, the texture of the earth and the animal droppings that indicate lizard burrows or small marsupials.

Nakakut grew up in the region around the sacred rocks at the Granites, an area that experienced two gold rushes in the first half of the 20th century. Suffering from drought, Warlpiri people were also attracted to the region because the ceremonial site at Yarturluyarturlu had water sources that dried up less than others. The miners complained about the influx of Aboriginal people. The government set up a ration depot there, which was quickly overwhelmed by the demand and miserable conditions of the Aboriginal people.

This population was moved to a reserve in the south in the late 1940s: Yuendumu. There, Nakakut and her sister married the same man they had been promised

---

1 In Warlpiri, you cannot call someone by the same name as yours but instead use the expression *narruku* "same name" or another name. The original French version of this chapter appeared after the mourning period following B. Gibson's passing. In this chapter, Glowczewski refers to B. Gibson either as "B." (standing for her English name, Barbara), or by Nakakut, a diminutive form of her subsection name "Nakamarra".

4 Dreaming to sing: Learning and dream creation in the Australian desert

to at birth. They worked at the clinic and had several children. Hundreds of people were settled there. Conflicts ensued, with spears, boomerangs and fighting clubs. To relieve this overcrowding, the government decided to create a new reserve. The chosen site, Hooker Creek, was in the territory of the Gurindji tribe, but a number of Warlpiri were taken there, including Nakakut's family. Some tried several times to walk the 600 kilometres of desert separating the new reserve from Yuendumu. But, each time, they were forcibly brought back. In 1967, all Aboriginal people in Australia benefited from a referendum that granted the federal government the right to legislate for Aboriginal people across the country. Soon after, the residents of the reserve were able to elect their first town council and replaced the name Hooker Creek with a traditional name: Lajamanu (Meggitt 1962; Munn 1973).

I arrived in Lajamanu in 1979. The Warlpiri had just won a land claim over part of their ancestral territory and were preparing to reoccupy places that had been inaccessible since they were sedentarised[2] at Yuendumu and Lajamanu (Peterson et al. 1978). Nakakut camped with her husband and three of her sisters on the edge of the women's camp. The mother of a 20-year-old son in initiation, she regularly participated in female rituals, singing, dancing and having her body painted. But, because she was still breastfeeding her youngest son, she sometimes had to interrupt these ritual activities to take care of him. I returned four years later, and she had become a businesswoman and caretaker of rituals, leading songs and dances. Her husband had used materials from an old windpump to build a few tin houses on their ancestral land, located 100 kilometres east of Lajamanu. The family camped there and returned once a week with an old tractor to stock up at the Lajamanu store.

By the early 1980s, the search for gold had resumed in the Tanami Desert, with the sophisticated equipment of open pit mines. The land title obtained by the Warlpiri granted them the right to an income from the region's mineral resources. To undertake explorations and exploratory trenches, interested companies had to negotiate with the Aboriginal people recognised as the traditional owners of the region. Sometimes, the traditional owners objected to exploration in certain places they wished to protect for religious reasons and sought their protection in the event that minerals were found. The area of the sacred site at the Granites, for which Nakakut's father had been the owner, was the subject of a request for exploration by a mining company. The knowledge she had inherited from him then took on an unforeseen importance.

---

2   This refers to the government reserves in which Warlpiri people were forced to settle in the period post-World War II.

The owners and rights holders for land and its associated totems are determined by a series of traditional rules. First, the care of totems and associated sacred sites is generally transmitted among the Warlpiri within the father's patrilineal clan. Sometimes, when a child is raised by an adoptive father, it is the land of the adoptive father that they will inherit. The most important clan is the one that initiates the child and in which all men have paternally inherited responsibilities to the *jukurrpa*. Due to the sedentarisation of Warlpiri people and their dispersal to different communities, the determination of the rights holders for a place subject to an exploration application requires the gathering of the traditional owners for meetings to negotiate with the relevant mining company. At such meetings, some representatives often mention the name of a person forgotten in the list of rights holders due to their distant residence. Thus, mining meetings are an opportunity to reunite with close or distant relatives that may meet with not only people from Yuendumu (Dussart 1988) but also from other communities of the Warlpiri language area (Willowra, Ali Curang, Papunya) and neighbouring areas (e.g., Balgo, Kiwirrkurra), as well as those who now live in the camps on the outskirts of the towns of Katherine, Alice and Darwin. Sometimes, the Warlpiri even seek to find children who have been adopted by non-Warlpiri families as far away as Arnhem Land or by non-Indigenous families in Queensland or South Australia.

In 1984, when the site at the Granites was the subject of a mining agreement, hundreds of people felt concerned because it was a ceremonial site shared by several groups, many of whose members had grown up in the region. Everyone knew that the Granites site, Yarturluyarturlu, was linked to the Possum, but no-one seemed to know all the songs and dances that told the story of the journey. Two women from Lajamanu received new songs and body paintings for the Possum *jukurrpa* associated with this site in dreams and taught them to other women.

This innovation was based on a longstanding tradition of dreaming new verses of songs and episodes celebrating Dreaming ancestors. Such dreams did not have the status of creation but of remembrance of something considered "forgotten" from the repertories of the *jukurrpa*. After much discussion, the authenticity of these dream revelations was attested by the fact that the dreamers had sung the correct sequence of sites associated with the Possum *jukurrpa* prior to the revelations. Some Elders were somewhat embarrassed by the incorporation of these ritual elements into Warlpiri cultural heritage; indeed, they claimed to be the only ones who could celebrate the Possum, saying that women should celebrate another totem associated with the Possum's travels. Nakakut knew all

4 Dreaming to sing: Learning and dream creation in the Australian desert

Figure 4.1. Barbara Gibson Nakamarra leading the Yawakiyi *yawulyu* dance.

of the Possum story and knew how to sing this journey alongside that of the Yawakiyi (Plum). She taught this cycle of songs to her kin.

Shortly after Nakakut and her relatives sang the songs and danced for Yawakiyi *jukurrpa* (see Figure 4.1), one of her Warlpiri nephews emerged as the leader of the negotiations, knowing the best way to defend Lajamanu's interests. At the time of the dream story presented here, Nakakut had just been recognised as one of the heirs to her father and was going to a mining meeting in Yuendumu community where she had lived with a double preoccupation: to prevent the destruction of the sacred site embodying the Possum ancestors and to ask for royalties from the exploitation of the minerals in the authorised region. A year later, the site would be protected by a large grid built around it, and alongside her sister and co-wife, she would receive a 4WD vehicle as compensation.

Karnanganja manu Ngapa (Emu and Rain Dreamings) Told by Barbara Gibson Nakamarra

The other night, after Yakiriya told you [Glowczewski] the Emu story, I dreamed that I was sitting with her and the ancestral women. We were getting ready for a ceremony and a crowd of non-Indigenous people were taking pictures of us!

My mother-in-law called out to me, very angrily, saying that she didn't want non-Indigenous people to take pictures of us, but I said: "Don't worry about it! They're going to give us a truck."

Indeed, the next day I had to fly to the meeting in Yuendumu, where I intended to ask the mining company for a truck as compensation for my ancestral rights for the Granites region, where they had interests. And the dream continued and revealed to me two new songs, one for the Yankirri (Emu) *jukurrpa* and the other for the Ngapa (Rain/Water) *jukurrpa*. The songs were given to me by the wooden female Emu egg, the poor thing, who is alone now that you have her male companion. I made them both years ago for Yakiriya, that's why she sang for me. She made me sick before my dream; I was cold without knowing why. Then, when I woke up, when I was on the plane, I felt very unwell. My husband asked me what was wrong and I replied that I was nauseous probably because I had not had breakfast. It is true that I was also nervous about speaking at the meeting. When I returned, I said to Yakiriya, "it was the 'cracked feet', the Emu, that made me feel so weird with this pain in my stomach. I took on the plane the two songs I had been given!"

Yakiriya knew because I told her my dream before I left. She is the one who with two other Nangala was singing in my sleep the new Emu song: *karnanganja nangunangu mangurrularna mangurrungurru … Karnanganja* refers to the parents of the egg, *nangunangu* is the waterhole they saw and the rest means that they sat there and then moved on. But as they sang Emu songs, all the women, myself included, were painted with the Rain/Water Dreaming designs.

Two Napanangka, Betty and Nyilirrpina, stood up the nullanulla (*mangaya*) imbued with ritual power. They erected it on the spot where the Emu and his wife covered their eggs, near the huge waterhole formed by the Initiated Man (Ngarrka) Dreaming that belongs to my husband. So I danced with the other women and we sang the new Rain/Water song: *murraninginti kutakuta jurdungku jurdungku luwarninya … murraninginti* means on the other side: that is, the west in relation to the east where the Emu travelled through; *kutakuta* is the storm and *jurdu*, the whirlwind. When it comes to *luwarni* "throwing", it evokes the lightning strikes. Suddenly a cloud of dust rushed over us. A very powerful wind lifted the sand. The whirlwind covered us with dust. At the same time the rain began to fall. We sang and danced the Ngapa (Rain/Water) *jukurrpa* song and got sent the sandstorm and were answered by the lightning bolts. These came from the sacred kurrajong trees of Lullju where the Rain/Water people brought them out when they filled the hole with water.

4 Dreaming to sing: Learning and dream creation in the Australian desert

All the women ran for cover, not to their shelters, but under the dome-shaped foliage of the trees as we once did. The dance ground was surrounded by them. I shouted to both Napanangka, "Come! There's too much wind and dust!" They continued to dance and to pull out the nullanulla they had erected. Still dancing, they then joined us to keep it safe.

That's when I woke up in the middle of the night. I thought of our traditional ceremonies for the Emu Dreaming and the Rain/Water Dreaming. I thought of the two Nangala, now deceased, who were the most expert in leading the rituals. Custodians of the Rain/Water Dreaming in the Kulpulurnu region and of the Emu Dreaming with the two rockholes in the rock where the Emu and his wife discovered the *miyaka* (kurrajong fruit). These two women taught me their knowledge, like at school. The whole Kulpulurnu clan was my family because my father's clan often visited them in times of drought. Thinking about those who have taught me, I had a lot of pain.

When I went back to sleep, I went back into the same dream. The sandstorm had subsided, the rain had stopped. We were only a small group of women: two Nakamarra, my sister Beryl and me, two Nangala, Yakiriya and another woman, a Nampijinpa and one of the two Napanangka, Betty Hooker, who led us. We danced for the big soakage Kuraja, which is near the town of Katherine. That's where the Rain/Water Dreaming ends. There are black stones all around there. We call them "Black clouds", an expression that also refers to the sea.

The Rain/Water Dreaming painted designs that we wore on our chests have turned into paintings of the Emu Dreaming. Napanangka said, "Now you will follow the Emu Dreaming to the salt water, the sea."

She took a large wooden dish, which she painted with the designs of the Emu Dreaming (see Figure 4.2). Dancing the Emu Dreaming, we found ourselves far north, in Jikaya, a site along this Dreaming trail, where there are many small waterholes. Still dancing, each of us dipped one foot in one of the holes and removed it as soon as she felt the water rise. It was funny, we tasted the water from all the holes with our feet!

All night we danced. At dawn, just before sunrise, the sea appeared, the salt water is black and vast. Napanangka said: "This is where you must end up, for here the brother and sister Emu went back into the ground."

Each of us tasted the sea with our feet as we had done from the Jikaya holes. Huge waves rose and I was very scared. Suddenly we found ourselves again at the great black-stone swamp where the Rain/Water Dreaming ends. I saw a circular ceremonial ground and a crowd of ancestral women with unknown faces. With

Figure 4.2. Sketch of the Emu designs on the wooden dish. Image by Barbara Glowczewski.

that, I woke up. The day was beginning. The women of the Dreaming had shown me, in its entirety, the ancient ceremony for Emu and Rain/Water by making me travel to the end of the two ancestral itineraries.

4 Dreaming to sing: Learning and dream creation in the Australian desert

We perform this ceremony alongside men every four to five years to introduce boys to the Yankirri (Emu) and Ngapa (Rain/Water) *jukurrpa* and clans. We dance all night, as in my dream: before night falls, we sing the verses corresponding to the Ngapa (Rain/Water) *jukurrpa* of Kulpurlunu. Around midnight, the songs and dances take us to Jikaya, the site of the Emu with the small waterholes that I saw in my dream.

Just before sunrise, we close the ceremony with the dance of the arrival of a brother and a sister Emu at the sea. There in the sea, the bodies of the two Emu children stay forever. It is their *kuruwarri* designs that inhabit the two wooden eggs that we paint on this occasion. At each ceremony, we paint them fresh in red with white markings similar to the footprints of the emus.

The same emu prints are painted on the ritual boards used to close the ceremony; they represent the parents of the two children, who did not go to sea but returned to the desert near Kulpurlunu, the site of the Rain/Water Dreaming. At one end of the dish, thick black lines represent the sea, undrinkable salt water that we call *karnta* (woman). These features are separated from each other by white lines, clouds. Two white arches on top correspond to the two Emu children. This part of the dish shows the end of the Emu's journey.

The middle of the dish corresponds to half of the journey coinciding with the end of the Rain/Water Dreaming section at the large black-stone swamp, Kuraja. Two black features represent the drinkable fresh water that we call *wirriya* (boy). Between these features and those representing the sea, two long yellow arches depict the male kurrajong fruits of the Jikaya region of the Yankirri (Emu) *jukurrpa*, while on the other half of the dish, the same yellow arches depict the female fruits of the Kulpurlunu region of the Ngapa (Rain/Water) *jukurrpa*. Between the yellow arches of the bottom (south) and the top (north), we draw a yellow oval corresponding to the dish (*parraja*), the hollow log that was used by the Emu parents to prepare the fruits. Around the two ovals, small yellow arches represent both the white skin of the fruit and the yellow powder from inside.

At sunrise, during the last dance with this painted dish, we insert the ritual pole into the ground, which is adorned in its upper part with black lines separated by white lines, representing (as on the dish) the sea and clouds. Then the respective owners of the Emu and Rain/Water *jukurrpa* bury the pole. We say that they bury the two *jukurrpa* until the next ceremony.

It is not enough to dream of a new song or a new painting and to say that they come from the ancestral heroes of the *jukurrpa*. In general, it is necessary to follow the corresponding route. In my case, the Emu egg, the little girl, led my *pirlirrpa* (spirit) through her *jukurrpa* so that I could identify the words of the song I had heard. In the same way the Rain/Water *jukurrpa* caused the sandstorm while I slept, confirming that the other song came from Lulju. Mungamunga (The Voices of the Night)[3] have different ways of making us understand things. For example, the sandstorm erupted just after my mother-in-law's anger that she didn't want non-Indigenous people to take a picture of us. When I told her to let them do it because they'd give us a truck, she shouted: "The truck is for you! Not for me."

Now my mother-in-law is a Nangala, an owner of the Ngapa (Rain/Water) *jukurrpa*. Like other women, I was painted with this *jukurrpa*, though for the most part we were not the custodians. Perhaps that's why she got angry and her *jukurrpa* inflicted the storm on us. Yakiriya told me that if I had received this nocturnal reminder of the *jukurrpa* tracks for Rain/Water and Emu and the revelation of two songs, it is because we do not celebrate these two *jukurrpa* enough.

By teaching women the new songs, we can revitalise the traditional ceremonies for Emu and Rain/Water Dreamings. It is true that here in Lajamanu, unlike Yuendumu, there are no longer many Nangala and Nampijinpa from Kulpulunu. The old ones have passed on and the others are too old or too young to dance. There are other Nangala but they come from the Lungkardajarra region and it is that part of the Ngapa (Rain/Water) *jukurrpa* that they look after. The Nangala may be jealous and will resent me for trying to teach them a new song about their Dreaming. But that's how it is, these Nangala have no ritual responsibility for the region I dreamed of. But me, I was initiated in my youth by several Nangala from Kulpurlunu. Also, I can direct this part of the celebration of the Rain/Water Dreaming with two other Nakamarra, Ngawalyungu and Puljukupari, whose maternal grandmothers were custodians of the same region.

As for my own maternal grandmother, she was the owner of the Rain/Water Dreaming from Pawu, that is to say for the final sequence of this route: her clan takes over the story looked after by the Kulpurlunu clan. My sons-in-law and my daughters-in-law come from both regions. *Ngulajuku* (That's all, I've finished).

Some keys to the Warlpiri interpretive system

Ngulajuku is the conventional way to close every story, of a myth, a dream or a simple conversation. Nakakut Nakamarra's dream and the comments she provides

---

3   This translation for Mungamunga was agreed upon with B. Gibson for *Desert Dreamers* (Glowczewski 2016). These invisible forces can take the shapes of different totemic ancestors, deceased people and contemporary strange beings who can seduce men, women and children.

4 Dreaming to sing: Learning and dream creation in the Australian desert

Figure 4.3. Barbara Gibson, Yakiriya, Beryl Gibson and Barbara Glowczewski with the male and female wooden emu eggs. Image supplied by Barbara Glowczewski.

in her narration refer to two totemic routes that stretch close to the Granites for hundreds of kilometres from south to north: the Rain/Water *jukurrpa* that created many water points by flooding the plains and the Emu *jukurrpa*. Nakakut says that she dreamed of the Emu because, shortly before, she had helped me translate the myth of the Emu told by her friend Yakiriya, whom she saw dancing in her dream and who, in exchange for a blanket, had given me a ritual object – a painted wooden emu egg – that Nakakut had made for her. Nakakut wanted the exchange to be photographed. It should be noted that the dream begins with her mother-in-law complaining that too many non-Indigenous people are taking pictures of them.

Women make wooden eggs that represent the fertility of the emus and are also used in rituals to encourage human fertility. The Emu Dreaming tells, among other things, the story of a male who follows a female and falls in love with her; when he finds her, he travels with her, and they have many children, some of whom travel far with them, over a thousand kilometres, outside their Country, to the sea. The Emu story offers an alternative family model for the Warlpiri, who are often polygamous. In fact, the emu is monogamous; moreover, the male incubates the eggs alternating with the female who goes in search of food. Emus are associated with a variety of plant foods, including *miyaka* (Red Kurrajong) fruits. The Emu ancestor passed on the method for preparation to prevent the yellow powder that covers them from blinding someone who rubs it in their eyes. The exchange of roles continues when the emus are small. Nakakut, who had made two wooden eggs (see Figure 4.3) – a male and a female – comments in her account that it was the one who stayed alone with Yakiriya, "the female, the poor one", who gave her the dream. The gift she gave me of a male egg followed two other gifts: in five years, I had received two baby carriers, although I had not yet had a child at the age of 28. When I gave birth to my two daughters, Nakakut's efforts finally made sense as, through the classificatory kinship system, I called her *ngati*, mother.

Since groupings and kinship relationships are very important in Aboriginal social organisation but also in dreams, it should be remembered that Warlpiri people practice a system of classification in eight subsections called "skin names". The eight names are taken two by two to form different kinship relationships so that everyone in their social world uses a kinship address term with respect to all other members, even if there is no biological connection. Similarly, all non-Aboriginal people living on site – teachers, nurses or ethnologists – are bound to enter this kinship network, which is the keystone of social and ritual organisation.

Indeed, everyone is owner *kirda* of their Dreamings and assistant/manager *kurdungurlu* of the Dreaming of their mother and their spouse. But, when a ceremony takes place, all members of the present group are automatically divided into one or the other role according to their skin names. People who have the same skin name as the person who is the owner of the Dreaming in question consider themselves "skin brothers"; as such, all those who have the skin name in the position of "father", "mother-in-law" or "father of the mother-in-law" of the real owners will also behave like *kirda* "masters/bosses" of the ritual (e.g., able to dance). All those whose skin name is in the "opposite" position – "father-in-law", "sister's child" or "brother/sister-in-law" – will be in a *kurdungurlu* position and will have to "work" for the ritual, either choreographing the dances, painting the ritual objects or preparing the ground (calling this job "worker", "manager", "lawyer" or "policeman"!).

The narrator of the dream is of Nakamarra skin. The owners of the Emu *jukurrpa* (as well as the Rain/Water *jukurrpa*) are Jangala/Jampijinpa for men and Nangala/Nampijinpa for women. A Nakamarra is mother of Nungarrayi and Jungarrayi, who marry Jangala and Nangala, respectively. The husband of a Nakamarra is Japaljarri, whose father is Jungarrayi, and mother is Nangala. Therefore, a Nakamarra woman is both "mother-in-law" for Jangala and Nangala (who marry her children) and daughter-in-law of Nangala, who is the mother of her husband. Therefore, she is a classificatory owner of the Emu and Rain/Water *jukurrpa* in

4 Dreaming to sing: Learning and dream creation in the Australian desert

two ways. In Nakakut's dream, we find several Nangala: first, her mother-in-law, who wants non-Indigenous people to stop taking pictures, then her friend Yakiriya, who told me the Emu myth and gave me the egg made by Nakakut. The dreamer further offers us her interpretation of their presence in her dream.

She also says that, during her dream, she woke up thinking of two other Nangala, the deceased owners of the Emu and Rain/Water *jukurrpa*, who instructed her when she lived in the Granites region. Thus, she associates her dream with the time of her childhood, before sedentarisation in Yuendumu, the community where she was to fly the day after this dream to defend her land and rights. Nakakut emphasised that her own maternal grandmother, a Nampijinpa, was the owner of the Rain/Water *jukurrpa* from Pawu: that is, the final sequence of this route because her clan takes over the story celebrated by the clan at Kulpurlunu. She adds that these sons-in-law and daughters-in-law (thus Jangala and Nangala) come from both regions and that, unlike in Yuendumu, in Lajamanu where she now lives, the Rain/Water Dreaming of this region of the Tanami Desert is not celebrated enough. She notes that the responsibility is to reactivate her connections, which would explain the purpose of the songs she heard in her dream.

In her dream, Nakakut stages two Napanangka, the skin name in a position of "mother" with regard to her own. It turns out that Beatty Napanangka, whom she sees leading the line of dancers, was the boss of the Kajirri ceremony, which, five years before, during my first stay in 1979, had served as the framework for the collective initiation of the dreamer's eldest son as well as that of his sister and her co-wife, another dancer in her dream. In the latter, the two Napanangka erect a sacred *mangaya* pole in the ground, then remove it by dancing exactly as the women do during the Kajirri ceremony. The dreamer evokes Mungamunga as the "Voices of the Night", which has various ways of making us understand things by giving different identities to dream characters and creating meaningful situations like the anger that becomes (or turns into) a sandstorm. Mungamunga is also said to take the form of various ancestral heroines, including the two Nampijinpa sisters associated with the secret ceremony Kajirri, as the maternal grandmother of Nakakut and the unidentified dancer who accompanies the dreamer and the other women mentioned in their journey to the sea.

In her dream, the dreamer thus relives the mythical path of the original Rain/Water *jukurrpa*, as well as that of the Emu *jukurrpa*, as recounted by the ancestors since the beginning of time. The authentication of the real sites through which they travelled is necessary to confirm the authenticity of the two new songs that she dreamed, respectively, for Emu and Rain/Water *jukurrpa*. It is necessary to renew the spiritual link with the land by singing and dancing the songs and dances inherited from previous generations as much as the new songs and dances received in dreams, which are the means of keeping the tradition alive, attesting to the memory of the dream and the ancestral beings as effectively always in the making. We have seen by this example how dream, myth, reality and ritual feed into each other. The narrator's self-reflection on her own dream helps us, through her clear perception and sense of humour, to understand that it is necessary to incorporate spoken narrative and elaboration to prevent confusion between dream, myth and reality. This distinction is often difficult to identify in Aboriginal statements (Poirier 1996), especially when, as in the case of dreams reported by Roheim (1988), the conditions of elaboration and the narrator's reference system are not given to us. The important thing to remember is that if everything has a prior context (Glowczewski 1991c), the story is like an "audiovisual" reading, deciphering traces, signs seen and heard in dreams, landscapes and everything in the environment that leaves footprints, be it humans, animals, rain and wind or even unknown forces.

In 1994, 10 years after the story of the dream told here, Nakakut came to visit me when I had just given birth to my second daughter in Broome, a small town on the north-west coast located 1,500 kilometres from Lajamanu. By then, widowed from her husband and after long ordeals of mourning, she had left Lajamanu and settled with an Aboriginal man from Tennant Creek in Kununurra, a small town in north-eastern Western Australia, halfway to Broome. It was the first time she had seen the Indian Ocean from the west coast. I showed her a cliff that the Aboriginal people of the region, the Yawuru and Djugun, of which my husband is a descendant, associate with the Dreaming of a giant Emu, Garnanganja, the same name as the ancestral Emu from the desert. This one left his footprints, arrow-like, more than a metre wide in diameter, engraved like fossils, in several places in the reefs; these traces were identified by specialists as those of different species of feather dinosaurs. On this cliff is an escarpment with many small holes that fill with seawater at high tide. As we dipped our feet into them, a strange feeling invaded us both – I felt transported into the desert; she recoiled, hugging my daughter and refused to go any further, sitting behind the cliff to protect herself from the "power" of this place. For me, it was like deja vu of the dream she had told me 10 years before when, in her words, "tasting" the site full of small waterholes in the rock, she had found herself – in her dream – at the edge of the salt water, the Pacific Ocean where the myth of the Emu ends, as it was told to me by her friend Yakiriya. Was the fertility egg she had painted for Yakiriya and which she had given me related to the birth of my daughter on the edge of the Indian Ocean? The myth and the dream seemed to come together in my reality.

References

Dussart, Françoise. 1988. Warlpiri Women's Yawulyu Ceremonies: A Forum for Socialisation and Innovation. PhD thesis, Australian National University, Canberra.

Glowczewski, Barbara. 1984. "Viol et Inviolabilité: Un Mythe Territorial en Australie Centrale". *Cahiers de Littérature Orale* 14: 125–50.

Glowczewski, Barbara. 1991a. *Du Rêve à la Loi Chez les Aborigènes: Mythes, Rites et Organisation Sociale en Australie.* Paris: Presses Universitaires de France.

Glowczewski, Barbara. 1991b. "Entre Rêve et Mythe: Róheim et les Australiens". *L'Homme* 118(31.2): 125–32.

Glowczewski, Barbara (ed.). 1991c. *Yapa. Peintres aborigènes de Balgo et Lajamanu/Aboriginal Painters from Balgo and Lajamanu.* Paris: Baudoin Lebon Editeur (bilingual catalogue).

Glowczewski, Barbara. 2000. *Pistes de Rêves. Art et Savoir des Yapa de Désert Australien (Dream Trackers. Yapa Art and Knowledge of the Australian desert)* (bilingual CD-ROM). Paris: United Nations Educational, Scientific and Cultural Organization Publishing.

Glowczewski, Barbara. 2002. "Mémoire des Rêves, Mémoire de la Terre: Jukurrpa". In *Rêves: Visions Révélatrices. Réception et Interprétation des Songes dans le Contexte Religieux*, edited by M. Burger, 75–97. Berne: Peter Lang.

Glowczewski, Barbara. 2016. *Desert Dreamers.* Minneapolis: Minnesota University Press/Univocal.

Glowczewski, Barbara. 2020. *Indigenising Anthropology with Guattari and Deleuze.* Edinburgh: Edinburgh University Press.

Glowczewski, Barbara and Barbara Gibson Nakamarra. 2002. "Rêver pour Chanter: Apprentissage et Creation Onirique dans le Désert Australien". *Cahiers de Littérature Orale* 51: 153–168.

Glowczewski, Barbara, Mary Laughren and Jerry Jangala Patrick. 2021. "Jurntu Purlapa: Warlpiri Songline for the Jurntu Fire Dreaming Site". *Cahiers de Littérature Orale* 87: 229–38.

Meggitt, Mervyn. 1962. *Desert People. A Study of the Walbiri Aborigines of Central Australia.* London: Angus & Robertson.

Munn, Nancy. 1973. *Walbiri Iconography.* Ithaca: Cornell University Press.

Peterson, N., P. McConvell, S. Wild, and R. Hagen. 1978. *Claim to Areas of Tradition Land by the Warlpiri, Kartangarurru–Kurintji.* Alice Springs: Central Land Council.

Poirier, Sylvie. 1996. *Les Jardins du Nomade. Cosmologie, Territoire et Personne dans le Désert Occidental Australien.* Münster: Lit (avec le concours du CNRS [French Scientific Research Center], Paris).

Roheim, Geza. 1988. *Children of the Desert II. Myth and Dreams of the Aborigines of Central Australia* (Oceania Ethnographies 2). Edited and introduced by John Morton and Werner Muensterberger. Sydney, University of Sydney.

Stanner, William Edward. 1958. "The Dreaming". In *Reader in Comparative Religion: An Anthropological Approach*, edited by William A. Lessa and Evon Z. Vogt, 23–40. Evanston, Illinois: Row, Peterson & Company (Australian Signpost, 1956).

Ruth Napaljarri Oldfield (c.1945–)

Ruth is an owner for the Ngarlu (Sugarleaf), Janganpa (Possum) and Warlawurru (Eagle) *jukurrpa* associated with the Country to the east of Yuendumu, near Mount Allan community. This is both Warlpiri and Anmatyerr Country. Ruth has lived in this area her whole life, walking through this Country as a young girl and then working as a housemaid and cook. When she moved into Yuendumu as a young adult, she was employed as a health worker. In her later life, she has become an internationally acclaimed artist, famous for her paintings of the Ngatijirri (Budgerigar) *jukurrpa*. Ruth lives in Yuendumu with her family and is a senior singer and custodian for many *yawulyu* songs.

> *Nganayi yangka kalalu-nganpa ngarrurnu kiyini, "Yiniwayi wajalu pina jarriya nyuntu-nyangurla yawulyurla". Yunparninjaku kalarnalu start jarrija. Wariyiwariyirlarnalu nganimpaju learn jarrija, nganimpajurnalu pina jarrija. Kalalu-nganpa learn-i manu yangka pinarri manu kalalu-nganpa yawulyurluju. Warrki-jangka yangka kalarnalu yanurra after work, kalalu-nganpa yirrarnu "Nyuntulku kanpa do mani waja jalangurluju, nyuntulurlulku waja kanpa yunparni". "Nyunturlulku kanpa do mani." Kalalu-nganpa ngarrurnu kujarlu, yuwayi. Kalarnalu-jana nyangu-jala, pina jarrija kalarnalu nyanjarla. Yuwayi yangka kalarnalu-jana nyangu yawuly- kurraju nganimparluju. Learn jarrijarna Yurntumurla ngajuju. Pina-manuju pimirdi-nyanurlu.*

They used to tell us "Learn your *yawulyu* (women's songs)." And we used to start singing. Yes, we were taught *yawulyu* (women's songs) at Wariyiwariyi (Mt Allan). Every day after work they used to paint us and then say, "You do it now, it's your turn to sing now." "You do it now," they used to tell us, and we used to watch them dancing. I also learned later at Yuendumu … with my aunties …

Wurlkumanujulpa palka nyinaja, nganayiji Jilaliki-palangujulpa palka nyinaja. Ngularralpalu palka nyinaja, ngularra kalarnalu-jana nyangu yangka wirntinja-kurra. Kalalu-nganpa ngarrurnu, "Wirntiyalu nyurrurla-nyangurla waja yungunpa pina jarri waja nyuntu-nyangurla yawulyurla, kurdijiki-ngarnti nganayiki-ngarnti yawulyuku-ngarnti waja karnta-kurlanguku-ngarnti." Kujarra kalalu-nganpa ngarrurnu. Yuwayi yijardu kalarnalu wirntija.

My old grandmother was here [in Yuendumu] and they [her and her sisters] were the ones who taught us. We used to watch them dance all the time and they used to tell us, "Dance your *yawulyu* (women's songs) so that you can know how to dance when it's time for *kurdiji* (big ceremony)." That's what they used to say to us and then we would dance.

Yangka jalangurlangu kujalpalpa nyinaja no songlpalu yunparnu wiyarrparlu. Yuwayi wiyarrpa, warraja-jala ka ngunanjayani yawulyu-wati yalumpuju. Yuwayi warraja ka ngunanjayani. Panukarirli right mardalu wajawaja-manu wiyarrparlu, some-palarluju kalu wajawaja-mani, yuwayi nganimparluju karnalu mardarni-jiki-jala.

Some, these days, must have lost theirs, and others are losing theirs, but we are still holding on to ours. Today people are just sitting down and no songs are being sung. Yes, poor things, [but] the *yawulyu* is still around. Yes it is still present and people do know it.

Coral Napangardi Gallagher (c.1935–2019)

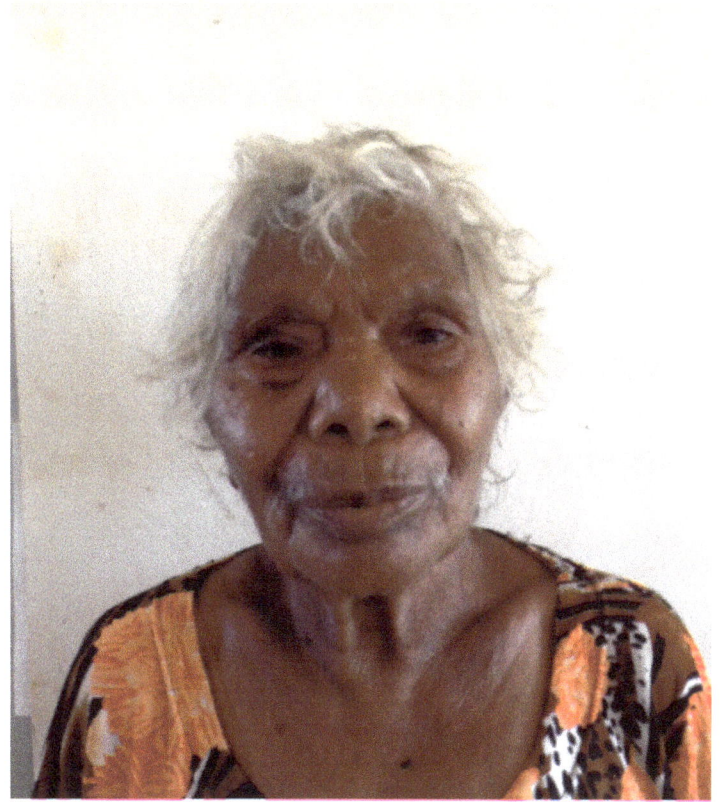

Napangardi was an important singer in Yuendumu until she passed away in 2019. She was an owner for the Mount Theo/Puturlu *jukurrpa* and *kurdungurlu* for the Jardiwanpa. In 2014, she published the book *Jardiwanpa Yawulyu* in collaboration with Peggy Brown, Barbara Martin and Georgia Curran. She worked tirelessly to teach younger generations traditional hunting skills, songs and dances. As a young woman, she lived with her husband and family at Wayililinpa outstation, to the south of Yuendumu.

Peggy Nampijinpa Brown (c.1941–)

Nampijinpa is a senior *juju-ngaliya* and leader for women's ceremonial life in Yuendumu. She is *kirda* (owner) for the Yankirri (Emu) *jukurrpa*, and also identifies with the Warlukurlangu (Fire) and Ngapa (Rain) *jukurrpa*. She was awarded an Order of Australia for her work founding the Mt Theo Program (now Warlpiri Youth Development Aboriginal Corporation, WYDAC). She lives in Yuendumu and is often at Mt Theo looking after young Warlpiri people.

Nyampu kuruwarri yungulu panungku nyanyi. And ngurrara nyuntu-nyangu warringiyi-kirlangu karnalu-nyarra kijirni nyampuju yungunparla marlaja mardarni.

We want lots of people to see these *jukurrpa*. And this is your grandfather's (father's father's) *jukurrpa* that I'm putting on you, so you can remember and carry it on.

Kuruwarriji tarnngangku-juku, kurdu karnalu-jana pina-pina-mani yangka, yungu kurdungku mardarni tarnngangku-juku ngula karnalu-jana pina-mani. Manu kuja new generation-ki karnalu-jana puta wangka, kuruwarri yungurnalu-jana jamulu yungkarla yilpalu yangka mardakarla nyanungurrarlulku.

The Dreaming is forever, we teach the young generations so they can learn and keep the culture with them. That's why we teach them. And we would like to give our culture to the new generations to keep and to carry on.

Ngulaku, yinyirra karnalu-jana, yungulu-nyanu tarnngangku mardarni warlalja warringiyi-kirlangu. Manu juju yungulu-nyanu mardarni ngurrara-nyanu yungu mardarni warringiyikirlangu tarnngangku-juku. Nuwu wajawaja-manta! Yungulu langangku mani, ngukunyparlu yungulu mardarni. Ngajuju yapa kalarnalu nyuyu jarrija yangka ring place-kirra, kalarnalu nyinaja wali kalalu yunparnu. Wurra-wiyi-jiki, wurulyparlu kalarna-jana pina-nyangu. Kalarna ngulajangkaju pina yanu. Kalarnarla think jarrija yaliki yawulyuku kuruwarriki. Pinarni yanu kalarna.

So they can keep their grandfather's (father's father's) country without losing them. To always have the knowledge of the country. People used to gather around at the ceremony place, they use to sing, then I would listen to them singing. Then I would go back thinking I should learn those songs, the *yawulyu*.

Kalalu yijardu yunparnu, kalarna-jana nyangu-wiyi, pingkangku kalarna yunparnu. Wirntinjakuju pina-jalalparna nyinaja. Wali yawulyulku yalumpu, pingkangku-wiyi, pingkangku-wiyi kalarna yunparnu. Warrajarlulku kalarna yunparnurra. Nyampu karna mardarni panu-kurlangu langangkulku, yangka kujakarna manngu-nyanyi. Milyapinyilki karna yawulyuju yalikari-kirlangu yalikari-kirlangu. Kalarnalu yangka jintangkarlu yunparnu.Ngulanya karnalujana marlaja mardarni nganimparluju. Ngula-warnuju kurdu-kurdukulku karnalu-jana yangka yunparni, pina-pina-mani karnalu-jana ngajarrarlulku, yilparnalu-jana jamulurra yungkarla or ngati-nyanurlulparla mardakarla.

They would sing, I used to watch and listen. Then I would sing softly, I already knew how to dance but I wanted to sing too. I can sing now, I have lots of songs, even other people's songs. We used to sing together, that's why we still carry it on, we want to teach our young ones to sing. We teach our young ones, so they can keep it and carry on with their mothers.

Kalalu-nganpa pina-pina-manu wirntinjarlu-wiyi. Wirntija-wiyi kalalu. Wali kalarnalu-jana nyangu, wali yangka kalarnalu jalajala jarrijalku, wirntijarralku kalarnalu. "Kari jungarni waja kanpa wirntimi ngurrju waja. Kuja wirntiya waja ngula karnangku pina yinyi." Wali yijardu kalarnalu-jana rdanparnu, kalarnalu wirntijalku. "Jungarni kanpa wirntimi, nyunturlurlu marda kapunpa mardarni jujuju, Tarnngangku-juku kapunpa mardarni. Kurdijirla, yawulyurla kapunpa mardarni tarnngangku-juku. Yaparla-nyanu-kurlangu jaja-nyanu-kurlangu, nyampuju kanpa mardarni warringiyi-nyanu-kurlangu nyuntuku-palangu-kurlangu. Tarnngangku-juku ngukunyparlu manta!"

They used to teach us by dancing at first. They would dance first. We would watch them then we would want to try and we would dance. "Dance like this" — we would dance alongside the elders. They taught us to dance, and they used to say to us, "You are dancing the right way, you are dancing the right way, maybe you will keep all these ceremony songs. You will have them at *Kurdiji* times and women's ceremony times. Ones belonging to your grandmothers (father's mother, mother's mother) and great aunts (father's father's sisters). You will keep this because it is your grandparents' *jukurrpa*, keep it in your head forever!"

Chapter 5

Minamina *yawulyu*: Musical change from the 1970s through to the 2010s

By Georgia Curran, Barbara Napanangka Martin and Linda Barwick

Minamina *yawulyu* are sung as a long series of verses by Warlpiri women[1] living in Yuendumu and Lajamanu. Associated with the travels of a group of ancestral women who came out from Minamina,[2] a site in the west of Warlpiri Country, the verses recount the travels of the Minamina women through a series of named places on their eastward journey. The verses sometimes refer to the women as *walarajarra* or *karrparnu*, the digging sticks they carry.[3] Together with the associated Country, designs and dances, Minamina songs and stories are owned by Warlpiri women of the Napangardi/Napanangka patricouple, *kirda* who are supported by *kurdungurlu* from the Nakamarra and Nangala subsection groups, although nowadays the *kurdungurlu* category tends to extend more generally to include any of the few senior women who still have knowledge of how to perform the songs. This is one indication that these songs are highly endangered. We discuss six recorded performances of Minamina

---

1 Warlpiri men also sing songs about the journey of the group of ancestral women, but this chapter is devoted to the women's songs. The Minamina songs that men sing are sung all night for *Kurdiji* ceremonies in Lajamanu (see Curran 2016).
2 There are many sites around Warlpiri country named Mina. In Warlpiri the word *mina* refers to a "[protective entity in which being lives or sleeps.] nest, lair, home, shell, living place, residence, niche, camp, enclosure, husk, shell, protective membrane, pericarp" (Laughren et al. 2022). In this chapter, Minamina is a specific place located in the far west of Warlpiri country, to the north-east of Lake Mackay.
3 The association of digging sticks with women is very salient. Females' umbilical cords are *karlangu* "digging stick" and males' are *karli* "boomerang" (Laughren et al. 2022: 1337).

yawulyu songs performed across a span of five decades by groups of singers in Yuendumu.[4] We compare these recorded performance instances to uncover some of the prominent changes, as well as stable features, across this period, illustrating a level of simplification and reduction in variability and complexity while maintaining the core essence of the songs and associated Country and the connections of individuals through inherited kinship rights.

The earliest known recordings of Minamina *yawulyu* songs were made by Rosalind Peterson in 1972 in Yuendumu with a large group of Warlpiri women who were painting up for a broader ceremony to be held that evening.[5] Many records of other performances exist (e.g., the recordings made by Richard Moyle in Balgo in 1979 and referred to in Moyle 1997); however, for this chapter, we focus on performances recorded in Yuendumu or led by women from Yuendumu. Some of the verses on this recording are still sung today by current generations of Warlpiri women, many of them descendants of the singers in the recording. Today's Minamina *yawulyu* songs are recognisably the same, using the same iconic tune and many similar lyrics referring to the landscape and the actions of the group of travelling ancestral women. Despite this (in many ways) remarkable level of continuity, there have also been significant changes to the performance contexts in which these songs are being sung, which have led to changes in selection of songs, musical setting and body designs.

In this chapter, we compare six recorded sets of Minamina *yawulyu* across a five-decade period. The recordings were made in three distinct blocks (1972, 2006 and 2016–2018). The earliest recordings were audio only, so they could not capture dancing and other important contextual features of the performance, although Rosalind Peterson took careful note of body designs and some other performative features in her field notes. Accordingly, our longitudinal analysis is limited to common features across the whole corpus. We will focus on 1) the song texts and overarching themes, 2) the ways rhythmic text verses are set to melodies and 3) the designs painted during the singing. We also make some general observations about the associated dancing.

To begin, we provide a general overview of the Minamina story and set out further details of the focal recorded performance instances, details of when and how they were made, and some observations of shifts in their performative features.

---

4 As there is relative fluidity of movement between Warlpiri communities, the singers would have had affiliations to a number of different Warlpiri communities.

5 Nicolas Peterson (2022 pers. comm.) has noted that the community was preparing for a *Jardiwanpa* ceremony that was being held in the evenings, but which was never finished due to a death in a nearby community.

5 Minamina *yawulyu*: Musical change from the 1970s through to the 2010s

The story of the ancestral women from Minamina[6]

In 2006, shortly after leading the singing of Minamina *yawulyu* for an elicited recording, Judy Nampijinpa Granites, as senior *kurdungurlu*, told the following story.

Yinya kujakarnalu yunparni ngulaju karnalu Minamina yinya yunparni karlarra, ngurra nyanungu Minamina. Karntalkulpalu miirn-nyinaja Napanangka, Napangardi, wati-wangurla. Karntakarilpalu, yalumpujuku, karnta-patunya.

This one that we're singing is really from Minamina. This song is the one from Minamina, way over to the west. At their home there at Minamina, the women are busying themselves. The women were really busy getting ready. All the Napangardis and all the Napanangkas – no men, there were only women there.

Karnta kanalyurr-pardinya kuja karrinja-pardija wurnaku-ngarnti. Milpirri mayi kalu-jana. Ngula-ngurlu nyampu wajarnalu ngurra-ngurlu nyampu-ngurlu yali-ngirli ngarna-ngurlu kuja karrinja-pardija. Yuwayi, yurna-kurralkulpalu nyampuju karrinja-pardijalpa, karrijalpa. Karrinjalu pardija ngarna[7]-ngurlu yinya-ngurlu.

The women stood up ready to travel. They rose up like rain clouds. From there, like that, they stood up to travel away from their home. Yes, they stood up to travel to another place from there, from their home, they stood up just like that.

Ngulalku karrparnu ready-manu. Yurnakulkulpalu wiyarrpalpalu yurnangkulkulpalu walarajarra-manu. Yurnangku ngula karnalu yunparni ngulaju kurrkara. Mirdijirrpi-jirrpi warlurr-wangkami ka kurrkara.

Then the digging sticks [the ancestral women] got ready to travel to another place – the dear things. Those *walarajarra* [the digging sticks/the ancestral women] [were going off to another place. We are singing about the desert oak country from afar. The bent-over [from the wind] desert oaks are making a sad sound.

---

6   See the book *Yurntumu-Wardingki Juju-Ngaliya-Kurlangu Yawulyu* (2017) by Warlpiri Women from Yuendumu and Curran, in which this story and some of the verses of Minamina *yawulyu* have been written down.

7   Ngarna is also the word used for an ant nests (as well as depressions in the country) indicating that the women moved away like ants move away from their nest.

Barbara Napanangka Martin is *kirda* for Minamina, her biological father's country and *jukurrpa*.[8] In 2017 she wrote down a further section to this story.

> *Yarnkajarnili Janyinki-wana jingijingi. Kujalu yukajarni Warrkakurrkukurra, ngunajayanirnili. Warrkakurrkurla ngunanjarlalu jukajuka-yirrarnu karrparnu. Kujaka yangka manja-wati karrimi Warrkakurrkurla.*

They went to Janyinki and then went straight through. Like that they all came in together, to Warrkakurrku (Mala Bore). They camped there. They left their digging sticks standing up there. Those mulga trees are still standing there like that today at Warrkakurrku.

> *Wirntinjayanulu jingijingi ngunanjarla. Kakarraralu yanu. Wirntinjayanulu kakarrara. Aileron-kurralu yanu. Ngula-kurralu yanu. Karrkungurrpa-lpalu pina nyinanjarla yirraru-jarrijalku. Yirraru-jarrijalu ngulajulu yarnkajarni jurujuru, nganayi karrparnu. Yurrujurujuru kujalu yanu walyangka karrparnuju karlarra-purdayijala. Kakarrumpayi-jangkalu pina yanu karlarrakurra. Kujalu kulpari-jarrija, yarnkajalu karlarrakurralku. Kulpari-yanulu karlarrajuku yurrujurujuru, nganayi karrparnu. Kanunjumparralu yarnkajarra, yinyalu pina yanu Minamina-kurra ngulalu yukaja. Tarnnga-jukulpalu nyinaja yinyajukuju.*

After camping there they danced along the way. They went eastwards dancing along. They went along past Aileron. After dancing they turned around and looked back [westward] and they all felt homesick, those digging sticks [the women]. They turned around, feeling homesick and then they all travelled back. They went past, back towards the west. They went all the way back to Minamina and they went back in there for good.

Minamina *yawulyu*: Six recorded performance instances

Warlpiri women's *yawulyu* are typically performed in a number of different community-based contexts. In recent decades, opportunities to perform have expanded to include new contexts, such as intercommunity women's meetings, showcases for openings and exhibitions, and staged performances (see Curran and Dussart 2023). When Warlpiri communities hold larger ceremonies,

---

8   Barbara's mother remarried when Barbara was a young girl so she grew up with a father from different Country. Although Barbara knew all her life that she was *kirda* for Minamina, it is only in the last five years that she has started learning from senior Warlpiri women about Minamina stories, songs and dances in the process of documenting them for the book, Warlpiri Women from Yuendumu and Curran (2017).

5 Minamina *yawulyu*: Musical change from the 1970s through to the 2010s

typically involving men's singing and women's dancing, beginning after sunset and going into the night, *yawulyu* are performed in the late afternoon in private women's spaces. Several hours before sunset, women sing and paint each other up with associated designs. On occasion, brief dancing will follow, typically finishing within half an hour. During the painting up, slower tempo *yawulyu* songs are sung, with some of the same verses being sung at a faster tempo for the dancing.

As with *yawulyu* more generally, Minamina *yawulyu* song items consist of the varied repetition of a fixed text (verse) of two (or occasionally three) lines, repeated over a period of approximately 30 seconds to one minute, until the completion of a longer melodic contour. Each of these song items is followed by a pause and another song item based on the same verse before moving on to new verses in subsequent items (see Barwick and Turpin 2016; Barwick, Laughren and Turpin 2013; Curran et al. 2019; Turpin and Laughren 2013). Each verse references places, features of the landscape and/or the actions of the group of ancestral women as they travelled from Minamina.

As mentioned, the six different recorded instances we consider in this chapter were made during three periods over the last five decades: Recording 1 was made in ceremonial contexts over several days in 1972; Recording 2 was made in an elicited context in 2006; and Recordings 3–6 were made in various performance contexts in 2016–2018.

We acknowledge the many limitations of recordings as documents of a performance instance. None of the six recordings we will discuss is a complete documentation of an entire performance – even if it was, many aspects of the surrounding social context cannot be captured in recordings (even those supplemented by additional information in accompanying written notes). For example, for Warlpiri women, each performance nurtures the particular relationships between the singers, other people present, and the Country and *jukurrpa* to which they are connected. In these dimensions, each performance instance is unique, and neat comparisons cannot be made between them. Notwithstanding these evident shortcomings, this body of recordings is regarded as a valuable resource for contemporary Warlpiri performers because it represents some of the only detailed documentation of the songs performed in older performances. Therefore, analysing features that are captured well by recording can give us some valuable perspectives on change over time.

Recording 1: Painting up with Minamina yawulyu (June 1972; Peterson 1972–1973)

In 1972–1973, Rosalind Peterson lived with her husband, anthropologist Nicolas Peterson, in Yuendumu, where he was undertaking ethnographic fieldwork. During this period, she participated in a number of women's *yawulyu* events and made notes and recordings on some of these, including a number of sessions on 24–26 June 1972, during which 14 verses of Minamina *yawulyu* were sung (for full details including the names of the singers, see Peterson 1972–1973).[9] R. Peterson also made detailed notes about the participants and their relationships to each other, as well as sketching in coloured pencil the designs painted on the women's chests and stomachs while they were singing.

In 2007, Curran, Jeannie Nungarrayi Egan and Thomas Jangala Rice listened to these recordings during a visit to Canberra and wrote down the words of many of the verses. Rice was *kurdungurlu* for Minamina because it was his mother's *jukurrpa* and Country; thus, he knew the songs well from hearing them sung frequently by his mother when he was a child. More recently, Barwick, Martin and Curran have reviewed these recordings with senior contemporary singers and *kirda* for Minamina, particularly Lynette Nampijinpa Granites (senior singer), Connie Nakamarra Fisher (senior singer), Elsie Napanangka Granites (*kirda*), Geraldine Napanangka Granites (*kirda*) and Valda Napanangka Granites (*kirda*). In part due to the poor sound quality at parts of the old recordings,[10] but also due to shifts in knowledge and difficulty in understanding the "hard" language used in these songs, these sessions raised many questions within this group. Only a few of the verses were recognisable, and most were unknown by the current singers of Minamina *yawulyu*, although L. Granites was able to identify a number of keywords in the songs.

---

9   These recordings are archived at the Australian Institute of Aboriginal and Torres Strait Islander Studies (AIATSIS) with Nicolas Peterson's recordings from Yuendumu (1972–1973).

10 The recording machine was positioned close to the stone in which ochres were being ground; in some sections, this dominates the audio recording, overriding the singer's voices.

5 Minamina *yawulyu*: Musical change from the 1970s through to the 2010s

Recording 2: The Warlpiri Songlines project (December 2006; Curran and Egan 2005–2008)

In 2005–2008, Curran and Egan worked together with a group of senior female singers to record and document various *yawulyu* for the "Warlpiri Songlines" project.[11] On 18 December 2006, Judy Nampijinpa Granites (older sister to Lynette Granites and grandmother to Geraldine, Valda and Elsie; see Granites' profile) led the singing of a Minamina *yawulyu* song set that was recorded and archived with the "Warlpiri Songlines" collection at AIATSIS. Judy had good knowledge of Minamina *yawulyu* because not only had she been a main leader for women's ceremonies in Yuendumu over many decades but also her husband was *kirda* for this *jukurrpa* (for further details on Judy's role as female ritual leader, see Dussart 2000).[12] She had the strong support of seven other singers who together sang 15 verses of Minamina *yawulyu*. Following the recording, Judy re-listened to these songs and provided detailed stories about each, unpacking their meanings. The stories were documented alongside the song texts in the book *Yurntumu-Wardingki Juju-Ngaliya-Kurlangu Yawulyu* (Warlpiri Women from Yuendumu and Curran 2017, 11–34). Martin has played a key role in writing down these stories both as *kirda* for Minamina and due to her strong bilingual skills in writing both English and Warlpiri. As Judy passed away before we started making this book, Lorraine Nungarrayi Granites assisted Martin in interpreting the song texts and stories for the written representation (see Curran, Martin and Carew 2019).

Recording 3: Making the Yurntumu-Wardingki Juju-Ngaliya-Kurlangu Yawulyu DVD (Warlpiri Women from Yuendumu and Curran 2017)

During the book's development, a group of Warlpiri women decided they wanted to make four short films to showcase the dances for the *yawulyu* song series represented in the project for inclusion as a DVD accompaniment to the book *Yurntumu-Wardingki Juju-Ngaliya Kurlangu Yawulyu* (Warlpiri Women from Yuendumu and Curran 2017). On 18 July 2016, a large group of Warlpiri women gathered at a women's ceremonial ground at Mijilyparnta (Mission Creek) with filmmaker Anna Cadden. The group began the session by painting

---

11 This was an Australian Research Council Linkage project between the Australian National University, University of Queensland, the Central Land Council and the Warlpiri Janganpa Association, with Chief Investigators Nicolas Peterson, Mary Laughren and Stephen Wild, PhD student Georgia Curran, and key research collaborators Jeannie Nungarrayi Egan and Thomas Jangala Rice.

12 Judy and her sisters were married to Japangardi brothers who were all *kirda* for Minamina.

Figure 5.1. Barbara Napanangka Martin leads the Minamina *yawulyu* dances for the film. Photo still taken from a video made by Anna Cadden, 2016.

up four women who all had patrilineal *kirda* rights for Minamina *yawulyu*. Lorraine Nungarrayi Granites led the singing of four verses, supported by only three other women, including Coral Napangardi Gallagher, who had been an important and knowledgeable singer during her life but was very elderly when the recording was made.[13] As part of the painting up-session, Granites also included a number of other verses of women's songs associated with *jilkaja*, a ritual women sing to escort a boy who is travelling to a community for his initiation.[14] Following the painting up, the women danced in a long line led by Martin to three different Minamina *yawulyu* verses (see Figure 5.1).

---

13 C. Gallagher was, however, one of the main singers accompanying Judy Granites in the 2006 recording, which was made when she was one of the main senior singers in Yuendumu.

14 These *jilkaja* songs have been excluded from this chapter as they are only intended for Warlpiri women to hear. Because Granites led the singing during this event, no other senior women picked up that these *jilkaja* songs were inappropriate to include. Lynette Granites, who had not been part of the recording as she was in Alice Springs at the time, complained about this to Lorraine Granites a number of years later and asked for them to be removed from public access points.

5 Minamina *yawulyu*: Musical change from the 1970s through to the 2010s

Recording 4: Painting up at the Southern Ngaliya dance camp (Curran 2017)

Since 2010, Incite Arts and the Warlpiri Youth Development Aboriginal Corporation have collaborated with Warlpiri women to hold biannual dance camps where Warlpiri women gather to sing *yawulyu* and teach younger generations. These events are held over a long weekend at the beginning of the school holidays at different outstations near Warlpiri communities. In April 2017, a dance camp was held at Mijilyparnta (Mission Creek), attended by a large number of Warlpiri women who had recently been reviewing proofs of the songbook to be published later that year. In the book is an old photo of a particular section of Minamina *yawulyu* known as *jintiparnta* (a native truffle that grows in the sandhill country in cold weather) painted on Yarraya Napangardi, a much-loved *yawulyu* singer and *kirda* from Minamina and relative for many people in attendance. Peggy Nampijinpa Brown decided she would paint Cecily Napanangka Granites, Yarraya's brother's daughter (*pimirdi*), and therefore also *kirda* for Minamina, with the same designs (for further details of this event, see Curran 2020c). Peggy, as a senior *kurdungurlu*, painted Cecily while a group of women sang five Minamina *yawulyu* verses; however, they did not dance Minamina *yawulyu* later that evening as originally planned because Cecily returned back to Yuendumu for medical reasons.

Recording 5: Painting up with Minamina yawulyu for the book launch at the Northern Territory Writers Festival (Deacon and Turpin 2017)

In 2017, a large group of Warlpiri women travelled to Alice Springs to launch the *Yurntumu-Wardingki Juju-Ngaliya-Kurlangu Yawulyu* (Warlpiri Women from Yuendumu and Curran 2017) book at the Northern Territory Writers Festival. On 21 May 2017, at a chilly morning hour, the group gathered at the Olive Pink Botanic Gardens and began to paint up. As the group planned to dance the *Yarlpurru-rlangu* ("Two Age-Brothers") *yawulyu* in the indoor section of the Olive Pink Cafe, which involves the meeting of Minamina and Mount Theo ancestors, a number of women were painted up with Minamina *yawulyu* in an outdoor space. Three verses of the Minamina *yawulyu* were sung as two sisters, Elsie Napanangka Granites and Alice Napanangka Granites, were painted with Minamina designs. At the same time, a larger group of women were simultaneously painting up with Ngapa *yawulyu* designs, so it was difficult to identify the number of Minamina *yawulyu* items performed for the painting up. Another dancer, Audrey Napanangka Williams, was painted with Mount Theo designs and danced as the Mount Theo ancestor. A growing

Figure 5.2. Two sisters, Alice Napanangka Granites and Elsie Napanangka Granites, dance as two ancestors from Minamina, who meet up with their age-brother from Mount Theo, danced by Audrey Napanangka Williams. Photo still taken from video footage by Ben Deacon.

crowd emerged to watch as the group painted up and then followed them as they danced into the room (see Figure 5.2). One Minamina *yawulyu* verse was sung while they danced, followed by an additional verse specific to the meeting up of the two different ancestors from the different Country at Minamina and Mount Theo.

Recording 6: Painting up with Minamina yawulyu for a performance at the Aboriginal Tent Embassy, Canberra (Macdougall and Duke 2018).

In 2018, when a group of 16 Warlpiri men and women travelled to Canberra, several dances of Warlpiri women's *yawulyu* and men's *purlapa* were performed at the Aboriginal Tent Embassy (for details of the *purlapa*, see Curran and Sims 2021). The Minamina group planned to dance the *Yarlpurru-rlangu yawulyu* with Barbara Napanangka Martin and Alice Napanangka Granites painted up as two Minamina ancestors and Jean Napanangka Brown as a Mount Theo ancestor (see Figure 5.3). These three women danced together while the rest of the group of women sang a *yawulyu* associated with the meeting of these

5 Minamina *yawulyu*: Musical change from the 1970s through to the 2010s

Figure 5.3. Barbara Napanangka Martin and Alice Napanangka Granites dance as the Two Age-Brothers from Minamina with Jean Napanangka Brown as the Age-Brother from Mount Theo. Photo by Georgia Curran.

two ancestral beings.[15] During the painting up of Martin and A. Granites, four verses of Minamina *yawulyu* were sung.

Made across varying contexts (public, private, women's only), the six recordings involved different women as song leaders, singers, dancers and in other participatory roles – all factors that influence the song choices and other features of the performance. Table 5.1 sets out a brief comparative summary of some of these features, including the reason for the performance, the number of singers, the overall duration of the event, the number of verses recorded and the number of song items recorded.

---

15 The *yawulyu* verse sung while the women were dancing is classified as being *Yarlpurru-rlangu* "Two Age-Brothers", referring to the *jukurrpa* story about the two ancestors who were initiated in the same ceremony and meet together to re-establish the special bond that they have for life.

Table 5.1. Comparison of features of the six recorded performance instances.

Performance event and date	Reason for performance	Number of participants (singers in brackets)	Overall duration	Number of verses	Number of items recorded (av. = average)
Recording 1 (1972) Women's ceremonial event (1972)	Women's painting up prior to a larger ceremony (women-only event)	42 (of whom unknown number of singers)	10 hrs approx. over 3 days (3 hrs recorded); painting up and some dancing	14	approx. 80 items per hour (8–25 items / verse)
Recording 2 (2006) Elicited recording (2006)	Documentation purposes (women-only event for public dissemination)	8 (7)	35 mins	15	42 items (2.8 items / verse)
Recording 3 (2016) DVD painting up and dancing (2016)	Documentation: video footage to be included with *yawulyu* book (women-only event for later public dissemination)	23 (4)	30 mins painting up plus 12 mins dancing	4 + 3 (not including *jilkaja* songs)	17 items painting up (av. 4 items / verse) 7 items for dancing (av. 2.2 items / verse)
Recording 4 (2017) Southern Ngaliya dance camp (2017)	Teaching and learning: women's camp focused on teaching young girls (women-only event)	approx. 50, including many younger women and children (4)	19 mins painting up	5	24 items (av. 4.6 items / verse)
Recording 5 (2017) Northern Territory Writers Festival performance (2017)	Public performance: to launch the *yawulyu* book	18 (6)	20 mins painting up (mixed *yawulyu*) plus 8 mins dancing	3 + 1	6 audible items (av. 1.5 items / verse)
Recording 6 (2018) Aboriginal Tent Embassy performance (2018)	Public performance: showcasing Warlpiri songs to Canberra audience	12 (3)	20 mins painting up and 10 mins dancing	4	17 items (av. 4.25 items / verse)

5 Minamina *yawulyu*: Musical change from the 1970s through to the 2010s

Some features in Table 5.1 may be interpreted as evidence of shifts in performance practice over time, while other variations may seem to be due instead to shifting performance contexts.

Reasons for performance: There is a trend in more recent times for performances of Minamina *yawulyu* to be more public. While many performance instances were held in women-only contexts, in recent years, younger Warlpiri women have often been the target audience for teaching and learning activities (e.g., at dance camps), as well as for documentary purposes (e.g., 2006 elicitation, 2016 DVD production). However, in the latter case, the performances were also designed to include non-Warlpiri female and male public audiences. Two events, the 2017 Northern Territory Writers Festival book launch and the 2018 Tent Embassy performance in Canberra, were explicitly designed for non-Warlpiri audiences that included both men and women.

Number of participants: In 1972, a large number of women participated, although we do not know exactly how many of these were singers. R. Peterson's fieldnotes (1972) list 42 performers, including a large group of *kirda* from Minamina, each of whom had to be painted up as the verses were sung. By contrast, in the 2016–2018 performances, only 2–3 *kirda* were painted up, and there were only 4–5 singers, even in larger-scale events, like the Southern Ngaliya dance camp. This represents a significant reduction in the number of singers compared to the unknown but certainly large group of singers audible in the 1972 recording, and even the 12 singers who participated in the 2006 documentation session.

Overall duration of performance: Together, the above factors resulted in a much shorter overall duration of more recent performances – under an hour, compared to more than 10 hours in 1972. The more public nature of some recent performances may also have had an effect on overall duration because performers often faced the pressures of external timeframes.[16]

Number of verses and their repetitions: Flowing from the above observations, recent performances held in 2016–2018 demonstrate a dramatic reduction in the numbers of verses sung compared to the older recordings of 1972 and 2006, as well as fewer repeated items of each verse. In the 1972 recording, the same verse would be repeated over and over again (between 8 and 25 times) as each *kirda* was painted up with the relevant body design (see Appendix 5.2 for examples). The constrained time frames and the small number of *kirda* for the more recent performances appear to have resulted in less time being devoted to

---

16 At the Northern Territory Writers Festival performance in 2017, the event organisers had an allotted time for the Warlpiri women's presentation and a livestream organised, creating pressures to hurry along the painting up and dancing.

painting up (average four items per verse) due to not only the smaller number of *kirda* but also less elaborate or less extensive body designs (see further below).

As we will illustrate in this chapter, these factors have a major influence on the ways in which Minamina *yawulyu* are being performed and passed on to younger generations.

The language and overarching themes of Minamina *yawulyu*

As is the case for many songs sung by Warlpiri women, the words used in Minamina *yawulyu* require interpretation from knowledgeable singers. Ruth Napaljarri Oldfield explained of Minamina *yawulyu* that "this is hard language, not like some other *yawulyu*. Not everyone can understand these songs, only the really old women" (Ruth Napaljarri Oldfield, cited in Curran 2010, 106). As discussed elsewhere, this is not so much because the words are radically different from spoken words in Warlpiri (as is often the case for songs) but more because the specific connotations of words require bringing together complex knowledge from many domains, which is only fully known by the senior singers (Curran 2010, 114).

Singers in Yuendumu today have difficulty discerning (i.e., identifying the words being sung) and explaining the lyrics of Minamina *yawulyu*, contrasting them to other Warlpiri *yawulyu* (e.g., Watiyawarnu), which are described as "easy". In 2021, senior singer Lynette Nampijinpa Granites was able to articulate some of the words of the songs on the 1972 recording so that we could write them down but could not expand significantly on their meanings. Nevertheless, in her discussion of the 1972 songs, she was able to identify some of the focal themes, many of which are also present in songs sung in more recent recordings, although some are not.

Theme 1: Swaying movement of the vertical figures

Listening to the 1972 recording in 2021, L. Granites identified dominant visual imagery of the Minamina *yawulyu*, evident in many verses sung in 1972, illustrated here in Example 5.1.[17]

---

17 Often the repeated lines in a verse differ in their final vowel qualities, though this is not perceived as linguistically significant by singers. In the following examples, the standard form of the line-final vowel is presented.

5 Minamina *yawulyu*: Musical change from the 1970s through to the 2010s

Example 5.1

Line A	Line B
♫♩♫♩♩	:‖: ♫♩♩♫♩♩
Janyinki wayurangka	**Warlurrumpu wayurangka**
"Janyinki swaying"	"Warlurrumpu swaying"

L. Granites was able to articulate the word *wayurrangka* (*wa-yurr-wang-ka*), which was tricky for others to hear because the syllables merged together in sung form and because the word does not appear in contemporary Warlpiri (e.g., Laughren et al. 2022).[18] L. Granites explained that this referred at once to the swaying of the trees and the movement of long upright figures of the travelling ancestral women. This word is sung often in various verses throughout the 1972 recording but has since gone out of use and does not appear in verses sung in more recent performances. Nevertheless, the theme of long, skinny, vertical objects with a swaying movement remains as dominant visual imagery in the verses recorded more recently. Example 5.2 from the 2006 recording was also sung in the 2017 and 2018 public performances.

Example 5.2

Line A	Line B	Line C
♫♩♪♩.	:‖: ♫♩♪♩.	:‖: ♫♩♪
Walarajarra	**Minyiranyira**	**Kanalyurrparna**
"Digging sticks"	"Smell of freshly wet earth"	"In one group"

In this verse, the word *walarajarra* was explained in 2006 by Judy Nampijinpa Granites as referring simultaneously to the digging sticks carried by the ancestral women, to the upright women's bodies as they walked and to the desert oak trees that grow in the Country around Minamina (see Figure 5.4). This imagery is also reflected in body designs painted on women's chests in the 1972 performances, which is now the main design featured in the 2016 and 2018 performances (discussed later in this chapter).

---

18 The word *wayurangka* may be an example of poetic language used only in song.

Figure 5.4. Minamina and the Country to the east are dominated by desert oak trees, symbolically representing the ancestral women as they travel and the digging sticks that they carry. Photo by Mary Laughren.

Theme 2: Ritual power or essence of the ancestral women and their Country

Another dominant theme still evident in verses from the 2016–2018 recorded performances is exemplified by the word *minyira* – literally "fat, lard, grease, marrow, butter, oil" (Laughren, 2022: 434) but metonymically referring to the women's oil-laden headbands. The oil dripping from the women's headbands as they dance symbolises their ritual power. In 2006, Judy Granites explained that *minyira* also meant the smell of the earth after rain, referring to the strong essence of the Country most prominent after rain (Young 2005).

The word *minyira* (sometimes partially reduplicated as *minyiranyira*) appears in Example 5.3 (1972) and Example 5.4 (2016), as well as elsewhere in the corpus.

Example 5.3

Line A	Line B
♪♩♩♪♩	:‖: ♪♩♩♪♩
Minyiranyira	**Kanalyurrparna**
"Headdress rubbed with fat"	"In one group"

Example 5.4

Line A

Minyira yinjilpirrpirrkari

"Headdress falling down in drops"

Line B

Kanalyurrkanalyurrpa

"In one group"

Theme 3: Place names

Across recent performances, verses centred on central place names for the Minamina *jukurrpa* are emphasised. This strong trend emerges in the telling of *jukurrpa* stories (evident in the story that began this chapter), as well as in songs for both Warlpiri men and Warlpiri women. The prominence of place names emphasises Country as perhaps the most essential aspect of *jukurrpa* and constitutes a core focus for many senior Warlpiri people in ceremonial performance. For example, the places Minamina and Janyinki are focal sites in the travels of the ancestral women, and these placenames feature prominently in song verses from across the five-decade period.[19]

Decline in songs with women-only subject matter and connotations

In the 1972 recording, songs on numerous other themes recur – themes that were drawn out by Egan and Rice, as well as by Granites.[20] Many of these songs contain subject matter restricted to women, including content focused on female sexual desire and menstruation. Many of these verses cannot be published because knowledge of their content is restricted to a senior female audience, but there are some examples from the 1972 performance that can be discussed here, including Example 5.5.

---

19 Janyinki is nowadays sung about in a "light" version of the verse due to the centrality of this site for the travels of the ancestral women; however, it has strong women-only knowledge that is not shared publicly.

20 Jeannie Nungarrayi Egan and Thomas Jangala Rice, pers. comm. 2006 and Lynette Nampijinpa Granites, pers. comm. 2017.

Example. 5.5

Line A Line B

♫♫ ♫♫ ♩.   :‖: ♫♩ ♩. ♫♩ ♩.

Wararrji kijirninya **Kanalyurrpa kijirninya**

"Putting on the snake vines" "Putting on the group"

For knowledgeable senior women, this verse alludes to the sexy way a woman walks when she has a baby in a coolamon tied around her shoulders and waist with the snake vine.[21] This song can be used in private contexts as a *yilpinji* to attract a particular desired man, but a "light" interpretation of the verse (as in Example 5.5) allows it to be sung in contexts involving younger children, with emphasis placed on the movement of the group of ancestral women, rather than its sexualised connotations. Nevertheless, this song does not occur in the more recent performances (all of which are either public performances or events involving younger generations) and has likely been lost from the repertory known by current senior Warlpiri singers. Despite the women hearing this song recently on the older recordings, it has not been reincorporated into recent more open performance contexts.

Sexual content was similarly avoided at the Southern Ngaliya women's bush camp in 2017, when Cecily Napanangka Granites was painted with the *jintiparnta* "native truffle" design. In this instance, the senior singers had requested a copy of the proofs of the forthcoming book from which to copy the design because they had not painted it for many years (Warlpiri Women from Yuendumu and Curran 2017). It was felt to be important to paint this design on Cecily as a way of carrying forward her specific relationship to her aunt (father's sister), who featured in the photo in the book (for further details, see Curran 2020c). The senior singers noted that they had forgotten the particular *yawulyu* verses associated with *jintiparnta*. While hinting at the sexual connotations of this particular design, they sang open songs as they painted Cecily. Despite this event being a private women's bush camp, there were many younger children and visitors for whom sexualised content was not appropriate.

---

21 The snake vine has many other uses, which the song may also evoke in other contexts.

Kurdaitcha birds: Reinforcing cultural values

A prominent theme throughout many *yawulyu* songlines is the sporadic appearance of ancestral figures in the form of birds who lustfully pursue groups of travelling women. These "kurdaitcha birds", as senior Warlpiri women refer to them, are always of the wrong skin group for marriage to those of the group of women, and any resulting sexual liaisons lead to negative outcomes for the women, ranging from humiliation to death.

As discussed elsewhere, the presence of these birds in songs represents a fear of loss of particularly valued aspects of Warlpiri identity, notably "of connections to country, of traditional social organisation, of control over women's sexuality, and of the gendered forms of sociality which have until recently typified Warlpiri life" (Curran 2020b, 128). Kurdaitcha birds are common figures in the verses from the 1972 and 2006 recordings; their significance is drawn out in deeper ways in the accompanying stories. Examples 5.6 and 5.7 are verses from the 2006 recording about the "Spotted Nightjar" bird – named in the songs as either *yinkardakurdaku* (Example 5.6) or *kunkurdakurdaku* (Example 5.7) – who pursues the group of women throughout their eastwards journey, flitting around them in the nearby bush and calling out repeatedly in the manner typical of this bird species (which is rarely seen but often heard).

Example 5.6

Line A   Line B

Yinkardakurdakurlu   **Yayirlinpirr kujurnu**

"Spotted nightjar"   "Throwing out their cries"

Example 5.7

Line A   Line B

Kunkurdakurdaku   **wakarrpungka**

"Spotted nightjar"   "Encircling"

Kurdaitcha birds like this do not feature as much in the more recent recordings from 2016 to 2018. This may indicate a possible classification of this type of cultural knowledge as inappropriate for broader public performances (e.g., women-only category). During the 2016–2018 period, the only occasions on which verses about the kurdaitcha bird were sung were women-only events: the DVD production and the Southern Ngaliya dance camp, despite both events being videoed for archiving and broader circulation. Example 5.8, sung in 2016 and 2017, is a version of Example 5.6 but uses the alternative name for the bird, "Kunkurdakurdaku", as found in Example 5.7.

Example 5.8

Line A   Line B

♪ ♩ ♪ ♩ ♩ ♪ ♩   :||:   ♪ ♩ ♪ ♩ ♩ ♪ ♩

Kunkurdakurdakurlu   **Yayirlinpirr kujurnu**

"Spotted nightjar"   "Throwing out their cries"

While the pursuit of the travelling women from Minamina by the spotted nightjar bird is central to the *jukurrpa* story, it seems that these verses are now held to be inappropriate for the contemporary public performance settings in which Warlpiri women today perform *yawulyu*. In the final DVD production intended to be viewed by the general public, in the story told by Martin guided by Lorraine Nungarrayi Granites (transcribed earlier in this chapter), she chose not to mention this aspect of the story. Although the verse in Example 5.8 was sung, its surrounding story remained unexplained in this context. Instead, the singers chose to emphasise the named places through which the ancestral women travel.

Changes in musical settings across time

Only one verse, presented below in Examples 5.9A and 5.9B, occurs in all three periods covered by our sample. These Examples were recorded in 1972, 2006 and three of the four performances in 2017–2018.[22] Usually performed as the first verse in the recording, it serves as an anchor to the focal site of Minamina, from where the group of ancestral travelling women begin their journey. By comparing the ways in which this verse has been performed across the performances, we uncover some shifts in the ways in which the rhythmic text of the verse is performed across the characteristic Minamina melody.

22   The verse was not performed for the 2016 DVD performance (Recording 3 in Table 5.1).

Contemporary shifts in setting of text-rhythm to melody: Comparing a verse performed across the five-decade period

It is normal in Warlpiri songs, as in other Central Australian songs, that each verse tends to have a fixed rhythmic setting (forming a unit often referred to as "text rhythm"). Example 5.9A shows the usual text-rhythm of the verse when performed for painting, as occurs in many instances across all five performances. In one performance at the 2017 Northern Territory Writers Festival, the verse was also performed for dancing, resulting in a change to the text-rhythm given in Example 5.9B.

Example 5.9A

Line A   Line B

♪♪♪ ♩ ♪♪♪ ♪♪♪ ♩   :||:   ♪♪♪ ♪♪♪ ♪♪♪ ♩

Minamina pirlarlany kijirninya   **Japingka pirlarlany kijirninya**

Example 5.9B

Line A   Line B

♪♪♪ ♩. ♪♪♪ ♪♪♪ ♩.   :||:   ♪♪♪ ♪♪♪ ♪♪♪ ♩.

Minamina pirlarlany kijirninya   **Japingka pirlarlany kijirninya**

While the text-rhythm of Example 5.9A can be classified as additive, with no regular pulse,[23] the text-rhythm of Example 5.9B demonstrates a regular pulse, notated here as a dotted crotchet, and the dancers' movements are synchronised by clapsticks beaten by the lead singer. Comparing the two settings, we can see that this regularity in the text-rhythm is achieved simply by reducing the duration of the long note to a dotted crotchet rather than a minim. We cannot be certain whether the use of this verse to accompany dancing is a recent innovation or was simply not previously recorded.

Another common feature of the Central Australian musical style is flexibility in text-melody layout – that is, the placement of the text-rhythm cycle onto the melodic contour characteristic of each song set (Barwick 1989; Ellis 1985; Pritam 1980; Turpin 2007b). The melodic contour typical of Minamina and

---

23   While clear groupings of the short notes into triplets can be observed, the long notes are consistently four quavers in length.

used across all five performances uses five pitches, approximating to degrees 8, 7, 4, 3, 2 and 1 of a gapped major scale, presented in the order 78/4321/4321 (where slashes represent breaths separating distinct melodic sections). These pitches are relative rather than fixed – in the 1972 and 2006 performances, the tonic (final) is F, but in the three recent performances, the tonic is variously C, B flat and E flat.

In 1972, the oldest Minamina performance analysed, we can observe a great variety of text-melody layouts across its 17 consecutive items (see Appendix 5.1). We have already noted that in the 1972 performance, a far greater number of items was performed per verse than in recent performances, where only 2–4 consecutive items were typical.

One notable feature of text-melody layout occurs only in the 1972 performance. Text line reversal occurs where the text line pairs AA and BB are presented reversed on the melody in consecutive items. This occurs nine times in the 17 items of the 1972 performance but not at all in the later performances. This reversal of the melodic placement of the text draws attention to the flexibility of the musical system and may be an important educational tool for novice learners (Barwick 1990).[24] By contrast, the later performances since 2006 all begin with the AA text line pair.

Another important variable is the overall duration of the song item. While the 1972 performance presents a minimum of two and a maximum of six melodic sections, with most being three or more, both items in the 2006 performance present four melodic sections (not counting the initial humming performed by the song leader Judy Nampijinpa Granites). By contrast, in the 2017–2018 performances the maximum number is three, with two or even one melodic section occurring on occasion. The duration of each section is relatively shorter also, with many sections presenting only two lines rather than the three or four lines commonly found in melodic sections in the 1972 and 2006 performances.

In summary, the constrained time frames of later performances have contributed to an apparent lessening in the complexity of the musical system. If we consider that teaching and learning of songs by Warlpiri women are usually inductive rather than explicit, the reduction in the number of presentations of verses, together with the reduction in the duration of melodic sections and song

---

24 Other clues to the flexibility of the system may be gained when the text line pair or a text line is split across two melodic sections (e.g., 1972, items xiv and xv), or when a text line is split across two sections, usually only possible when there is a mid-line long note (e.g., Minamina / *pilarlany kijirninya*, found in Deacon and Turpin 2017, items ii and iv).

5 Minamina *yawulyu*: Musical change from the 1970s through to the 2010s

items, makes it more difficult for the novice learner to pick up that the melodic system is actually very flexible. This perhaps encourages a more rote learning approach, where the alignment of textual and melodic units suggests a more fixed placement of the text on the melody. However, as Marett has suggested, such simplification of the musical system may facilitate greater participation by learners (2007). The most important features of this Minamina verse, its text-rhythm setting and the core melodic contour characteristic of the song set, are preserved more or less intact.

Number and variation of body painting designs

Five of the six song events analysed in this chapter are accompanied by the painting of body designs. It is evident that painting up is a far lengthier component and is valued and given more attention by Warlpiri women despite dancing often receiving more public attention. In the instances where dancing did occur, it was short in duration.[25] Due to its elicited nature, no painting up was done as part of the 2006 performance, but all others feature the painting of red, black, white and sometimes yellow ochre designs. Over the three days in 1972 when Peterson recorded the Minamina *yawulyu* ceremonies, she copied 13 different designs painted on women's breasts, décolletage and upper arms. Each of these designs was painted on numerous women, and their relationships to each other were noted by Peterson too (see Appendix 5.2). Peterson also documented designs drawn on stones, one design painted on a woman's belly (around her belly button), one design painted on a woman's upper knees, one design painted on a *kuturu* "ceremonial pole" inserted into the centralised ceremonial ground, and one design painted on a *yukurrukurru* "dancing board" held by women during the brief stints of dancing that Peterson noted occurring sporadically during the painting up. Peterson noted that the belly design was "covered over quite quickly". Nowadays, these belly designs are rarely painted and are often only associated with specific *nyurnukurlangu* "healing songs" performed in non-public contexts. By contrast, the designs painted on chests are paraded around with pride and often not washed off for several weeks. A woman who is being painted up is said to be imbued with ancestral power as the painted designs and oil are applied to her body.

Across the recordings made during the 2016–2018 period, it is evident that the variety of designs had greatly reduced, with only three designs painted –

---

25 Often, for public performances, Warlpiri women paint up in a private space before entering a staged area to dance. The audiences that attend these performances see only the dancing component of *yawulyu*.

Figure 5.5. Barbara Napanangka Martin and Joyce Napangardi Brown painted up with Minamina designs in 2016. Photo by Georgia Curran, 2016.

one being copied directly from a photograph from the 1980s and the other two being variations on a single design. The main Minamina design painted on women's chests during 2016–2018 has long vertical lines down each breast and arm, which are said to also represent the "digging sticks' that are a key theme in both past and contemporary Minamina *yawulyu* performances (see Appendix 5.3).

In three of the four performances in recordings 2016, 2017 and 2018, a variation on a single design was painted on all women present with connections to Minamina as *kirda*. In 2016, all Napangardi/Napanangka women were painted with the same design for Minamina – a series of long vertical lines representing the digging sticks (see Figure 5.5). In the public performances in 2017 and 2018, a variant of this design was painted that did not incorporate the circular designs on the shoulders and lower arms.

Despite the overt loss of variation of design in the more recent performances, the strict rules apparent around who paints whom have been maintained across the five-decade period. As a rule, only *kirda* are painted by their *kurdungurlu*, senior women with the authority and knowledge to do so. In the more recent recordings, one obvious exception is Lorraine Nungarrayi Granites' role in painting up. Despite not being in the right kin category for *kurdungurlu*, her

5 Minamina *yawulyu*: Musical change from the 1970s through to the 2010s

late husband was *kirda* for Minamina, as was the case for other Nampijinpas in the 1970s who held key *kurdungurlu* roles. Granites is one of the main senior singers who lead most *yawulyu* singing and performance in Yuendumu today and has been described as "*kurdungurlu* for everyone" due to her broad-ranging ritual knowledge.

Conclusion

It is evident that, as there are fewer senior singers and differing performance contexts in the more recent period of 2016–2018, there is a reduction or simplification (or both) of many aspects of what were previously more complex systems of knowledge surrounding performances of Minamina *yawulyu*. The performances in our sample reveal an overall reduction in the number of verses, the number of repetitions of each verse and the number of associated body designs painted on the women's bodies as part of the performances. This reduction in the repertory makes sense given the dramatically reduced number of knowledgeable singers today compared to the 1970s when most women over 30 living in Yuendumu were active participants in regular *yawulyu* events.[26]

Also observable from these comparisons is a reduction in variability in the setting of verses to melody, indicating various kinds of simplification of song form. In the more recent performance instances, a possibly more westernised and simplified approach is used where the same text line pair always begins each song item. The flexibility of text and melody placement is one aspect of *yawulyu* singing that is difficult to learn in the contemporary context; knowledge of how to do so relies on a lifetime of participation in different kinds of *yawulyu* events. Nevertheless, today's singers take care to perform the correct verses to the correct melodic contour, thus maintaining the core facets of Minamina musical identity.

While several of the more public themes have been carried forth into the recent performances, others that are more restricted to women-only contexts led by groups of knowledgeable senior singers have been dropped from the repertories sung in more recent times. This is likely because, in past decades, *yawulyu* ceremonies were held in more private women's contexts where there was also space to discuss surrounding stories and explain the connotations of the songs. In more recent performances, many of which are performances to the broader public, key themes are carried forward but only in their "open" forms, and there

---

26 Attrition of song knowledge has been further exacerbated by demographic shifts of recent decades that have seen significant proportional increases in Yuendumu's youth population.

is often little chance to articulate the deeper – and less public – meanings of these songs. When Warlpiri women nowadays hold *yawulyu* in women-only contexts, there is also often an emphasis on teaching younger dancers and children through demonstration and showcasing songs and dances to visitors. Many themes are deemed inappropriate in such contexts, resulting in their loss from the repertories known by the contemporary group of singers.

In a similar way, the reduction in the number of designs may be due to the increase in public performances and youth-focused events where there is a tendency to paint up large groups of young women and children with generic designs, with significant time pressure placed on senior women to ensure that these events are successful. Certainly, the much longer periods devoted to painting up in the 1972 performance, reflected in the high number of items performed for each verse, facilitated more careful and more detailed selection and application of designs.

The overall tendency to reduce variability and complexity observed in multiple dimensions across this chapter has resulted in a notable reduction in the variety of Minamina *yawulyu* verses known and performed by senior Warlpiri singers. We suggest that such changes allow the song leaders to maintain performances and ensure that younger generations are inheriting the core and deemed essential parts of their cultural identity. Allan Marett (2007) described a similar but perhaps more conscious decision by senior performers of the Walakandha *wangga* from Wadeye (Port Keats), suggesting that previously complex musical and dance practices were strategically simplified "in order to strengthen the articulation of a group identity in ceremonial performance" (2007, 63). For Warlpiri women, we suggest that musical simplification may be one way in which senior song leaders (in some cases reduced to a single person) can manage the pressures they face to hold together the singing while also instructing younger dancers and guiding other aspects of ceremonial performance. Where once there would have been large groups of women, in more recent performance instances, there are often only a few singers, and sometimes a single leader who knows the songs, guides the dancing and other ritualised movement, and instructs on how to paint the designs. The simplifications we have pointed out may be one way in which song leaders are making their immense role doable, with various performance aspects adapted on the fly when leaders feel overwhelmed by their many responsibilities.

In a contemporary context where Warlpiri women are concerned about the intergenerational transfer of knowledge and practices surrounding *yawulyu*, Minamina is by no means unusual in making these adaptations. The efforts of senior women to ensure that contexts still exist for younger generations to learn about and understand *yawulyu* are testament to the important cultural value placed on this song genre. Although some performative aspects may change in response to changing circumstances, it is evident that core knowledges of places in Warlpiri Country and individual women's family connections are prioritised in the varying ways Minamina *yawulyu* are being carried forward. The choice to focus on these aspects of Warlpiri place-centred connections ensures that younger women can carry forth a strong cultural identity. The simplification or reduction of some aspects of the performance is a practical means for Warlpiri women today to ensure that they can maintain Minamina *yawulyu* and a strong female cultural identity for younger generations of Warlpiri women, enabling them to know about and feel connection to their Country and its associated kinship networks and ceremonial practices.

References

Barwick, Linda. 1989. "Creative (Ir)regularities: The Intermeshing of Text and Melody in Performance of Central Australian Song". *Australian Aboriginal Studies* 1: 12–28.

Barwick, Linda. 1990. "Central Australian Women's Ritual Music: Knowing through Analysis versus Knowing through Performance". *Yearbook for Traditional Music* 22: 60–79.

Barwick, Linda and Myfany Turpin. 2016. "Central Australian Women's Traditional Songs: Keeping *Yawulyu/Awelye* Strong". In *Sustainable Futures for Music Cultures*, edited by Huib Schippers and Catherine Grant, 111–144. New York: Oxford University Press.

Barwick, Linda, Mary Laughren and Myfany Turpin. 2013. "Sustaining Women's *Yawulyu/Awelye*: Some practitioners' and Learners' Perspectives". *Musicology Australia* 35(2): 191–220.

Bell, Diane. 1983. *Daughters of the Dreaming*. Minneapolis: University of Minnesota Press.

Curran, Georgia. 2010. "Linguistic Imagery in Warlpiri Songs: Some Examples of Metaphors, Metonymy and Image-Schemata in *Minamina yawulyu*". *Australian Journal of Linguistics* 30(1): 105–15.

Curran, Georgia. 2016. "Travelling Ancestral Women: Connecting Warlpiri People and Places through Songs". In *Language, Land and Song: Studies in Honour of Luise Hercus*, edited by Peter K. Austin, Harold Koch and Jane Simpson, 425–455. London: EL Publishing.

Curran, Georgia. 2018. "The Poetic Imagery of Smoke in Warlpiri Songs". *Anthropological Forum* 28(2): 183–96.

Curran, Georgia. 2020a. *Sustaining Indigenous Songs*. New York: Berghahn Books.

Curran, Georgia. 2020b. "Bird/Monsters and Contemporary Social Fears in the Central Desert of Australia". In *Monster Anthropology: Ethnographic Explorations of Transforming Social Worlds through Monsters*, edited by Yasmine Musharbash and Geir Henning Presterudstuen, 127–142. London: Bloomsbury.

Curran, Georgia. 2020c. "Incorporating Archival Cultural Heritage Materials into Contemporary Warlpiri Women's *Yawulyu* Spaces". In *Archival Returns: Central Australia and Beyond*, edited by Linda Barwick, Jennifer Green and Petronella Vaarzon-Morel, 91–110. Sydney: Sydney University Press.

Curran, Georgia and Françoise Dussart. 2023. "'We Don't Show our Women's Breasts for Nothing': Shifting Purposes for Warlpiri Women's Public Rituals—*Yawulyu*—Central Australia 1980s–2020s". *Studies in Religion/Sciences Religieuses*. https://doi.org/10.1177/00084298231154430

Curran, Georgia and Otto Jungarrayi Sims. 2021. "Performing *Purlapa*: Projecting Warlpiri Identity in a Globalised World". *The Asia Pacific Journal of Anthropology* 22(2–3): 203–19.

Curran, Georgia, Barbara Napanangka Martin and Margaret Carew. 2019. "Representations of Indigenous Cultural Property in Collaborative Publishing Projects: The Warlpiri Women's Yawulyu Songbooks". *Journal of Intercultural Studies* 40(1): 68–84.

Dussart, Françoise. 2000. *The Politics of Ritual in an Aboriginal Settlement: Kinship, Gender and the Currency of Knowledge*. Washington: Smithsonian Institution Press.

Ellis, Catherine. 1985. *Aboriginal Music, Education for Living*. St. Lucia: University of Queensland Press.

Laughren, Mary, Kenneth Hale, Jeannie Egan Nungarrayi, Marlurrku Paddy Patrick Jangala, Robert Hoogenraad, David Nash and Jane Simpson. 2022. *Warlpiri Encyclopaedic Dictionary*. Canberra: Aboriginal Studies Press.

Marett, Allan. 2007. "Simplifying Musical Practice in Order to Enhance Local Identity: The Case of Rhythmic Modes in the Walakandha *Wangga* (Wadeye, Northern Territory)". *Australian Aboriginal Studies* 2: 63–76.

Moyle, Richard. 1997. *Balgo: The Musical Life of a Desert Community*. Nedlands: Callaway International Resource Centre for Music Education.

Peterson, Rosalind. 1972. Fieldnotes from Yuendumu [unpublished].

Pritam, Prabhu. 1980. "Aspects of Musical Structure in Australian Aboriginal Songs of the South-West of the Western Desert". *Studies in Music* 14: 9–44.

Turpin, Myfany. 2007. "Artfully Hidden: Text and Rhythm in a Central Australian Aboriginal Song Series". *Musicology Australia* 29(1): 93–108.

Turpin, Myfany and Mary Laughren. 2013. "Edge Effects in Warlpiri *Yawulyu* Songs: Resyllabification, Epenthesis, Final Vowel Modification". *Australia Journal of Linguistics* 33(4): 399–425.

Warlpiri Women from Yuendumu and Georgia Curran (ed.). 2017. *Yurntumu-Wardingki Juju-Ngaliya-Kurlangu Yawulyu: Warlpiri Women's Songs from Yuendumu* [including DVD]. Batchelor: Batchelor Institute Press.

Young, Diana. 2005. "The Smell of Greenness: Cultural Synaesthesia in the Western Desert". *Etnofoor* 18(1): 61–77.

Archival references

Curran, Georgia and Jeannie Nungarrayi Egan. 2005–2008. "Warlpiri Songlines (Minamina Yawulyu)". [AIATSIS accession no. PETERSON_CURRAN_01]

Curran, Georgia. 2017. "Southern Ngaliya Dance Camp at Mijilyparnta" [unpublished field recording, video].

Deacon, Ben and Myfany Turpin. 2017. "Northern Territory Writers Festival" [unpublished field recording, video].

Macdougall, Colin and Nathan Duke. 2018. "Warlpiri Performance at the NT Tent Embassy" [unpublished field recording].

Peterson, Nicolas. 1972–1973. "Nic Peterson Collection (Y7 Women's Ceremony)" [43 audiotape reels, approx. 60 minutes each, digital access copies]. [AIATSIS accession no. PETERSON_N03]. Recorded at Yuendumu, NT.

Warlpiri women from Yuendumu (produced by G. Curran). 2017. *Yurntumu-wardingki juju-ngaliya-kurlangu yawulyu*: *Warlpiri women's songs from Yuendumu* [DVD]. Batchelor: Batchelor Institute Press.

Appendix 5.1. Melody/text layout across 26 items of MI01 (common verse across all performance instances analysed).

Line A: minamina pilarlany kijirninya
Line B: japingka pilarlany kijirninya
Abbreviations: melodic section (MS), text line reversal (TLR), text line phasing (TLP), Northern Territory Writers Festival (NTWF), Tent Embassy (TE).

Item	MS1	MS2	MS3	MS4	MS5	MS6	Comment
1972 i	BB	AA	BBA				
1972 ii	AA	BBAA	BBA(A)				TLR
1972 iii	AA	BBAA	BBA(A)				
1972 iv	AA	BBA(A)	BBA(A)				
1972 v	BBAA	BBA(A)	BBA(A)				TLR disagreements MS1
1972 vi	BB	AABB	AAB(B)				TLR
1972 vii	BB	AABB	AAB(B)				
1972 viii	AA	BBAA	BBA(A)				TLR
1972 ix	BB	AA	BBA(A)	BBA(A)			TLR
1972 x	-	BB	AA	BB	AA	BB	TLR straight on, no MS1, maybe MS5, 6, 7, 8, 9
1972 xi	[A]AA	BBA	BBA				NB: note incomplete text cycle MS2 – 3 lines/MS
1972 xii	BB	AABB	inaudible				TLR talking
1972 xiii	AA	BBA	ABB	AAB			TLR
1972 xiv	BA	ABB	AA	BB	AA	BB	straight on – TLP
1972 xv	-	AB	BAA	BB	AA	BBA	nearly straight on – TLP
1972 xvi	[A]AA	BBAA	BBA(A)				TLR
1972 xvii	AA	BBA					
2006 i	[-?]	[A]A	BBA(A)	BBAa1	a2BB		recorder on mid-item
2006 ii	[hum]	AABB	Aa1	a2BB	AABB		cued by TR
2017 NTWF iii	Aa1	a2BB	AA(B)				items i, ii, iv inaudible due to competing singing
NTWF iv	Aa1	a2BB	AA(B)				dancing
NTWF v	-	AA	BB	AA			dancing
SNDC i		AAB(B)					fragment
2018 TE i		AA	BB	AA			
2018 TE ii		AA	BB	AA			
2018 TE iii		AA	BB				

5 Minamina *yawulyu*: Musical change from the 1970s through to the 2010s

Appendix 5.2. Designs painted in 1972 based on Rosalind Peterson's notes (orthography changed to standardised version).

Note: the yellow-coloured pencil represents white ochre used during the painting up

Date/Design #	Design	Who painted who (relationship)
24/6/1972 Design 1		Maggie Napangardi painted by Dolly Nampijinpa (*mantirri* "sister-in-law")
24/6/1972 Design 2		Judy Napangardi painted by Jeanie Napurrurla (*yurntalpa* "brother's daughter" > *ngati* "mother")
24/6/1972 Design 3		Millie Napangardi painted by Helen Napanangka (*jukana* "cross-cousin" for each other)

Date/Design #	Design	Who painted who (relationship)
24/6/1972 Design 4		Polly Napangardi painted by Dolly Nampijinpa (*yabala*?)
24/6/1972 Design 5		Mary Napangardi painted by Jeanie Napurrurla (*yurntalpa* "brother's daughter" > *ngati* "mother")
24/6/1972 Design 6		Jeanie Napurrurla painted by Judy Nampijinpa

5 Minamina *yawulyu*: Musical change from the 1970s through to the 2010s

Date/Design #	Design	Who painted who (relationship)
25/6/1972 Design 7		*Details not provided in Peterson's notebooks*
25/6/1972 Design 8		*Details not provided in Peterson's notebooks*
25/6/1972 Design 9		*Details not provided in Peterson's notebooks*
26/6/1972 Design 10		*Details not provided in Peterson's notebooks*

Date/Design #	Design	Who painted who (relationship)
26/6/1972 Design 11		*Details not provided in Peterson's notebooks*
26/6/1972 Design 12		*Details not provided in Peterson's notebooks*
26/6/1972 Design 13		*Details not provided in Peterson's notebooks*

5 Minamina *yawulyu*: Musical change from the 1970s through to the 2010s

Appendix 5.3. Designs painted in performances (2016–2018).

Date/Event	Design	Key features	Who painted who?
18/7/2016	Design 1	Vertical lines down breasts and arms represent digging sticks	Joyce Napangardi Brown and Barbara Napanangka Martin painted by Lorraine Nungarrayi Granites; Cecily Napanangka Granites painted by Peggy Nampijinpa Brown
March 2017/ Southern Ngaliya dance camp	Design 2	Circular designs across chest represent the truffles	Cecily Napanangka Granites painted by Peggy Nampijinpa Brown with guidance from Lucky Nampijinpa Langton
May 2017/ Northern Territory Writers Festival	Design 3 (variation of #1)	Vertical lines down breasts and arms represent digging sticks	Alice Napanangka Granites and Elsie Napanangka Granites both painted by Lynette Nampijinpa Granites
2018/Tent Embassy	Design 3 (variation of #1)	Vertical lines down breasts and arms represent digging sticks	Alice Napanangka Granites and Barbara Napanangka Martin both painted by Lynette Nampijinpa Granites

Fanny Walker Napurrurla

Photo by Gertrude Stotz. Used with permission.

Fanny Walker (c. 1926–2019) was a traditional Warlpiri woman who maintained a very strong connection to her father's Country of Jipiranpa, its stories and rituals. She was born in the Pawurrinji area near a rockhole called Karlampi from which her personal name Karlampingali derived. Napurrurla lived at the Phillip Creek Native Settlement before being moved with two of her daughters to the Warrabri Aboriginal Reserve, now known as Alekarenge, established by the government in 1956. Napurrurla had a great love and knowledge of Warlpiri *yawulyu* and was an active performer until her death in 2019. In 2009, she and her sisters collaborated with their son Brian Murphy and his Ali Curung Band Nomadic to create innovative performances that combined her traditional *yawulyu* singing with western-style country rock music, including a song about Jipiranpa. In 1996–1997, Napurrurla was among a large group of Alekarenge women recorded by Linda Barwick singing two series of Ngurlu *yawulyu* songs associated with Jipiranpa and Pawurrinji. In 2010, she collaborated with

Barwick and Laughren in their documentation of the Jipiranpa song series by again singing the verses, speaking them in Warlpiri and explaining their meaning and geographic context.

Chapter 6

Expert domains of knowledge in Ngurlu *yawulyu* songs from Jipiranpa

*By Fanny Walker Napurrurla, Linda Barwick and Mary Laughren
with contributions from Sarah Holmes Napangardi,
Jessie Simpson Napangardi, Judith Robertson Napangardi
and Theresa Napurrurla Ross*

This chapter focuses on Ngurlu *yawulyu* "Edible Seed" songs from the Warlpiri homeland of Jipiranpa, as performed and explained by Fanny Walker Napurrurla (c. 1926–2019). The associated story concerns a man of the Jakamarra skin from Jipiranpa, who lusts after his mothers-in-law: two Nangala women from Kulpurlunu, whose Dreaming is Ngapa (Rain/Water). As they travel across Jipiranpa Country,[1] the two Nangala women collect and process many different types of edible seed, observed and tracked by Jakamarra. We reflect on some of the challenges for contemporary Warlpiri people in accessing and passing on to future generations the expert knowledge of Country, Dreamings and performance conventions that are integrated within the songs.

Recordings of the songs were made in 1996 and 1997, when a group of Warlpiri women living at Alekarenge, including Napurrurla, performed Ngurlu *yawulyu* "Edible Seed" songs for Linda Barwick, David Nash and Jane Simpson. The Jipiranpa songs that form the subject of this chapter were performed intermingled with a second set of Ngurlu *yawulyu* songs from the Warlpiri homeland of Pawurrinji. Years later, in 2010, Napurrurla and her daughters,

---

1   In previous publications, the place name "Jipiranpa" has also been transcribed as "Jiparanpa".

Sarah Holmes Napangardi, Jessie Simpson Napangardi and Judith Robertson Napangardi, worked alongside Laughren and Barwick to transcribe and translate the Jipiranpa verses and record additional stories and commentary. In 2018–2021, Barwick and Laughren checked the recordings and transcriptions of the 47 Jipiranpa verses with Napurrurla's daughters and Warlpiri translator Theresa Ross Napurrurla.

In the main part of the chapter, we introduce the songs and stories associated with them, as explained by Fanny Walker Napurrurla, reflecting on some of the difficulties inherent in working with the multiple domains of expert knowledge inherent in the ancestral story and the songs. These include knowledge of Jipiranpa Country and its various ancestral tracks and stories, knowledge about seed-processing practices, knowledge of musical conventions and knowledge of the "hard language" of song. Appendix 6.1 contains text transcriptions, linguistic glosses, rhythmic transcriptions and commentary for each of the 47 Jipiranpa verses.

Social history of the Jipiranpa Ngurlu songs

In 2010, Fanny Walker Napurrurla explained to Barwick and Laughren how the Ngurlu *yawulyu* songs had been brought to Alekarenge along with other Warlpiri Dreamings:

> I was a young woman (adult) when I came to Alekarenge. People had been at Philip Creek first, and there was no water, so we were moved to Kaytetye people's country at Alekarenge. The old people brought the songs and ceremonies for Miyikampi. They brought the Ngurlu Seed ceremonies for Jipiranpa and for Pawurrinji. They brought the Ngapa Rain/Water ceremony for Kulpurlunu.
>
> The Nangalas and Nampijinpas danced for Ngapa (rain/water).
>
> The Napanangkas and Napangardis danced for Miyikampi.
>
> The Nakamarras and Napurrurlas danced for Jipiranpa (my side) and for Pawurrinji.
>
> Also the Jarrajarra groups (Napaljarri-Nungarrayi) had their business and the women would dance for their own father's father's country and Dreaming.

6 Expert domains of knowledge in Ngurlu *yawulyu* songs from Jipiranpa

> It was the old people who have since passed away who taught me and the others the songs and dances and paintings. They used to paint up.[2]

Napurrurla was very strong in her identification with her Country, Jipiranpa. In 2021, Napurrurla's daughters, Jessie Simpson Napangardi and Sarah Holmes Napangardi, reminisced about Napurrurla's last visit to Jipiranpa:

> We went with our mother to Jipiranpa around … 2018 or 2019. She asked us to take her. She talked to all of us to take her one last time to see her country.

> That Jipiranpa is on the south side. Rangers from Willowra go and look after that country.

> Jipiranpa is a beautiful place. Not too rocky. Stones that sparkle in the moonlight. It was really hot when we went, so we had to make shade.

> It was a long, long road to Jipiranpa. We slept halfway on the trip, and we went to other people's country too.

> We stayed for two nights at Jipiranpa. First, we settled in and found a place to camp. The next day we went in the Toyota. Our mum was showing us that place – the rockholes. She was telling stories and singing. We were just driving around going from one rockhole to another.

> Our mum and that old man J. Bird Jangala were talking for that milarlpa "spirit people". She was saying that it was her last trip and was telling them that it was OK for her family to keep visiting that place after she was gone.

> We had feeling for that country. We could feel those milarlpa around us. If we woke up at night, we had to wake up others for company.[3]

This statement shows how visits to Country can create strong memories and instil attachment to Country, ancestors and Dreamings.

---

2   Edited summary by Mary Laughren from her interview in Warlpiri with Fanny Walker Napurrurla and Jessie Simpson Napangardi (T100718a-03.wav). This recording was made by Myfany Turpin, and fieldwork was funded by the Australian Research Council Linkage project LP0989243. See Chapter Appendix for details of these comments.
3   Written statement created with Gretel Macdonald, 15 October 2021.

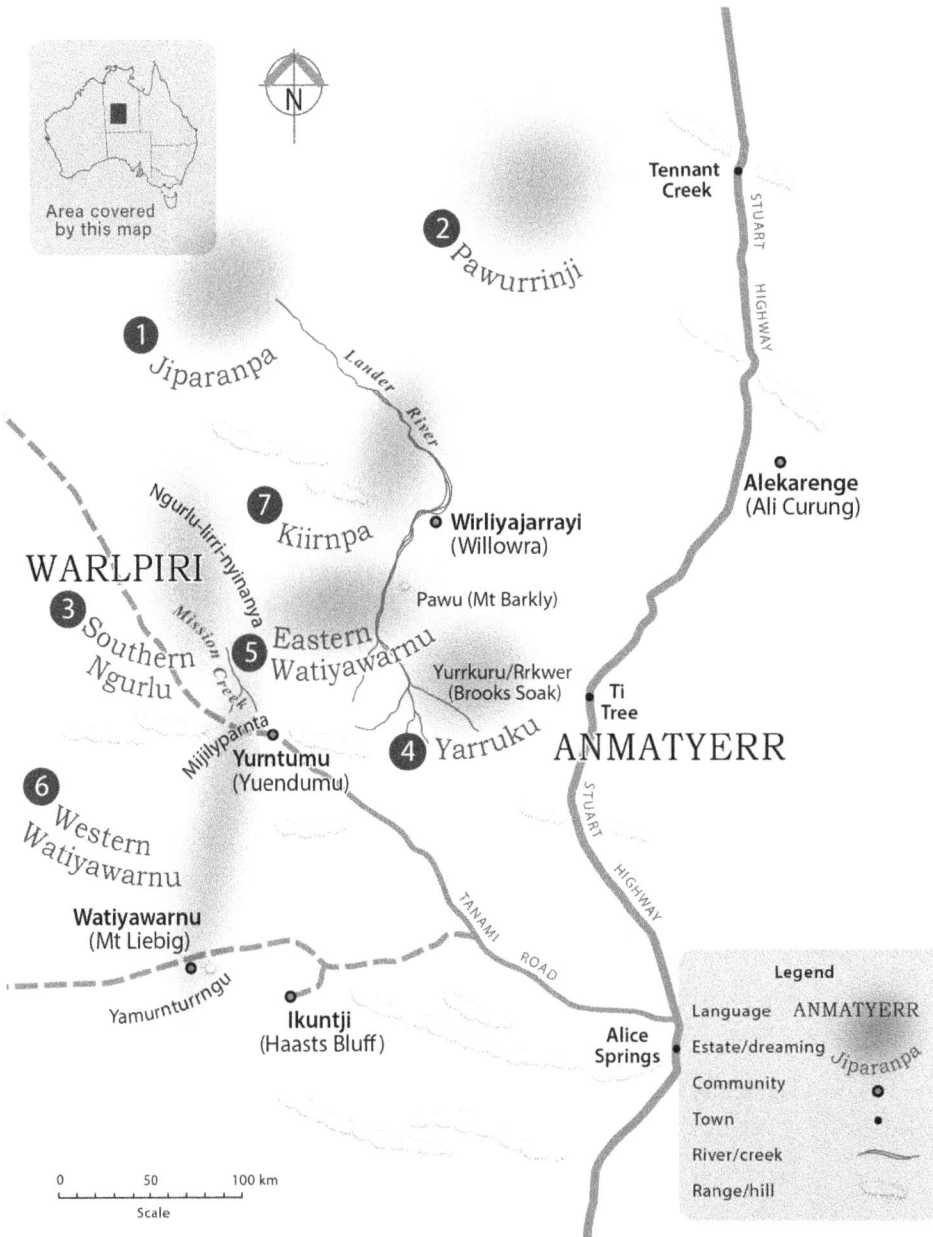

Figure 6.1. The general location of Warlpiri and Anmatyerr "Edible Seed" *yawulyu*, including (in the north) Jipiranpa and Pawurrinji (from Curran et al. 2019). Map by Brenda Thornley.

Edible Seed Dreamings

Jipiranpa and Pawurrinji are just two of a number of different Warlpiri Countries associated with Edible Seed Dreamings (Curran et al. 2019; see Figure 6.1). The various seed Dreamings have in common a stock of women's knowledge and understandings about how to gather and process edible seeds, but each Dreaming is embedded within its own characteristic ancestral places and histories and often has its own ways of structuring the songs and their music. Some Dreaming tracks cross different Countries, and this is the case for the Ngurlu Dreaming for the Countries of Jipiranpa and Pawurrinji. Several verses in the Ngurlu Jipiranpa song set also occur in other *yawulyu* song sets, including the Ngurlu *yawulyu* from Pawurrinji (Barwick 2023), the Arrwek/Yarruku *yawulyu* (Watts et al. 2009; Yeoh and Turpin 2018), and the *Jardiwanpa yawulyu* (Gallagher et al. 2014).

This chapter will focus on the Jipiranpa songs for which Fanny Walker Napurrurla was principal *kirda* (owner). Most of these songs were discussed at length with her by Barwick and Laughren when we replayed these sessions to her and her family when visiting Alekarenge in 2010 (Figure 6.2).[4] Napurrurla did not want to comment on any Pawurrinji songs included in the recordings.

Background to the 1996–1997 recordings

In 1996 and 1997, Barwick and linguist David Nash recorded four sessions of Ngurlu *yawulyu* singing at Alekarenge. These were non-ceremonial performances staged primarily for the purpose of recording. Facilitated by Nash and fellow linguist Jane Simpson, Barwick was visiting Alekarenge at the request of a senior Warlpiri songman, Engineer Jack Japaljarri, who wanted to record his knowledge of men's *yilpinji* songs (selected public men's songs that could be heard by women).[5] At Japaljarri's request, each day, Barwick also moved to the nearby *jilimi* "single women's quarters" to record women's ceremonial *yawulyu* songs from a number of different Dreamings, including Ngapa "Rain" *yawulyu* and Ngurlu "Edible Seed" *yawulyu*.

---

4   See Chapter Appendix for further details and summary of these Barwick-Turpin recordings T100718a, T100719a.

5   Japaljarri and his close friend Joe Bird Jangala led the men's singing and decided what was to be recorded and who else needed to be included in the performance group. Men's singing sessions recorded under the direction of Japaljarri and Jangala included several different Dreamings, including Yilpinji Ngapa (Rain/Water Dreaming), Yilpinji Malikijarra (Two Dogs Dreaming) and Yilpinji Ngurlu (Edible Seed Dreaming).

Figure 6.2. Fanny Walker Napurrurla discusses her *yawulyu* Jipiranpa songs with Mary Laughren and Linda Barwick, witnessed by her daughters and other family members, Alekarenge, 19 July 2010. Photo by Myfany Turpin. Used with permission.

As explained above by Fanny Walker Napurrurla in 2010, holders of the Ngurlu "Edible Seed" Dreaming at Alekarenge at this time came from two different Warlpiri estates ("Countries"): Jipiranpa, in the Tanami Desert west of Alekarenge, and Pawurrinji, north-west of Alekarenge (rough locations shown in Figure 6.1). In the 1920s and 1930s, many Warlpiri people from these and other Countries left their homelands, driven out by drought and the Coniston massacres (Kelly and Batty 2012; Nash 1984). Napurrurla and the other women who performed Ngurlu *yawulyu* for Barwick in 1996 and 1997 had previously lived and performed together on Warumungu Country at Phillip Creek Reserve, established in the 1930s, which was transferred, due to lack of water, in the 1950s to a new government settlement on Kaytetye Country that was initially given the name "Warrabri"[6] and later renamed Alekarenge (Bell 1993; Nash 1984, 2002).

---

6   The name "Warrabri" was a portmanteau based on Warramungu (Warumungu) and Warlbri (Warlpiri), the home languages of many of the people moved to the settlement, although the settlement itself was on Kaytetye Country.

6 Expert domains of knowledge in Ngurlu *yawulyu* songs from Jipiranpa

The *kirda* for Jipiranpa and Pawurrinji Countries belong to the same Napurrurla-Nakamarra semi-moiety.[7] In the four performances in our corpus, the principal *kirda* were Fanny Walker Napurrurla and Mary O'Keeffe Napurrurla (for Jipiranpa) and Ada Dickenson Napurrurla (for Pawurrinji). The *kirda* were supported in holding and performing their songs by senior *kurdungurlu* "managers", who had inherited Ngurlu Country and Dreaming affiliation through their mothers (so belonging to the Nungarrayi and Napangardi subsections) or mother's mothers (Nampijinpa, Nangala). In these performances, the principal *kurdungurlu* were Irene Driver Nungarrayi, Edna Brown Nungarrayi and Lillian Napangardi.[8] The principal performers on each occasion are listed in Table 6.1.

As is usual in Central Australian traditional singing, each singing session consisted of several short song items, separated by stretches of silence or quiet discussion. Song items are grouped into sets of 2–5 repetitions of a single verse. A given verse may recur later in a singing session or in a different session.[9] Although the verse order is said by some to follow a fixed sequence of events and sites to form a "songline", in practice, ordering is flexible and can be based on several factors, typically discussed between *kirda* and *kurdungurlu* in the breaks between song items.[10]

---

7   See Peterson and Long (1986) for explanation of Warlpiri kinship and land tenure systems.

8   Maggie Green Nampijinpa was also present for Performances 3 and 4; Suzie Newcastle Nampijinpa was also present for Performance 4.

9   For example, in Performance 1, Verse 7 recurs three times, as song items 18–20 and 44–45 on tape AT97/13A and song items 22–23 on tape AT97/13B, and also in Performance 1 as song items 11–13 on tape AT96/18A (archived with AIATSIS Collection BARWICK_L01).

10 For discussion of song ordering in various Australian song traditions, see Ellis (1970), Moyle (1979) and Treloyn (2007).

Table 6.1 Four performances of Ngurlu *yawulyu* recorded at Alekarenge by Linda Barwick and David Nash in 1996 and 1997.

Performance #	Date performed and session title	*Kirda*	*Kurdungurlu*	Recording ID
Performance 1	17 September 1996 "Yawulyu Ngurlu at Jipiranpa"	Fanny Walker Napurrurla, Mary Napurrurla, Ada Dickenson Napurrurla, Annette Nakamarra, Marjorie Limbiari Nangala-Napurrurla	Irene Driver Nungarrayi, Lillian Napangardi, Peggy Napangardi, Jessie Rice Nungarrayi, Edna [Brown] Nungarrayi	Barwick AT96/18, DT96/5, notebook 96/1:17–28
Performance 2	21 September 1996 "Yawulyu Ngurlu coming in to Pawurrinji"	Ada Dickenson Napurrurla, Fanny Napurrurla	Irene Driver Nungarrayi, Lillian Napangardi, Nancy Jones or Downes Nungarrayi, Nancy Lauder Nungarrayi, Rosie Napangardi	Barwick AT96/23–24; DT96/10–11; notebook 96/1: 87–99 Nash: V53
Performance 3	19 August 1997 "Yawulyu Ngurlu at Jipiranpa"	Mary Small O'Keeffe Napurrurla, Ada Dickenson Napurrurla, Annette Nakamarra, Ivy Napurrurla, Lorraine Napurrurla	Edna Brown Nungarrayi	Barwick AT97/13AB; DT97/8, notebook 97/2; Nash: V61
Performance 4	20 August 1997 "Yawulyu Ngurlu Pawurrinji and Jipiranpa mixup"	Mary Small O'Keeffe Napurrurla, Ada Dickenson Napurrurla, Amy Morrison Nakamarra, Lorraine Limbiari Napurrurla, Ivy Limbiari Napurrurla, Elaine Driver Nakamarra, Maudie Fishhook Nakamarra, Annette Nakamarra Jackson	Edna Brown Nungarrayi	Barwick AT97/16AB–17A, DT97/11; notebook 97/2; Nash: V64

Each Ngurlu *yawulyu* performance comprised over 100 song items (see second column of Table 6.2). The third column of Table 6.2 shows the total number of discrete verses in each session. In total, 19 of the total 47 Jipiranpa verses occurred in more than one performance. In the fourth and fifth columns of Table 6.2, we have subdivided the verses in each Ngurlu *yawulyu* performance into those belonging to Jipiranpa and those belonging to Pawurrinji. We can see that in both 1996 and 1997, the women chose to perform first a session focused on Jipiranpa verses (Performances 1 and 3) and, on a later day, a session focused on Pawurrinji verses (Performances 2 and 4). Nevertheless, each performance recorded includes verses from both Jipiranpa and Pawurrinji.

Table 6.2 Distribution of song items and verses from Jipiranpa and Pawurrinji across the corpus.

Performance	Number of song items	Total number of discrete verses	Number of Jipiranpa verses	Number of Pawurrinji verses
Performance 1 (1996)	104	37	33	4
Performance 2 (1996)	191	51	3	48
Performance 3 (1997)	110	35	30	5
Performance 4 (1997)	110	32	6	26

The verses selected and the sequence in which they are performed can vary considerably from one performance to another, but particular verses are generally chosen to highlight stories and connections relevant to the purpose of the performance and the people who are participating. For example, in these song sessions, the mixing of Jipiranpa and Pawurrinji verses reflects the affiliations of those participating in the performances, as well as their shared Dreamings, histories and migration stories.

Texts, rhythms, translations and comments for each of the 47 Jipiranpa verses identified in our recordings are included in Appendix 6.1, together with an indication of where to find the songs on the recordings. Most verses were discussed intensively by Fanny Napurrurla and Mary Laughren in 2010. For several verses, Fanny Walker Napurrurla provided additional versions as part of her commentary. Translations and comments for four of the verses (Verses 25, 31, 32, 40) are tentative because we were not able to discuss them directly with Fanny Walker Napurrurla in 2010. In 2020, Theresa Ross Napurrurla assisted with translations, and some additional commentary was also provided in 2021 by Napurrurla's daughters, Sarah Holmes Napangardi, Jessie Simpson Napangardi and Judith Robertson Napangardi.

What Ngurlu *yawulyu* Jipiranpa songs are about

The songs interweave several themes related to the Dreaming story associated with the song. In 2010, Fanny Walker Napurrurla explained to Barwick and Laughren that the story concerns an ancestral Jakamarra from Jipiranpa who is following (and lusting after) two Nangala sisters (whose Dreaming is Ngapa "Rain") as they travel across his Country. These Nangala women stand in the classificatory mother-in-law relationship to Jakamarra, the most prohibited "wrong way" social relationship in the Warlpiri marriage exchange system. Normally, any form of social contact between mothers-in-law and sons-in-law is strictly avoided. In this way, the story highlights the Warlpiri Law of marriage exchange (Curran 2020; Laughren et al. 2018).

Napurrurla explained:

> *Parajalpa-palangu Nangala-jarra, Jakamarrarlu, Yimarimarirli. Wrong-way.*

Yimarimari[11] Jakamarra followed the two Nangala women. Wrong way [they were his classificatory mothers-in-law]

> *Wiiwii-jarrinjinanu-pala. Mawu-palangu nyangu. "Nyampu nyurruwarnu waja". Tuurn-kijirninja-yanu. "Nyurruwarnu-juku, nyurruwarnu waja nyampuju. Wurnturulpa-pala yanu karlarra." Jutu-pungu-palangu.*

They [the two women] urinated as they went along. He saw where they had urinated. "This is an old one" [Jakamarra said to himself]. He kept going [following their tracks]. "Still an old one, this is an old one. The two of them have gone far west." He stopped following them.

> *"Yanirni kapala, kutulku waja!" Finishi-manu jutulpa-palangu …*
>
> *Nguru-nyanu-kurra-pala yanu, Kulpurlunu-kurra marda-pala yanu.*

"They are coming this way, getting closer now!" He finished going after them …

They [the two Nangalas] went back to their own place. Maybe they went to Kulpurlunu [principal site for Ngapa (Rain/Water) Dreaming].[12]

---

11 The personal name "Yimarimari" is discussed further below.
12 Discussion with Mary Laughren and Linda Barwick, recorded by Myfany Turpin in July 2010. Translation by Mary Laughren.

Expert knowledge of edible seeds

As they travel, the two Nangala women gather seeds and sit down in various places to make food from them. Specific seed-processing actions referenced in the songs include gathering seeds, threshing them, winnowing to remove chaff and husks, yandying to separate seeds from other material, and grinding and preparing seedcakes (Curran et al. 2019).[13] For example, Verse 2 refers to specific winnowing actions performed by the ancestral Nangala women (using a coolamon, sitting on their heels to winnow by tossing the seeds up in the air for the wind to blow away the chaff; Example 6.1).

Example 6.1

Wajiparlu-kula yarrarra mardarni :||: **Murdupurrjurlurna yarrarra mardarni**

"With a coolamon winnowing"   "Kneeling I winnow"

(Verse 2, Appendix 6.1)[14]

For those who know Jipiranpa Country well, the specific plants and animals mentioned in the songs (e.g., Verses 23 and 8) may provide indirect clues to the specific tracts of Jipiranpa Country where the named biota typically occur (Example 6.2).

Example 6.2

Kirlkirlajalu maninjintarra :||: **Warlarlajalu maninjintarra**

"Go and gather the kirlkirlaja seeds"   "Go out and get [the seeds]"

(Verse 23, Appendix 6.1)

Expert knowledge of ancestral ceremonies and stories

The Jakamarra who is following the two Nangalas is referred to by various special names that evoke specific aspects of the ancestral story. The Jakamarra's names include Yimarimari (e.g., Verse 11, Example 6.3) and Kalajirti (e.g., Verse 12, Example 6.4).

---

13 Note that many of these actions are repetitive and rhythmic in nature, as are songs and their associated dances that enact these ancestral actions.
14 For all examples, see Appendix 6.1 for breakdown of words and possible translations.

Example 6.3

Yimarimarirla yimarimarirla	:‖:	**Mujurdujurdu mujurdujurdu**
"Gecko, gecko"		"Short and stumpy one"

(Verse 11, Appendix 6.1)

The Warlpiri word *yimarimari* (alternate pronunciation *yumarimari*)[15] refers to a specific lizard that is light in colour. Fanny Walker Napurrurla commented that this Jakamarra was also light-skinned. Napurrurla's daughter Sarah Holmes Napangardi identified *yimarimari* as a lizard like a gecko but bigger with a colourful back. The word *yimarimari* can be analysed as a partial reduplication of *yimari*, a word that occurs in several other songs in the Jipiranpa set (sometimes in the form *yimarinji*), and that is variously translated into English as "wooden scoop", "coolamon" or (in Laughren et al. 2022) "women's dancing board" (see Verses 20, 27, 36, 37, 38) – all implements of similar shape that are specifically associated with women. This name for Jakamarra, then, is related to women's activities including ceremonial activities. The other word in Verse 11, *mujurdujurdu* is another name for *yimarimari* (possibly referring to the gecko's short fat tail; the spoken Warlpiri form is *mujurdu* "stumpy").

Example 6.4

Ngurlungka yurrkalyparla pantirni	:‖:	**Kalajirti japarna pantirni**
"Spearing into the seeds, into the mucus-like ones"		"Shall I spear Kalajirti?"

(Verse 12, Appendix 6.1)

Jakamarra's other name, based on the Warlpiri word *kalajirti*, refers to spinifex, a dominant and defining species of the Tanami Desert region, where Jipiranpa is located. The prickly qualities of spinifex are repeatedly referenced by the songs' recurrent use of the verb *pantirni* "spear, poke" (Verses 3, 4, 12). In discussing this song in 2021, Napurrurla's daughter Sarah Holmes Napangardi commented that people who are married wrong skin, which is common these days, are called *wingki* "immoral", a concept that is related to *kalajirti*. This name for Jakamarra, then, evokes his activities in pursuit of his mothers-in-law.

---

15 The Warlpiri language of the verses contains many forms that are characteristic of the eastern dialect, Wakirti Warlpiri (Simpson and Nash 1990).

Expert knowledge of Jipiranpa Country and its ancestral songlines

Several texts (e.g., Verse 18, Example 6.5) refer to the meeting of Jakamarra and the Nangala sisters.

Example 6.5

Ngarralalanpa rdipija :||: **Wurnamirinpa rdipija**
"You appeared from the opposite direction"   "You met up along the way"
(Verse 18, Appendix 6.1)

Verse 6 (Example 6.6) references Ngapa *jukurrpa*, the Nangalas' Rain/Water Dreaming, the story of which also includes the generation of rainclouds from clouds of smoke. In the Jipiranpa song set, references to fire often seem to be associated with Jakamarra.[16]

Example 6.6

Ngapa kiyalkiyal kiyalku karri :||: **Kurupurna kiyalku karri**
"Rainclouds are gathering, gathering"   "Cloud of smoke is rising"
(Verse 6, Appendix 6.1)

As the women travel, the Jakamarra is following their tracks and spying on them (Verse 17, Example 6.7).

Example 6.7

Wirliyakurnarla tarnpirni tarnpirni :||: **Wirliyakurnarla wayirninjinani**
"I'll follow in her tracks coming this way"   "I'll go along looking for her tracks"
(Verse 17 [variant], Appendix 6.1)

Jakamarra performs sorcery to get the Nangala women.

Sometimes, Jakamarra performs various acts of sorcery (e.g., Verse 42, Example 6.8; see also Verse 38) to bring the Nangala sisters under his control.

---

16 See Curran (2019), Morton (2011), Peterson (1970), Vaarzon-Morel et al. (Chapter 8, this volume) for discussions of the cultural significance of fire in relation to marriage exchange.

Example 6.8

Wanjitarra	**luwarni**	:‖:	**Kilmirr-luwarni**
"Spinning [hairstring] on a spindle"			"He was spinning hairstring"

(Verse 42, Appendix 6.1)

Some of Jangala's tricks include shapeshifting as a type of spider or lizard (as already seen in Verse 11, Example 6.3 above). The women notice various odd things as Jakamarra manifests in a variety of forms (e.g., Verse 10, Example 6.9; see also Verse 34).

Example 6.9

Mamupururnparlurna yarrarra mardarni	:‖:	**Yawarnturrurlurna yarrarra mardarni**
"I am winnowing it with a barking spider"		"I am winnowing with the grass seed"

(Verse 10, Appendix 6.1)

The *mamupururnpa* winnowed by the Nangalas along with their grass seed provides a dilemma for interpretation and, thus, translation. While the definition in the *Warlpiri Encyclopaedic Dictionary* (Laughren et al. 2022) is "barking spider" (a translation affirmed by Napurrurla's daughters in 2021), in 2010, Napurrurla herself commented that *mamupururnpa* was "a tiny lizard mixed in with the seeds being winnowed". Warlpiri translator Theresa Ross Napurrurla suggested that in this context, the translation could be "thing making a humming sound", a common attribute of both barking spiders and some species of gecko. It is possible that the word *mamupururnpa* could be derived from *mamu* (the word used in Pintupi and other Western Desert languages for an evil spirit, as well as in expressions meaning "clever, knowing, skilful, tricky") with the addition of *puru* "hidden, covered" (plus the endings -rn + -pa). According to the Pintupi dictionary, *mamu* is an invisible spirit that hides in dark places and looks out to harm humans (Hansen and Hansen 1992, 53–54). In this light, it is plausible that in this verse, *mamupururnpa* refers to Jakamarra under a different guise – a man hiding away from the Nangalas but intending to have sex with them, so needing to get close to them surreptitiously.

6 Expert domains of knowledge in Ngurlu *yawulyu* songs from Jipiranpa

Expert musical knowledge

Although musical settings of *yawulyu* verses can be quite diverse in terms of text repetitions and other conventions for text-setting,[17] there are well-established norms for Central Australian song performance. These norms are established and communicated in performance, in which a group of women, led by one or two senior singers (usually *kirda*), sing verses in a sequence decided by the song leaders in discussion with senior *kirda* and *kurdungurlu*. Although there may be some negotiation in the musical details of the verse, especially when a new verse first begins to be sung, the ideal is strong unison singing of the ancestral verses. Most of the Jipiranpa verses conform to these widespread norms. For the purposes of this chapter, we will focus on expert musical knowledge of the rhythmic setting of text while noting that the performance of other musical features, including melody and the alignment of text to melody, requires similar expertise.

Verses typically consist of a fixed text string, usually subdivided into two, or rarely three, lines. Sometimes, these lines can be further subdivided into two or three text-rhythm segments. Normally the same text string will be set to an identical rhythm whenever it occurs, although there are some exceptions to this rule (discussed below). As an example, let us consider Verse 15 (Example 6.10).

Example 6.10

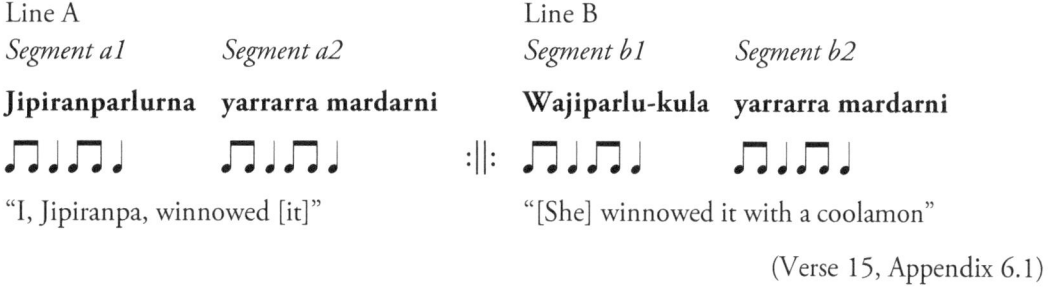

(Verse 15, Appendix 6.1)

As is often the case, the two lines share part of their text (segments a2 and b2, *yarrarra mardarni* "winnowed") while the first segment differs (a1 *jipiranparlurna* "I, Jipiranpa" and b1 *wajiparlu-kula* "with a coolamon"). The whole text-rhythm cycle, in this case consisting of consecutive repeats of both

---

17 See many works of Turpin and her collaborators, including San and Turpin (2021), Turpin (2007a, 2007b), Turpin and Laughren (2013) and Yeoh and Turpin (2018).

lines (form AABB), is repeated over and over in the course of a single item until the complete melody is presented, usually in 3–4 melodic phrases.[18]

In one instance (Verse 31, Example 6.11), the same text is set to two different rhythmic settings in consecutive items of Performance 1, first presenting the "slow" version (Warlpiri *yanku*; 31A, transcribed in 3/4 time), then the "fast" (Warlpiri *yaruju*; 31B, transcribed in 2/4 time). In full performances including dance, different dance movements would be performed to match these "slow" and "fast" rhythmic types.

Example 6.11

	Waji-rirririrrirli	maninya	:‖:	Wirringka	wirringkarna	maninya
Yanku "slow"	♫♪♫♩	♫♩		♫♩	♫♪.	♫♩
Yaruju "fast"	♫♫♫♩	♫♩		♫♩	♫♫	♫♩
	? "On the ?? I'm getting it"			"On the water runoff area, on the water runoff area I am getting it"		

(Verses 31A and 31B, Appendix 6.1)

Due to the existence of these two rhythmic settings for Verse 31, there are 48 rhythmic texts in total across the 47 verses in the Jipiranpa corpus.

Standard features of rhythmic text in Jipiranpa verses

We have identified five common features of the text-rhythm settings of Jipiranpa verses, whose distribution across the corpus of 48 Jipiranpa rhythmic texts is shown in Table 6.3.[19] In each case, the vast majority of verses adhere to a pattern we will call "standard", shown on the left of the table, with a minority, shown on the right, displaying non-standard features.

---

18   The placement of the rhythmic text on the melody is decided in performance, and often varies between consecutive items. See Barwick (2023, 1989) for examples and discussion of the principles of text-melody alignment in the Central Australian musical system.

19   For the purposes of this musical analysis, the sample size is 48, counting the fast and slow versions of Verse 31 as different rhythmic text combinations.

Table 6.3. Standard and non-standard forms of five rhythmic text features and their distribution across the corpus of 48 rhythmic texts.

Feature	Standard	n/48	Non-standard	n/48
Verse structure	AABB	44	Other (A, AB)	4
Line length equality	Equal (lines equal duration)	37	Unequal (4:3, 3:2, 5:4, 9:7)	11
Text meter type	Simple: 2/4 (fast), 3/4 (slow)	30	Other (3/8, 5/8, 6/8, additive)	18
Stress alignment (left edge)	Yes	35	No	13
Longest note (right edge)	Final	45	Non-final	3

1. <u>Verse structure:</u> 44 of the 48 rhythmic texts in the corpus have the text repetition pattern AABB (i.e., where the text/rhythm cycle is "doubled" – comprised of two consecutive repetitions of each text line pair). Only four rhythmic texts (7, 11, 13 and 33) follow a non-standard pattern, with a single line A (texts 7 and 33) or two unrepeated lines AB (texts 11 and 13).

2. <u>Line length:</u> 37 of the 48 rhythmic texts in the corpus have the same rhythmic duration in both lines of a text couplet or, in the case of a single line text, each segment (Verses 7 and 33).

3. <u>Text meter type:</u> A majority of verses in the corpus (30) are in a simple meter: 2/4 for fast songs and 3/4 for slow songs. A variety of other rhythmic meters can be found: some verses are set in 3/8, 5/8, 6/8 or additive meter.

4. <u>Stress alignment (left edge):</u> The standard for this corpus (in 35 out of 48 rhythmic texts) is for the musical stress to align with phonological stress in Warlpiri on the first syllable of the phonological phrase (the "left" edge of the text segment; Turpin and Laughren 2013). From a rhythmic perspective, we could say that the first syllable falls on a beat. In 13 of the 48 rhythmic texts, the initial syllable of the text string is unstressed (i.e., set to an upbeat or anacrusis); thus, rhythmic stress is misaligned with normal word-initial stress in spoken Warlpiri.

5. <u>Longest note (right edge):</u> 45 of the 48 rhythmic texts follow the general convention of having the final note of a line or segment (the "right" edge of the phonological phrase) being the longest or equal longest in the line.[20] Three rhythmic texts violate this convention (Verses 18, 25 and 33).

---

20 Correspondingly, short notes typically mark the beginning of a structural unit.

As an example of standard text-setting, consider again Verse 15 (Example 6.12):

Example 6.12

Jipiranparlurna yarrarra mardarni :‖: **Wajiparlu-kula yarrarra mardarni**

♫♩♫♩   ♫♩♫♩   ♫♩♫♩   ♫♩♫♩

"I, Jipiranpa, winnowed [it]"   "[She] winnowed it with a coolamon"

(Verse 15, Appendix 6.1)

1. <u>Verse structure</u>: Each line of rhythmic text is repeated, yielding the **standard** verse structure AABB.

2. <u>Line length equality</u>: The two lines are exactly equal in rhythmic duration and thus **standard**. Indeed, in this case, they are also identical in rhythm, each consisting of 4 repetitions of the core rhythmic cell (quaver-quaver-crotchet).

3. <u>Text meter type</u>: The rhythmic meter is a simple type (2/4) and thus **standard**.

4. <u>Stress alignment (left edge)</u>: On the left edge, stress is **standard**, aligning with the first syllable of each line and, indeed, of each word within the line.

5. <u>Longest note (right edge)</u>: On the right edge, the final note in each line is equal to the longest note occurring within the line (a crotchet) and thus **standard**.

Verse 15 thus conforms to all five of the standard text-setting conventions for this song set, as outlined in Table 6.3.

6 Expert domains of knowledge in Ngurlu *yawulyu* songs from Jipiranpa

Transgression of musical norms in Ngurlu *yawulyu* from Jipiranpa

By contrast to the text-setting norms set out above, the predominantly non-standard text-setting of Verse 11 is set out below (Example 6.13).

Example 6.13

Line A		Line B	
Segment a1	*Segment a2*	*Segment b1*	*Segment b2*
Yimarimarirla	**yimarimarirla** :‖:	**mujurdujurdu**	**mujurdujurdu**
♪♫♫♩.	♪♫♫♩	♫♩♩♩	♫♩♩♩.
(8 quaver pulses)	(7 quaver pulses)	(8 quaver pulses)	(9 quaver pulses)
"Gecko, gecko"		"Short stumpy one"	

(Verse 11, Appendix 6.1)

1. <u>Verse structure:</u> This text appears to be AABB in form, but the duration of the final long note in each half-line varies between a dotted crotchet (when the immediately following segment begins with an upbeat) and a crotchet (when the immediately following segment aligns word stress and musical stress on the first syllable). Therefore, it must be analysed as AB in form and thus **non-standard**.

2. <u>Line length equality:</u> The two lines are of unequal rhythmic duration, with Line A consisting of 15 quaver values (8 + 7) and Line B consisting of 17 quaver values (8 + 9). This feature is classified as **non-standard**.

3. <u>Text meter type:</u> The base rhythmic meter is indeterminate, totalling 15 quaver pulses in Line A and 17 quaver pulses in Line B. This meter is classified as **non-standard**.

4. <u>Stress alignment (left edge):</u> Stress alignment differs between the two lines, with Line A beginning with an unstressed short note, misaligning with Warlpiri's word-initial stress, while Line B begins on the beat, thus aligning with expected word stress. The misalignment in Line A means that for this feature, too, the text-setting is classified as **non-standard**.

5. <u>Longest note (right edge):</u> This is the only text-setting convention this rhythmic text seems to follow, but even here the situation is complex. In Line A, the longest note value (dotted crotchet) occurs at the end of segment a1, rather than at the end of the whole line (where segment a2 finishes with a crotchet). In Line B, the dotted crotchet occurs at the end of segment b2,

coinciding with the line-final position. Because both lines end with a longer note value, on balance, we have classified this feature as **standard**.

Thus, Verse 11 uses non-standard text-setting conventions in four of the five features identified in Table 6.3, and even the fifth feature (placement of longest note) differs in some respects from the norm.

Distribution of text-setting features according to song theme

In these Ngurlu *yawulyu* songs from Jipiranpa, particular themes seem to be marked by the use of standard or non-standard musical conventions. We have classified the 48 rhythmic texts in the corpus into three thematic groups according to the type of activity represented or referenced. Twenty-one of the 48 verses are about seed processing or related activities of the Nangala women; 19 refer directly or indirectly to Jakamarra and his activities; and a further eight verses are presently unclassified or ambiguous, sometimes due to lack of discussion with Fanny Walker Napurrurla.

If we consider the distribution of these thematic groups against the proportion of standard to non-standard musical features for each of the 48 rhythmic texts, the following pattern emerges (see Table 6.4).

Table 6.4. Distribution of standard text-rhythm features according to thematic groups.

	Thematic groups			
Feature distribution strength	Seed processing	Jakamarra	Unclassified	TOTAL
5/5 standard	15	2	3	20
4/5 standard	2	9	4	15
3/5 standard	3	3	1	7
2/5 standard	1	4	0	5
1/5 standard	0	1	0	1
TOTAL	21	19	8	48

Table 6.4 shows that the majority of rhythmic texts associated with the Nangalas' seed processing (15 of 21 verses) conform completely to the standard text-rhythm features as outlined in Table 6.3, while all except two verses (17/19) dealing with the activities of Jakamarra and his encounter with the women have at least one non-standard feature. Thus, we suggest that Jakamarra's norm-defying behaviour in pursuing his two mothers-in-law is reflected in the

preponderance of non-standard text-rhythm conventions in verses that concern him. Perhaps the musical rule-breaking in Jakamarra's verses reflects his pursuit of "wrong way" social relationships.

Conclusion

As is widely recognised, song texts can be very difficult to interpret.[21] Deciphering and interpreting song texts can be even more difficult when the principal performers and owners have passed away and ways of life have changed dramatically so that there is no longer a wide understanding of some of the practices and domains of expert knowledge that are embedded in the song texts. This is the situation of many contemporary Warlpiri people who may now have grown up in communities far from their ancestral homelands (Barwick, Turpin and Laughren 2013; Wild 1987).

Sarah Holmes Napangardi, Fanny Walker Napurrurla's eldest daughter and *kurdugurlu* for these Ngurlu songs from Jipiranpa, stated, "I grew up on *ngurlu*";[22] however, by the time their family was living in Alekarenge, her mother would still sing *yawulyu*, but only a few. She taught Sarah some songs. In 2010, Napurrurla herself commented that:

> The young girls still dance and get painted up, but they don't sing. They don't know the songlines. We older women paint up the young women and young girls. The young girls dance with the paintings we put on them.[23]

Napurrurla's daughters agree that understanding their mothers' songs now can be "a little bit hard".[24] We suggest that Elders' often-expressed wishes for teaching and learning of *yawulyu* songs to take place "on Country" (Barwick, Laughren and Turpin 2013) recognise the power of situational learning to integrate multiple domains of expert knowledge. Contemporary Indigenous Ranger programs across Australia are increasingly incorporating

---

21 For discussion of Australian examples, see among others, Barwick, Birch and Evans (2007), Dixon (1980), Donaldson (1979), Koch and Turpin (2008), Garde (2006), Hale (1984), Turpin and Stebbins (2010), Walsh (2007) and Wild (1984).

22 Personal communication to Gretel Macdonald, 2021.

23 Edited summary of interview by Mary Laughren [T100718a-03.wav] in AIATSIS collection BARWICK_J01. Warlpiri text of relevant section: ML: Manu kamina-kamina? FW: Yuwayi. Yirntija-gain kalalu. Yeah. Yirntija kalalu. ML: Pina-pina-manulu-jana yawulyuku yunparninjaku? FW: Lawa. Yawulyu-mipalpalu-jana kujurnu. […] ML: Nuu kalu yunparni young-people-rlu? FW: Walku. ML: Wirntimi kalu? FW: Yirntimi kalu. Jessie: Kamina-kaminalu wirntija. ML: Kuruwarri-kirli. FW: Kuruwarri kujurnu-rnalu-jana.

24 Jessie Simpson Napangardi, personal communication to Gretel Macdonald, 15 October 2021.

cultural activities into their land management activities (Ens et al. 2016). For example, the already cited account of Napurrurla's final visit to Jipiranpa was facilitated by the Indigenous Rangers from the nearby Warlpri community of Willowra and bolstered her daughters' "feeling for that Country" and its *milarlpa* (ancestral people).[25] Similarly, the Southern Tanami Ranger Group, with leadership from Enid Nangala Gallagher, Alice Nampijinpa Henwood and other Elders, has supported the creation of resources for song learning that are recorded and developed on Warlpiri Country.[26] This seems to be one important arena for Warlpiri people to expand their activities to support intergenerational transmission of expert knowledges and their contexts.

In compiling this chapter, Barwick and Laughren have been mindful of the general risk of misinterpretation in intercultural contexts and of the related specific issue that our attempts to write down and interpret the "hard" language of the *yawulyu* Jipiranpa verses may contain errors. Recovering the correct text from audio recordings – the starting point of our work – is an exercise fraught with difficulty (Bracknell 2017; Hercus and Koch 1995; Turpin and Laughren 2013), and there are also acknowledged difficulties in translating poetic language with its use of esoteric, oblique and sometimes ambiguous language (Barwick 2011; Koch and Turpin 2008; Walsh 2007), not to mention the required specialist contextual knowledge of seed-processing practices, Jipiranpa Country and its ancestral stories. Musical features of Central Australian songs are similarly highly complex and sometimes difficult to interpret (Ellis 1985; Ellis and Barwick 1987). Any errors we have made risk misleading or disempowering contemporary and future Warlpiri people, who are the rightful holders of this knowledge tradition. We have tried to counter these risks by checking our part of the work, firstly with Fanny Walker Napurrurla and her family and secondly with Warlpiri experts in language and culture. We respectfully offer our part of this work as a tribute to our co-author, the great ceremony woman, Fanny Walker Napurrurla, asking that readers take the written versions of the songs we present here not as authoritative exegesis but more as suggestions or pointers to the full richness of *yawulyu* as performed.

---

25 Written statement created by Jessie Simpson Napangardi and Sarah Holmes Napangardi with Gretel Macdonald (15 October 2021).

26 See List of Contributors for further details on Enid Nangala Gallagher and profile for Alice Nampijinpa Henwood this volume.

Acknowledgements

Thank you to the family of Fanny Walker Napurrurla, including Sarah Holmes Napangardi, Jessie Simpson Napangardi and Judith Robertson Napangardi, for their interest, comments and permissions. Thanks also to Theresa Ross Napurrurla for assistance with Warlpiri translations; to David Nash, Jane Simpson and Myfany Turpin for their ongoing support through the many years it has taken to complete this research; and to Gretel Macdonald for research assistance in the latter stages of the project. At various times, fieldwork has been funded by the Australian Research Council Queen Elizabeth II Research Fellowship (1992–1996), the Australian Research Council Linkage project LP0989243 (for interviews undertaken in 2010), the Australian Research Council Linkage project LP160100743, the Kurra Aboriginal Corporation, Pintubi Anmatjere Warlpiri Media and Communications, and the University of Sydney. Thanks to Myfany Turpin and anonymous peer reviewers for additional comments that have improved the chapter.

References

Barwick, Linda. 1989. "Creative (Ir)regularities: The Intermeshing of Text and Melody in Performance of Central Australian Song". *Australian Aboriginal Studies* 1: 12–28.

Barwick, Linda. 2011. "Including Music and the Temporal Arts in Language Documentation". In *The Oxford Handbook of Linguistic Fieldwork*, edited by Nicholas Thieberger, 166–79. Oxford: Oxford University Press. https://doi.org/10.1093/oxfordhb/9780199571888.013.0008

Barwick, Linda. 2023. "Songs and the Deep Present". In *Everywhen: Australia and the Language of Deep History*, edited by Ann McGrath, Laura Rademaker and Jakelin Troy, 93–122. Lincoln: University of Nebraska Press and the American Philosophical Society.

Barwick, Linda, Bruce Birch and Nicholas Evans. 2007. "Iwaidja Jurtbirrk Songs: Bringing Language and Music Together". *Australian Aboriginal Studies* 2: 6–34.

Barwick, Linda, Mary Laughren and Myfany Turpin. 2013. "Sustaining Women's *Yawulyu/Awelye*: Some Practitioners' and Learners' Perspectives". *Musicology Australia* 35(2): 191–220. https://doi.org/10.1080/08145857.2013.844491

Bell, Diane. 1993. *Daughters of the Dreaming*. 2nd ed. Sydney: Allen & Unwin.

Bracknell, Clint. 2017. "Maaya Waab (Play with Sound): Song Language and Spoken Language in the South-West of Western Australia". In *Recirculating

Songs: Revitalising the Singing Practices of Indigenous Australia, edited by Jim Wafer and Myfany Turpin, 45–57. Canberra; Newcastle: Pacific Linguistics & Hunter Press.

Curran, Georgia. 2019. "'Waiting for Jardiwanpa': History and Mediation in Warlpiri Fire Ceremonies". *Oceania* 89(1): 20–35.

Curran, Georgia. 2020. "Bird/Monsters and Contemporary Social Fears in the Central Desert of Australia". In *Monster Anthropology: Ethnographic Explorations of Transforming Social Worlds through Monsters*, edited by Yasmine Musharbash and Geir Henning Presterudstuen, 127–42. London: Bloomsbury Academic. https://doi.org/10.5040/9781350096288.ch-008

Curran, Georgia, Linda Barwick, Myfany Turpin, Fiona Walsh and Mary Laughren. 2019. "Central Australian Aboriginal Songs and Biocultural Knowledge: Evidence from Women's Ceremonies Relating to Edible Seeds". *Journal of Ethnobiology* 39(3): 354–70. https://doi.org/10.2993/0278-0771-39.3.354

Dixon, R. M. W. 1980. *The languages of Australia*. Cambridge: Cambridge University Press.

Donaldson, Tamsin. 1979. "Translating Oral Literature: Aboriginal Verses". *Aboriginal History* 3: 62–83.

Ellis, Catherine. 1985. *Aboriginal Music, Education for Living*. St. Lucia: University of Queensland Press.

Ellis, Catherine. 1970. "The Role of the Ethnomusicologist in the Study of Andagarinja Women's Ceremonies". *Miscellanea Musicologica* 5: 76–208.

Ellis, Catherine and Linda Barwick. 1987. "Musical Syntax and the Problem of Meaning in a Central Australian Songline". *Musicology Australia* 10: 41–57.

Ens, Emilie, Scott Mitchell L., Yugul Mangi Rangers, Craig Moritz and Rebecca Pirzl. 2016. "Putting Indigenous Conservation Policy into Practice Delivers Biodiversity and Cultural Benefits". *Biodiversity and Conservation* 25: 2889–2906. https://doi.org/10.1007/s10531-016-1207-6

Gallagher, Coral Napangardi, Peggy Nampijinpa Brown, Georgia Curran and Barbara Napanangka Martin. 2014. *Jardiwanpa Yawulyu: Warlpiri Women's Songs from Yuendumu*. Batchelor: Batchelor University Press.

Garde, Murray. 2006. "The Language of *Kun-Borrk* in Western Arnhem Land". *Musicology Australia* 28: 59–89.

Hale, Kenneth L. 1984. "Remarks on Creativity in Aboriginal Verse". In *Problems and Solutions: Occasional Essays in Musicology Presented to Alice M. Moyle*, edited by Jamie C. Kassler and Jill Stubington, 254–62. Sydney: Hale & Iremonger.

Hansen, Kenneth L. and Lesley E. Hansen. 1992. *Pintupi/Luritja Dictionary*. 3rd ed. Alice Springs: IAD Press.

Hercus, Luise and Grace Koch. 1995. "Song Styles from Near Poeppel's Corner". In *The Essence of Singing and the Substance of Song: Recent Responses to the Aboriginal Performing Arts and Other Essays in Honour of Catherine Ellis* (Oceania Monograph 46), edited by Linda Barwick, Allan Marett and Guy Tunstill, 106–20. Sydney: Oceania Publications.

Kelly, Francis Jupurrurla, dir, and David Batty, dir. 2012. *Coniston*. Yuendumu/Brunswick: Pintubi Anmatjere Warlpiri Media and Communications/Rebel Films.

Koch, Grace and Myfany Turpin. 2008. "The Language of Central Australian Aboriginal Songs". In *Morphology and Language History in Honour of Harold Koch*, edited by Claire Bowern, Bethwyn Evans and Luisa Miceli, 167–83. Amsterdam: John Benjamins.

Laughren, Mary, Georgia Curran, Myfany Turpin and Nicholas Peterson. 2018. "Women's *Yawulyu* Songs as Evidence of Connections to and Knowledge of Land: The Jardiwanpa". In *Language, Land and Song: Studies in Honour of Luise Hercus*, edited by Peter K. Austin, Harold Koch and Jane Simpson, 425–455. Batchelor: Batchelor Institute Press.

Laughren, Mary, Kenneth Hale, Jeannie Egan Nungarrayi, Marlurrku Paddy Patrick Jangala, Robert Hoogenraad, David Nash and Jane Simpson. 2022. *Warlpiri Encyclopaedic Dictionary*. Canberra: Aboriginal Studies Press.

Morton, John. 2011. "Splitting the Atom of Kinship: Towards an Understanding of the Symbolic Economy of the Warlpiri Fire Ceremony". In *Ethnography and the Production of Anthropological Knowledge: Essays in Honour of Nicolas Peterson*, edited by Yasmine Musharbash and Marcus Barber, 17–38. Canberra: ANU Press.

Moyle, Richard M. 1979. *Songs of the Pintupi: Music in a Central Australian Society*. Canberra: Australian Institute of Aboriginal Studies.

Nash, David. 1984. "The Warumungu Reserves 1892–1962: A Case Study in Dispossession". *Australian Aboriginal Studies* 1: 2–16.

Nash, David. 2002. "Mary Alice WARD (1896–1972)". In *Australian Dictionary of Biography* (Volume 16; 1940–80 Pik–Z), edited by John Ritchie and Dianne Langmore, 490–91. Melbourne: Melbourne University Press. http://www.adb.online.anu.edu.au/biogs/A160582b.htm

Peterson, Nicolas. 1970. "Buluwandi: A Central Australian Ceremony for the Resolution of Conflict". In *Australian Aboriginal Anthropology: Modern Studies in the Social Anthropology of the Australian Aborigines*, edited by Ronald M. Berndt, 200–15. Nedlands: University of Western Australia Press.

Peterson, Nicolas and Jeremy Long. 1986. *Australian Territorial Organization: A Band Perspective*. Sydney: University of Sydney.

San, Nay and Myfany Turpin. 2021. "Text-Setting in Kaytetye". In *Proceedings of the 2020 Annual Meeting on Phonology*, edited by Ryan Bennett, Richard Bibbs, Mykel Loren Brinkerhoff, Max J. Kaplan, Stephanie Rich, Amanda Rysling, Nicholas Van Handel and Maya Wax Cavallaro, 1–9. Columbia: Linguistics Society of America. https://doi.org/10.3765/amp.v9i0.4911

Simpson, Jane and David Nash. 1990. *Wakirti Warlpiri: A Short Dictionary of Eastern Warlpiri with Grammatical Notes*. Tennant Creek: Jane Simpson and David Nash.

Treloyn, Sally. 2007. "'When Everybody There Together … then I Call That One': Song Order in the Kimberley". *Context: A Journal of Music Research* 32: 105–21.

Turpin, Myfany. 2007a. "Artfully Hidden: Text and Rhythm in a Central Australian Aboriginal Song Series". *Musicology Australia* 29(1): 93–108.

Turpin, Myfany. 2007b. "The Poetics of Central Australian Song". *Australian Aboriginal Studies* 2: 100–115.

Turpin, Myfany. 2012. *Kaytetye to English Dictionary*. Alice Springs: IAD Press.

Turpin, Myfany and Mary Laughren. 2013. "Edge Effects in Warlpiri *Yawulyu* Songs: Resyllabification, Epenthesis, Final Vowel Modification". *Australian Journal of Linguistics* 33(4): 399–425.

Turpin, Myfany and Tonya Stebbins. 2010. "The Language of Song: Some Recent Approaches in Description and Analysis". *Australian Journal of Linguistics* 30(1): 1–17.

Walsh, Michael. 2007. "Australian Aboriginal Song Language: So Many Questions, So Little to Work With". *Australian Aboriginal Studies* 2: 128–44.

Watts, Lisa, April Ngampart Campbell, Clarrie Kemarr and Myfany Turpin. 2009. *Mer Rrkwer-Akert* [DVD]. Alice Springs: Charles Darwin University Central Australian Research Network.

Wild, Stephen A. 1984. "Warlbiri Music and Culture: Meaning in a Central Australian Song Series". In *Problems and Solutions: Occasional Essays in Musicology Presented to Alice M. Moyle*, edited by Jamie C. Kassler and Jill Stubington, 41–53. Sydney: Hale & Iremonger.

Wild, Stephen A. 1987. "Recreating the Jukurrpa: Adaptation and Innovation of Songs and Ceremonies in Warlpiri Society". In *Songs of Aboriginal Australia* (Oceania Publications), edited by Margaret Clunies Ross, Tamsin Donaldson and Stephen Wild, 97–120. Sydney: University of Sydney.

Yeoh, Calista and Myfany Turpin. 2018. "An Aboriginal Women's Song from Arrwek, Central Australia". *Musicology Australia* 40(2): 101–26. https://doi.org/10.1080/08145857.2018.1550141

6 Expert domains of knowledge in Ngurlu *yawulyu* songs from Jipiranpa

Appendix 6.1 Verses and rhythms for Ngurlu *yawulyu* from Jipiranpa

Ngurlu *yawulyu* songs from Jipiranpa are ordered in this Appendix following the order of Performance 3 (tape AT97/13AB), then Performance 1 (tape AT96/18AB), then Performance 4 (tape AT97/16AB_17A).

Each distinct verse is numbered 1–47 (four have text variants, and one has both slow and fast versions, making a total of 48 distinct rhythmic texts). The verse number is followed by an indication of how many times the verse occurs in the corpus (giving song item codes as per Barwick's database). For each verse, the lines in the text (usually two) are presented in a series of text/rhythm tables following the order and line repetition structure first heard; it is not uncommon for text line order to be reversed in some items.

We use the musical repeat symbol :||: for internal repetition of each line (AABB); and the slash symbol / to separate unrepeated lines (AB).

The first line indicates syllabic rhythm; the second line is the Warlpiri text written in standard Warlpiri;[27] the third is morphemic representation of the text; the fourth morpheme-by-morpheme glossing; and the last line is a free translation.

Comments by *kirda* Fanny Walker Napurrurla (FW) on 18–19 July 2010 (recorded on T100718a and T100719a), by *kurdungurlu* Sarah Holmes Napangardi (SH) in 2021, by translator Theresa Ross Napurrurla (TR), or by the transcribers (Mary Laughren [ML] and Linda Barwick [LB]) are presented when relevant beneath the text/rhythm tables.

Abbreviations used in glosses:

1 = first person; 2 = second person; 3 = third person; 12 = first and second person dual (inclusive); AUX = auxiliary; CS = changed state; DAT = dative case; EL = elative case; ERG = ergative case; FOC = focus; IMP = imperative; IMPF = imperfective aspect; INC = incipient; INF = infinitive; LOC = locative case; NPST = non-past tense; PERL = perlative case; PL = plural; PRES = present tense; PST = past tense; Q = question; REDUP = reduplication; S = subject; TOP = topic.

---

27 In this summary of the verses, we have opted for standard Warlpiri rather than phonetic text as sung because the latter may include vowel alterations that tend to be inconsistent from one rendition of the text line to the next, and that may also vary between individual singers in group performance.

Verse 1

5 items (AT9618A-s20_22; AT9713A-s01_02)

Line A				Line B			
♪♫♩	♪♪♩	♪♪♩	:‖:	♪♫♩.	♪♫♩	♪♪♩	♪♪♩
Punangkarna	yarrarra-	mardarni		**Punanjarlu**	punanjarlu	yarrarra-	mardarni
puna-ngka-rna ash-LOC-1S	yarrarra- winnow-	marda-rni have-NPST		puna-njarlu ash-much	puna-njarlu ash-much	yarrarra- winnow-	marda-rni have-NPST
"I winnow ashes"				"Winnow lots of ashes"			

Comments:

FW: *Puna-lpa yarrarra-mardarnu* "She was winnowing ashes". Cooking *ngurlu* "seeds" in hot ashes.

ML: The frequent ending *-rna* (as on *puna-ngka*) is ambiguous between the first-person singular subject enclitic pronoun "I" and an epenthetic "vocable" element added to a phrase to provide enough syllables to match the rhythmic pattern (Turpin and Laughren 2013, 400). We will gloss all instances as "1S", but some should probably be analysed as a vocable.

Verse 2

3 items (AT9713A-s03_05)

Line A				Line B			
♫♩♫♩	♫♩	♫♩	:‖:	♫♩♫♩	♫♩	♫♩	
Wajiparlu-kula	yarrarra-	mardarni		**Murdupurrjurlurna**	yarrarra-	mardarni	
wajipa-rlu-kula coolamon-ERG-indeed	yarrarra- winnow-	marda-rni have-NPST		murdupurrju-rlu-rna kneeling-ERG-1S	yarrarra- winnow-	marda-rni have-NPST	
"With a coolamon winnowing"				"Kneeling I winnow"			

Comment:

ML: *Murdupurrju* in line B, based on *murdu* "knee", is equivalent to *murdujirrpijirrpi* in Verse 44 and *murdujirrpi* in Verse 2 (variant) and Verse 45.

6 Expert domains of knowledge in Ngurlu *yawulyu* songs from Jipiranpa

Verse 2 (variant)

4 items (AT9618A-s23_26)

Line A				Line B		
Wajipa kularna	**yarrarra**	**mardarni**	:||:	**Murdujirrpirlirna**	**yarrarra**	**mardarni**
wajipa-kula-rna	yarrarra-	marda-rni		murdujirrpi-rli-rna	yarrarra-	marda-rni
coolamon-indeed-1S	winnow	have-NPST		kneeling-ERG-1S	winnow	have-NPST

"It's a coolamon I winnow [with]"   "Kneeling I winnow [it]."

Verse 3

2 items (AT9713A-s11_s12)

Line A				Line B	
Kalajirti	**japarna**	**pantirni**	:||:	**Jarnangkarna**	**pantirni**
kalajirti	japa-rna	panti-rni		jarna-ngka-rna	panti-rni
kalajirti	Q=1S	spear-NPST		bushfire-LOC-1S	spear-NPST

"Shall I spear Kalajirti?"   "I'll spear [it/her/him] at the leading edge of the fire"

Comments:

SH: Sarah explains that people who are married wrong skin, which is common these days, are called *wingki*, which is related to *kalajirti*.

ML: *Jarna* refers to a bush or grass fire, particularly the leading edge where the flames are active, and where animals escaping fire were more easily speared.

ML: *Kalajirti* is a type of Gummy Spinifex grass and is also the name of a man who is one of the ancestral beings celebrated in this ceremony.

Verse 4

3 items (AT9618A-s34; AT9713A-s13_14)

Line A					Line B			
♫♪.	♫♩	♪♪♪♪	♫♩	:‖:	♫♪.	♫♩	♪♪♪♪	♫♩
Kalajirti	**japarna**	**wuyuwuyu**	**yirrarnu**		**Kalajirti**	**japarna**	**turdurr-turdurr**	**yirrarnu**
Kalajirti	japa-rna	wuyuwuyu	yirra-rnu		Kalajirti	japa-rna	turdurr-turdurr	yirra-rnu
Kalajirti	Q-1S	rub	put-PST		Kalajirti	Q-1S	?	put-PST
"Did I rub against Kalajirti?"					"Did I affect Kalajirti?"			

Comment:

FW: Women sing this song to attract their boyfriends. It is a "love" song or *yilpinji*.

Verse 5

6 items (AT9618A-s36_38; AT9713A-s15; AT9713A-s39_40)

Line A				Line B		
♫♩	♫♩♩	♫♩	:‖:	♫♪.	♫♩	♫♩
Marnangka	**yurrkalyparla**	**pantirni**		**Kalajirti**	**japarna**	**pantirni**
marna-ngka	yurrkalypa-rla	panti-rni		Kalajirti	japa-rna	panti-rni
spinifex-LOC	mucus-LOC	spear-NPST		Kalajirti	Q-1S	spear-NPST
"In the spinifex, in the mucus[-like] spearing"				"Will I spear Kalajirti?"		

Comments:

FW: *Ngurlu, panturnulpa Kalajirtirli* "Kalajirti was piercing/poking the seeds".

ML: The verb *pantirni* denotes a sharp pointed entity coming into contact with something: corresponding to English verbs "poke", "stab", "pierce", "spear". Although we gloss all occurrences as "spear", these other verbs might better describe some events.

ML: *Yurrkalypa* in this context may refer to the shiny melted spinifex resin following bushfire.

Verse 6

5 items (AT9618A-s04_06; AT9713A-s16_17)

Line A			Line B	
♫♩♩♩	♫♩♩	:‖:	♫♩♩	♫♩♩
Ngapa kiyalkiyal	**kiyalku karri**		**Kurupurna**	**kiyalku karri**
ngapa kiyal-kiyal- rain rise-rise	kiyalku-karri rise-stand		kurupu-rna smoke-1S	kiyalku-karri rise-stand
"Rainclouds are gathering, gathering"			"Cloud of smoke is rising"	

Comment:

FW: The cloud of smoke from the bushfire rises and causes rainclouds to form.

Verse 7

10 items (AT9618A-s11_13; AT9713A-s18_20; AT9713A-s44_45; AT9713B-s22_23)

Line A

♫♩♪.	♫♩♫♩	♫♩♪.
Yukurlukurlu	**jarijalparnarla**	**winiwinirla**
yukurlukurlu burnt_ground	jari-ja-lpa-rna-rla walk(?)-PST-IMPF-1S-3DAT	wini-wini-rla burnt_ground-REDUP-LOC

"I was walking searching for it on the burnt ground"

Comments:

FW: The people were walking on the burnt ground.

ML: The origin and meaning of past tense verb *jari-ja* is unclear. *Jari* denotes thick scrub.

Verse 8

5 items (AT9713A-s21_22; AT9713A-s53_55)

Line A			Line B		
♫♩♩	♩♩	♩♩	:‖: ♫♩♩	♩♩	♩♩
Warrilyirla	**karli**	**nyina**	**Wajarnpirla**	**karli**	**nyina**
warrilyi-rla	ka-rli	nyina	wajarnpi-rla	ka-rli	nyina
mallee-LOC	PRS-12	sit	ironwood-LOC	PRS-12	sit

"We [you and I] are sitting under the Red-bud Mallee"

"We are sitting under the Ironwood"

Comment:

LB: Musical settings of this verse vary. In AT9713A-s21_22, singers consistently perform the long notes as minim, used here. In AT9713A-s53_55, singers audibly disagree regarding the duration of long notes; some singers perform consistent dotted minims.

Verse 9

2 items (AT9713A-s23_24)

Line A		Line B	
♫♩♫♩	♫♩♫♩	:‖: ♫♩♫♩	♫♩♫♩
Wajiparlu-kula	**yarrarra mardarni**	**Wumurljumurljurlu**	**yarrarra mardarni**
wajipa-rlu kula	yarrarra-marda-rni	wumurljumurlju-rlu	yarrarra-marda-rni
coolamon-ERG-indeed	winnow-have-NPST	close_together-ERG	winnow-have-NPST

"With a coolamon winnowing"

"Close up winnowing"

Verse 10

6 items (AT9618B-s02_04; AT9713A-s25_27)

Line A		:||:	Line B	
♫♫♩	♫♩♫♩		♫♩♫♩	♫♩♫♩
Mamupururnparlurna	**yarrarra mardarni**		**Yawarnturrurlurna**	**yarrarra mardarni**
mamupururnpa-rlu-rna name-ERG-1S	yarrarra-marda-rni winnow-have-NPST		yawarnturru-rlu-rna grass_seed_sp.-ERG-1S	yarrarra-marda-rni winnow-have-NPST
"I am winnowing it with a Barking Spider"			"I am winnowing with the grass seed sp."	

Comments:

FW: *Mamupururnpa* was a tiny lizard mixed in with the seeds being winnowed; *yawarnturru* seeds were winnowed by the Dreaming ancestor.

SH and JL: *Mamupururnpa* identified as barking spider.

TR: In translating this text, suggested "thing making a humming sound" – as do both barking spiders and fat-tailed geckos.

ML: An alternative reading would be that both *mamupururnpa* and *yawarnturru* are names of the ancestor(s) this verse celebrates: A. "I, Mamupururnpa, am winnowing"; B. "I, Yawarnturru, am winnowing".

Verse 11

5 items (AT9618A-s17_19; AT9713A-s37_38)

Line A			Line B	
♪♫♫𝅗𝅥.	♪♫♫♩	:‖:	♫♩♩♩	♫♩♩𝅗𝅥.
Yimarimarirla	yimarimarirla		**Mujurdujurdu**	mujurdujurdu
yimarimari-rla	yimarimari-rla		mujurdu-jurdu	mujurdu-jurdu
Fat-tailed Gecko-LOC	Fat-tailed Gecko-LOC		short_&_stumpy-REDUP	short_&_stumpy-REDUP

"Gecko, gecko" "Short stumpy one"

Comments:

FW: *Mujurdujurdu* was another name for *Yimarimari*, a Jakamarra from Jipiranpa who followed his mothers-in-law, two Nangala women.

SH: Sarah identifies *yimarimari* as the tiny lizard mixed in with the seeds. She explains that it is like a gecko but bigger with a colourful back. *Mamupururnpa* is identified as a barking spider.

ML: Spoken form is unreduplicated *mujurdu*. Partial reduplication (*mujurdu-jurdu*) is commonly employed in songs.

Verse 12

1 item (AT9713A-s41)

Line A				Line B		
♫♩	♫♩♩	♫♩	:‖:	♫♪.	♫♩	♫♩
Ngurlungka	yurrkalyparla	pantirni		**Kalajirti**	japarna	pantirni
ngurlu-ngka	yurrkalypa-rla	panti-rni		Kalajirti	japa-rna	panti-rni
seeds-LOC	mucus-LOC	poke-NPST		Kalajirti	Q-1S	poke-NPST

"Spearing into the seeds, into the mucus-like ones" "Shall I spear Kalajirti?"

Verse 13

2 items (AT9713A-s42_43)

Line A		:‖:	Line B	
♩ ♪♪.	♩ ♪♩.♩.		♩ ♪♩.♩.	♩ ♪♩.♩.
Kanarna	**warangka wara**		**Yukurrukurru**	**wirnpiwirnpirna**
kana-rna	warangka wara		yukurrukurru	wirnpiwirnpi-rna
digging_stick-1S	across_shoulder REDUP		dancing_board	thin&narrow-1SG
"I'm [carrying] a digging stick on my shoulder"			"Dancing board, long skinny one"	

Comments:

FW: *Kanalpa jinta kangu yukurrukurrurlu wijilpajilparlu.* "The *yukurrukurru* 'Dancing Board' Dreaming carried one digging stick across her shoulders."

ML: Another type of partial reduplication found in songs is exemplified by *warangka wara* in which only the initial two syllables are reduplicated; in spoken Warlpiri, the fully reduplicated *warangka-warangka* may be used.

ML: Verse 13 evokes women dancing and acting out part of the story of this song set.

LB: Note text repetition varies. Mostly AABB text: AABA/BAA/BBAAB.

Verse 13 (variant)

2 items (AT9618B-s15_16)

Line A		:‖:	Line B	
Kanarna	**warangka wara**		**Yukurrukurru**	**wijilwijilpa**
"I'm [carrying] digging stick up on shoulder"			"Dancing board, dancing board"	

Comments:

FW: *Wijilwijilpa* and *yukurrukurru* both refer to the "Dancing Board" Dreaming.

LB: Note (mostly) AB text – order of segments in second line sometimes reversed: AA'BABA/BABA.

LB: Compared to Verse 13, this version substitutes the last word in Line B *wirnpiwirnpirna* "thin and narrow" with the word *wijilwijilpa*, a synonym for *yukurrukurru* "dancing board".

Verse 14

5 items (AT9618B-s32_34; AT9713A-s46_47)

Line A			Line B	
♪♪♩♪♪♩	♪♪♩♪♪♩	:‖:	♪♪♩♪♪♩	♪♪♩♪♪♩
Lakati lakati	**parrarna yirrarnu**		**Lurlupujupuju**	**parrarna yirrarnu**
l-(w)akati l-(w)akati	parra-rna yirra-rnu		lurlupujupuju	parra-rna yirra-rnu
Portulaca-redup (seeds)	everywhere-1S put-PST		kneeling	everywhere-1S put-PST

"Portulaca seeds, I put them all over"   "Kneeling put them all over"

Comment:

ML: Vowel-initial Arandic words incorporated into Warlpiri songs, such as the word for *Portulaca sp.* in Line A, are typically sung with an initial "l" (e.g., *lakati-lakati*, a reduplicated word). The spoken Warlpiri name of this species is *wakati* as in Verse 44, line A. Note that *parrarna* is similar to *parrarla*, the name of an edible seed, which appears in Verse 39, Line B.

Verse 15

2 items (AT9713A-s48_49)

Line A			Line B	
♪♪♩♪♪♩	♪♪♩♪♪♩	:‖:	♪♪♩♪♪♩	♪♪♩♪♪♩
Jipiranparlurna	**yarrarra mardarni**		**Wajiparlu-kula**	**yarrarra mardarni**
Jipiranpa-rlu-rna	yarrarra-marda-rni		wajipa-rlu-kula	yarrarra-marda-rni
Jipiranpa-ERG-1SG	winnow-have-NPST		coolamon-ERG-indeed	winnow-have-NPST

"I, Jipiranpa, am winnowing"   "Winnowing with a coolamon"

Comment:

ML: Jipiranpa is both a place name and the name of the ancestor.

Verse 16

3 items (AT9713A-s50_52)

Line A			Line B	
♫ ♩ ♩	♩ ♩. ♩ ♩.	:‖:	♫ ♩ ♩	♩ ♩. ♩ ♩.
Ngajangaja	**ngajangaja**		**Jalajala**	**jalajala**
[??]			[??]	
"[One said] 'Ngajangaja'"			"[The other said] 'Jalajala'"	

Verse 17

3 items (AT9713A-s56_58)

Line A

♫ ♪ ♪ ♪   ♫ ♪ ♪ ♪

Wirliyakurnarla   tarnpinya tarnpinya

wirliya-ku-rna-rla   tarnpi-nya tarnpi-nya
track-DAT-1SG-3DAT follow-PRES follow-PRES

"I'm following her tracks"

Verse 17 variant

[not on original recording – sung by FW in 2010 elicitation session]

Line A			Line B	
Wirliyakurnarla	**tarnpirni tarnpirni**	:‖:	**Wirliyakurnarla**	**wayirninjinani**
wirliya-ku-rna-rla track-DAT-1SG-3DAT	tarnpi-rni tarnpi-rni follow-hither follow-HITHER		wirliya-ku-rna-rla track-DAT-1SG-3DAT	wayirni-nji-na-ni search-INC-CONT-NPST
"I'll follow in her tracks coming this way"			"I'll go along looking for her tracks"	

Verse 18

6 items (AT9618B-s21_23; AT9713A-s59_AT9713B-s01_02)

Line A		Line B	
Ngarralalanpa	**rdipija**	**Wurnamirinpa**	**rdipija**
ngarralala-npa	rdipi-ja	wurnamiri-npa	rdipi-ja
opposite_direction-2S	go_to-PST	travel-2S	go_to-PST

"You appeared from the opposite direction"   "You met up along the way"

Comments:

FW: The paths of the Dreamings crossed as they came from opposite directions.

LB: Myfany Turpin (personal communication) points out that this verse also occurs in the Arrwek (edible seed) song set (see Yeoh and Turpin 2018, 103, verse labelled "rrwek24"). It also occurs in *Jardiwanpa yawulyu* (see Song 38 in Gallagher et al. 2014, 86).

In both lines, the rhythmic notation is intended to show the strongly stressed triple grouping that crosses word boundaries. This is an example of misalignment of musical stress with normal first syllable word stress in spoken Warlpiri. Note the almost identical text in Line A, Verse 41. The text here in Verse 18 is set in *yaruju* "fast" style, in contrast to the *yanku* "slow" style of Verse 41.

Verse 19

9 items (AT9618A-s07_09; AT9713B-s03_06; AT9713B-s29_30)

Line A			Line B	
♫ ♩ ♪.	♫ ♩ ♪.	:‖:	♫ ♩ ♫ ♩	♪ ♩.
Warlu yumpurlu	**y-analyurrparlu**		**Ngamanjimanjirli**	**kangu**
warlu-yumpu-rlu	(l/y)-analyurrpa-rlu		ngamanjimanji-rli	ka-ngu
fire-burning(?)-ERG	flame(?)-ERG		wild-ERG	carry-PST
"The bright burning fire, the flames"			"The wild angry one took it."	

Comments:

FW: Smoke was rising up from the burnt ground after the fire had passed on. [Glossed *analyurrpa* as *jarra* "flame".]

ML: The initial consonant of the vowel-initial word *analyurrpa* is sung variably as "y" or "l". This word is possibly related to *ngalyurrpa* "flickering, blazing", as suggested by meaning given by FW; it is also similar to *kanalyurrpa* "many together".

Verse 20

2 items (AT9713B-s07_08)

Line A			Line B		
♪ ♩ ♩ ♪	♪ ♩ ♩ ♪	:‖:	♪ ♩ ♩ ♪	♪ ♩ ♩	♪ ♩ ♩ ♪
Yimarinjirli	**yirrarnu-nyanu**		**Rdanjirdarrardarra**	**rdamara**	**yirrarnu-nyanu**
yimarinji-rli	yirra-rnu-nyanu		rdanjirdarrardarra	rdamara	yirra-rnu-nyanu
wooden_scoop-ERG	put-PST-SELF		(? meaning uncertain)	(?lots)	put-PST-SELF
"S/he put it for her/himself with a coolamon"			"S/he put lots of it for her/himself"		

Comments:

SH: Sarah suggests that *rdanjirdarrardarra* refers to lots of people or things there. She mentions a potential synonym *jirdangarra*, meaning lots of people there, as in *jirdangarra nyinami kalu*.

ML: Narrow wooden scoop is recorded as *yimari* in spoken language; *yimarinji* may be a song form.

Verse 21

4 items (AT9618B-s50_51; AT9713B-s09_10)

Line A			Line B		
♫♩♩♩	♫♩♫♩	:‖:	♫♪.	♫♩	♫♩♫♩
Ngaju-japa karna	**yilpirrki-yirrarni**		**Pirdijirri**	**japarna**	**yilpirrki-yirrarni**
ngaju-japa ka-rna	yilpirrki-yirra-rni		pirdijirri	japa-rna	yilpirrki-yirra-rni
I-Q-AUX-1S	ash-put-NPST		seed-cake	Q-1S	ash put-NPST

"Am I cooking [it] in the hot ashes?"   "Will I cook the seed-cake in the hot ashes?"

Comments:

FW: *Yilpirrki-yirrarni* is the same as *julyurl-yirrarni* "put into fire".

ML: In one instance, Line B was sung as: *pirdijirri-rna japa yilpirrki-yirra-rni*.

Verse 22

4 items (AT9713B-s11_14)

Line A			Line B	
♫♫♪	♫♫♫♩.	:‖:	♫♫♪	♫♫♫♩.
Marukurdurlu	**warrampal-kijirninya**		**Kirliwarlunya**	**warrampal-kijirninya**
marukurdu-rlu	warrampal-kiji-rninya		kirliwarlu-nya	warrampal-kiji-rninya
Spinifex_Pigeon-ERG	scatter-throw-PRES		[Seeds?]-FOC	scatter-throw-PRES

"Spinifex Pigeon is scattering [them]"   "It is scattering [the seeds?]"

Comment:

ML: We did not have the opportunity to discuss this verse with Fanny Walker Napurrurla, hence there is some uncertainty about the translation. One reviewer noted a similarity between Warumungu *kiirli* "seed" and *kirliwarlu* in Line B; however, *kiirli* refers to non-edible seeds that must be cleaned out of fruits before eating (equivalent to Warlpiri *kurla*), as opposed to edible seeds that are ground to prepare for eating. *Kirliwarlu* might be the name of a seed being scattered by the pigeon. Another possible parsing is *kirli warlu-nya* where *kirli* refers to something belonging to another (typically son-in-law) and *warlu* "fire", so the free translation of this line might be "scattering fire belonging to son/mother-in-law".

Verse 23

6 items (AT9618B-s05_07; AT9713B-s15_17)

Line A			Line B	
♩ ♪♩. ♪♪ ♩.	♩ ♪♩. ♪♪ ♩.	:‖:	♩ ♪♩. ♪♪ ♩.	♩ ♪♩. ♪♪ ♩.
Kirlkirlajalu	**maninjintarra**		**Warlarlajalu**	**maninjintarra**
kirlkirlaja-lu	mani-nji-nta-rra		warlarlaja-lu	mani-nji-nta-rra
seed sp.-PL.S	get-INC-IMP-THITHER		hunting-PL.S	get-INC-IMP-THITHER
"Go and gather the *kirlkirlaja* seeds"			"Go out and get [the seeds]"	

Comments:

FW: They were collecting seeds while out gathering food.

ML: A reviewer alerted us to the link between Warumungu *walala* and *warlarlaja* "hunting" in line B; *-ja* may be an assertive marker added to the word of Warumungu origin.

Verse 24

3 items (AT9713B-s18_20)

Line A			Line B	
♪♩♩♪♩♩	♪♩♩	:‖:	♪♩♩♪♩♩♪♩♩	♪♩♩
Purlkakulparnarla	**wayurnu**		**Jungarntungarntukulparnarla**	**wayurnu**
purlka-ku-lpa-rna-rla	wayu-rnu		Jungarntungarntu-ku-lpa-rna-rla	wayu-rnu
old_man-DAT-IMPF-1S-3DAT	search-PST		Name-DAT-IMPF-1S-3DAT	search-PST
"I was searching for the old man"			"I was searching for Jungarntungarntu"	

Comments:

FW commented: *ngurra-ku-lpa-rna-rla* "camp-DAT-IMPF-1S-3DAT", which FW said was that they were looking for where the old man was sleeping/camping.

ML: Jungarntungarntu may be the name of a place.

LB: The line quoted by FW occurs in Verse 43.

Verse 25

4 items (AT9713B-s21; AT9713B-s39_41)

Line A

Yankuyankukurla **ngirirrangkanya**

yanku-yanku-ku-rla ngirirr-(wa)ngka-nya
slowly-slowly-DAT?-3DAT grind-do-PRES

"Slowly slowly grinding [them]" [or,
"Grinding them for Yankuyanku"]

Line B

Pirlirnardakurla **ngirirrangkanya**

pirlirnarda-ku-rla ngirirr-(w)angka-nya
?-DAT-3DAT grind-do-PRES

"Grinding them for Pirlirnarda" (?)

Comment:

ML: Text and interpretation are tentative, because we were unable to check the song with Fanny Walker Napurrurla in 2010. The first words of lines A and B present parallel forms, which suggests that both *yankuyanku* and *pirlirnarda* are names: *yanku* "slow", *pirli* "stone, hill".

Verse 26

8 items (AT9618A-s01_03; AT9713B-s24_28)

Line A

Yukurlukurlu **kurlpurr-pardinya**

yukurlukurlu kurlpurr-pardi-nya
burnt_ground ?-rise-PRES

"Burnt ground is ?"

Line B

Jarnangka karna **kurlpurr-pardinya**

jarna-ngka ka-rna kurlpurr-pardi-nya
bushfire-LOC AUX-1S ?-rise-PRES

"At the front of the bushfire I am ?"

Verse 27

3 items (AT9713B-s31_33)

Line A			Line B	
♫ ♫	♫ ♩	:‖:	♫ ♩ ♩	
Warnparla-rna	**kujurnu**		**yimarirla**	
warnparla-rna	kuju-rnu		yimari-rla	
?-1S	throw-PST		coolamon-LOC	
"I tossed ?"			"In the coolamon"	

Verse 28

3 items (AT9713B-s34_36)

Line A

♫ ♩ ♫ ♩	♫ ♩ ♫ ♩	:‖:	♫ ♩ ♫ ♩	♫ ♩ ♫ ♩
Wumurljumurljurlu	**yarrarra mardarni**		**Mamupururnparlurna**	**yarrarra mardarni**
wumurljumurlju-rlu	yarrarra-marda-rni		mamupururnpa-rlu-rna	yarrarra-marda-rni
close_together-ERG	winnow-have-NPST		Barking_Spider-ERG-1S	winnow-have-NPST
"Close up winnowed it"			"I, Barking Spider/Lizard(?), winnowed it"	

Comment:

FW: Identified *mamupururnpa* as a small lizard that people used to eat; it was mixed in with the seeds being cleaned.

Verse 29

4 items (AT9713B-s42_45)

Line A			Line B	
♪♩♩♩♩♩.		:‖:	♪♩♩♪♩.	♪♩♩♪♩.
Pirli	**karna**	**kanyi**	**Warakukurlu**	**kurlukukurlu**
pirli	ka-rna	ka-nyi	Waraku-kurlu	Diamond Dove-ERG
stone	AUX-1S	carry-NPST	[black_stone?]-WITH	
"I'm carrying a stone"			"Diamond Dove [is carrying the black stone]"	

Comment:

ML: This is likely to be *waraku-kurlu* "black stone-WITH" from Kaytetye *arake*: "black stone used for making stone knives and axes; burnt wood used for painting ceremonial designs; soft black stone used for painting ceremonial designs" (Turpin 2012, 150–51). The ERG on *kurlukuku* "Diamond Dove" indicates that this is the name of the one carrying the black stone (also referred to more generally as *pirli* "stone" in the A line). Further adding to the complexity of interpretation, *pirli* is also used to refer to some seeds; and in this case, the use of *waraku* in Line B could further specify black seeds (like those in *wakati* in Verse 14). Note that the sound pattern *kukurlu* occurring at the end of both segments of Line B derives from different sources.

LB: Myfany Turpin (personal communication) advised that this verse also occurs in the Arrwek song set. Although not published in Yeoh and Turpin (2018), it can be seen in the 2009 film *Mer Rrkwer Akert* (Watts et al. 2009).

Verse 30

3 items (AT9713B-s48_50)

Line A		Line B	
♫♩♫♩ ♪♩.	:‖:	♫♩	♫♩♫♩
Ngurlu-japa karna	**kanyi**	**Ngurlungka**	**yulkarlilkarlirla**
ngurlu-japa ka-rna	ka-nyi	ngurlu-ngka	yulkarlilkarli-rla
seeds-Q AUX-1S	carry-NPST	seeds-LOC	lush_green_growth-LOC
"Am I taking the seeds?"		"There are seeds, lush green plants"	

Verse 31A (slow version)

1 item (AT9618A-s14)

Line A			Line B		
♫♪♩.♫♩	♫♩	:‖:	♫♩	♫♪.	♫♩
Waji-rirririrrirli	**maninya**		**Wirringka**	**wirringkarna**	**maninya**
waji-rirririrri-rli	ma-ninya		wirri-ngka	wirri-ngka-rna	ma-ninya
?-?-ERG	get-PRES		water_channel-LOC	water_channel-LOC-1S	get-PRES

? "On the ?? I'm getting it"   "On the water runoff area, on the water runoff area I am getting it"

Comment:

ML: Based on discussion with Fanny Walker Napurrurla, unknown form *waji-rirriririrri* (Line A) may have same meaning as *wirri* (Line B). This is where seed-bearing grasses grow best.

Text and interpretation are tentative, because we were unable to check the song in detail with FW in 2010.

Verse 31B (fast version)

2 items (AT9618A-s15_16)

Line A			Line B		
♫♫♫♩	♫♩	:‖:	♫♩	♫♫	♫♩
Waji-rirririrrirli	**maninya**		**Wirringka**	**wirringkarna**	**maninya**

"On the ?? I'm getting it"   "On the water runoff area, on the water runoff area I am getting it"

Verse 32

3 items (AT9618A-s27_29)

Line A			Line B	
♪♫♩♪♪	♩♪♩♪ :‖:		♪♫♩♪♪	♩♪♩♪
Warlarrpirdipirdi	**muurl-pantirninya**		**Yaliwanajangka**	**muurl-pantirninya**
warlarrpirdipirdi shin(?)	muurl-panti-rninya accurately-pierce-PRES		yali-wana-jangka there-PERL-EL	muurl-panti-rninya accurately-pierce-PRES
"[It] pierces the shin" (?)			"From [being] near there it pierces through"	

Comment:

ML: Text and interpretation are tentative, because we were unable to check the song with Fanny Walker Napurrurla in 2010. *Warlarrpirdipirdi* has been analysed as a partially reduplicated form of the spoken form *warlarrpirdi*.

Verse 33

3 items (AT9618A-s30_32)

Line A

♫♩♪♪	♫♫♪	♫♩♪♪
Jurtarnpijirna	**marnta yarriyarri**	**turnma wantija**
Jurtarnpi-ji-rna Name-TOP-1S	marnta-yarriyarri ?	turnma wanti-ja ? fall-PST

"I, Jurtarnpi ?? fell"

Comments:

FW: Jurtarnpi was the name of a Nakamarra woman, aunt of FW, who had passed away. It is the name of the Dreaming who is singing herself in this song.

ML: The name "Jurtarnpi" may be built on the verb *tarnpi* "follow tracks of", as in Verse 17. The future form of this verb is *tarnpi-ji*.

Verse 34

3 items (AT9618A-s39_41)

Line A Line B

Warraparnu ka **wiirnpinyi** :||: **Kana** **rirrija** **rirrija**

warraparnu ka | wiirn-pi-nyi | kana | rirri-ja | rirri-ja
Great_Desert_Skink AUX | cut-do-NPST | digging_stick | move-PST | move-PST(?)

"Cutting the Great Desert Skink"   "The digging stick moved" (?)

Comments:

FW: The skink *warrarna* breaks up into pieces while cooking.

ML: In glossing, I have assumed that *rirri-ja* is a variant of the verb recorded as *yurirri-ja* "move" in spoken language. *Warraparnu* (eastern Warlpiri) and *warrarna* (western Warlpiri) refer to the same skink species (dialect variation).

Verse 35

3 items (AT9618A-s46_48)

Line A Line B

Ngayikutu **ngayikutu** **yirrarnu** :||: **Kampularna** **yirrarnu**

ngayikutu | ngayikutu | yirra-rnu | kampula-rna | yirra-rnu
tree sp. | tree sp. | put-PST | handle-1S | put-PST

"Put on [a handle made of] *ngayikutu* wood"   "I put a wooden handle"

Verse 36

4 items (AT9618A-s49_52)

Line A

♪ ♩ ♩ ♪ ♩   ♪ ♩ ♩ ♪ ♩   :||:

Jangartpangartparlu   **yirrarnu-nyanu**

Jangartpangartpa-rlu   yirra-rnu-nyanu
Bird sp.-ERG   put-PST-SELF

"Jangartpangartpa put [seeds] on/for himself"

Line B

♪ ♩ ♩ ♪ ♩   ♪ ♩ ♩ ♪ ♩

Yimarinjirli   **yirrarnu-nyanu**

yimarinji-rli   yirra-rnu-nyanu
wooden_scoop-ERG   put-PST-SELF

"With a wooden scoop put [seeds] for himself"

Comments:

FW: Jangartpangartpa is the name of a bird, which is also the old man's name. It lives in the Jipiranpa area.

ML: There may be an association with the place name Jangarlpangarlpa north of Jipiranpa.

Verse 37

2 items (AT9618A-s53_54)

Line A

♪ ♩ ♩ ♪   ♪ ♩ ♩ ♪   :||:

Yimarinjirli   **yirrarnu-nyanu**

yimarinji-rli   yirra-rnu-nyanu
wooden_scoop-ERG   put-PST-SELF

"With a small digging scoop to put [seeds] for himself"

Line B

♪ ♩ ♩ ♪ ♩   ♪ ♩ ♩ ♪

Nyinirtirlkirtirlki   **yirrarnu-nyanu**

nyinirtirlkirtirlki   yirra-rnu-nyanu
any-old-way   put-PST-SELF

"He put [the seeds] for himself any old way"

6 Expert domains of knowledge in Ngurlu *yawulyu* songs from Jipiranpa

Verse 38

1 item (AT9618A-s55)

Line A		Line B	
♪♩♩♪	♪♩♩♪	:‖: ♪♩♩♪	♪♩♩♪
Yimarinjirli	**yirrarnu-nyanu**	**Kiwirnin-karrarlu**	**yirrarnu-nyanu**
yimarinji-rli	yirra-rnu-nyanu	kiwirnin-karra-rlu	yirra-rnu-nyanu
wooden_scoop-ERG	put-PST-SELF	sound-WHILE-ERG	put-PST-SELF

"With a small digging scoop he put [the seeds] for himself"

"He put them for himself while making the sound 'kiwirnin'"

Verse 39

4 items (AT9618B-s08_11)

Line A		Line B		
♫♩♫♩	♫♩	:‖: ♫♩	♫♩	♫♩
Wajiparlu-kula	**luwarni**	**Parrarla**	**karnarla**	**luwarni**
wajipa-rlu-kula	luwa-rni	parrarla	ka-rna-rla	luwa-rni
coolamon-ERG-indeed	yandy-NPST	seed sp.	AUX-1S-3DAT	yandy-NPST

"With a coolamon yandying them"

"I'm yandying the white parrarla seeds"

Verse 40

4 items (AT9618B-s17_20)

Line A		Line B	
♫♩♫♩	♫♩♫♩	:‖: ♫♩♫♩	♫♩♫♩
Walurnarrirlirna	**yarrarra mardarni**	**Wumurljumurljurla**	**yarrarra mardarni**
walurnarri-rli-rna	yarrarra-marda-rni	wumurljumurlju-rla	yarrarra marda-rni
Honey_Grevillea-ERG-1S	winnow-have-NPST	close_together-3DAT	winnow-have-NPST

"I winnow [the seeds] with [the thing made from] honey grevillea"

"Close up winnowing"

Verse 41

2 items (AT9618B-s24_25)

Line A		:||:	Line B	
♫♩♩♩	♫♩♩		♫♩♩♩	♫♩♩
Ngarralalanpa	**rdipijampa**		**Yalumpu-japanpa**	**rdipijampa**
ngarralala-npa	rdipi-ja-mpa		yalumpu-japa-npa	rdipi-ja-mpa
opposite_direction-2S	go_to-PST-ACROSS		that-Q-2S	go_to-PST-ACROSS
"You went past coming from the opposite direction"			"Did you go past there?"	

Comments:

FW: The old Jakamarra man, Kalajirti, went back to Jipiranpa, his own Country, after he had chased and had illicit sex with his two mother-in-laws (two Nangala women).

LB: Note text line placement on melody is reversed in second item, to start with BB text line pair. Note the almost identical text Line A in Verse 18. In this case the rhythm is *yanku* "low", and there is an extra syllable (-*mpa* ACROSS).

Verse 41 (variant)

Sung by FW in elicitation session, 2010.

Line A		:||:	Line B	
♫♩♫♩	♫♩♩		♫♩♫♩	♫♩♩
Yalumpu-japanpa	**rdipijarni**		**Yalumpu-japanpa**	**rdipijarra**
yalumpu-japa-npa	rdipi-ja-rni		yalumpu-japa-npa	rdipi-ja-rra
that-Q-2S	go_to-PST-HITHER		that-Q-2S	go_to-PST-THITHER
"Was that where you came to?"			"Was that where you went?"	

Comments:

LB, ML: This text was offered by FW in 2010 (recording T100719a) when discussing Verse 41 as sung on the 1996 recording. Both lines of this version are based on Line B of Verse 41. The two lines are identical apart from the contrasting morphemes -*rni* "hither" and -*rra* "thither".

Verse 42

3 items (AT9618B-s26_28)

Line A			Line B	
♪♪♪♪	♪♪♪	:||:	♪♪	♪♪♪
Wanjitarra	**luwarni**		**Kilmirr-**	**luwarni**
wanjitarra	luwa-rni		kilmirr-	luwa-rni
spindle(?)	spin-NPST		?	spin-NPST

"Spinning [hairstring] on a spindle"   "He was spinning hairstring" (?)

Comments:

FW: The old man was spinning string from other people's hair on his spindle.

ML: *Kilmirr-* is analysed as a preverb (of unknown meaning) because Warlpiri words must end in a vowel. This is also justified by the anacrusis on the first syllable of the verb *luwarni*.

LB: The rhythm is notated in 3/8. Note that in both lines the second element *luwarni* begins on an anacrusis (meaning the second syllable of *luwarni* bears musical stress).

Verse 43

3 items (AT9618B-s29_31)

Line A			Line B	
♪♪♪♪♪	♪♪♪	:||:	♪♪♪♪♪	♪♪♪
Purlkakulparnarla	**wayurnu**		**Ngurrakulparnarla**	**wayurnu**
purlka-ku-lpa-rna-rla	wayu-rnu		ngurra-ku-lpa-rna-rla	wayu-rnu
old_man-DAT-IMPF-1S-3DAT	search-PST		camp-DAT-IMPF-1S-3DAT	search-PST

"I was looking for the old man"   "I was looking for his camp"

Comment:

LB: Line B was quoted by FW as a comment on Verse 24.

Verse 44

3 items (AT9618B-s35_37)

Line A			Line B	
♪♩♩♩♩	♪♩♩	:‖:	♪♩♩♩♩	♪♩♩
Wakati wakati	**larrarna**		**Lurlupujupuju**	**larrarna**
wakati wakati	l-arrarna		lurlupujupuju	l-arrarna
Portulaca REDUP	(l)-put		kneeling	(l)-put
"Putting Portulaca seeds"			"Crouched on knees putting [seeds]"	

Comment:

ML: *Larrarna* is analysed as vowel-initial "put" verb *arrarna* from an Arandic language source, with initial "l" prefixed to provide a consonant-initial word. In spoken Warlpiri, *yirra-rni* "put", as in Verse 38, is also an Arandic borrowing.

Verse 44 (variant)

[Not on original recording; FW explanation and "correction" in 2010]

Line A			Line B	
Wakati wakati	**larrarna**	:‖:	**Murdujirrpijirrpi**	**larrarna**
wakati wakati	l-arrarna		murdujirrpijirrpi	l-arrarna
Portulaca REDUP	(l)-put		kneeling	(l)-put
"Putting Portulaca seeds"			"Crouched on knees putting [seeds]"	

Comments:

FW: The women were down on their knees gathering up the Portulaca seeds.

LB: Compared to Verse 44, this version substitutes *lurlupujupuju* "kneeling" with the synonym *murdujirrpijirrpi*, based on the stem *murdu* "knee", also pronounced *mirdi*.

Verse 45

4 items (AT9618B-s38_41)

Line A   Line B

♪♩♪♩ ♪♩♪♩ :||: ♪♩♪♩ ♪♩♪♩

Wajiparlu-kula	**kipirninja-yanu**	**Murdujirrpirlirna**	**kipirninja-yanu**
wajipa-rlu-kula	kipi-rninja-ya-nu	murdujirrpi-rli-rna	kipi-rninja-ya-nu
coolamon-ERG-indeed	yandy-INF-go-PST	kneeling-ERG-1S	yandy-INF-go-PST

"Winnowed [seeds] with a coolamon"   "Crouched on knees I was winnowing [seeds]"

Comment:

ML: *Murdujirrpi* in Line B, based on *murdu* "knee", is a shorter form of *murdujirrpijirrpi* "kneeling", which appears in Line B of Verse 44 variant. In spoken Warlpiri, the longer form *murdujirrpijirrpi* is more common.

Verse 45 (variant)

[Not on original recording; FW explanation and correction in 2010]

Parrarla karnarla	**luwaninja-yanu**	:||:	**Murdujirrpirlirna**	**kipirninja-yanu**
parrarla ka-rna-rla	luwa-ninja-ya-nu		murdujirrpi-rli-rna	kipi-rninja-ya-nu
seed_sp. AUX-1S-3DAT	winnow-INF-go-PST		kneeling-ERG-1S	yandy-INF-go-PST

"I was winnowing white *parrarla* seeds"   "Kneeling I was yandying [seeds]"

Comment:

LB: Compared to Verse 45, this version has a different Line A.

Verse 46

4 items (AT9618B-s42_45)

Line A		Line B	
♫ ♩♫ ♩	♫ ♩♫ ♩ :‖:	♫ ♩♫ ♩	♫ ♩♫ ♩
Kumururnturlarna	**kipirninja-yanu**	**Warilyirrilyirri**	**kipirninja-yanu**
kumururntu-rla-rna	kipi-rninja-ya-nu	warilyirrilyirri	kipi-rninja-ya-nu
seed_sp.-LOC-1S	winnow-INF-go-PST	seed_sp.	winnow-INF-go-PST
"I was yandying *kumurruntu* seeds"		"Yandying *warilyirrilyirri* seeds"	

Comment:

ML: *Warilyirrilyirri* is the Warumungu name of a wren species. Seeds can be named after birds because of the shape of the seed or seed cluster, e.g. *puntaru* "little buttonquail"; "Quail's Foot Grass seed".

Verse 47

4 items (AT9618B-s46_49)

Line A		Line B	
♪♪♩♩	♪♩♩. :‖:	♪♪♩♩	♪♩♩.
Wirrijirna	**pakarnu**	**jarnangkarna**	**pakarnu**
wirriji-rna	paka-rnu	jarnangka-rna	paka-rnu
hairstring-1S	strike-PST	bush_fire-1S	strike-PST
"I made hairstring"		"I made it near the fire" (?)	

Comments:

FW: He was spinning hairstring near the fire.

ML: Alternative glossing for *jarnangkarna*: *jarna-ngka-rna* "shoulder-LOC-1S" is "I made/struck it on the shoulder".

Nellie Nangala Wayne

Nangala was born in 1952 and grew up on Mount Doreen cattle station west of Yuendumu. When she was a young girl, she moved to Yuendumu, where she went to school. When she was a young woman, she married and had three children. Nangala has worked at the Yuendumu Old People's Program and the Yuendumu Women's Centre. She has also been an important member of the Yuendumu Women's Night Patrol. Nangala has been central to recent projects to record and document women's *yawulyu*, particularly in her involvement in the production of *Yurntumu-Wardingki Juju-Ngaliya-Kurlangu Yawulyu* (Warlpiri Women from Yuendumu and Curran 2017), as well as public performance events. Nangala is an important ceremonial leader for the Southern Ngaliya women's dance camps.

Ngajuju Nangala, ngapa jukurrpa, kuruwarri ngula karnalu yirrarni, yunparni, jukurrpaju ngapa. Yuwayi ngapa dreamingji. Milyapinyi karna jukurrpa kujakarnalu-jana yirrarni kurdu-kurduku every nganayi yangka school-rlangurla culture day ngula karnalu-jana ngapa jukurrpa yirrarni jukurrpaju and jirrnganja nguna karnalu-jana ngapangka-juku yuwayi.

I am Nangala, belonging to the Ngapa (Rain/Water) *jukurrpa*. We sing and paint the Ngapa Dreaming. I know the *jukurrpa* that we put on the kids at school when there is a culture day, and sometimes we go out and do the Ngapa ceremony with the kids.

Ngula karnalu follow mani song, ngaju-nyangu big sister-rluju learn manurra yuwayi right up. Ngapa yanu yatijarra, yinya kajana yatijarra karrimirra ngapa panukarikilki nyampu nganayi-ngirli nyampu kulkurru yangka my brother-kurlangu Jiwaranpa, far as there. Nganimpa-nyanguju ngulalpa nganimpa-nyangu big brother nyinaja yalumpurla Jiwaranparla outstationrla, yinyaju panukarikilki ka-jana karrimirra yatijarra ngula yanu yuwayi nyampuju ngapa yuwayi.

We follow the songs my big sister taught me, yeah. The Ngapa went up north, and the *Ngapa jukurrpa* on the northern side belongs to those people on that side, our *Ngapa jukurrpa* goes far as my big brother's outstation called Jiwaranpa. The *Ngapa jukurrpa* on the northern side belongs to those people from that area.

Reference

Warlpiri Women from Yuendumu and Georgia Curran. 2017. *Yurntumu-Wardingki Juju-Ngaliya-Kurlangu Yawulyu: Warlpiri Women's Songs from Yuendumu* [including DVD]. Batchelor: Batchelor Institute Press.

Maisie Napurrurla Wayne

Napurrurla was born in Ti-Tree. When she was young, she came down to Yuendumu and grew up around Cockatoo Creek, to the north of Yuendumu. She is a *kirda* for the Ngurlu "edible seed" *jukurrpa* from near Mijilyparnta (Mission Creek) as well as Yumurrpa "white yam" in the Southern Ngaliya part of Warlpiri Country. She is a senior leader for *yawulyu* in Yuendumu and a leader for the biannual Southern Ngaliya dance camps through which she teaches this cultural knowledge to younger generations. Napurrurla has worked as a health worker at the Yuendumu clinic, as a childcare worker and at the Yuendumu Women's Centre.

> *Yuwayi kurdu-warnu-patulku, yuwayi yangka pina-pina-mani-jala karnarlu-jana yuwayi. Yuwayi ngurrju kajikarlipa-jana pina-pina-mani yunparninjaku, yunparninjaku and nganayiki yangka yawulyuku kaji wirnti yinga mardarnirra nyanungurlulku yangka ngalipakariji. Ngajurlangu kajirna lawa-jarrimi yingalu kurdu-warnu-paturlulku mardarnirra nyanungurrarlulku, yuwayi. Pina-pina-jarrijarna ngulaju kamina-wiyi yangka kaminarnalu pina-pina-jarrija jaja-nyanurla, yapirliyi-nyanurla pina-pina-jarrijarna, yuwayi, and pimirdi-nyanurla.*

Yeah pina-pina-jarrijarnalu. Kurdu-warnu-wiyilparna lampunu-wangu-wiyi yangka lampunu turnturnpa kalarnalu nyinaja yuwayi.

Yes we are already teaching our younger generations. It's really good for us to teach the young girls to sing and dance the *yawulyu* so they can keep it and carry on with it when they get older, and when I pass away they can keep it. I was taught by my grandmothers when I was just a young girl, and also my aunties taught me when I was a young girl.

Yangkalpajulu pina-pina-manu ngulaju yalilparna nganayi-pinki kuturu-pinki grab-manu and parraja wali ngulangkulpaju pimirdi-nyanurlu, yapirliyi-nyanurlu marda. "Manta ngula waja", kalajulu kujarlu jiiny-ngarrurnu, "Manta waja and wirntinjayanta yalumpu-kurlu" yuwayi. "Parla-kurlu-ngurlulku manta waja yalumpu parrajalku manta waja! Jungarni wirntiya ngula-kurluju!" Yijardulparna wirntija, nganayi pimirdirlilpaju manu yapirliyirli, jajangku, especially yapirliyi-nyanurlu, pimirdi-nyanurlu. Yuwayi, wurlkumanu yalirli tardungku yuwayi. Yuwayi, ngampurrpa karna nyina yangka yingalu, karlipa-jana wangka purdangirli-warnu-watilki, "Nyuntulku waja yungunpa mardarnirra, ngampurrpa karnangku wangka waja yeah nyuntulku waja kajirna ngajurlangu nyurnurra jarrimi yungunpa nyunturlulku run- mani, kanyinpa nyampuju, kanyi nyunturlurlulku." Yuwayi.

When I grabbed the coolamon or the dancing pole my grandmother and my auntie would say to me, they used to point to me and say "Get that thing for you to dance with!" That's what they used to say to me. Then I would dance with my grandmothers and my aunties, that old lady *Tardu* taught me. Yes, I am interested so we can tell [the young people] "You keep this [knowledge] now so that you can be responsible when I pass away."

Peggy Nampijinpa Martin

Nampijinpa is the daughter of Maudie Nungarrayi and Fuzzy Martin Jangala. Peggy is *kirda* for Pawu (including Warnajarra) and *kurdungurlu* for Patirlirri and the Ngatijirri *jukurrpa* complex. Peggy is a leader in women's business in Willowra. Growing up and living in Willowra, she participated in *yawulyu* – women's ceremonial business – as much as a mother of six could. She learned from the older women over the years. Since 2016, she has helped explain the meanings and ownership of the songs, along with Lucy Nampijinpa Martin and Helen Napurrurla Morton; Peggy has been key in the documentation of Warlpiri women's *yawulyu*. In 2019, she provided a newly received *yawulyu* design for Warnajarra, thereby demonstrating continuity of tradition. Today she is one of two leading businesswomen in Willowra who knows the songs, designs and stories and sings loudly and clearly. She is a co-author of Morais et. al (in press 2024, Aboriginal Studies Press) *Yawulyu: Art and song in Warlpiri women's ceremony*.

Reference

Morais, Megan, Lucy Nampijinpa Martin, Peggy Nampijinpa Martin, Helen Napurrurla Morton, Janet Nakamarra Long, Maisie Napaljarri Kitson, Maureen Nampijinpa O'Keefe, Clarrie Kemarr Long, Jeannie Nampijinpa Presley, Marjorie Nampijinpa Brown, Selina Napanangka Williams, Leah Nampijinpa Martin and Myfany Turpin. In press 2024. *Yawulyu: Art and Song in Warlpiri Women's Ceremony.* Canberra, ACT: Aboriginal Studies Press.

Lucy Nampijinpa Martin

Lucy Nampijinpa Martin was born out bush near Willowra around 1930 to Ruth Nungarrayi and Fuzzy Martin Jangala. Lucy is *kirda* for Pawu (Mount Barkly), including Warnajarra. She is *kurdungurlu* for Patirlirri and Ngatijirri *jukurrpa*. Lucy grew up participating in *yawulyu*. She was an integral part of the women's business documented in 1981–1982, and the Warnajarra series discussed in this book. She has been essential in the repatriation of materials to the community. It is via Lucy that the revitalisation of culture can take place. She is one of the leading businesswomen in Willowra today. As such, it is she who knows the songs and designs. She is a beacon of knowledge. In 2019, when playing songs previously recorded in 1981–1982, it was Lucy Nampijinpa Martin who would join in and sing loudly and clearly. Afterwards, she and Peggy Nampijinpa Martin would explain the songs. Younger women gathered around to listen and to learn. Lucy's work features throughout Chapter 7 – it includes the songs she sang in 1981–1982 and has sung since for further recording purposes.

Chapter 7

Warnajarra: Innovation and continuity in design and lyrics in a Warlpiri women's song set

By Myfany Turpin, Megan Morais, Mary Laughren, Peggy Nampijinpa Martin and Helen Napurrurla Morton

This chapter describes a Warlpiri women's *yawulyu* song set referred to as Warnajarra. The interdependence of design and dance with song warrants some discussion of all three components; however, we focus predominantly on the song texts. These texts make great use of repetition and words from neighbouring languages. Warnajarra is from Pawu, an area south of Willowra community in Central Australia on the Eastern edge of Warlpiri Country (Vaarzon-Morel 1995; Wafer and Wafer 1980). To the east are Anmatyerr and Kaytetye people, whose closely related languages are of the Arandic subgroup – quite different from the Ngumpin-Yapa subgroup to which Warlpiri belongs.

Pawu is often translated as "Mount Barkly", the English name for a prominent hill and outstation on the Pawu homelands (see Figure 7.1). The patrilineal owners or *kirda* for the north-east side of Pawu, including its *jukurrpa* and songs, belong to the Jangala/Nangala and Jampijinpa/Nampijinpa subsections or "skins" (hereafter referred to as J/Nangala and J/Nampijinpa). Warnajarra "Two Snakes" is a major *jukurrpa* associated with Pawu and the J/Nangala and J/Nampijinpa subsections, and the snakes are said to be of Jangala skin.[1] The Warnajarra travel north to Jarrajarra, an area whose patrilineal owners belong to the J/Nungarrayi and J/Napaljarri subsections and that is also associated

---

1   *Warna* "snake", *-jarra* "two of".

with the neighbouring Arandic language Kaytetye. These subsections, along with the J/Napangardi and J/Napanangka, are in the opposite patrimoiety to J/Nangala and J/Nampijinpa, who marry into them. *Jukurrpa* associated with Jarrajarra include Jurlarda "Sugar Bag", and several of the Warnajarra songs relate to Jurlarda *jukurrpa* and the ancestral Moon Man *jukurrpa*.

It is not clear to which type of snakes Warnajarra refers. It may be that the referent of Warnajarra is intentionally vague; however, when asked, Nampijinpa described the snakes as "two little ones, quiet ones, grey ones",[2] which suggests they may be of the species *Lialis burtonis*, Burton's legless lizard. While referred to as *warna* "snakes", these two ancestors are, at some level, also human beings. In addition to the Warnajarra songs described in this chapter, Pawu also has *yawulyu* that celebrate a number of other ancestors, some of which are described in Turpin and Laughren (2013, 2014), Curran (2019) and Warlpiri Women from Yuendumu (2017).

The Warnajarra "Two Snakes" *yawulyu* described in this chapter was recorded by Megan Morais (nee Dail-Jones) in 1981 and 1982 as part of her research on Warlpiri women's ceremonial dance (Dail-Jones [Morais] 1984, 1998).[3] The singers also explained the meanings and words of the songs, which were translated at the time by Janet Nakamarra Long (Morais 1981–1982). Since then, *yawulyu* performance has declined at Willowra, as in other Warlpiri communities. The authors of this chapter subsequently worked with Willowra women in 2016–2019 to gain further understanding of the songs as part of a larger song documentation project.[4] This created opportunities for younger women to hear and practise the songs, as well as learn their significance from Elders. An outcome of the project is a book of the 1981–1982 *yawulyu* (Morais et al., in press).

This chapter assembles work from these two fieldwork periods, almost 40 years apart, to draw attention to aspects of *yawulyu* where there is creativity, an indicator of vitality, such as that found in body designs, and where it is absent, as is the case in the songs – suggesting that this reflects the degree of exposure to and practice of visual arts versus ceremonial singing, respectively. The chapter argues that the poetic structure of songs is founded on knowledge of neighbouring languages and complex patterns of poetic reduplication; that is,

---

2   Peggy Nampijinpa to Helen Morton and Myfany Turpin, 18 August 2019, recording 20190816-1, 6'33". To be archived at AIATSIS.
3   This research was supported by a grant from AIATSIS in 1981.
4   This research was supported by three Australian Research Council grants: LP0560567, FT140100783 and LP140100806.

7 Warnajarra: Innovation and continuity in design and lyrics in a Warlpiri women's song set

Figure 7.1. Map of the Warlpiri region (Morais et al 2024). Warnajarra *yawulyu*, the subject of this chapter, relates to Pawu (Mount Barkly), in the centre of the map.

patterns of syllable reduplication not found in speech. We put forward that the absence of new songs and the decline in the number of singers reflect a lack of familiarity with these structures.

We first discuss the corpus of recordings and then creativity in *yawulyu* designs. We then discuss the relationship between the meaning of verses and visual aspects (dance and design) and issues in identifying words and their meanings. We then discuss aspects of meter and focus on two salient features of Warnajarra song texts: the intermingling of neighbouring Arandic language vocabulary with Warlpiri and poetic reduplication. While both features are present in other Central Australian *yawulyu* (Koch and Turpin 2008), they are particularly prevalent in the Warnajarra verses.

The recordings

The analysis presented in this chapter draws on the two periods of fieldwork mentioned above: 1981–1982 and 2016–2019. A brief description of these events follows. Recordings of Warnajarra, on which the analysis presented here is based, are summarised in Tables 7.1 and 7.2 and described below.

Table 7.1. The 1981/1982 recordings by Megan Morais.

Date	Recording name	Number of song items and verses
28, 29 May 1981	DJ_M01-019516–8	119 song items, 30 verses
23 April 1982	DJ_M02-021717 copy of P. Wafer's recording	37 song items, 9 verses

The recording name refers to the archive number at the Australian Institute of Aboriginal and Torres Strait Islander Studies (AIATSIS).

In 1981, Warnajarra was performed during a *yawulyu* session of singing and painting up for Pawu (Mount Barkly). The main singers were Millie Nangala Kitson, Topsy Nangala, Molly Nungarrayi Martin, Ruby Nampijinpa Forrest, Mitipu Nampijinpa and Lady Napaljarri Morton, with many other women participating. The next day, Warnajarra was performed again, but with dancing following the painting up, and singing accompanying both these activities. This was a typical ceremonial procedure: painting up one day, followed by painting up and then dancing the next (or two days later). There is no doubt that the first *yawulyu* session strengthened the subsequent session.

Another recording of Warnajarra was made on 23 April 1982. This was in preparation for the Mount Barkly Land Claim. The performance was at Mount Barkly Station just after a hunting trip. Both Megan Morais and anthropologist Petronella Wafer (Vaarzon-Morel) were there, and the archived recording is a copy of P. Wafer's recording. This did not include painting up (consequently, *kirda*, the patrilineal ceremonial owners, were not instilled with the power of the ancestors and did not become the embodiment of Warnajarra), but there was spontaneous dancing during the singing, which Morais documented in Benesh Movement Notation (Dail-Jones [Morais] 1984, 1992).[5] A third performance of Warnajarra was held three days later, on 26 April 1982, with painting up and dancing at Pawu. Unfortunately, the recordings are of poor quality due to windy conditions; therefore, they could not be analysed. However, drawings of

---

5   Later in 1982, the audio recording was translated during a meeting with the women, and the accompanying dance movements were discussed.

the ceremonial designs were made, and notes on songs were written down as the women painted up (see Figure 7.2).

In 2013, Myfany visited Megan in California. Following from this, a request for Megan's collection (audio, drawings, notes, photos) was made to AIATSIS for Myfany to bring to Willowra. In 2016, Mary and Myfany worked with Willowra women to transcribe and translate the songs on these recordings, which often resulted in further singing; in 2019, Megan also came to Willowra. Only the sessions relating to Warnajarra are listed below.

Table 7.2. The 2016–2019 recordings in which Warnajarra was performed or translated.

Date and recorders	Location	Content	Number of song items and verses
30 June 2016 (Laughren and Turpin)	Willowra	Discussion of songs on DJ_M01-019517 followed by a performance of Warnajarra: Peggy Nampijinpa, Lucy Nampjinpa, Leah Nampijinpa and Marilyn Nampjinpa	48 song items, 22 verses
16 August 2019 (Turpin and Morton)	Alice Springs	Discussion of songs on DJ_M01-019517 and M01-019518 with Peggy Nampijinpa and Helen Morton	
25 Nov 2019 (Turpin and Morais)	Willowra	Discussion of songs from Pawu with Peggy Nampijinpa, Lucy Nampijinpa, Marilyn Nampijinpa and Marjorie Brown Nampijinpa	

Relationship between design, dance and song text

Body painting and dance are integral to a full *yawulyu* performance. Both only occur with song and can provide further information or alternate understandings of the accompanying song. A brief look at body painting gives insight into the vitality and change that is currently taking place in *yawulyu* in Willowra.

Figure 7.2 is a copy of a body painting design that the Warlpiri women painted frequently during *yawulyu* in 1981–1982. This accompanied multiple song sets, including Majardi (hairstring waistbelt) that women use in Pawu dances. As Munn (1973, 146) stated, Warlpiri people perceive designs and songs as a single complex and treat them as "complementary channels of communication about an ancestor". A design is sung on. The women doing the painting up must sing. Painting up and singing activate the *kuruwarri* (power) of the

Figure 7.2. Women's Warnajarra body design that represents Majardi (hairstring waistbelt, see Figure 7.4), 26 April 1982. Drawing by Megan Morais.

jukurrpa. The designs, songs and dance movements are comparable in that the different components of each can be perceived to be multifaceted, with many levels of interpretation (Morais et al., in press). This creates a potential avenue for changing associations or meanings.

While Myfany and Megan were going over Pawu designs and archived recordings in 2019, Lucy Nampijinpa Martin and Peggy Nampijinpa Martin sang one of the Warnajarra verses. At the end of the singing, Peggy said she had a new design. It came to her while singing the verse in Figure 7.3 (Verse 33).[6] She had Selina Napanangka Williams draw the design as she explained it. Peggy said it was Majardi from Pawu. She included a drawing of a Majardi (hairstring waistbelt) she intended to make (see Figure 7.4).

---

6   The musical Figures represent a verse. The top row is the speed of the clap beat ("x") accompanying the singing (showing both 1982 and 2019 tempo). Where the verse is divided into two lines, these are indicated as "A" and "B". The row underneath is a rhythmic representation of the vocal line, and the dotted double lines show that the line repeats before moving on to the other line. The row beneath this is the sung syllables. The rows beneath this show the Warlpiri and/or Arandic speech equivalents with an English gloss or linguistic abbreviation in small caps underneath. Poetic words and reduplication are shown in grey. Where possible, a free English translation is provided underneath. See Appendix 7.1 for list of linguistic abbreviations.

7 Warnajarra: Innovation and continuity in design and lyrics in a Warlpiri women's song set

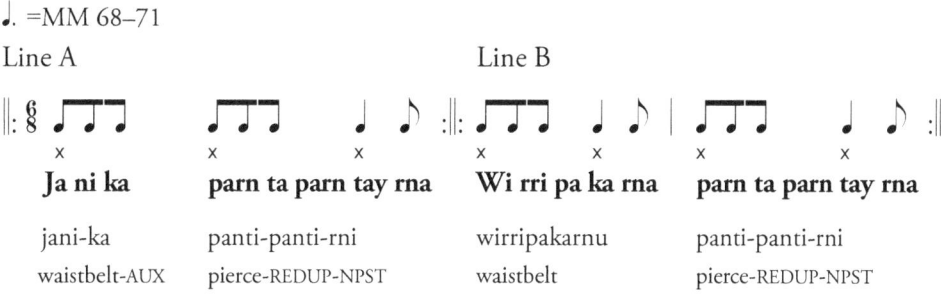

"Sewing the waistbelt, Sewing the ceremonial skirt"

Figure 7.3. The Warnajarra verse from 1982 (Verse 33, DJ_M02-021714, song items 1–3) that inspired Peggy's new design, which was drawn after Peggy sang this verse on 25 November 2019 (audio recording 20191125_6).

Peggy's new design (Figure 7.4) is significantly different to the 400 designs copied during *yawulyu* performances in 1981–1982. Differences in the design style include the break-up of the yoke, which predominantly had 1–3 lines painted under the neck going from shoulder to shoulder (see Figure 7.2). In the 2019 design, Peggy had created the yoke lines with small red, white and yellow squares. In effect, these squares create, as well as break up, the yoke lines. Significantly, the Warlpiri hand sign for *yawulyu* replicates the lines across the yoke, moving without pause from one shoulder to the other. In other words, in the past, the unbroken yoke represented *yawulyu*. Thus, now we have an altogether different rendition of *yawulyu* designs.

In addition to a change in the format of the yoke, Peggy's 2019 design on the arms has changed in that it replicates the design on the yoke – multiple times over. This differs from the 1980s designs, where the arm designs usually replicated those on the breasts rather than the yoke. Figure 7.5 shows how arm designs replicated breast designs in 1981. Additionally, in the past, women painted circles and dots rather than small squares. Interestingly, Peggy's breast elements are somewhat reminiscent of a 1981 Warnajarra body design from Pawu, demonstrating some continuity within her innovation.

Peggy's 2019 design (see Figure 7.4) is indicative of changes that are occurring in *yawulyu* designs today: a new design inspired by a Warnajarra song sung 40 years ago and still being sung in 2019.[7]

Designs, songs and dance movements are comparable in that the different components of each can be perceived to be multifaceted, with many levels of

---

7   For further information on changes in *yawulyu* today, see Morais et al. (in press).

Figure 7.4. The 2019 *yawulyu* design created by Peggy Nampijinpa Martin after singing the Warnajarra verse in Figure 7.3 (Verse 33). Penned by Selina Napanangka Williams. Underneath is the Majardi (hairstring belt) penned by Peggy. Both were later redrawn by Megan Morais and are presented here.

interpretation. Just as body designs provide multi-symbolic information, dance typically includes gestures and the use of highly symbolic props. The dance gestures can relate to the meaning of the text, or dance may add something extra about the text. Here we provide one example of each and refer readers to Dail-Jones [Morais] (1984, 1992, 1998) for further information about Warlpiri dance.

7 Warnajarra: Innovation and continuity in design and lyrics in a Warlpiri women's song set

Figure 7.5. Warnajarra yawulyu body design from Pawu. Representation on paper by Megan Morais, 1981.

Dance related to the meaning of the text

As in many *yawulyu*, dance is often a symbolic representation of the meaning of the verse it accompanies. In the early 1980s, Willowra women did not allow video recording or still photography, so Megan notated the dance using Benesh movement notation. Thus, Megan's descriptions of the dance are based on both analysis through transcription, as well as field notes from the time. Consider the verse described in Figure 7.7 (Verse 13) and its accompanying dance described below. The senior women explained that ancestral women sang this verse while mending the traditional Majardi (hairstring waist belt) they were wearing.[8] (A detailed discussion of the words in this verse and their meanings is provided following Figure 7.7.)

The accompanying dance movement involved hands near one's lap, palms facing in towards the stomach and forefingers touching, fingertips pointing down, and doing a slight patting action of 3–5 beats (down on the main beat) as the hands move to the left of the body while the upper torso and head turn to the left, following the action of the hands. The action was repeated alternately to the right side and the left. One person threw dirt over her back during these

---

8   Majardi are worn as a ceremonial sporran or apron by men and women. They are referred to in the early ethnographic literature as a "pubic tassel". They are often the subject matter of *yawulyu*.

movements (the Benesh notation of this dance can be seen in Appendix 7.2). The movements in this dance relate to both the meaning and the rhythm of the verse. The rhythm of the verse is made up of a 5-syllable/note pattern (♪♪♪♩♩) that repeats four times (Figure 7.3, Verse 13). This vocal rhythm may correspond to the "slight patting action of 3–5 beats". The body painting worn by the performers is also said to represent the word in the text, Majardi (hairstring waist belt) (see Figure 7.2).

Dance not directly related to the literal meaning of the song text

The dance can also be a symbolic representation of actions or objects that are not mentioned in the text. For example, the dance accompanying the verse in Figure 7.6 (Verse 6) involves turning the torso and the head to the right, and down, and then to the left and down, *ad lib*. This symbolises how the snakes were looking around as they were hunting. Literally, the verse text is "Make a gully, you two snakes!" The song evokes a small gully or water channel at Pawu, where water flows from a spring. The Two Snakes got to this site where they made this gully for the water to run through. The dance action symbolises the looking-around action by the Two Snakes, an action not overtly referred to in the verse.

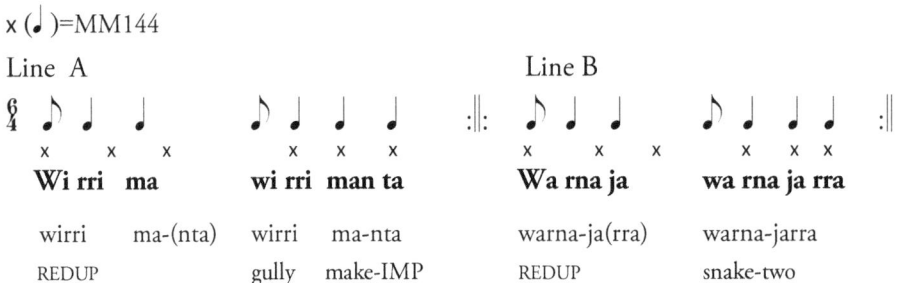

Figure 7.6. A verse of Warnajarra where the dance represents the Two Snakes ancestors looking around (Verse 6).

Like most Warnajarra verses, the verse in Figure 7.6 shows reduplication. The sequences *wirrima wirrimanta* in Line A and *warnaja warnajarra* in Line B are both examples of reduplication. In both cases, the reduplication is partial rather than full – as the full words are *wirri-manta* and *warna-jarra*. Partial reduplication can copy from either the beginning of a word (left edge) or from the end of a word (right edge). In this verse, both reduplications copy from the left edge of the word, omitting the final syllable: *wirrima(nta)*, *warnaja(rra)*. Both leftwards and rightwards reduplication is

7 Warnajarra: Innovation and continuity in design and lyrics in a Warlpiri women's song set

present in Warnajarra. Finally, the entire line is a reduplication – there is no unaccounted-for text in either line. Here, we can say that reduplication is a method of line formation. The remainder of this chapter outlines the many different patterns of reduplication: partial and whole reduplication, from the left edge or right edge, and even more complex patterns. The discussion thus far has assumed that identifying the underlying words is uncontroversial; however, this is rarely the case in song.

Issues regarding identifying words in songs

It can be difficult to identify words in Aboriginal songs, as many researchers have observed (Brown et al. 2017; Clunies Ross, Donaldson and Wild 1987; Koch and Turpin 2008; see also Vaarzon-Morel et al., Chapter 8, this volume). Varying degrees of certainty about a speech equivalent have led researchers to talk about songs ranging from complete transparency (where the words are unanimously agreed upon) to opacity, where speakers may not know the speech equivalent (Walsh 2007). Opacity can be due to sound changes imposed on words or because foreign, archaic or special poetic words ("spirit language") are used (Brown et al. 2017). The task is even more challenging because songs are often highly elliptical and enjoy multiple possible interpretations. Vagueness and ambiguity seem to be highly prized, possibly to maximise the relevance of a verse in multiple contexts.

Even the most transparent song texts can have a degree of ambiguity. By way of illustration, consider the Warnajarra verse in Figure 7.7 (Verse 13). Note that the final hemistich (half-line) is identical in both lines, as is common in *yawulyu*.

Figure 7.7. Ambiguity in the words of a Warnajarra verse (Verse 13).

There are three possible speech equivalents for the final hemistich in each line. It could be *panti-panti-rni* "sewing" or the past form *pantu-pantu-rnu* "sewed", or *parnta-parnta* "covering", followed by either *-rna* "I" or *rna*, a common song vocable (with no known meaning) occurring at the end of a bar as an upbeat (Turpin and Laughren 2013).⁹ It is the presence of the auxiliary *ka* in Line A that determines the correct interpretation shown as "a)". In addition, there are two possible referents of the song: a group of ancestral women or the two ancestral Jangala Snake Men, who were later described as sewing string on their belt to make a hairstring waist belt.¹⁰

This verse also illustrates two further points about how *yawulyu* verses are formed. First, notice the recurrence of *wirri* in this verse and the previously considered verse (Figures 7.6 and 7.7), in seemingly semantically unrelated words: *wirri* "gully" and *wirripakarnu* "hairstring belt", also present in the everyday Warlpiri word *wirriji* "hairstring". The use of *wirri* may serve to unite the images to which these songs relate. Repetition of syllables may thus become associated with particular meanings.

Second, the verse is made of two nearly identical lines. Their rhythm is the same, and the text in the second hemistich is the same; further, while the words in the first hemistiches differ (*ngajularri*, *wirripakarnu*), their meaning "waistbelt" is the same. Such parallelism between lines is a common way of forming a *yawulyu* verse. Such methods of line formation are particularly prevalent in Warnajarra and are the focus of this chapter.

Vocabulary from neighbouring languages

A striking feature of the Warnajarra song texts is the large number of words from neighbouring Arandic languages and a small number likely from Warumungu, spoken further north. Pawu is close to the eastern extremity of Warlpiri Country, and there is a long history of people from this area interacting with Anmatyerr- and Kaytetye-speaking people to the east (Vaarzon-Morel 1995; Wafer and Wafer 1980). In the 1980s, many older *yawulyu* performers at Willowra spoke or understood either or both Anmatyerr and Kaytetye, as well as Warlpiri.¹¹ Arandic languages and Warlpiri have different sound systems. One of the main differences is that Warlpiri words start with a consonant and end in a vowel and have stress on their first syllable, while Arandic words mostly

---

9   Given a tendency for verbs to occur in line-final position and to be in non-past forms, we suggest that *panti-panti-rni* "sewing" is the most likely speech equivalent.
10 Peggy Nampijinpa to Helen Napurrurla and Myfany Turpin, 16 August 2019 (audio file 20190816-01, to be deposited at AIATSIS).
11 Despite their similar sound systems, Kaytetye and Anmatyerr use different spelling systems. Throughout this chapter, the Anmatyerr spelling system based on that in Green (2008) is used for all Arandic words to simplify the comparison of Arandic words with Warlpiri.

start with a vowel and have stress on their second (i.e., first post-consonantal) syllable (Breen 2001). Arandic words are woven into poetic lines altered to adhere to the Warlpiri sound system. This usually involves adding a consonant to the beginning of a word and turning central vowels into a high vowel, "i" or rounded "u" and changing the quality of the final vowel (not written in Anmatyerr orthography), which is typically "a" when sung although a high vowel in Warlpiri speech. For example, consider the final word of Lines A and B in Figure 7.8 (Verse 18). This is likely an Anmatyerr verb meaning "sitting around", *internerl-anek*, which becomes *l + intirnirl-aniki* in song. It can be seen that the added consonant "l" is actually the final consonant of the relativiser *-arl* from the end of the previous word, transferred to the beginning of the next word *internerl-anek*. The "e" is altered throughout to "i" when borrowed into Warlpiri.[12] Note that the line-final vowel is "a", not "i", which is a common line-final vowel in *yawulyu*, especially in Arandic. In Line B, the speech equivalent could be Kurraya, as pointed out by a reviewer, an important place that features in Warumungu *yawulyu*, or Arandic *kwerray* "girl-VOC". Lexical ambiguity arising from Arandic, Warumungu and Warlpiri words as possible speech equivalents is one source of ambiguity in song meaning.[13]

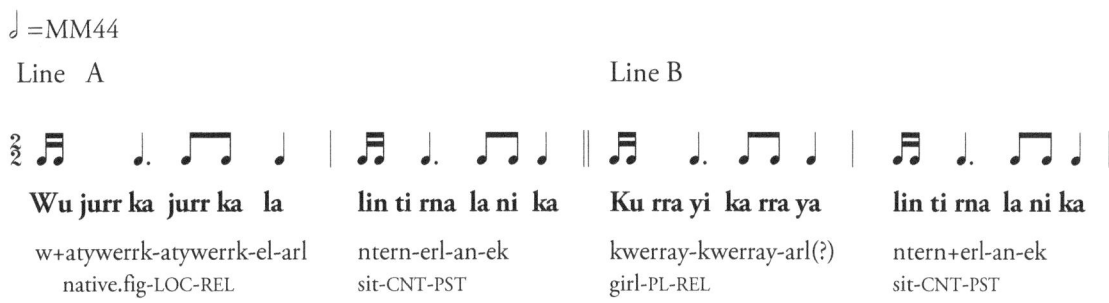

Figure 7.8. A Warnajarra verse with speech equivalents from neighbouring language varieties, here showing Arandic words on which the song text is likely based (Verse 18).[14]

---

12 In spoken Warlpiri, words of Arandic origin are pronounced with a final high vowel "i" or "u", subject to vowel harmony conventions.

13 Meggitt (1966, 26–28) discusses the interpretation of song lines inherited from non-Warlpiri sources based on phonetic similarity, and the accompanying vagueness as to their literal meaning.

14 The tempo of this slow meter song is based on the minim, as this is closest duration to the clap beat that occurs in other slow meter verses. Bar lines correspond to both the grouping of two beats in a bar and the hemistich.

Most Arandic words begin with a vowel, but Warlpiri words must begin with a consonant – hence the insertion of "w" before "*atywerrk*" in Line A in Figure 7.8. Typically, the consonants "w" or "y" are added to the beginning of Arandic words borrowed into Warlpiri. For example, *wijirrki* is the Warlpiri, and Warumungu, word for the native fig (*Ficus brachypoda*). In *yawulyu* also, additional consonants are inserted word-initially, including nasal consonants "m" and the lateral "l", which have their origin in the Arandic song practice of transferring the final consonant of a monosyllabic suffix to the beginning of a word (as on the verb in Figure 7.8). In Arandic *yawulyu*, when there is no available final consonant to be transferred, a glide is inserted line-initially, as in Line A in Figure 7.8, or the initial vowel is dropped (Turpin 2005, 193, 2007). The retention of rounding on the vowel following "j" in *wujurrka* (Figure 7.8) mirrors the Arandic spoken form of *atywerrk*.

Some Arandic words have been incorporated into Warlpiri and have a set form, such as *yalkiri* "sky"; however, in song, we find that there can be a different consonant at the beginning of the word. For example, "sky" is sung with an initial "m" not "y" in the verse in Figure 7.9 (Verse 30). This is the result of transferring the final consonant of the Arandic verbal inflection *-em* (non-past), "m" to the beginning of the line. Note that while the speech equivalents in the middle of the line are not known, it is possible they end with either the locative (*-el*) or relativiser (*-arl*), and that this is the source of the "l" at the beginning of the Anmatyerr verb. This is the same resyllabification seen in Figure 7.8, a process that also occurs in connected speech.[15] In contrast, the line-initial consonant "m" is transferred from the previous line-final suffix, a process documented in Hale (1984, 260) and Turpin (2005, 236) in other Warlpiri and Arandic songs respectively. The line, as a poetic structure, is not a feature of speech; thus, line-final consonant transfer is unique to central Australian singing traditions. Notice too that the transfer of final consonants in Figures 7.8 and 7.9 is limited to monosyllabic root-level suffixes: a constraint also found in other Arandic–Warlpiri songs (Hale 1984; San and Turpin 2021).

---

15 See Hale (1984) for a discussion of this phenomenon, which also contributes to the Warlpiri spoken lexicon.

7 Warnajarra: Innovation and continuity in design and lyrics in a Warlpiri women's song set

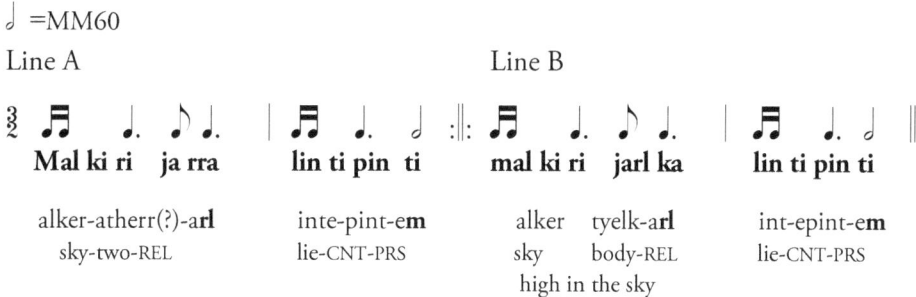

Figure 7.9. A Warnajarra verse with Arandic vocabulary and final consonant "l" transferred to the beginning of the next word and "m" to the beginning of the next line (Verse 30).

Variability in the initial consonant of the word is a further telltale sign that these are not everyday Warlpiri words but purely song forms. For example, the verse in Figure 7.7 has the word *ngajularri* "waistbelt", but this is sometimes sung as *majularri*, varying the initial consonant.[16]

Meter

Most of the 28 Warnajarra verses fall into one of two broad meters: a slow meter and a fast syncopated meter. Contrasting meters within a song set are also found in other Warlpiri *yawulyu* (Turpin and Laughren 2013, 2014), as well as in neighbouring Kaytetye (Turpin 2005). Only one Warnajarra verse has a meter other than these two fast and slow meters. This is the verse considered in Figure 7.7 (Verse 13). It has a compound triple meter, a meter frequently used in Ngatijirri "Budgerigar" *yawulyu* (Turpin and Laughren 2013). The Warnajarra and Ngatijirri *jukurrpa* tracks intersect, and it may be that this triple meter verse in the context of a Warnajarra performance alludes to the Ngatijirri *jukurrpa* associated with Wirliyajarrayi (Willowra) where the performers were living.

Approximately half the Warnajarra verses are in the fast syncopated meter, which often consists of some repeated text. Figure 7.10 (Verse 3) shows a verse in the fast meter, where reduplication can be seen with *jartampa* in Line A and *lingkaji* in Line B (*lingkaji* is, in fact, a triplication, as identified by the underlining). Clapping occurs on every crotchet beat. Figure 7.11 (Verse 2) shows a verse in the slow meter – in this case, slow triple meter with a regular clap accompaniment (marked by "x") at a tempo of MM = 50 bps (represented as a

---

16 Warlpiri *mawulyarri* and Warumungu *makkulyarri* are alternate words for *ngajularri*; in both languages, *majardi* also refers to a hairstring belt.

dotted minimum in Figure 7.8). Slow meter often has no clap accompaniment (e.g., Figures 7.7 and 7.8). The slow meter may allude to the Moon Dreaming, which also intersects with Pawu.[17]

The slow meter verse in Figure 7.11 (Verse 2) has the same words as the verse in Figure 7.10 (Verse 3): *jartampa* and *lingkaji*. Comparing these two verses with the same words reveals how different patterns of reduplication and the use of different meters can produce vastly different verses.

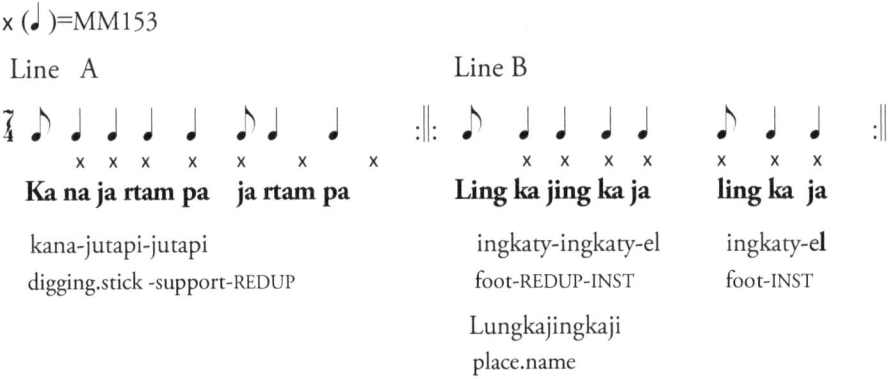

Figure 7.10. A Warnajarra verse in the fast meter, with 153 clap beats per minute (Verse 3). It is based on the words *kana*, *ingkatyel* and a form of either *jurtampi* or *jutapi*.

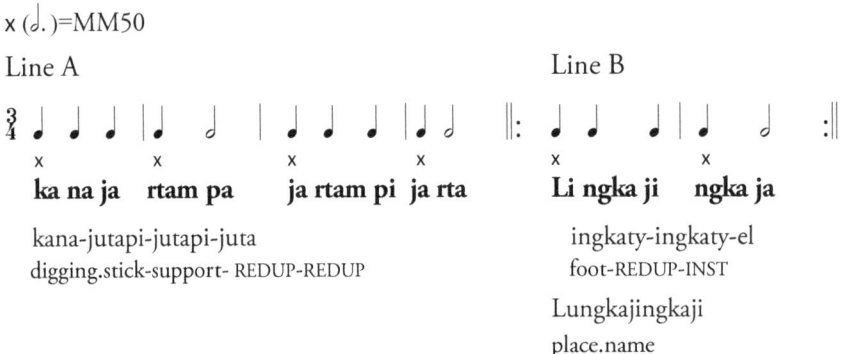

Figure 7.11. A Warnajarra verse in the slow meter, with 50 clap beats per minute (Verse 2). Note that it is based on the same words as the verse in the fast meter in Figure 7.10 above.

---

17 A *yawulyu* performance relating to the Pawu and Patirlirri areas includes one verse in this same slow meter, which is said to be associated with the Moon Dreaming (Turpin and Laughren 2013, 408).

In Figures 7.10 and 7.11, the immediate reduplication is either partial (e.g., *lingkaji-ngkaji*; *jartampi-jarta*) or, if it is identical, its rhythm contrasts (e.g., *jartampa jartampa*). Note that in the identical triplication, there is an intervening partial reduplication (*lingkaji ngkaji lingkaji*). Partial reduplication can be from the right edge, leaving out the initial syllable (*li-ngkaji ngkaji*), or from the left edge, leaving out the final syllable (*jarta-mpi jarta*).

These different patterns of reduplication can lead to different interpretations of what the speech words are, depending on whether one "hears" Warlpiri or Arandic speech equivalents. For example, *lingka* is a word for "snake" in Warlpiri, while *ingka* or *angkety* is "foot" in various Arandic languages. We return to this verse in more detail below, where we discuss triplication and the relationship between linguistic variety and reduplication type.

Reduplication

One of the most striking features of the Warnajarra verses is the use of reduplication. In speech, reduplication can be a means of word formation (e.g., English "hanky-panky", "riff-raff") or mark grammatical information, commonly plurality or repeated action. Other types of reduplication occur only in poetry and song, where it may be associated with specific meanings or used as a marker of the genre and a method of line formation. Reduplication can involve only part of a word, such as the consonants in "riff-raff" or the "anky" part of "hanky-panky", or it can be an exact copy of the word, as is the case for contrastive focus in English. In poetry and song, reduplication can also be a means of line formation. In this section, we illustrate the different functions of reduplication and their many different forms found in Warnajarra. Reduplication, both total and partial, is a more significant feature of the Warlpiri lexicon than of the English lexicon (see Nash 1986).[18]

Lexical reduplication

Lexical reduplication is common in spoken Warlpiri and song texts, including Warnajarra. Figure 7.12 (Verse 22) shows a Warnajarra verse that contains the Warlpiri word *munga-munga* "dark" (when sung, it is pronounced *minga-minga*), a lexical reduplication of *munga* "darkness, night". This reduplicated word is also one of the names of Ancestral Dancing Women who travel from

---

18 See Fabricius (1998) for a wider discussion of reduplication patterns in Australian languages.

west to east in association with male initiation ceremonies. The reduplication forms the entire line (Line B).[19]

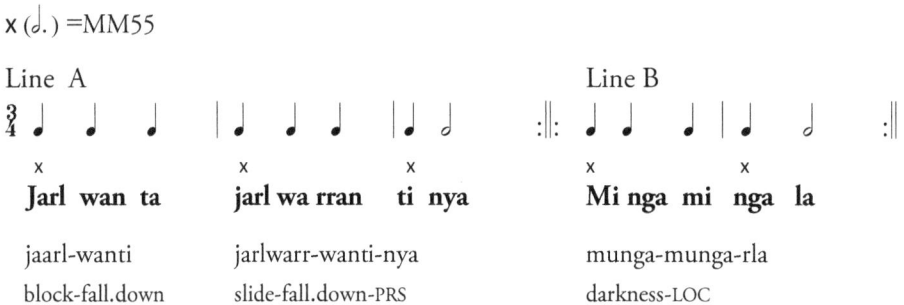

Figure 7.12. An example of lexical reduplication, *munga-munga* "darkness", forming an entire line (Line B) in Warnajarra (Verse 22).

Lexical reduplication can also form just part of a line. This can be seen in both lines of the verse in Figure 7.13 (Verse 1), where the second (and final) word of each line is *jarna-jarna*.

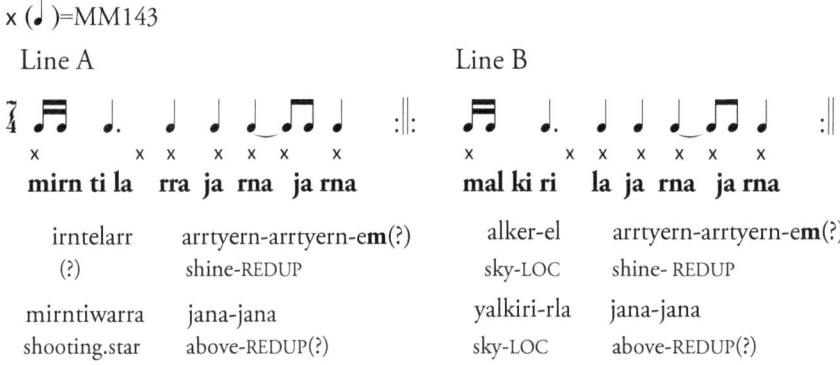

Figure 7.13. A lexical reduplication *jarna-jarna* in the second half of the lines (A and B) in Warnajarra (Verse 1).

Jarna-jarna may be the Warlpiri word *jarna-jarna*, a genre of men's ceremony, or (as a reviewer suggested) the reduplicated form of the everyday Warumungu word *jana* "above, high", which is appropriate in this context.[20] However, the

---

19   We discuss the partial poetic reduplication in Line A, *jarlwa-nta jarlwa*, below.

20   The *Warlpiri Encyclopaedic Dictionary* defines *jarna-jarna* as "songs sung by men during dance with *witi* poles performed prior to initiation". Note that *jarna-jarna* also means "loads carried on the shoulder", leading to further ambiguity of the verse (Laughren et al. 2022).

7 Warnajarra: Innovation and continuity in design and lyrics in a Warlpiri women's song set

line initial "m" suggests an Arandic source for both lines, as shown at the end of both lines in Figure 7.13.

Grammatical reduplication

Grammatical reduplication is far more common in Warlpiri than English; unsurprisingly, it is also found in song texts, including Warnajarra. Figure 7.14 (Verse 4) shows a verse in the fast meter that contains grammatical reduplication, which signals a distributive action or multiple subjects. The second word of Line A, *warangka* "across the shoulders", is reduplicated; thus, the phrase (and line) as a whole means "(multiple people) going along with a digging stick across their shoulder". Line B contains a similar reduplication, although the speech equivalent of *-jutapi* "for support" is less certain.

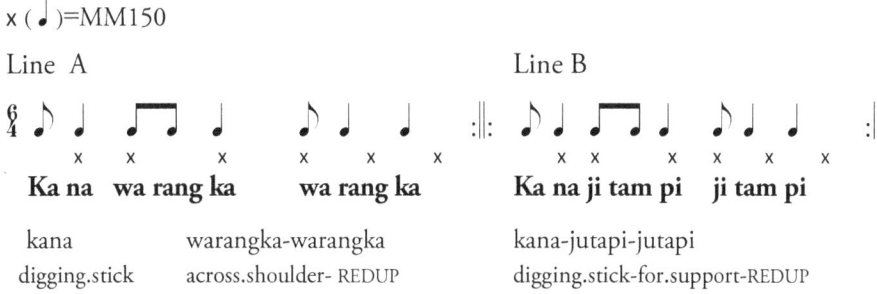

"With a digging stick on my shoulder and a digging stick for support I travel"

Figure 7.14. Grammatical reduplication marking distributive action (Verse 4).

Notice that, in both lines, the base is set to a different rhythm than the reduplicant: ♫♩ (base) and ♪♩ ♩ (reduplicant). In the fast meter, the base has two short (S) notes followed by one long (L) note (i.e., SSL), while the reduplicant has SLL (short-long-long). In the fast meter, we see the greater use of long notes in the reduplicant as if it is an emphatic rendition of the base.

Word repetition

In Warnajarra, repetition of a nominal occurs, and it is unclear whether this is lexical or grammatical reduplication to create a word with a slightly different but related meaning[21] or simply the repetition of a word forming two separate

---

21 Warlpiri has grammatical reduplication that marks a non-default reading of a word; that is, it may indicate plurality, or repeated actions, or it may denote something similar to the denotation of the simple term (e.g., *yalyu* "blood", *yalyu-yalyu* "red" (i.e., blood-like); *kunjuru* "smoke", *kunjuru-kunjuru* "smoky, grey").

225

noun phrases. Figure 7.15 (Verse 19) shows a verse with word repetition in both lines. The second word of Line A repeats *kunjuru* "smoke"; and in Line B, lirranji – the only word in the line – repeats. The reduplicant in both words is in line-final position. The difference in the final vowel of the words (*kunjura/kunjuray*) is due to a process found only in song, where alteration of line-final vowels occurs to form a diphthong (written "ay") in accordance with an ABBA pattern of line repetition (Turpin 2022).

Figure 7.15. Grammatical reduplication marking plurality (Lines A and B, Verse 19) in the slow meter (Verse 19).

There is no evidence from explanations given by singers that such word repetition creates a different meaning. Notice also how the repeated word is set to a different rhythmic pattern than the former: ♫ ♩. ♫ ♩, which may suggest a repeated word rather than a lexical reduplication. To the researcher's ear, it is as if it is an emphatic or exaggerated repetition of the base.

In Figures 7.13, 7.14 and Line A of 7.15, the reduplication accounts for only some of the line as the first word in these lines is not reduplicated (*mirntiwarri, kana, warlu*). In contrast, the repetition in Figure 7.15, Line B (*lirranji lirranji*) accounts for the whole line; thus, this is also a method of line formation.

Poetic reduplication

The term "poetic reduplication" refers to reduplication that occurs only in song rather than speech; thus, its meaning is particular to and associated with *yawulyu* and presumably other aspects of the *jukurrpa* as this is what *yawulyu* pertains to. If such reduplications were used in speech, presumably, they would be used deliberately to allude to *yawulyu*. As a point of comparison, consider child-directed speech words, such as "wee-wees", that connote a context of children. Poetic reduplication in Aboriginal song has been noted in other Central Australian songs (Strehlow 1971, 189; Turpin 2005, 204, 212), including in another *yawulyu* song from Pawu (Turpin and Laughren 2013). The remainder of the chapter identifies the different types of reduplication patterns, relating these to whether the speech equivalent is Warlpiri or Arandic and whether the accompanying meter is fast or slow.

Partial reduplication

In spoken Warlpiri, there are two principal types of partial reduplication, both of which involve the reduplication of a metrical foot that contains two (or three) vocalic mora. At the left edge of a word, the initial morpheme can be reduplicated and preposed to the base. This is especially productive with preverbs and verbs. Considering first preverbs, one example is *jaka-jakarr-(w) apa* "walk squeaking foot". The partial reduplication of the manner preverb *jakarr* as *jaka* is in free variation with the total reduplication of the preverb (i.e., *jakarr-jakarr-*). Verb stems minus the inflectional suffix also reduplicate, such as *panti-rni* "pierce/poke" -> *panti-panti-rni* "pierce/poke many/repeatedly". These productive grammatical reduplications contrast with lexical reduplication where the reduplicant is monomoraic, as in *jarnjarn-paka-rni* "chop into pieces", *kunykuny-ngarni* "suck on".[22] Non-productive lexical reduplication is also a feature of some nouns, such as *kirlil-kirlil-pa* "Galah" or *jintirr-jintirr-pa* "Willy Wagtail" where *-pa* is added to the consonant-final reduplicant, thus creating a vowel-final word as required. Right edge reduplicants are of the form (C)CVCV, and these are not productive. The reduplicated CVCV foot may follow a monomoraic base (e.g., *ji-wiri-wiri* "rising smoke"; *ja-rlantu-rlantu* "roomy, spacious") or a bimoraic foot (e.g., *jirnta-rarra-rarra* "squirting"; *jurda-warra-warra* "skipping"; *laja-warra-warra(-pi-nyi)* "get lots of"). These lexical right edge reduplicants can also be of the form CCVCV, where the initial C acts as a syllable coda to the preceding CV sequence (e.g., *ja-rntarru-rntarru* "on knees"). Warlpiri words cannot begin with a CC sequence, nor can they begin with the consonant "ly", which is at the left edge of the reduplicant in *ji-lyiwi-lyiwi* "sizzle". Preverbs or verb stems longer than two syllables may also be reduplicated, but always as total reduplications (e.g., *pirltarru-pirltarru-yani* "stretch out visible for a long way"). These are productive.

Taking Kaytetye as an example of a neighbouring Arandic language, total reduplication indicates plurality or an increase or decrease in the intensification of meaning and occurs with nominals, preverbs and noun formatives. Examples include the nominal *arrilpe* "sharp" -> *arrilp-arrilpe* "very sharp"; the preverb *pererre* "back and forth", as in *pererre ape-* "go back and forth" -> *pererre-pererre ape-* "go back and forth lots of times"; and the noun formative *awap-* "block", as in

---

22 There is no *kuny-ngarni* since preverbs must be minimally bimoraic (with two vowel morae); instead, there is *kuuny-ngarni* "suck" with a long vowel. Productive reduplication would give *kuuny-kuuny-ngarni*.

awap-arre- "block" -> *awap-awap-arre-* "block lots of things". There is also partial reduplication of final CVCV in lexical items *pwe-lyerrelyerre* "dust, marks".[23] With some words, there are two possible analyses for the reduplication pattern, such as the Kaytetye word for "galah", *kelkelkelke*, which could be analysed as *ke-lelkelelke* (12323) or *kelelkelel-ke* (12123). The 12323 reduplication patterns also occur in Kaytetye *yawulyu*, occurring in 14 of 90 lines (Turpin 2005, 221). The reduplication is also attested in the occasional longer lexical item, such as *elerterre-kamekame* "Australian kestrel". Partial verb stem reduplication is more complex and not discussed here (for details, see Panther 2020).

Poetic reduplication is typically partial reduplication. Figure 7.16 (Verse 8) is a partial reduplication that forms the entire line. It is in the fast meter. The "base" of the reduplication is a four-syllable word *warna-jarra* "snake-two", and the "reduplicant" copies only the first three syllables (*warnaja*), leaving off the final syllable "*rra*"; thus, it copies from the left edge in a manner not found in the spoken language. Notice how the copied element *warnaja* has the exact same rhythm (SLL) in both the base and the reduplicant. Only the relationship between the clap beat (x) and the vocal line differs. In the base, the beat coincides with the second syllable; in contrast, in the reduplicant, it coincides with the first syllable. Copying of the rhythm is only attested in partial reduplication; whole reduplication always employs a different rhythm in the base and reduplicant.

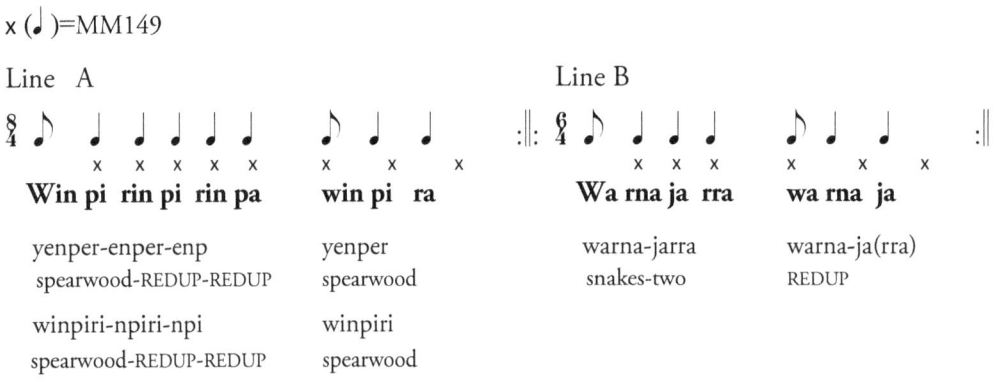

Figure 7.16. Partial reduplication from the left edge – *warnaja* – with identical rhythm, base preceding reduplicant. Line B is in three Warnajarra verses: Verse 8 (shown here), 12 and 14.

The reduplication in Line A is discussed in subsection "Triplication".

---

23   Cognate with Eastern Warlpiri and Warumungu *pulyurrulyurru* "red".

7 Warnajarra: Innovation and continuity in design and lyrics in a Warlpiri women's song set

Partial reduplication from left edge, base before reduplicant

In Figure 7.16 (Verse 8), the partial reduplication starts from the left edge of the base; that is, syllables 123 (*wa.rna.ja*) are copied but not syllables 234 (*rna.ja.rra*). Left edge reduplication is frequently associated with words of Warlpiri origin, such as *warna* "snake". In some left edge reduplication, a syllable is added rather than deleted before the word is repeated. This can be seen in Figure 7.17 (Verse 23), where the word *mangkuru* "swamp" has the syllable *rna* added before the word is repeated.[24] This ensures the reduplication is not identical; here, there is an additional syllable and note in the "base", while the reduplicant is only three syllables. The syllable *rna* is a vocable in other Warlpiri *yawulyu* (Turpin and Laughren 2013) and Kaytetye *yawulyu* (Turpin 2005, 212), where it occurs as the final syllable of a metrical unit. Note that this is homophonous with the 1sg pronoun "I".

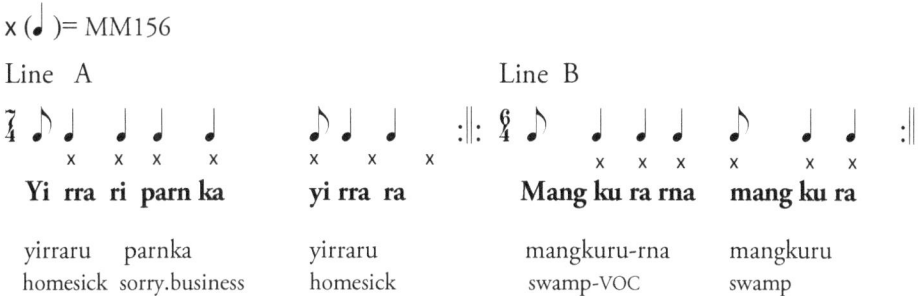

Figure 7.17. Base that has a vocable as its final (fourth) syllable. Reduplication from left edge of word, base followed by reduplicant. Fast meter (Verse 23).

The same pattern of partial reduplication from the left edge, with the same rhythm, can be seen in Line B of the verse shown in Figure 7.18 (Verse 15). In this instance, the fourth syllable appears to be part of a suffix. The base is a phrase "*ninjaparnta*", whose meaning is unknown. The final element "*rnta*" is omitted in the reduplicant. This pattern of partial reduplication can be represented as 1234 123.

---

24 This word for swamp may also be cognate with Warumungu *mangkkuru* "black soil plain", which is also used for "sea".

Figure 7.18. Partial reduplication from the left edge – *ninjapa* – with identical rhythm, base followed by reduplicant. Line B, fast meter (Verse 15).

Partial reduplication from left edge, base after reduplicant

Thus far, we have seen partial reduplication from the left edge where the base precedes the reduplicant (Figure 7.18, Verse 15; Figure 7.17, Verse 23; Figure 7.16, Verse 8). In the line *Warnajarra-warnaja* (Figure 7.16, Verse 8), we know that *warna-jarra* is the base because it is a word, while *warnaja* is not a word and is thus considered the reduplicant. Consider the line in Figure 7.19 (Verse 6). Here, the base comes *after* the reduplicant. That is, the four-syllable word *warna-jarra follows* the three-syllable reduplicant. Line A of this verse follows the same pattern, with the three-syllable reduplicant preposed to the four-syllable base. While it is possible to analyse *warnaja* in Line B as *warna-ja* or *warna-ju* where the third syllable is an assertive or topic-marking clitic, such an analysis of *wirrima* in Line A is not available as this is not a word and there is no monosyllabic suffix or enclitic -*ma*. If the base contains the imperative verb *ma-nta*, then this reduplication differs from the productive reduplication of a preverb or verb stem since both are copied here. Notice that the partial reduplication again copies the rhythm of the base; however, as it omits the final syllable, it is not identical reduplication.

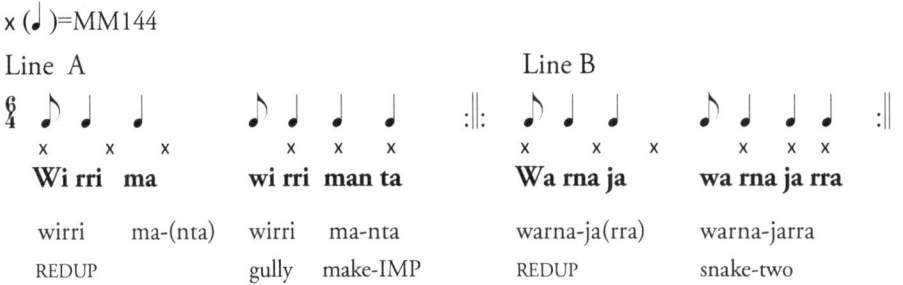

Figure 7.19. Base after reduplicant in both lines of the verse. Partial reduplication from the left edge base after reduplicant. Fast meter (Verse 6).

In Figure 7.19 (Verse 6), the three-syllable reduplicant *warnaja* precedes the base. What is so striking about this verse is not so much that the base comes after the reduplicant but that the same text is used for both orderings: *warnajarra-warnaja* (base + reduplicant), *warnaja-warnajarra* (reduplicant + base).

Figure 7.19 represents the verse as sung in the 1981 performance. In the 1982 performance, this verse was sung with the hemistiches reversed in each line: *wirrimanta wirrima / warnajarra warnaja*, thus changing the reduplication pattern to base *before* reduplicant, as in Figures 7.17 and 7.18. This is the only verse where the order of hemistiches differs in a subsequent performance.

Partial reduplication from right edge

Another pattern of partial reduplication is 12323. Here, the initial syllable of the line is not repeated. Such "right edge" reduplication occurs when the speech equivalent is of Arandic origin. Figure 7.20 (Verse 17) shows a line comprised of this pattern. The line is based on the Arandic word *atywerrk* "native fig" (*Ficus platypoda*).[25] This word is reduplicated, and the consonant "w" added to the beginning.[26] Thus, what appears as partial reduplication from the right edge is constructed from whole reduplication of an Arandic word, and a consonant is added as lines must be consonant initial (Turpin 2007a). Although *wijirrki* "native fig" exists in Warlpiri, and neighbouring Warumungu, its origins are possibly Arandic as the rounded vowel in song points to the Arandic form.

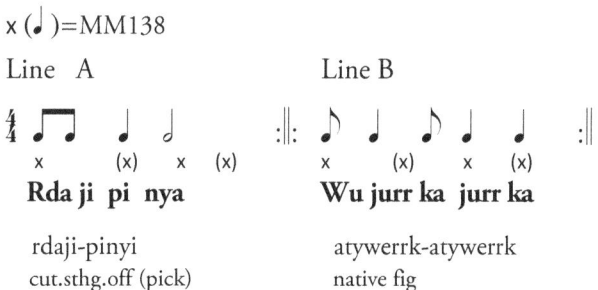

Figure 7.20. Partial reduplication from right edge: Arandic base *atywerrk* reduplicated and consonant added to beginning (Verse 17).

---

25 This word *atywerrk* has an optional initial vowel, either "e" or "a", depending on the Arandic variety. Its pronunciation can have an initial rounded vowel, central vowel or no vowel.

26 Note that long vowels are subject to assonance patterns that affect every other repetition of a line in performance: that is, A<u>A</u>B<u>B</u>, where a line and its repetition have a different vowel quality.

The 12323 partial reduplication is widespread in the neighbouring Kaytetye language not only as a form of lexical words (e.g., *pwelyerrelyerre* "dust")[27] but also as a method of line formation in *yawulyu*. Turpin (2005, 212) found that 14 lines of a Kaytetye rain song set conform to this pattern.[28]

Triplication

In Figure 7.21 (Verse 3), we see partial reduplication from the right edge: *lingkaji-ngkaja*.[29] Right edge reduplication in Warnajarra is frequently associated with words of Arandic origin, as argued in the previous section. We suggest that Line B is based on an Arandic word *ingkaty* "foot", which has various forms in Arandic languages today.[30] The word is reduplicated (*ingkaty-ingkaty*), and the consonant "l" is added to the beginning of the word, thus conforming to lines starting with a consonant (the source of the "l" is discussed below the Figure). The first three syllables are further repeated (a pattern 123 23 123), forming a line of eight syllables through "triplication".

Figure 7.21. Partial reduplication from the right edge: Line B consists of syllables that repeat in a triplication pattern of 123 23 123 (Verse 3).

---

27 *Pulyurrulyurru* also means "red" in Eastern Warlpiri and Warumungu.
28 It may be significant that this song set also belongs to the same patricouple.
29 Singer Peggy Nampijinpa stated that "*Lingka-jingkaja*" refers to a place; however, no speech equivalents were given.
30 Some reflexes of *ingkatye* "foot" include Kaytetye *angketye* (Turpin and Ross 2012, 118) Anmatyerr *ingka* "foot" (Green 2008, 323) and *ingkatyel-wem*, which means to walk in someone's footprint (Green 2008, 324) in Anmatyerr, Arrernte and Alyawarr.

The initial consonant "l" is most likely the Arandic instrumental suffix *-el*; thus, the phrase is *ingkaty-el* "(go) by foot".[31] The suffix *-el* marks each as a separate word, as opposed to the internal reduplication in *ingkaty-ingkaty-el*.

As in most verses from this song set, each line is repeated before commencing the other line. The process of transferring the final consonant of the line-final suffix to the beginning of a line, followed by repetition for a Warlpiri verse (in Anmatyerr language), is one outlined by Hale (1984, 261). In the figures the transferred consonant is in bold face. In the fast meter, many Warnajarra lines, such as that shown above, are formed through this pattern of triplication. On the surface, it appears to be a partial reduplication from the right edge; however, as we have shown, it is partial reduplication from the left edge of an Arandic base *ingkaty-ingkatyel* followed by consonant transfer and resyllabification.

Some lines of the 123 23 123 pattern add an initial consonant rather than transferring the final consonant. As has been observed for Arandic *yawulyu*, such consonant transfer is only possible if the final consonant is a monosyllabic suffix – not when it is part of the root (Hale 1984; Turpin 2005). Figure 7.22 (Verse 15) shows one such line. The line is based on the Arandic word *akwerlp*, which has related but different meanings in Arandic languages.[32] The word *akwerlp* is reduplicated, and a consonant "w" is added to the beginning of the word/line: *w+akwerlp-akwerlp-a*, creating a five-syllable form. The three-syllable "base" is then repeated: *w+akwerlp-akwerlp-a w+akwerlp-a*. As with *wijirrki* "native fig", *Wakurlpu* also exists in Warlpiri as a place name, but this place name is not what this verse refers to.

Figure 7.22. Triplication with partial reduplication from the right edge. Fast meter (Verse 15, Line A).

---

31 The form *ingkatyel* "by foot" with consonant transfer is similarly in a verse of the Kaytetye Rain *yawulyu* (Turpin 2005, 238).

32 In Anmatyerr, *akwerlp* means "riverbank, creek bank; slope or top of a hill"; in Kaytetye and Alyawarr, it means "sandhill".

Notice how the rhythm differs in every iteration of the repeated syllables: SLS SL SL SLL. The 123 23 123 pattern of line formation through triplication can be seen in both lines of Verse 26 (see Figure 7.23). Line A may be based on the Arandic word *arnerre* "rockhole", reduplicated, and the consonant "*w*" again inserted at the beginning of the word.[33] Line A again has a unique rhythm for each repeated sequence, the same rhythm as seen in Figure 7.22 (Verse 15). In contrast, Line B has the same rhythm for the base and the "triplicant" SLL LL SLL; however, the final vowel differs in the base *litarrpi* from the reduplicant and triplicant *litarrpa*. In this line, a syllable has the same rhythm in all three iterations. It is not known what speech equivalent (if any) corresponds to the base, although the initial "l" and the reduplication from the left edge of the line suggests an Arandic speech equivalent.[34]

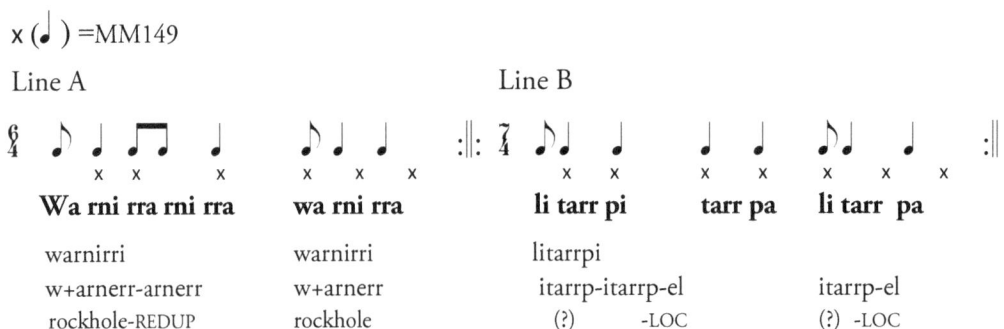

Figure 7.23. Triplication with partial reduplication from the right edge. Contrasting rhythm in Line A; identical rhythm in line B. Fast meter, Verse 26.

A more complicated triplication can be seen in Figure 7.24 (Verse 8). Here, a three-syllable base is repeated, and a syllable is added to form a nine-syllable line. Given that words do not end in a consonant, the base can be considered *winpiri*. This has a number of possible speech equivalents: one is "spearwood" (*Pandorea doratoxylon*), a borrowing from Arandic *(u)yenpere* "spearwood".[35] While the speech equivalent is uncertain, we can say that the base is partially reduplicated from the right edge, reduplicating all but the initial consonant

---

33 The Warlpiri equivalent is *warnirri* and the Warumungu *warnirr*.
34 Peggy Nampijinpa identified litarrpitarrpi as the name of the rockhole referred to in Line A.
35 Another possible speech equivalent is *elper* "quickly" (K), one of the meanings given for this verse; another is *anper* (A), which has two meanings, "fantastic" and "beside". It could also be Warumungu *wirnppar(i/a)* "break-fut/imperative".

win.pirin.pirin. The syllable *-pa* is added to this consonant-final string, *win.pirin.pirin.pa.*[36]

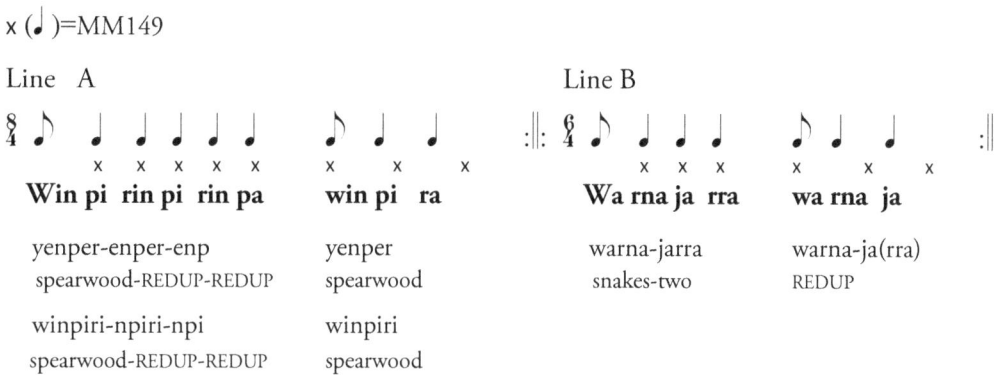

Figure 7.24. Triplication with partial reduplication from the right edge and additional syllable. Fast meter (Verse 8).

This pattern of reduplication can also be seen in Chapter 6, with Song 30, Line B, second hemistich:

winpirin   pirinpa
yalkarlirl   karlila
  1 2 3   2 3 4

As we have seen, reduplication from the right edge is associated with words of Arandic origin as these words are vowel initial, and Warlpiri adds a consonant to the front of these, which is not reduplicated. In contrast, left edge reduplication is associated with words of Warlpiri (and possibly Warumungu) origin, as we saw with *warna* "snake", *mangkuru* "swamp in open country" and *wirri* "gully".

A further right edge triplication is illustrated in Figure 7.25 (Verse 7). This is a verse comprised of only one line, based on a single Arandic word *arlerlk-arlerlk* "Sandover Lily" (*Crinum flaccidum*; Green 2008, 66).[37] This word is a lexical reduplication and serves as the base for the partial reduplicant that follows. The source of the line-initial consonant "*rr*" – which is not a permitted word-initial consonant in Warlpiri – may be the Kaytetye relative suffix *-arr*. Line-final "*rr*" is transferred to the line-initial position, and the word-final "*rr*" internal to the line resyllabifies to form the

---

36 In Warlpiri phonotactics, the syllable *-pa* is added to a consonant-final word to make it vowel final; however, it may also be a partial triplication.

37 It may also be based on a reduplication (and partial reduplication) of *iylerlkarr* (Turpin and Ross 2012, 31) "white headband": *ilerlk iylerlkarr iylerlkarr* (see Appendix 7.1).

onset of the reduplicant. This pattern is the same as discussed regarding Figure 7.21 (Verse 3): *alyerlk-alyerk-arr alyerlk* > *rr-alyerlk-alyerlka- rr-alyerlka-*.

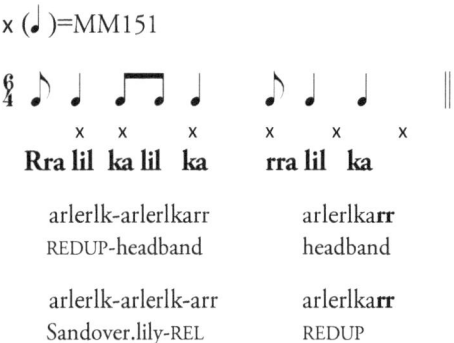

Figure 7.25. Right-edge triplication: 123 23 123. Fast meter (Verse 7, one line only).

Here, we have another interesting instance of "deliberate" ambiguity. A competing analysis of the word in Figure 7.25 (Verse 7) is the phonologically similar word for a woman's white headband used in *yawulyu* performances: *iylerlkarr* is the Anmatyerr respect language term. The semantic association between these two words lies in their whiteness; the white headband stands out on the women's heads, while the white flower of the Sandover Lily stands out when it blossoms after good rains. There is also a shared erotic connotation; *yawulyu* enhances female attractiveness and may attract illicit relations, while the onion-like tuber of the Sandover Lily is poisonous, a symbol of illicit relations in some *yawulyu* verses. In both cases, what may appear attractive is dangerous if consumed. As the final "*rr*" in *iylerlkarr* "headband" belongs to the word and is not an inflectional suffix or enclitic, it is not a candidate for consonant transfer. Thus, we retain the *alyerlk-alyerlk* "Sandover Lily" analysis of the literal text.

Partial reduplication, partial line

In addition to various patterns of partial reduplication as a method of line formation, partial reduplication can also occupy only some of a line. This can be seen in Figure 7.26 (Verse 27), which is a verse in the slow meter. Here, the initial text, *pijingka*, which means "pinching with the fingers", is *not* reduplicated, whereas the last five syllables contain a partial reduplication, *lardi-lardila*, a sequence of 12 123. Although the word from which the reduplication is derived is unknown, it is likely that the base follows the reduplicant because the longer form, *lardila*, is likely the base.

7 Warnajarra: Innovation and continuity in design and lyrics in a Warlpiri women's song set

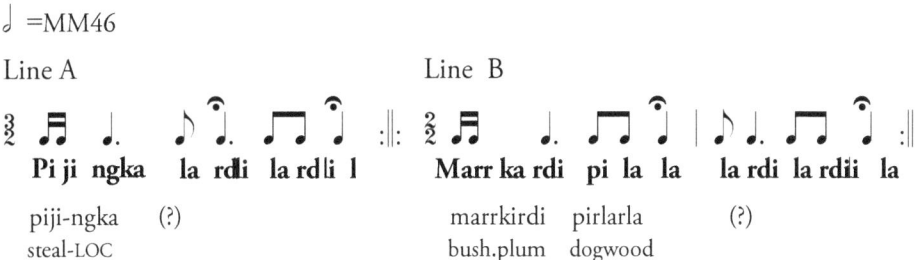

Figure 7.26. Partial reduplication *lardi-lardila*. Slow meter (Verse 27).

Reduplication that forms only part of the line was also seen in *kana-jutampi-jutampi* (Figures 7.10, Verse 3 and 7.11, Verse 2), where the speech equivalent may be a single phrase comprised of a lexical reduplication.

Conclusion

Warnajarra is characterised by much poetic reduplication of varying patterns: partial and whole; from the right edge and left edge of the line; word repetition; and even "triplication", including patterns not found in spoken Warlpiri. This contrasts with many other Warlpiri and Arandic *yawulyu*, where the text appears closer to spoken language. While other *yawulyu* have examples of reduplication, the reduplication in these is more like reduplication found in everyday speech: grammatical and lexical reduplication. Like other *yawulyu* from the eastern Warlpiri region, which contain both Arandic and Warlpiri vocabulary, Warnajarra shows up different patterns of reduplication tied to the language variety – Arandic vocabulary is associated with reduplication patterns from the right edge and may involve line-initial consonant addition and transfer. In contrast, productive Warlpiri reduplication occurs only from the left edge.

A feature of reduplication in Warnajarra is that the base and its reduplicant are either not textually identical or, if they are, these are set to different rhythms. This near-identity convention is also found in other *yawulyu*, including that from Pawu (Turpin and Laughren 2014) and in neighbouring Kaytetye (Turpin 2007a, 103). While reduplication occurs in verses of both meters of Warnajarra (fast and slow), it is a more characteristic feature of verses in the fast meter. Fast meter verses tend to relate to the Warnajarra ancestors, whereas the slow meter verses seem to relate to other *jukurrpa* whose path is crossed by Warnajarra. The association of musical style with different sociopolitical groups was noted early on by musicologists such as Catherine Ellis:

> The portion of a song which refers to sacred places within the care of a local group may be performed only by members of that group and it is in their own musical idiom. (Ellis 1966, 138)

Later, Ellis (1985, 92) argued that melody encodes the essence of an ancestral being in Western Desert songs. In the case of Warlpiri *yawulyu*, rhythm and tempo may also play a significant role in musical representation of the ancestral being. The relationship between the Warnajarra meters and their subject matter requires further investigation.

Without knowing the conventions of song creation, including the complex reduplication patterns we find in Warnajarra, and the different treatment of Arandic vocabulary, it would not be possible to "find" new Warnajarra *yawulyu* song texts. This knowledge was traditionally acquired through frequent attendance at *yawulyu* performances and engagement in singing alongside older and more knowledgeable singers. Notably, we find an example of innovation in the *yawulyu* visual design accompanying song. Perhaps the modern and transformative practices of Indigenous painting on canvases (as well as, e.g., paper, material, cars), widespread across Australia, has somehow influenced Peggy Nampijinpa's "finding" of a new *yawulyu* design. Young and old Warlpiri people participate in creating visual designs that relate to traditional *jukurrpa* and employ traditional graphic motifs while introducing many innovative features, with economic opportunities arising from this. In contrast, fewer people have learned traditional song over the past 40 years. The unfamiliarity of this style of singing was evident to Mary Laughren in 2014 when Elder Jerry Jangala Patrick taught a *purlapa* (created in the 1980s) to younger Warlpiri people in the Lajamanu Church; they had difficulty mastering the rhythmic texts, whose conventions differ from speech in many ways, some of which have been demonstrated in this chapter. This contrasted with Mary's experience in the 1980s when these songs were created and learned by Warlpiri with ease. Certainly, Warlpiri people today are fluent in a wide variety of musical genres, composing and performing in Warlpiri; yet rarely (if ever) are the traditional conventions for associating text and rhythm incorporated into these other genres. This contrasts with the visual arts where elements of traditional Warlpiri iconography are drawn on in contemporary artistic practices.

References

Breen, Gavan. 2001. "The Wonders of Arandic Phonology". In *Forty Years On: Ken Hale and Australian Languages*, edited by Jane Simpson, David Nash, Mary Laughren, Peter Austin and Barry Alpher, 45–69. Canberra: Pacific Linguistics.

Brown, Reuben, David Manmurulu, Jenny Manmurulu, Isabelle O'Keeffe and Ruth Singer. 2017. "Maintaining Song Traditions and Languages Together at Warruwi (Western Arnhem Land)". In *Recirculating Songs: Revitalising the Singing Practices of Indigenous Australia*, edited by Jim Wafer and Myfany Turpin, 257–74. Canberra: Pacific Linguistics.

Clunies Ross, Margaret, Tamsin Donaldson and Stephen Wild (eds). 1987. *Songs of Aboriginal Australia* (Oceania Monograph 32). Sydney: University of Sydney.

Curran, Georgia, Linda Barwick, Myfany Turpin, Fiona Walsh and Mary Laughren. 2019. "Central Australian Aboriginal Songs and Biocultural Knowledge: Evidence from Women's Ceremonies Relating to Edible Seeds". *Journal of Ethnobiology* 39(3): 354–70. https://doi.org/10.2993/0278-0771-39.3.354

Dail-Jones [Morais], Megan. 1984. "A Culture in Motion: A Study of the Interrelationship of Dancing, Sorrowing, Hunting, and Fighting as Performed by the Warlpiri Women of Central Australia". Master of Arts thesis, University of Hawaii, Honolulu.

Dail-Jones [Morais], Megan. 1992. "Documenting Dance: Benesh Movement Notation and the Warlpiri of Central Australia". In *Music and Dance of Aboriginal Australia and the South Pacific* (Oceania Monograph 41), edited by Alice Moyle, 130–43. Sydney: University of Sydney.

Dail-Jones [Morais], Megan. 1998. "Warlpiri Dance". In *The International Encyclopedia of Dance* (vol. 1), edited by Selma Jean Cohen, 227–29. New York: Oxford University Press.

Ellis, Catherine. 1966. "Aboriginal Songs of South Australia". *Miscellanea Musicologica* 1: 137–90.

Ellis, Catherine. 1985. *Aboriginal Music, Education for Living: Cross-Cultural Experiences from South Australia*. St Lucia: University of Queensland Press.

Fabricius, Anne H. 1998. *A Comparative Survey of Reduplication in Australian Languages* (Studies in Australian Languages 3). Munich: Lincom Europa.

Green, Jennifer. 2008. *Eastern and Central Anmatyerr to English Dictionary*. Alice Springs: IAD Press.

Ghomeshi, Jila, Ray Jackendoff, Nicole Rosen and Kevin Russell. 2004. "Contrastive Focus Reduplication in English (the SALAD-Salad Paper)". *Natural Language & Linguistic Theory* 22(2): 307–57.

Hale, Ken. 1984. "Remarks on Creativity in Aboriginal Verse". In *Problems and Solutions: Occasional Essays in Musicology Presented to Alice M. Moyle*, edited by Jamie C. Kassler and Jill Stubington, 254–62. Sydney: Hale & Iremonger.

Koch, Grace and Myfany Turpin. 2008. "The Language of Central Australian Aboriginal Songs". In *Morphology and Language History. In Honour of Harold Koch*, edited by Claire Bowern, Bethwyn Evans and Luisa Miceli, 167–83. Amsterdam; Philadelphia: John Benjamins.

Laughren, Mary, Kenneth Hale, Jeannie Nungarrayi Egan, Patrick Marlurrku, Paddy Jangala, Robert Hoogenraad, David Nash and Jane Simpson. 2022. *Warlpiri Encyclopaedic Dictionary*. Canberra, ACT: Aboriginal Studies Press.

Meggitt, Mervyn. 1966. *Gadjari Among the Walbiri Aborigines of Central Australia* (Oceania Monograph 14). Sydney: The University of Sydney.

Morais, Megan. 1981–1982. "Fieldnotes of [Warlpiri] Women's Ritual Business at Willowra, NT (3) Meetings: 120–130" [unpublished manuscript]. Canberra: Australian Institute of Aboriginal and Torres Strait Islander Studies.

Morais, Megan, Lucy Nampijinpa Martin, Peggy Nampijinpa Martin, Helen Morton Napurrurla, Janet Nakamarra Long, Maisie Napaljarri Kitson, Maureen Nampijinpa O'Keefe, Clarrie Kemarr Long, Jeannie Nampijinpa Presley, Marjorie Nampijinpa and Brown, Selina Napanangka Williams, Leah Nampijinpa and Martin and Myfany Turpin. In press. *Yawulyu: Art and Song in Warlpiri Women's Ceremony*. Canberra: Aboriginal Studies Press.

Munn, Nancy. 1973. *Walbiri Iconography: Graphic Representation and Cultural Symbolism in a Central Australian Society*. Ithaca: Cornell University Press.

Nash, David. 1986. *Topics in Warlpiri Grammar* (Outstanding Dissertations in Linguistics, Third Series). New York: Garland Publishing Inc.

Panther, Forrest. 2020. Topics in Kaytetye Phonology and Morpho-Syntax. PhD thesis, University of Newcastle, Newcastle.

San, Nay and Myfany Turpin. 2021. "Text-setting in Kaytetye". In *Proceedings of the 2020 Annual Meeting of Phonology*, edited by Ryan Bennett, Richard Bibbs, Mykel Loren Brinkerhoff, Max J. Kaplan, Stephanie Rich, Amanda Rysling, Nicholas Van Handel and Maya Wax Cavallaro, 1–9. Columbia: Linguistics Society of America. https://doi.org/10.3765/amp.v9i0.4911

Strehlow, T.G.H. 1971. *Songs of Central Australia*. Sydney: Angus & Robertson.

Turpin, Myfany. 2005. Form and Meaning of Akwelye: A Kaytetye Women's Song Series from Central Australia. PhD thesis, University of Sydney, Sydney. https://ses.library.usyd.edu.au/handle/2123/1334

Turpin, Myfany. 2007a. "Artfully Hidden: Text and Rhythm in a Central Australian Aboriginal Song Series". *Musicology Australia* 29: 93–107.

Turpin, Myfany. 2007b. "The Poetics of Central Australian Song". *Australian Aboriginal Studies* 1: 100–15.

Turpin, Myfany. 2022. "End Rhyme in Aboriginal Sung Poetry". In *Rhyme and Rhyming in Verbal Art, Language, and Song*, edited by Venla Sykäri and Nigel Fabb, 213–28. Helsinki: Finnish Literature Society. https://doi.org/10.21435/sff.25

Turpin, Myfany and Mary Laughren. 2013. "Edge Effects in Warlpiri *Yawulyu* Songs: Resyllabification, Epenthesis and Final Vowel Modification". *Australian Journal of Linguistics* 33(4): 399–425.

Turpin, Myfany and Mary Laughren. 2014. "Text and Meter in Lander Warlpiri Songs". In *Proceedings of the 43rd Australian Linguistic Society Conference 2013*, 1–4 October, 398–415. Melbourne, University of Melbourne.

Turpin, Myfany and Alison N. Ross. 2012. *Kaytetye to English Dictionary.* Alice Springs: IAD Press.

Vaarzon-Morel, Petronella (ed.). 1995. *Warlpiri Women's Voices: Warlpiri Karntakarnta-Kurlangu Yimi: Our Lives Our History.* Alice Springs: IAD Press.

Wafer, James and Petronella Wafer. 1980. *The Lander Warlpiri/Anmatjirra Land Claim to Willowra Pastoral Lease.* Alice Springs: Central Land Council.

Walsh, Michael. 2007. "Australian Aboriginal Song Language: So Many Questions, So Little to Work With". *Australian Aboriginal Studies* 2: 128–44.

Warlpiri Women from Yuendumu and Georgia Curran (ed.). 2017. *Yurntumu-Wardingki Juju-Ngaliya-Kurlangu Yawulyu: Warlpiri Women's Songs from Yuendumu* [including DVD]. Batchelor: Batchelor Institute Press.

Appendix 7.1 Warnajarra Verses

Poetic words, reduplication and words of Arandic origin are shown in grey. These may be words from neighbouring languages and/or words only used in song. Following an Aboriginal word, (?) signals that this is not a confirmed speech equivalent; following an English word, it signals that this is not a confirmed meaning.

Linguistic glosses are as follows:

1sg = 1st person singular; aux = auxiliary; cnt = continuous aspect; imp = imperative; inst = instrumental; loc = locative case; np = non-past tense; pl = plural; prs = present tense; RDPL = reduplication; rel = relativiser, voc = vocable.

Verse 1

x (♩)=MM143

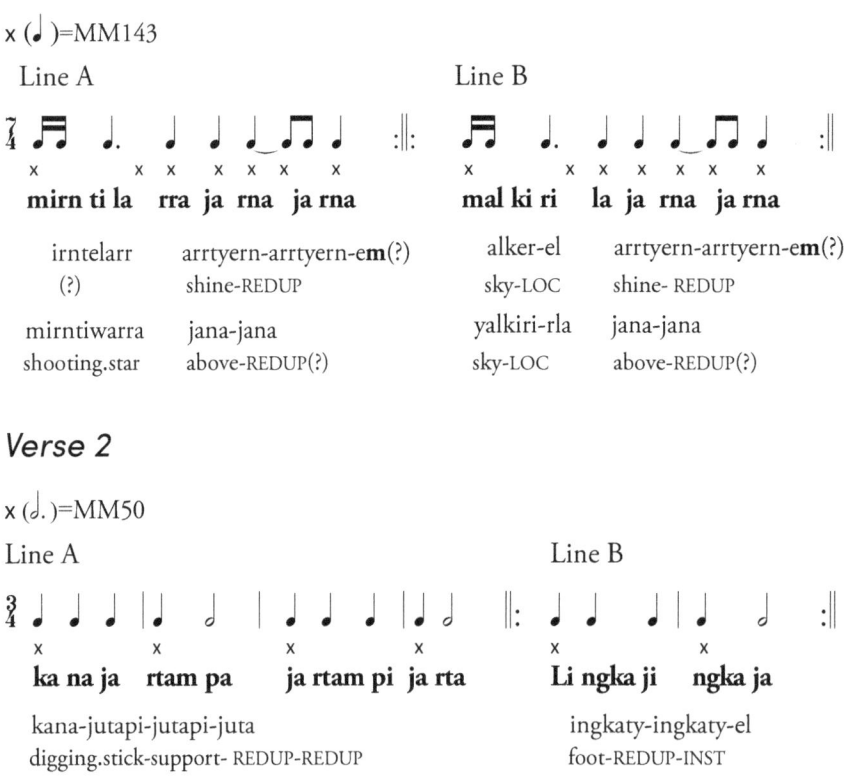

7 Warnajarra: Innovation and continuity in design and lyrics in a Warlpiri women's song set

Verse 3

x (♩)=MM153

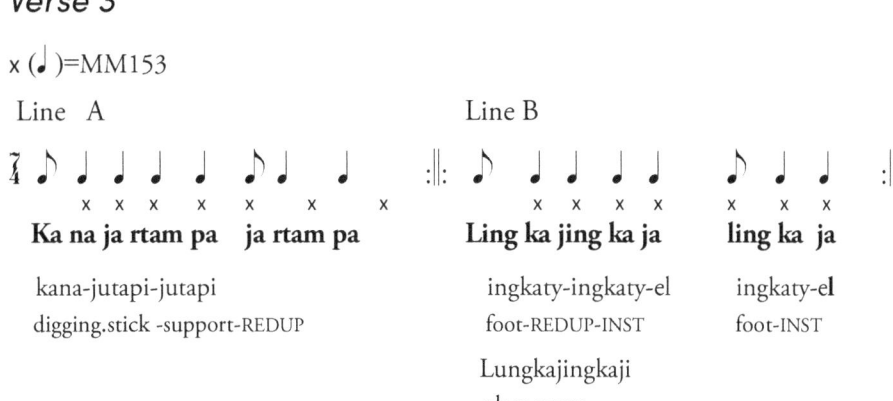

Line A	Line B
Ka na ja rtam pa ja rtam pa	**Ling ka jing ka ja ling ka ja**
kana-jutapi-jutapi	ingkaty-ingkaty-el ingkaty-el
digging.stick -support-REDUP	foot-REDUP-INST foot-INST
	Lungkajingkaji
	place.name

Verse 4

x (♩)=MM150

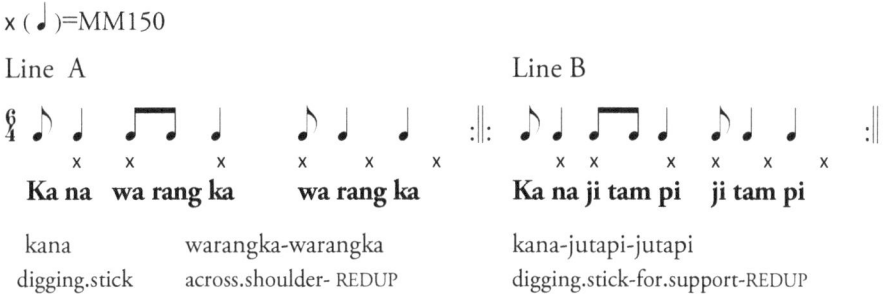

Line A	Line B
Ka na wa rang ka wa rang ka	**Ka na ji tam pi ji tam pi**
kana warangka-warangka	kana-jutapi-jutapi
digging.stick across.shoulder- REDUP	digging.stick-for.support-REDUP

"With a digging stick on my shoulder and a digging stick for support I travel"

Verse 5

♩=MM42

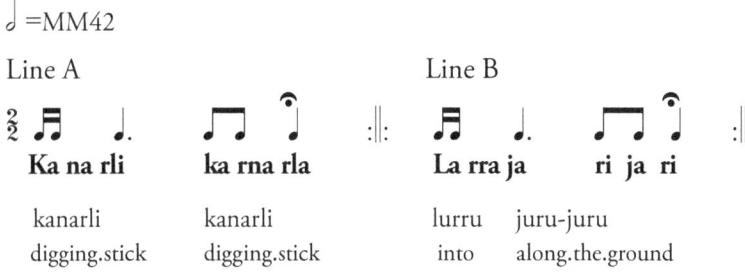

Line A	Line B
Ka na rli ka rna rla	**La rra ja ri ja ri**
kanarli kanarli	lurru juru-juru
digging.stick digging.stick	into along.the.ground

"The digging stick [is] along the ground"

Verse 6

x (♩)=MM144

Line A 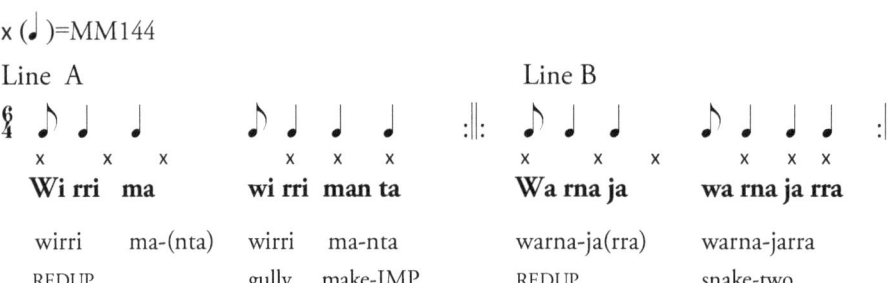 Line B

Wi rri ma	**wi rri man ta**	**Wa rna ja**	**wa rna ja rra**
wirri ma-(nta)	wirri ma-nta	warna-ja(rra)	warna-jarra
REDUP	gully make-IMP	REDUP	snake-two

Verse 7

x (♩)=MM151

Rra lil ka lil ka	**rra lil ka**
arlerlk-arlerlkarr	arlerlka**rr**
REDUP-headband	headband
arlerlk-arlerlk-arr	arlerlka**rr**
Sandover.lily-REL	REDUP

Verse 8

x (♩)=MM149

Line A 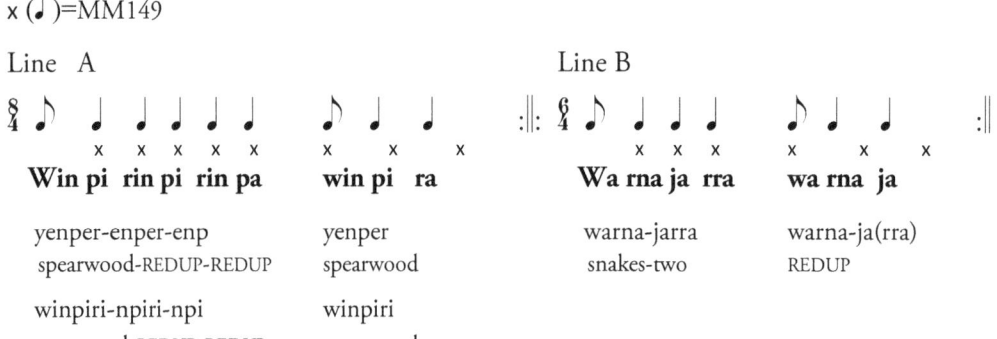 Line B

Win pi rin pi rin pa	**win pi ra**	**Wa rna ja rra**	**wa rna ja**
yenper-enper-enp	yenper	warna-jarra	warna-ja(rra)
spearwood-REDUP-REDUP	spearwood	snakes-two	REDUP
winpiri-npiri-npi	winpiri		
spearwood-REDUP-REDUP	spearwood		

7 Warnajarra: Innovation and continuity in design and lyrics in a Warlpiri women's song set

Verse 10

x (♩)=MM140

Man ti ra rri rnay   man ti ray

anter arrern-e**m**   anter-a**m**
fat put_on-PRS   fat-EMPH

Verse 11

♩=MM48

Line A   Line B

Wa ra kin pa rta   **Mal ki ra li rri ya**

wara! Kiirnpa (?)   alker-arl-irr-eya**m**(?)
hey   name   sky-ALL-INCH-DO.AFTER
                          into the sky

Verse 12

♩=MM139

Line A   Line B

Wu ri ku ri ku   wu ri ku   **wa rna ja rra   wa rna ja**

wuru-kuruku   wuru-ku   warna-jarra   warna-ja(rra)
shedding skin   REDUP   snake-two   REDUP

Verse 13

♩.=MM125

Line A   Line B

Nga ji la rray ka | parn ta parn tay rna   **Wi rri pa ka rna | parn ta parn tay rna**

ngajularri   ka   panti-panti-rni   wirripakarnu   panti-panti-rni
waistbelt   AUX   pierce-REDUP-NPST   waistbelt   pierce-REDUP-NPST

245

Verse 14

x (♩)=MM136

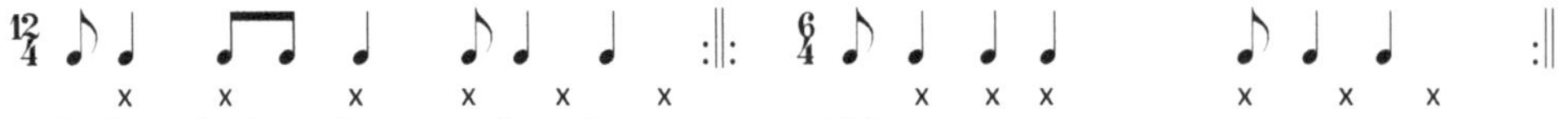

Line A Line B

Ji lang ka lang ka | **ji lang ka** | **Wa rna ja rra** | **wa rna ja**

jila-ngka -langka | jila-ngka | warna-jarra | warna-ja(rra)
waterhole-LOC REDUP | waterhole-LOC | snake-two | REDUP

Verse 14 (variant)

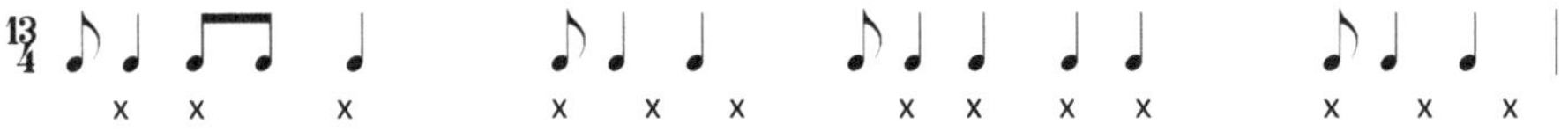

Ji la ngka la ngka | ji la ngka | ji la ngka la ngka | ji la ngka

Verse 15

x (♩)=MM133

Line A Line B

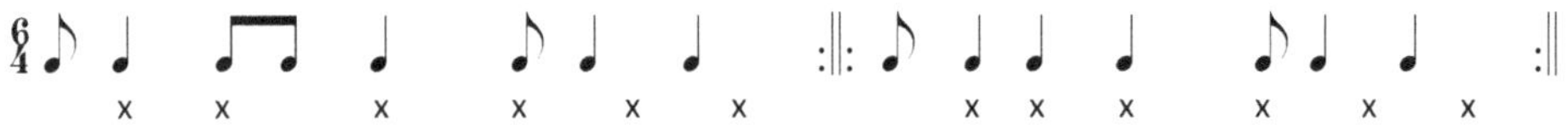

Wa kurl pa kurl pa | **wa kurl pa** | **Nin ja pan ta** | **ni nja pa**

w+akwerlp-akwerlp | w+akwerlp | (?) -parnta(?) | (?) -pa(rnta)(?)
sandhill-REDUP | sandhill | -with | -with

Verse 16

x (♩.)=MM81

Line A Line B

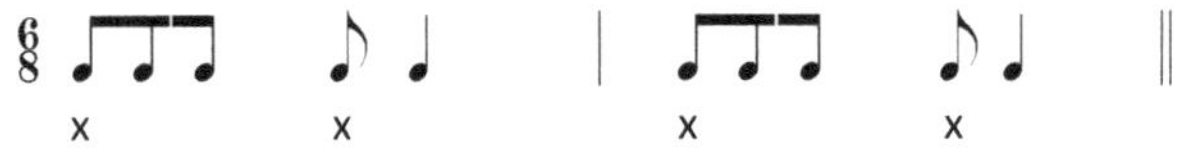

Wa kurl pa kurl pay | **wa kirl pi li nya**

w+akwerlp-akwerlp | Warlilpilinyi ~ Wakurlpilinyi
sandhill-REDUP | place name
place name

7 Warnajarra: Innovation and continuity in design and lyrics in a Warlpiri women's song set

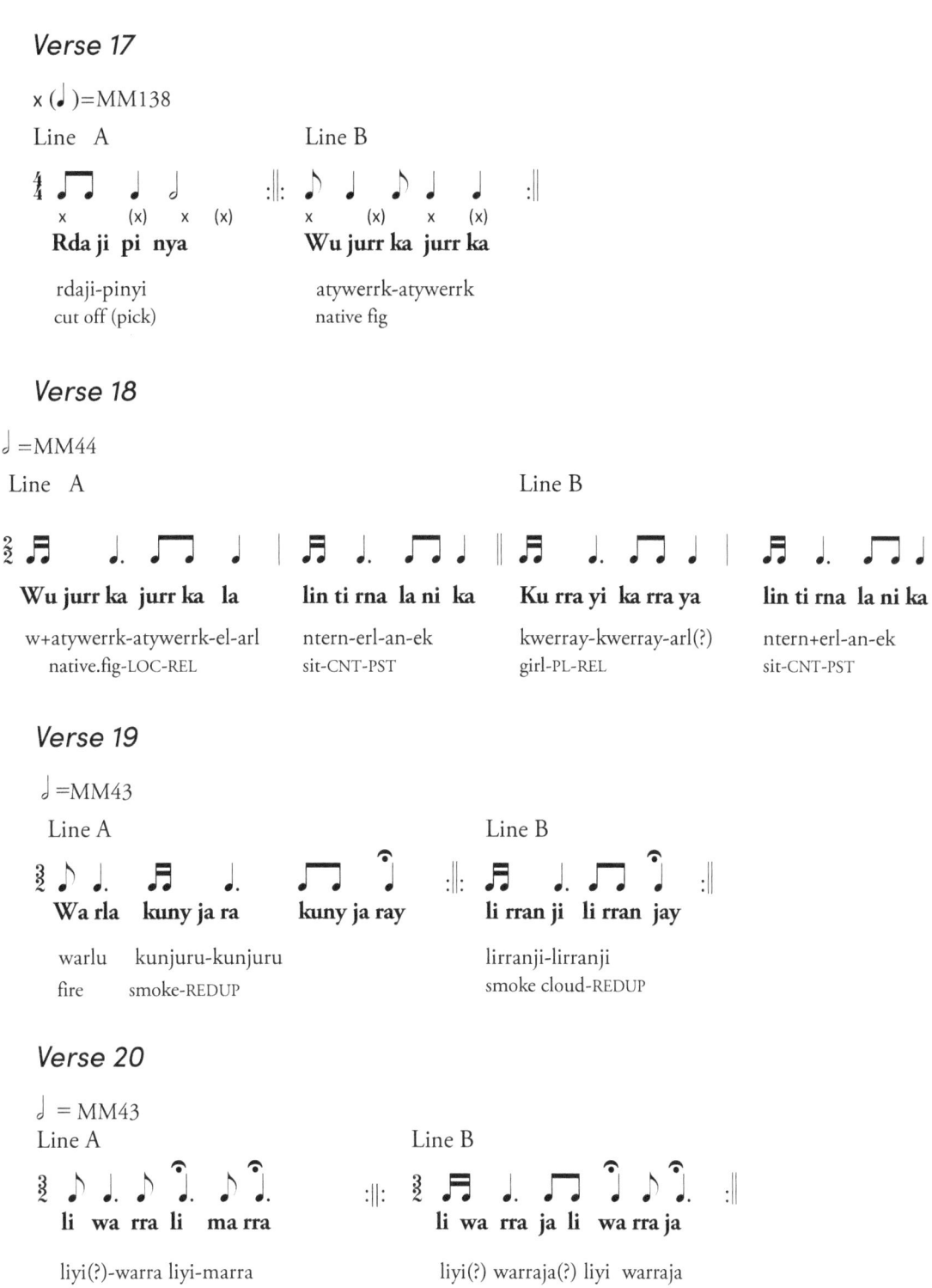

247

7 Warnajarra: Innovation and continuity in design and lyrics in a Warlpiri women's song set

249

Verse 33

♩. =MM 68–71

Line A   Line B

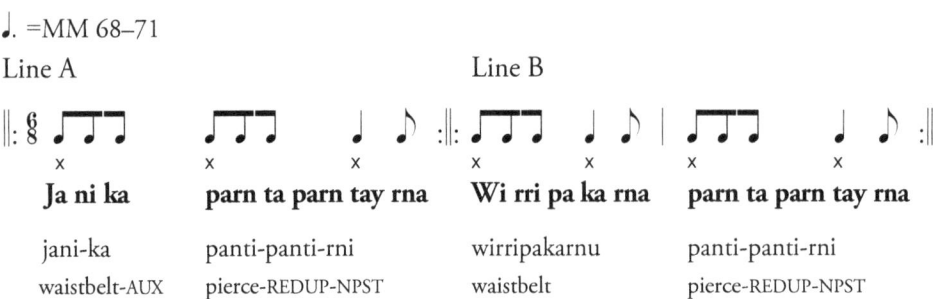

Ja ni ka	parn ta parn tay rna	Wi rri pa ka rna	parn ta parn tay rna
jani-ka	panti-panti-rni	wirripakarnu	panti-panti-rni
waistbelt-AUX	pierce-REDUP-NPST	waistbelt	pierce-REDUP-NPST

"Sewing the waistbelt, sewing the ceremonial skirt"

Appendix 7.2 Benesh notation for the dance accompanying (Verse 13 and 33)

MBW-A: 'majardi'

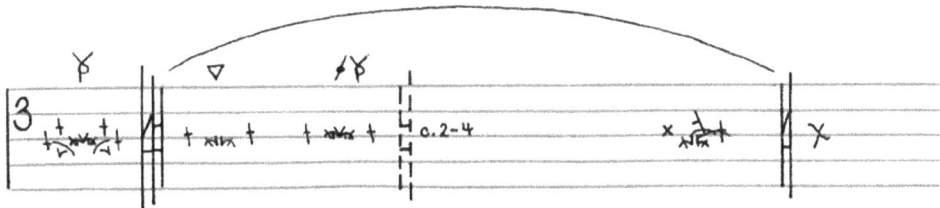

Lorraine Nungarrayi Granites

Nungarrayi grew up in Willowra but lived a lot of her adult life in Yuendumu after she married. She is *kirda* for the Wurrpardi and Ngatijirri *jukurrpa* from the Country near Willowra. She is a senior female song leader and knows and sings a large repertory of *yawulyu* songlines as she has participated in ritual life since she was a young girl. Nungarrayi has worked tirelessly on the recording and documentation of women's *yawulyu*, especially in the DVD production *Yurntumu-Wardingki Juju-Ngaliya-Kurlangu Yawulyu: Warlpiri Women's Songs from Yuendumu* (Warlpiri Women from Yuendumu and Curran 2017) and is central to the biannual Southern Ngaliya dance camps through which she teaches this cultural knowledge to younger generations. Nungarrayi was involved in the establishment and maintenance of the Yuendumu Old People's Program in Yuendumu, where she worked for many years.

Jalangukuju yangka yawulyulkurlupa-jana milki-yirrarnilki … Nyampunya karnangku kijirni nyampuju nyuntu-nyangu ngurrara karnangku kijirni nyampuju, nyuntu-nyangu warringiyi-kirlangu.

Today, we sing the *jukurrpa* for our young generations and we say to them while we paint them that these are their grandfather's (father's father's) songs.

Yunparnilki karnalu nyampu nawu, kijirni kujakarnalu, yunparninja-karrarlu. Yuwayi warringiyi-kirlangu papa-kurlangu. Yuwayi warringiyi-kirlangu papa-kurlangu.

We sing about the Country, and we paint while singing. The grandfather's and the father's *jukurrpa*.

Kajikanparla wait-jarri kurdungurluku yinyaju, you can wait kurdungurluku.

Kajinpa juju-wardingki nyina, ngulaju yantarni. Kajikanparla wait-jarri kurdungurluku yinyaju, you can wait kurdungurluku. Kaji kangku ngula-juku yanirra kajikangku yajarnilki, "Yantarni nyanjaku!"

You have to wait for the *kurdungurlu*. If you are a ceremonial person, well, just come along. You have to wait for the *kurdungurlu*. They are the ones that say you can come to the ceremony. "Come to see!"

George (Cowboy) Jungarrayi Ryder

Known to many as "Cowboy", Jungarrayi sadly passed away in 2020. As a senior Warlpiri man and *kirda* for Ngunulurru and Yinapaka in the Lander region, Jungarrayi led the Willowra Ngajakula revitalisation project. Jungarrayi's deep knowledge was gained through a life lived on the land. He was born about 1935 "in the bush" near Mungakurlangu on the Lander. Jungarrayi recalled that his father, Fred Japaljarri Karlarlukarri, and mother, Beryl Nakamarra, took him around the Country and:

Taught me everything. They told me, "Don't do the wrong thing, you've got to follow your grandfathers." The *kurdungurlu* and old people taught me the stories about Country way, *jukurrpa*, the law. I walked everywhere, all over, without shoes, in the early days, no flour, in the bush before Welfare.

One day, while young, Jungarrayi was picked up on a truck and taken to work around Willowra station. On that occasion, he ran away, but later he worked as a stockman on Anningie, Willowra and other stations, building windmills, yards and fences, and droving cattle. He was given the name "Ryder" because he was "among horses all the time". Throughout this time, Jungarrayi maintained an intimate relationship with the land and continued to learn "from the old people". He remembered them as "really knowledgeable, important old men, living together *jintangka* ["in one, united"], *jurdalja* way,[38] *kirda* and *kurdungurlu*, no argument".

---

38 That is, observing reciprocal and respectful relations between people related through marriage.

Jungarrayi was *kurdungurlu* for the Jardiwanpa *jukurrpa* "as far as Tilkiya" and *kirda* for Ngajakula on the lower Lander. He was an expert, *juju-ngaliya*, running all the business. As an Elder, Jungarrayi took seriously his responsibility to instruct younger generations about *jukurrpa*. He shared his knowledge generously, teaching his family and other Lander families about their Countries. He also taught *kardiya*, while working tirelessly for his people on numerous collaborative intercultural projects, including the Willowra cultural mapping project, native title claims, and with Warlpiri rangers and Central Land Council land managers regarding fire and other caring-for-Country activities. Jungarrayi was a wise, dignified teacher and a deeply caring family man who left a rich legacy. He was pleased to have recorded Ngajakula and happy to share the story. The following chapter is in memory of Jungarrayi.

Chapter 8

Reanimating Ngajakula: Lander Warlpiri songs of connection and transformation

By Petronella Vaarzon-Morel, George Jungarrayi Ryder†, Teddy Jupurrula Long, Jim Wafer and Luke Kelly

Ngajakula is a major public Warlpiri ceremonial complex associated with the Japangardi-Japanangka-Japaljarri-Jungarrayi patrimoiety. It complements the *Jardiwanpa* fire ceremony, which belongs to the opposite patrimoiety. Although Dreamings associated with Ngajakula continue to be sung, the ceremony has not been performed in its entirety for many years. In 2018, the Willowra community, concerned that detailed knowledge of the songs would be lost, decided to record a Ngajakula song cycle as part of the Lander Warlpiri Cultural Mapping Project.

This chapter reflects on the initial phase of the Ngajakula project, when over 60 songs connected with the northern Lander region were recorded, and Elders Kumunjayi Jungarrayi Ryder[1] and Teddy Jupurrula Long instructed younger people about Dreamings and sites associated with the ceremonial complex. While both men and women participated in the event and sang Ngajakula, our focus here is on the portion of the songline led by Jungarrayi through his Country to the north of Willowra, along the Lander River and east (see Figure 8.1). Our account builds on long-term collaboration between Warlpiri

---

1   Sadly, Jungarrayi has since passed away, but his legacy lives on through his songs. Jungarrayi was also known in daily life as "Cowboy George". Out of respect, we refer to him here as "Kumunjayi" and "Jungarrayi" throughout the remainder of this paper.

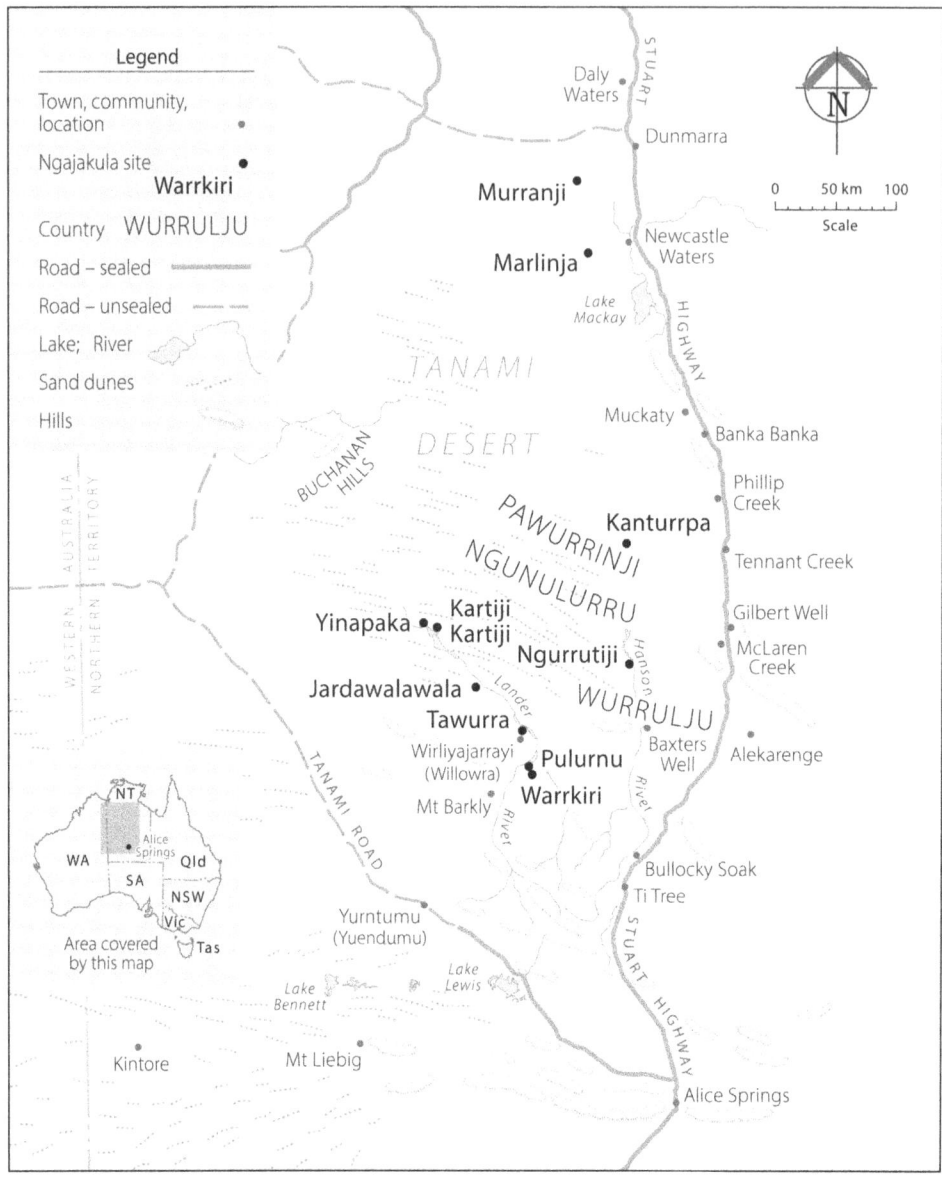

Figure 8.1. Ngajakula sites along the Lander River, north of Willowra. Map by Brendy Thornley.

and Anmatyerr knowledge holders and non-Indigenous researchers who have worked on the Willowra mapping project. The remainder of the chapter is in five main parts.

We begin by describing the context in which Ngajakula songs were recorded during the mapping project and introduce the Dreamings and associated Countries sung during the recording sessions. Then, drawing on historical

8 Reanimating Ngajakula: Lander Warlpiri songs of connection and transformation

sources, including written records and audiovisual material, in the second section, we discuss the findings of earlier ethnographic accounts of fire ceremonies, with a particular emphasis on Ngajakula. As we will see, ethnographers' evolving understandings of the fire ceremonies are instructive, revealing dimensions of Ngajakula that warrant further examination throughout the chapter.

Our discussion of the history of fire ceremonies in the different Warlpiri communities highlights both differences and similarities. There is no single authoritative reading of fire ceremonies, and the variations reveal the significance of placing ceremonial performances (and their interpretations) within the appropriate historical and socio-geographic contexts. The Warlpiri song texts discussed in this chapter are both emplaced and relational, and our chapter attempts to show how issues of scale, sociality and ecology, and the interchangeability of human and non-human beings, inflect understandings of relationality (and its embeddedness) over time. Accordingly, in the third section, we discuss the history and significance of Ngajakula in Willowra people's lives. We also consider the role Ngajakula has played historically in aligning relations between sociolinguistic groups and Countries through space and time.

The fourth section provides a condensed overview of the stories and songs of the north-eastern Ngajakula songline. The selected details offered at this point allow us to better appreciate the issues raised in the fifth section of the paper. There, we consider what it means to Willowra people to learn about the Ngajakula songs in the present and reflect on the implications of the ongoing documentation and revitalisation of Ngajakula songs and ceremony for the future.

The detailed information provided in these two sections is not primarily intended for the ethnographic archive. The collaborative authorship of this chapter reflects Willowra people's desire to utilise different technologies and approaches for promoting knowledge of Lander Warlpiri cultural heritage and engaging younger generations. The recent performance of the Ngajakula fire ceremony, a public ceremony involving men and women at Willowra, together with recordings and observations presented in this chapter, form part of the Willowra community's efforts to promote intergenerational transmission and understanding of the ceremony. This reflects the present volume's broader themes of vitality, continuity and change.

Figure 8.2. *Kurdungurlu* Teddy Jupurrurla Long instructing younger people about *jukurrpa* places (Willowra, 2018). To the left is Dwayne Ross. Photo by Petronella Vaarzon-Morel.

Recording the Ngajakula songlines

Over the past few years, the Willowra community has undertaken a cultural mapping project, in the course of which Elders have instructed younger people about their Dreamings and sites while visiting their Country (Vaarzon-Morel and Kelly 2020). In the process, those collaborating on the project have mapped sites associated with ancestral actors involved in Ngajakula, *Jardiwanpa* and other ceremonial complexes. While locating sites within estates, Elders have emphasised the significance of ceremonial associations in linking different Dreamings and social groupings concerned with the reproduction of Warlpiri social life. In recognition of the fact that Ngajakula is no longer performed, it was decided to record a particular portion of the Ngajakula songline that relates to sites to the north and east of Willowra. As Jungarrayi commented, "we can sing first and later put places on the map for young fellas to learn".[2] To date, we

---

2   Personal comment to Petronella Vaarzon-Morel.

8 Reanimating Ngajakula: Lander Warlpiri songs of connection and transformation

Figure 8.3. Preparing to record Ngajakula song cycle (Willowra, 2018). Photo by Petronella Vaarzon-Morel.

have completed the first phase of the project, which involved the recording of Jungarrayi's Ngajakula songline.

In preparation for the recording session, the ceremonial ground at Willowra was swept, firewood gathered and a windbreak erected. Jungarrayi then proceeded to carve clapsticks to beat the rhythm of the verses. Meanwhile, a large canvas map of sites visited in the Lander region was hung from a Toyota parked near the ceremony ground (see Figures 8.2 and 8.3). With women gathered a short distance away, Jungarrayi (*kirda* for Ngajakula) and Jupurrurla (his *kurdungurlu*) introduced the session by describing the importance of the project and providing an overview of Countries and key Dreamings that crisscross the Lander region. They then traced the path of Ngajakula along a north–south route as it linked different *jukurrpa* (Dreamings) and Countries and intersected two Jardiwanpa lines.

In discussing Ngajakula, they stressed that they celebrate the *jukurrpa* for Country over which they hold responsibility as *kirda* and *kurdungurlu* and that they "use proper ceremony for our area". As Jungarrayi stressed: "I can't touch that southern side [Ngaliya Warlpiri Ngajakula and Jardiwanpa songlines], only Purluwanti and Willowra and Ngunulurru area sites." Further distinguishing his songline from the southern one, Jungarrayi contrasted the vocal style of each, pointing out that he sang Ngajakula "light and high" not "*pirrjirdi*, heavy like Yuendumu mob south".

The series of Ngajakula songs that were then sung and recorded focused on encounters between ancestral beings in the section of the Ngajakula songlines that connects Marlinja (near Newcastle Waters), Ngunulurru (sandhill Country between the Lander and Hanson floodouts) and Yinapaka (Lake Surprise). The Dreamings celebrated in the songs were Purdujurru "Brush-Tailed Bettong" (*Bettongia penicillata*), Panungkarla "Ramsay's Python" (*Aspidites ramsayi*), Milwayi "Central Bandy-Bandy, Common Bandy-Bandy" (*Vermicella vermiformis*), Ngapangarna "Water bird" (also referred to as *kalwa* – the generic Warlpiri gloss for "Heron, egret"), Jurrurlujurru "Mulga Parrot (?)",[3] Jarnpa ("malevolent being"), Jurlarda ("Sugarbag", i.e., "bush honey"), Purluwanti "Eastern Barn Owl" (*Tyto javanica*), Jutiya "Desert Death Adder" (*Acanthophis pyrrhus*)[4] and Jinjiya (tree species said to be "like bloodwood").[5]

Although the Ngajakula songline also passes through Countries and celebrates Dreamings associated with the J/Napangardi and J/Napanangka semi-moiety, their songs were not sung during our recording session. We explore the recorded songs later in this chapter. In the next section, we discuss earlier ethnographic accounts of Ngajakula to contextualise our material.

---

3   This word may be a variant of *jarrurlujarrurlu*, which the *Warlpiri Encyclopaedic Dictionary* glosses as "Princess Parrot". The species is variously identified as *Psephotus varius*, *Polytelis alexandrae* and *Leptolophus hollandicus*.

4   Unlike other terms noted here, Jutiya does not appear in the *Warlpiri Encyclopaedic Dictionary*. Our identification is based on the description of the snake – its characteristic appearance and behaviour – as given by George Jungarrayi.

5   The name may be related to the Warlpiri word *jinjirla*, one meaning of which is the tip of the tail of the Rabbit-eared bandicoot. *Jinjirla* can also refer to any flower or blossom; at Willowra, it can designate flowers used in a ritual headdress.

The written history of Ngajakula: Anthropological accounts

Over a hundred years ago, ethnographers Baldwin Spencer and Francis J. Gillen (1904) wrote that Warumungu, Jingili and Wakaya tribes possessed an elaborate fire ceremony that involved both male and female participants. The ethnographers were fortunate to witness a fire ceremony performed at Tennant Creek between 24 August and 7 September 1901. They noted that it was called *Nathagura* in Warumungu and was owned by the Uluuru moiety but controlled by Kingilli, the opposite moiety. The Kingilli moiety owned the *Thaduwan* ceremony, which in turn was controlled by the Uluuru moiety (Spencer and Gillen 1904, 376). As Peterson (1970) observed, the names of these two ceremonies – *Nathagura* and *Thaduwan* – are cognate, respectively, with the Warlpiri Ngajakula and *Jardiwanpa*. These ceremonies are owned by paternally related Warlpiri patrimoieties, which are equivalent to those of the Warumungu (i.e., Japangardi-Japanangka-Jungarrayi-Japaljarri for Ngajakula and Jupurrurla-Jakamarra-Jangala-Jampijinpa for *Jardiwanpa*).

According to Spencer and Gillen, the old men told them that the purpose of the ceremony was to resolve old quarrels (1904, 387). It was, reflected the ethnographers, "a method of settling accounts up to date and starting with a clean page – everything in the nature of a dispute which occurred before this is completely blotted out and forgotten. It may, perhaps, be best described as a form of purification by fire" (Spencer and Gillen 1904, 387). Notably, the central Dreaming celebrated in the Warumungu ceremony was recorded by Spencer and Gillen as Tjudia (Jutiya in standardised Warlpiri orthography), the Death Adder. As we will see later, Jutiya Dreaming is associated with Warlpiri Countries Ngunulurru and the neighbouring Kanturrpa, both of which lie east of the Lander River and west of Tennant Creek.[6]

In August 1967, several decades after Spencer and Gillen witnessed the Warumungu fire ceremony, Nicolas Peterson and Roger Sandall filmed a Warlpiri performance of the fire ceremony at Yuendumu. The following year, Peterson witnessed the final part of another such ceremony at the settlement (1970, 203). Then, in 1970, he published a trailblazing analysis of the 1967 ceremony referred to as *Buluwandi* (Purluwanti), said to be one of "three versions" of the fire ceremony, the other two being *Djariwanba* (*Jardiwanpa*) and *Ngadjagula* (Ngajakula). The mythology of *Jardiwanpa* concerns "the travels of *Yaripiri*,

---

6   The historical association of Ngajakula with Warlpiri is attested by Laurie Reece, who noted that the "ngatjukula" [Ngajakula] ceremony is "for general viewing and participation" (1979, 28). Although Reece's dictionary was published in 1979, it is based on his research conducted at Yuendumu 30 years earlier.

a snake of the djuburula and djagamara subsections, who went from Winbago (Blanche Tower) to an unknown destination north of Hooker Creek" (Peterson 1970, 201; see also Mountford 1968). Over the years, this songline has received much ethnographic attention (Curran 2019; Dussart 2000; Gallagher et al. 2014; Langton 1993; Laughren et al. 2016; Michaels 1986; Morton 2011)[7] and will not be discussed further here except in passing.

To return to Ngajakula, Peterson identified the mythological focus of the ritual as being concerned with "the travels of a rat kangaroo, *mala*, from Mowerung [Mawurrungu], south of Yuendumu, to Walaya near Hooker Creek" (1970, 201). At the time, he stated that the mythology of what he thought was a third ceremony, *Buluwandi* (Purluwanti),[8] featured "a bird and a snake resident at Inabaga [Yinapaka] on the Lander River flood-out" (1970, 201).

A decade after filming the 1967 ceremony, the Australian Institute of Aboriginal Studies released an edited film of the original footage (Sandall, Peterson and McKenzie 1977), in which Peterson refers to the Purluwanti ritual as Ngajakula.[9] As we discuss later, although there are connections between the two Ngajakula ceremonies, which are centred (respectively) on the ancestral beings Mala and Purluwanti, Elders at Willowra regard the two songlines as different. From an eastern Warlpiri perspective, the former is said to have travelled from the Arabana region in northern South Australia via Uluru, thence to Mawurrungu and north, whereas the songline associated with Purluwanti originates north of Newcastle Waters and travels south.

In relation to the Purluwanti stories, Peterson noted that, as Purluwanti travelled "he observed ancestral men holding a fire ceremony and descended to participate in parts of it. At a number of stages he transformed himself into various other forms, a snake *Banangula* [Panungkarla], an owl, a cockatoo and a *Gurrgurrba* [Kurrakurraja] bird" (1970, 202). Then, at the end of the ceremony, Purluwanti returned to Yinapaka. Peterson observed that although Purluwanti belonged to the Japaljarri and Jungarrayi semi-moiety, if Japangardi and Japanangka men from the other semi-moiety "wished to emphasise their role they introduce song cycles, emblems and mythology that are directly associated with their subsection" (1970, 202).

---

7   See Curran (2019) for a detailed account of the history of documentation of fire ceremonies at Yuendumu.
8   Initially identified by Peterson as a stork or pelican (see later discussion).
9   In 1987, Vaarzon-Morel viewed this film with Elders at Willowra who were critical of the way the Ngajakula ceremony was performed, stating that it mixed up *Jardiwanpa* with Ngajakula. This may be due to the way the film was edited, truncating songlines, but also, as Peterson (1970) noted, because Willowra leaders were not present at the ceremony.

Regarding the purpose behind the Ngajakula and *Jardiwanpa* ceremonies, Peterson stated that Warlpiri "offer the same explanation for holding the ceremonies today as the Warramunga gave to Spencer and Gillen in 1901" (1970, 200): that is, to resolve quarrels. However, he also noted that the ceremony is concerned with not just any quarrel but aggression arising from arguments about "rights to and over women" (1970, 211). During the ceremony, some of the workers (*kurdungurlu*) attack the owners (*kirda*) with burning branches, showering sparks upon them. Explaining the reason for the aggression of the workers towards the owners of the ceremony, Peterson suggested that it is because the owners have been bestowing their daughters without respecting the rights of matrikin: that is, the patrikin have failed to acknowledge the rights of the workers in arranging their nieces' marriages (1970, 213). As Peterson demonstrated, this explanation rests on a model of sisters exchanging daughters, upon which anthropologist John Morton subsequently elaborated.

Building on Peterson's account, Morton re-analysed the symbolism of Warlpiri fire ceremonies, explaining why "conflicts conditioned by bestowal arrangements should be mediated by fire" (2011, 17). Morton observed that, although fire Dreamings are not celebrated in Warlpiri fire ceremonies, fire is not only central to the ceremonies "but also central to Aboriginal relationships as a whole" (2011, 17). In a brilliant, if complex analysis, he shows how fire is implicated symbolically in "splitting the atom of kinship" to create relations of affinity: that is, in-law relations. Drawing on Lévi-Strauss, Morton concluded that the atom is split along a generational axis "by 'integrating the opposition between self and others' and making 'individuals into partners' across a gendered moiety divide" (2011, 29). Thus, "while the singular atom is split, plural atoms are joined, so that unity lost (chaos) is also unity regained (order)" (2011, 29). Of relevance to this current chapter is Morton's insight that fire has both "masculine and feminine elements" (2011, 27). Although Morton does not explore its implications in relation to the roles of female participants in the fire ceremony, Françoise Dussart (2000) and Georgia Curran (2019) have deepened our understanding of this dimension of the ceremony.

Dussart observed that, beyond the explanation of the ceremonies being performed to resolve conflicts caused by the violation of marital relations and bestowals, "these cycles establish alliances between widows of both genders with future spouses" (2000, 78).[10] Further, they encourage the maturation of the individual. Dussart highlighted the mentoring role of the maternal uncle in the

---

10 Several years ago, reflecting on the performances of fire ceremonies over time, Nicolas Peterson observed a shift in focus of the ceremonies from conflict resolution to memorial commemoration (personal communication to Petronella Vaarzon-Morel, 2019).

ceremony and the importance of specific kinship relations in structuring lines of attack with fire and protection from assault by fire during the ceremony (2000, 80). Following Peterson's lead, Dussart positioned *Jardiwanpa*, *Kura-kurra*, Ngajakula and *Purluwanti* as distinct ceremonial cycles, stating that "*Ngajikula* coordinate[s] the managers and owners of the Rat Kangaroo Dreaming (*Marlu* [Mala] *jukurrpa*)", while "*Kura-kurra* coordinate the activities of the reciprocally allied kin associated with the Budgerigar Dreaming (*Ngatijirri jukurrpa*), Bush Onion Dreaming (*Janmarda jukurrpa*), and Brown Bird Dreaming (*Jalalapinypinypa jukurrpa*)". Distinguishing Purluwanti from Ngajakula, Dussart relates that the former is concerned with "conflict resolution and marital realliance among the *kirda* and *kurdungurlu* of Dreamings for three Ancestral beings: the Bookbook Owl (*Kurrkurrpa*), Green Parrot (*Jarrurlu-Jarrurlu*), and a Snake (*Warna*)" (2000, 79).

The accounts discussed so far highlight different aspects of the songlines. While Dussart recorded different Dreamings associated with the four Fire song cycles, Spencer and Gillen (1904), Peterson (1970) and Wild (1975, 134) observed that the focus of fire ceremonies is a single Dreaming. Thus, Peterson reported that, although other ancestral figures are associated with Purluwanti, the Owl transformed himself into these other figures during his travels (1970, 202).

Nonetheless, in a recent paper on the history of fire ceremonies at Yuendumu, Curran presented a different interpretation. She affirmed that *Jardiwanpa* differs from other Warlpiri ceremonies "focused centrally on the journey of one particular ancestral being" (2019, 22). Unlike these ceremonies, the fire ceremonies "emphasise several different Dreaming itineraries, owned by different Warlpiri groups and therefore implicate more people" (2019, 21–22).[11] Integrating these different interpretations, Laughren et al. (2016, 3) observed that, in relation to *Jardiwanpa*, different Dreaming ancestors followed the paths of Yarripiri ("Inland Taipan"), the central figure of the ceremony. Importantly, these *Jardiwanpa* ancestors did not celebrate all the Dreamings whose tracks they crossed – only those with whom they had in-law relations, thus "emphasising a key concern of the Jardiwanpa ceremony was marriage relations or *jurdalja*" (2016, 4).

Drawing on Dussart (2000), Curran surmised that the difference between *Jardiwanpa* and Warlpiri site-specific ceremonies may be attributable to the north-eastern origins of *Jardiwanpa*. The provenance of Warlpiri fire ceremonies is intriguing, and we will have more to say on the topic later in this chapter. Here, we note that Dussart recorded being told that the *Jardiwanpa* ceremony

---

11   See also Gallagher et al. (2014).

8 Reanimating Ngajakula: Lander Warlpiri songs of connection and transformation

at Yuendumu dated from the first decades of the 20th century, when it was performed by Mudburra "in an exchange event between Warlpiri, Mudbura and Warrumungu" (2000, 32).

On the other hand, Peterson contrasted the then-recent introduction of Purluwanti to Yuendumu with the more longstanding traditions of *Jardiwanpa* associated with Yarripiri and the Ngajakula line associated with the site of Mawurrungu. Specifically, he remarked that, although Purluwanti was performed regularly at Lajamanu (Hooker Creek), "unlike *Djariwanba* and *Ngadjagula* it is only of recent standing in its present form at Yuendumu" (1970, 201). By this, he meant that "the current style of performance" was recent, but not the ceremony (1970, 214).

What is clear from our discussion so far is that while there are similarities and overlaps in the various ethnographic accounts of Warlpiri fire ceremonies, there are also differences. Variations in the stories undoubtedly reflect the Dreamings owned by *kirda* participating in the rituals, as Curran has shown regarding *Jardiwanpa* held at Yuendumu, but historical changes may also influence the ceremonies themselves and people's interpretations of their meaning. Reflecting on the history of fire ceremonies, Curran (2019) suggested that the intensification of social life in settlements such as Lajamanu and Yuendumu led to an increase in large-scale ceremonies such as *Jardiwanpa*, *Kurdiji* and cult ceremonies that have a "clear social purpose". In relation to the latter, she quoted the late Harry Jakamarra Nelson, who told her that "a primary reason for holding *Jardiwanpa* was to open up the restrictions on remarriage for widows of deceased men who were associated with the Jardiwanpa Dreaming ancestors" (2019, 22).[12]

Nonetheless, according to Curran, neither the finishing up of widowhood nor conflict resolution remains central to Yuendumu people's understandings of fire ceremonies today. Moreover, as a result of people's declining knowledge of Dreamings and associated sites and the influence of monetary payments received for the staging of *Jardiwanpa* to be filmed for an intercultural audience, the

---

12 Although this explanation was also offered by Dussart, it was not explicitly mentioned by Spencer and Gillen or Peterson. The question then arises as to whether the emphasis of the ceremonies changed over time. Let us return to Spencer and Gillen's account. Although the ethnographers do not discuss an association between the fire ceremony and mourning, the fact that the bodies of some performers were daubed in white pipeclay (Spencer and Gillen 1904, 389), which is used for Sorry Business, strongly suggests such an association. Further, the ceremony involved mockery, concealment and inversion (Spencer and Gillen 1904, 377–379, 386–388), which "often are associated with the periodicity of transition" (Handelman 1988, 247). It seems likely then that the fire ceremony, which followed upon a final mortuary ritual involving "bone breaking", was concerned with the ending of a widow's period of mourning as well as conflict resolution.

relevance of the ceremonies has changed (Curran 2019, 29). Hence, she argued that "this ritual has lost something of its emergent nature as a social conflict resolution ceremony" (2019, 33). At the same time, despite the changing meaning of *Jardiwanpa* in people's lives, the fixed-filmic representations of past *Jardiwanpa* have come to signify Warlpiri tradition for the wider public.

In this section, we have tracked various ethnographic analyses of Ngajakula and *Jardiwanpa*. This survey of our interlocutors' accounts of the rituals makes it clear that, with the exception of Peterson's work, most have been Yuendumu-centred and are concerned with the *Jardiwanpa* songline associated with the travels of the Yarripiri ancestor through southern Warlpiri Country. In this next section, we present a view from the Lander and the north-east, one centred on Ngajakula and the travels of the ancestral beings Purluwanti and Kurrakurraja. Drawing on discussions of the song performance with Jupurrula Long, Jungarrayi Ryder and others in the course of the Willowra cultural mapping project and on Vaarzon-Morel's earlier field research, we discuss the history of Ngajakula performances at Willowra and note the differences from their evolution at Yuendumu.

Histories of Ngajakula in the Lander Warlpiri region

The written record of Ngajakula and *Jardiwanpa* performances at Willowra dates to 1976, when two of the authors of this chapter (Wafer and Vaarzon-Morel), who were schoolteachers at the time, were invited to participate in the ceremonies. However, fire ceremonies had been performed on earlier occasions at Willowra and by Willowra residents at other places. Thus, Curran noted that in the 1970s, when Mary Laughren and Nicolas Peterson lived at Yuendumu, "Ngajakula was held more often than Jardiwanpa as the eastern Warlpiri from Willowra were then dominant in ceremonial activity" (2019, 22).

Still earlier, as Peterson indicated, Purluwanti was performed regularly at Lajamanu during the 1960s (1970, 210). Living there at the time were some older traditional owners of Yinapaka and Countries to the north and east who knew the *jukurrpa* landscape intimately. According to Elder Jerry Jangala Patrick, with the passing of these Elders, Lajamanu ritual life became oriented to Ngaliya Warlpiri and Western Desert traditions, and Purluwanti ceased to be performed at the settlement.[13]

---

13   Jerry Jangala Patrick, personal communication to Petronella Vaarzon-Morel, 8 June 2016. The information in this section is based on Vaarzon-Morel's fieldnotes from the period when she lived at Willowra and conducted research at the invitation of the Willowra community.

Fire ceremonies are ideally performed after the beginning of August, when Napaljarri-warnu, the Pleiades constellation associated with the Ancestral Dancing Women,[14] rises from the horizon in the night sky and ushers in warmer weather.[15] Vaarzon-Morel has noted that fire performances were held around this time at Willowra during 1976, 1977, 1979, 1980, 1987 and 1988. Following the death of a Jungarrayi leader of Ngajakula, the ceremony was closed for a period and appears not to have been held again until the early 1990s.[16]

Ngajakula rituals typically began at dusk, with people gathering on the ritual ground across the Lander River, where, for a period of two weeks or more, verses from the Ngajakula repertory were sung. Clapping boomerangs, men sat separately from but within earshot of women, who sang *yawulyu* associated with Ngajakula and danced. Typically, the owners sat facing north, the direction of travel of the ancestral beings (see also Peterson 1970; Wild 1977, 17).

It was sometimes the case that the Ngajakula song cycle was sung without culminating in a full-scale fire ceremony, which required the involvement of male and female *kirda* and *kurdungurlu* living at Alekarenge,[17] Tennant Creek and elsewhere. However, if the ceremony had progressed to the stage where a decorated pole was planted in the ceremony ground, widows' mourning rituals might still be undertaken, with widows and helpers applying yellow ochre to their hair and bodies and other ritual actions. The mothers of widows would place blankets and damper at the foot of the ritual pole to be exchanged with the maternal uncle of the deceased. Thereafter, discussions may be held between the widow, her uncle and the younger brother of the widow's deceased husband concerning custodianship of her children. However, the end of a widow's period of seclusion, which enabled remarriage, was not regarded as complete until the owners of the ceremony (the patricouple of the widows) were symbolically burned with fire.[18] What was clear is that the ceremony related to themes of death, conflict resolution and revitalisation.

---

14 The prevailing winter wind comes from the south and is associated with the dust kicked up by the Dancing Women as they travelled.

15 The connection with this constellation is intriguing, and it may be the case that different astronomical phenomena are involved, as occurs in other Warlpiri ceremonies. See, for example, Chapter 3 of this volume where Peterson discusses a performance of the Warlpiri winter solstice ceremony involving the "Daylight Star", also called the "Morning Star" (Venus).

16 They may also have been held at other times.

17 Previously known as "Warrabri".

18 Following the culmination of the fire ceremonies at Willowra, it was a widow's choice if she decided to stay in the *jilimi* ("single women's camp") or if she took a partner.

The unfolding of fire ceremonies was generally a complex affair involving much intricate coordination, reflecting a continuing history of exchange among different language groups. Thus, in March 1987, Willowra people discussed introducing Ngajakula to Pintupi people at Kintore. At the time, Willowra people were attending an initiation ceremony at Kunayungku outstation near Tennant Creek, during which women were painted with *yawulyu* designs for Yinapaka, Ngunulurru, Ngarnalkurru and other Countries whose Dreamings are celebrated in Ngajakula. The event emphasised ritual ties among Lander and other eastern Warlpiri Countries, including Kanturrpa, Miyikampi, Ngurratiji, Pawurrinji and Wurrulju.

The plan was to meet up at Yuendumu for a ritual exchange between Warlpiri and Pintupi; in April, some Elders from Willowra travelled to Yuendumu to begin preparations. However, as Kintore people had still not arrived by May, they returned to Willowra. Then, in August, a *Jardiwanpa* ceremony was held at Willowra. Like the earlier ceremony at Kunayungku, it involved weeks of singing and the widows' ritual but was not completed because the spectacular ritual involving the burning of owners did not happen. It was then planned to begin Ngajakula again after a few weeks' break, when it was hoped that Kintore people would arrive to stage the Ngajakula fire ceremony, followed by the conclusion of *Jardiwanpa*. After waiting some weeks, in November, Willowra people brought the Ngajakula ceremony to Kintore for a ceremony involving people from Kiwirrkura, Kintore and Amunturrngu (Mount Liebig).

The men gave Vaarzon-Morel various reasons for undertaking the ritual exchange, including that "Kintore mob really wanted it"[19] and that, unlike Yuendumu, where promised marriages were no longer undertaken and young people "married any way", Kintore was a place of "strong law" like Willowra, where people knew their Dreamings. As one Napaljarri expressed it, "right way marriage comes from knowing Dreamings and learning about country".[20] While it is beyond the scope of this paper to examine the ceremonial exchange, we note that Engineer Jack Japaljarri and other Elders from Alekarenge accompanied Willowra men and women to Kintore where the full-scale fire ceremony was performed, for which Warlpiri *kirda* and *kurdungurlu* were paid with money and blankets. The leaders of the ceremony on this occasion were Japangardi and Japanangka affiliated with Ngarnalkurru Country. Reflecting on the event some

---

19 Japangardi Williams, personal communication to Petronella Vaarzon-Morel, 6 November 1987.
20 Napaljarri, personal communication to Petronella Vaarzon-Morel.

years later in 1990, Jungarrayi commented: "they got that Purluwanti now at Kintore: we connect together, Willowra, Kintore and Mount Liebig".

Establishing new ceremonies in a place enables Elders from that place to link the songlines to yet other places. Linking songlines across different cultural landscapes may also facilitate the exchange of new ceremonies.[21] In fact, the two processes are intimately connected.

Early Ngajakula exchanges

Although the *jukurrpa*[22] that feature in Ngajakula are said to have existed in place *tarnngaku* ("forever"), it is clear the ceremony itself has long moved across the landscape.[23] In the 1990s, the late C. Jampijinpa Martin told Vaarzon-Morel that he first saw Ngajakula performed at Warrabri settlement shortly after people were moved there from Phillip Creek and Bullocky Soak[24] and that Engineer Jack Japaljarri was the ceremonial leader. Teddy Jupurrula also recalled attending Ngajakula at Warrabri, stating that "we went for big training from Willowra" with the "old people" from Newcastle Waters, Muckaty and Banka Banka who brought the ceremony to the settlement. The Elders included Pharlap Dixon Japaljarri (Jalyirri) and Andy Japaljarri from Elliott region who, along with Engineer Jack, were considered ceremonial leaders.

Then, in the late 1960s, Pharlap visited Willowra on a government works program and helped stage a Ngajakula performance involving Jimmy Jungarrayi Kitson, Long Mick Jungarrayi, Long Paddy Japaljarri, Engineer Jack Japaljarri, Jimmy Newcastle Japaljarri and Chicken Jack Japaljarri.[25] Jupurrurla recalled that "we used to sing all night, no sleep for three and a half weeks, all day and night, before next morning finish up".[26] He described old Wirtilki Japanangka from Ngarnalkurru as a senior Willowra leader, noting that Johnny Martin Jampijinpa was "the right *kurdungurlu* for Ngajakula" while Johnny Kitson was "Purluwanti himself". Sadly, these people have all passed away.

---

21 For example, Vaarzon-Morel noted this to occur in the 1980s, when a senior *kirda* for the *mala* (Rufous Hare-Wallaby) Dreaming at Ngarnalkurru visited Uluru and connected the Warlpiri songline to that of Yankuntjatjarra owners of Uluru. Not long after, people from Uluru visited Willowra and exchanged ceremonies.
22 And kin-based relationships among countries.
23 During discussions of Ngajakula as part of the mapping project in 2016, Jupurrurla cryptically remarked that "them Anmatyerr people used to have ceremony like Ngajakula, but they forgot about it".
24 Martin Jampijinpa, personal communication to Petronella Vaarzon-Morel, 2008.
25 The last few men travelled from Warrabri.
26 T. Long Jupurrurla, personal communication to Petronella Vaarzon-Morel, 9 April 2021.

Prior to this event, Jungarrayi and other Willowra people had worked on the cattle stations in the north, where they mixed with Jingili, Mudburra and Warlmanpa people. Jupurrurla recalled that while Willowra people figured out how they were related to others through the skin system, they were perplexed by *ngurlu*[27] – that is, Mudburra matrilineal social totemism. In this system, a person cannot marry someone of the same *ngurlu*, regardless of whether they are members of subsections that would be otherwise marriageable. As Jupurrurla explained it, a man might think a woman was the right one for him, but she might say "sorry [*ngurlu* way] I'm your mother".

It is apparent from discussions with Elders that the earlier days of intracultural gatherings were marked by an excess of tension sparked by arguments between local and visiting men over women.[28] Ngajakula provided a way to create unity. Thus, Jungarrayi described one occasion when they were camped near Elliott and participated in a Ngajakula performance led by local Japaljarri and Jungarrayi and involving Japanangka and Japangardi from Country on Muckaty station.[29] Jupurrurla recalled people saying to each other, "we thought, we are all *warlalja* [countrymen][30] and we need to finish up, say sorry, start fresh". Jupurrurla recounted that large quantities of material items including money, blankets, flour, tea, sugar, and kangaroo and emu meat were exchanged during the ceremony.

It is clear from our discussion that Ngajakula is an incorporative songline. However, it differs from initiation and other ceremonies that have dramatically expanded in recent years (Peterson 2000). These stress inclusiveness and represent a move away from "site-based ceremonies" (Peterson 2000, 213) and "rituals based on specific knowledge of Dreamings" (Curran 2011, 48). While Ngajakula worked to create a sense of relatedness and community among people from disparate language and cultural groups, it did so through songlines

---

27 This word is distinguished from the Warlpiri term *ngurlu* (meaning "seed") because it refers to a form of totemism inherited through the matriline (mother's brother). It is not estate-based like Warlpiri Dreamings. Nonetheless, we gratefully note an anonymous reviewer's observation that, while it's possible the Warlpiri term for *ngurlu* totemism may be only accidentally homophonous with the Warlpiri term for "seed", several "ngurlu" in the Elliott region are actually the names of seeds. M.J. Meggitt is the only ethnographer to have noted that "the Walbiri belief in matrispirits is historically connected with the *ngulu* beliefs of the neighbouring Mudbara, Djingili and Warramunga" (1962, 193). He likened the "Walbiri stress [on] the solidarity of the matriline at the betrothal or death of a member" (1962, 193) to the support that Murinbata *ngulu* clansmen give each other further north.
28 See also Meggitt (1962, 29, 35–36).
29 Jungarrayi named "One Fella Boot" Jangala as a main *kurdungurlu*.
30 Cf. Peterson (2000, 207).

that connect Dreamings and places associated with particular estates, aligning marriage relations among people from the estates that stand in a *jurdalja* ("in-law") relationship to each other.[31]

Stories and songs associated with north-eastern Ngajakula songline

It is beyond the scope of this chapter to list all the Ngajakula sites recorded in the songs and to analyse the relevant stories in detail, so here we limit ourselves to an overview of Dreaming stories and songs central to the Lander Ngajakula.

From the perspective of Willowra people, their Ngajakula starts at Murranji and travels through Jardawalawala, Pulurnu, Kartiji-Kartiji, Ngunulurru, Kanturrpa, Ngurrutiji and Ngarnalkurru, among other places, and south to Wirliyajarrayi (Willowra) area. Ngajakula is said to "change colours" and "changeover" (switch, transform and exchange) as the songline travels through different Countries. As noted previously, Purluwanti, "Eastern Barn Owl" (*Tyto javanica*) is one of the two main ancestral beings associated with the north-eastern Ngajakula, the other being Kurrakurraja, the Channel-Billed Cuckoo (*Scythrops novaehollandiae*), commonly referred to as "Storm Bird".[32]

Ngajakula, unlike *Jardiwanpa*, is concerned with waterbirds, which Purluwanti "keeps singing" to bring rain. Kurrakurraja is a long-distance traveller who brings rain from the far north and creates swamps in the sandhill Country east of Yinapaka. Willowra Elders trace its path through Jingili, Mudburra and Warlmanpa territories, noting that a branch also travelled through the Warumungu region. A migratory bird, Kurrakurraja lays its eggs only in the nests of other birds and is the classic troublemaker. The Kurrakurraja Dreaming is primarily associated with Japangardi and Japanangka subsections, whereas Purluwanti is associated with Japaljarri and Jungarrayi.

Purluwanti and Kurrakurraja Dreamings are regarded as *malirlangu*, or *jurdalja*,[33] travelling "side by side".[34] The two Dreamings unite the Countries that they visit. Thus, despite being associated with different subsections in the

---

31 It is beyond the scope of this paper to address the symbolism of the Dreamings except in passing.
32 Warlpiri sometimes also refer to Kurrakurraja as a "pelican" or *kalwa* "stork", which likely accounts for Peterson's (1970) initial identification of a "stork" or "pelican" as the main ancestral figure of Purluwanti.
33 This term refers to in-law pairs. People in *jurdalja* relationships "exchange their children as mother-in-laws (*malirdi*)" and also gifts such as boomerangs and shields. The *jurdalja* relationship is reciprocal (Laughren et al. 2022, 141).
34 Not necessarily in the same direction.

same moiety, they are considered to be *jintangka*, "in one". Countries associated with this patrimoiety are referred to as *ngurrayatujumparra*. Although it is beyond the scope of this chapter to discuss the Kurrakurraja stories further, we note that Kurrakurraja flies from Murranji to Yinapaka, then to a site in Ngarnalkurru Country, before returning to Ngunulurru and Murranji.

Purluwanti travels from Ngurruwaji to Murranji and Marlinja (near Newcastle Waters Homestead) before returning to Yinapaka, thence to sites such as Tawurra (in Ngarnalkurru area), Warrkiri near Willowra and back to Yinapaka. We noted earlier Peterson's observation that as Purluwanti travelled, "he observed ancestral men holding a fire ceremony and descended to participate in parts of it" (1970, 202). Kurrakurraja is similar. In describing the mirroring of everyday life in *jukurrpa* cosmology, Jungarrayi remarked that the ancestral beings "get together and finish 'em up. Same like *yapa*, *jukurrpa* does the same way again. They all finish 'em together in ceremony. They all get satisfied. They get [suffer] pain and it's finished. The troublemakers then went back to his country." Yinapaka is both a main place for Purluwanti and something of a crossroad, a "main centre" for Countries in the *ngurrayatujumparra* relationship, where certain Dreamings change over from one patricouple to the other in the same moiety.

The 2018 performance of Ngajakula songs at Willowra

The north-eastern Ngajakula song sets we recorded in 2018 were performed over two days (27–28 June), each divided into morning and afternoon sessions. The final video, compiled and edited to remove extraneous material, includes two hours of singing, interspersed with an additional half-hour of commentary (mostly in Warlpiri, with some English).[35] In geographical terms, the songs were concerned principally with two sets of sites located on longitudinally opposite sides of the sandhill Country of the northern Tanami Desert and with the relationship between them.

The southern sites, such as Kartiji-Kartiji and Ngunulurru, are situated between (and a little to the north of) the termini of two river systems: the Lander floodout at Lake Surprise (Yinapaka) and the Hanson floodout near Emu Bore (Yankirri-kurlangu). The northern sites are located in the region around Newcastle Waters and Murranji, with a focus on the site of Marlinja. Note, however, that the songs sung at Willowra in 2018 went only "halfway"

---

35 At the request of Jungarrayi Ryder and other Willowra Elders, copies of this material are deposited on a designated cultural heritage computer at Willowra Learning Centre; the material is also archived at Central Land Council for Willowra people's future use. Work on further analysis of the material with Willowra community is not yet completed.

to Marlinja. North of the site of Kulunganjalpa ("Buchanan Hills"),[36] they are regarded as belonging to others.

The performance was divided into seven song sets, with breaks between them: four on 27 June 2018 and three on 28 June. In the overview given here, the song sets are numbered 1–7, with the relevant site names given first and the Dreamings following in brackets.

1. Kartiji-kartiji to Kulunganjalpa (Purdujurru, Panungkarla, Milwayi)
2. Kulumpujuju to Ngunulurru; Parnparri (Ngapangarna, Jurrurlujurru)
3. Ngunulurru (Ngapangarna, Jurlarda)
4. Ngunulurru (Jurlarda)
5. Murranji to Yinapaka to Ngunulurru (Purluwanti)
6. Kulunganjalpa, en route to Marlinja (Panungkarla, Milwayi)
7. Ngunulurru (Jutiya, Jinjiya, Jurlarda)

Sets 1 and 6 pertain to the route between Kartiji-Kartiji and Kulunganjalpa, which is said to be "halfway" between Kartiji-Kartiji (near Lake Surprise) and Marlinja (near Newcastle Waters). Sets 2–5 and 7 all focus on the site (and "Country") known as Ngunulurru, in the sandhills between Lake Surprise and the Hanson floodout.

It is noteworthy that the "mobile" Dreamings from the two groups of songs travel in different directions, using different ambulatory modes. In sets 1 and 6, Panungkarla slithers overland from south to north; in sets 3 and 4, Jurlarda comes on tiny wings from further south, via Kanturrpa, to Ngunulurru.[37] By contrast, in set 5, Purluwanti flies in the opposite direction, from north to south; in set 2, Ngapangarna takes to the air at Kulumpujuju, west of Willowra, and flies eastwards to Ngunulurru. (Most of the other Dreamings in both sets are localised.)

The songs in sets 1 and 6 clearly belong to a single narrative complex. Part of the evidence is that the only time a song was repeated *between* sets was when the first song in set 1 was sung again at the beginning of set 6. Repetitions were otherwise infrequent and occurred only *within* a set (twice in set 1, once in set 5, twice in set 6 and once in set 7).

---

36 Named "Buchanan's Hills" on 10 June 1900 by Allan A. Davidson, leader of the Central Australian Exploration Syndicate, to honour a member of the expedition called George Buchanan (Davidson and Winnecke 1905, 26). The low range is located 77 kilometres south-east of Lajamanu, near Duck Ponds outstation (Mirirrinyungu).

37 Jurlarda travels from Muntarri (Gilbert Well, south of Tennant Creek) through Kanturrpa to Yirrinirli (on the Lander) and Ngunulurru.

The songs in the other four sets all pertain, as mentioned, to Ngunulurru. However, whereas the movements of Panungkarla give coherence to the narrative of sets 1 and 6, there is no single Dreaming that performs the same function for the Ngunulurru songs. Instead, there are three mobile Dreamings (Ngapangarna, Purluwanti and Jurlarda) associated with different, overlapping narrative lines. The following synopsis is thus divided into four narrative complexes, based on the travels of Panungkarla (*Aspidites ramsayi* "Ramsay's Python"[38]), Ngapangarna "Water Bird",[39] Purluwanti "Eastern Barn Owl" (*Tyto javanica*) and Jurlarda "Sugarbag".[40]

The travels of Panungkarla (song sets 1 and 6)

Kartiji-Kartiji is the home of Purdujurru "Brush-Tailed Bettong" (*Bettongia penicillata*), who occupies himself with digging for roots of the *wayipi* "Tar Vine" (*Boerhavia diffusa*). Panungkarla arrives on the scene hunting for Jungunypa "Spinifex Hopping-Mouse" (*Notomys alexis*), but the Mouse keeps getting away. Panungkarla gets sweaty from the chase and gives up in hunger and frustration. It is already dark when he gets back to his camp. During the night, he turns into an Emu.

The next morning, when he wakes up as a Snake again, he hurries on his way, still hungry, towards Marlinja. But, about halfway, at Kulunganjalpa, he meets Milwayi[41] "Central Bandy-Bandy, Common Bandy-Bandy" (*Vermicella vermiformis*), and they have an argument. They draw their knives and get ready for a fight,[42] jumping round and challenging each other. But they are too scared to stab each other, so they decide to continue on their way.

---

38 Also known as *pirntina* and *malilyi* in southern dialects of Warlpiri and as "woma" in English (a borrowing from Diyari, according to Dixon, Ramson and Thomas 1990, 106). The word *panungkarla* is no doubt related to *baningkula*, glossed by the *Mudburra to English Dictionary* (Green et al. 2019, 73) as "Water Python" (*Liasis fuscus*) and said to be a creator of "the central Dreaming track for Jingili people. All the other Dreaming tracks connect with or cross this one."

39 Also known as *kalwa* in southern dialects of Warlpiri. This may suggest an association with the "White-Necked Heron", called *jarlwa* in Gurindji (Meakins et al. 2013, 88; these authors identify the species as *Egretta pacifica* [*Ardea pacifica*?]) or, alternatively, with the "Blue Crane", called *darliwa* in Jingulu (Pensalfini 2011, 136), probably *Egretta novaehollandiae*. Pensalfini (2011, 198) noted that *darliwa* is specifically associated with Murranji.

40 Honey (and honeycomb) produced by Minikiyi "Native Bees" (*Trigona* sp.).

41 This name may be related to Warumungu/Warlmanpa *milywaru*, tentatively glossed as "quiet snake species" by Nash (1990, 212).

42 The name of the site of these events, Kulunganjalpa, is no doubt based on the Warlpiri word *kulu* "a fight".

Commentary: Jungarrayi, the lead singer, said he knows the songs for the section of the songline that continues on to Marlinja, but he stops at Kulunganjalpa. North of there, the songs belong to some now-deceased Warlmanpa people.

The travels of Ngapangarna (song sets 2 and 3)

Ngapangarna flies from Kulumpujuju to Ngunulurru. An associated Dreaming is Jurrurlujurru "Mulga Parrot", whose home is a site called Parnparri (near Emu Bore). At Ngunulurru, Ngapangarna's path crosses that of Jurlarda.

The travels of Purluwanti (song set 5)

Purluwanti flies from Murranji Country to Yinapaka, then across the plain to Ngunulurru. It does not land but is just looking around, "like a satellite" (as Jupurrula put it). Then it flies back to Murranji.

The travels of Jurlarda (song sets 3, 4 and 7)

Jurlarda comes from the south in the form of Minikiyi "Honey Bees". From their nest inside a tree at Ngunulurru, they try to get out of the entrance hole (called *wilpiri*), but the lump of honeycomb ("Sugarbag") they have produced is too big, and the hole is blocked by sand. One Bee manages to get through, but the sun dries him out, and he falls to the ground. Later, a Bee comes back in through the "eye" (*milpa* – a synonym for *wilpiri*).

Associated Dreamings include a bloodwood-like tree called Jinjiya (also known as Warlamarti) and its flower, called Yurrkulju, as well a snake called Jutiya "Desert Death Adder" (*Acanthophis pyrrhus*). The Jutiya changes colour, from red to orange to yellow, then turns itself into a human being.

Linguistic and musical features of the songs

At this stage of the revitalisation process, we have transcribed 12 of the approximately 60 songs that were sung at Willowra in 2018.[43] Transcription of the texts is complicated by the fact that many of the songs are in "song language" rather than standard Warlpiri. The phonology is consistent with Warlpiri, and some morphemes and phrases are readily recognisable. For example, the lines *Jutiya warna-jarrayi / Jutiya yapa-jarrayi* that occur in the second song of set 7 translate without difficulty as "Jutiya turned into a snake / Jutiya turned into a man". However, many lexemes in the recorded songs are not found in Warlpiri –

---

43 Textual transcriptions by Jim Wafer, musical transcriptions by Benjamin Lambert.

at least, as the language is recorded in the monumental *Warlpiri Encyclopaedic Dictionary* produced by Laughren et al. (2022).

Further research may reveal that some of the "song language" derives from one or more languages spoken to the north of Warlpiri. In light of the historical evidence suggesting that Ngajakula was brought to Warlpiri Country from the north, the most likely source languages are Warlmanpa, Mudburra, Jingulu, Gurindji and Warumungu. Alternatively, the songs may have originated even further away or even been received in "spirit language".[44]

On the surface, the musical features of the songs have much in common with those sketched out in previous research on Warlpiri men's singing practices (e.g., Wild 1975, 1977, 1979, 1984, 1987). However, there is a marked deficit of transcriptions of Warlpiri *men*'s songs – in contrast with a recent relative abundance of studies of Warlpiri women's songs – which makes comparison difficult. Further work is needed, and we are hoping to produce a more detailed account of the texts and music of the north-eastern Ngajakula cycle in a future publication.

Learning about the Ngajakula songs in the present

Referring to the southern Ngajakula songline, Liam Campbell reported that [the late] "Jakamarra Nelson, who has sung the Mawurrungu songs as a ceremonial leader, said it was not until late in his life, when he finally went to Mawurrungu, that he understood them" (2006, 29). A person's understanding of the deeper metaphorical meaning of songs and related rituals is clearly based on an embodied knowledge of places – but not only on that. It also depends on their seniority and the right to speak for the places and associated songs as either *kirda* or *kurdungurlu*.

Even in this scenario from earlier times, learning was an ongoing and patchy process[45] influenced by context (political and historical), social relatedness and opportunities to visit Country. With the increasingly mobile and diasporic nature of the Willowra community and the passing of Elders, opportunities for learning about Ngajakula have declined. Discussions of past Ngajakula events can evoke memories of lost kin and relationships. As Jupurrurla commented regarding the recording we made in 2018, "when old women see this video

---

44 Songs of the latter type are generally regarded as untranslatable (see Apted 2010).
45 As we have discussed earlier in the chapter, in relation to differing ethnographic accounts of the fire ceremonies, this is the case not only for Aboriginal people but also for their non-Indigenous interlocutors.

8 Reanimating Ngajakula: Lander Warlpiri songs of connection and transformation

they may get sad and very emotional, remembering the old people who used to sing the ceremony". However, it is also by teaching young people about the Ngajakula songlines that connections between Countries can be revitalised.

The process of learning about Ngajakula is complicated further by its changing pertinence. It is not so much that people no longer know the sites mentioned in fire ceremony songs, as Curran (2019) has suggested is the case with *Jardiwanpa* at Yuendumu, but rather that promised marriages no longer occur and *jurdalja* alliances between proximate Countries have substantially diminished. Although most marriages among the younger generation are still contracted "right way" in terms of subsection affiliations, they are no longer moored in Country in the same way as in the past.

By teaching the younger generations about the eastern Warlpiri Ngajakula songline, Jungarrayi and Jupurrurla hoped to promote greater understanding of the historically complex and interdependent nature of relationhips between Countries in the wider Willowra region. Specifically, the travels and activities of ancestral beings associated with the songlines articulate relations of both exchange and cooperation among Countries in the *ngurrayatujumparra* relationship, as well as their reciprocal relationships with *kurdungurlu* from the opposite moiety. Although not detailed in this chapter, they also reveal culturally significant connections among plants, animals and topography of the Countries with which the songline is concerned.

Conclusion

In his analysis of *Jardiwanpa*, Morton convincingly shows how fire mediates social relations by splitting the atom of kinship to create affinal relations. However, he does not directly address why the fire ceremonies take the form they do, involving long-distance songlines.

The late Marshall Sahlins, in his theory of kinship, argued that kinship is a "mutuality of being" (2013, 18) in which kinship is built on two kinds of mutuality. The first includes forms reckoned from birth, including consanguineal and affinal (thus symbolic, not biological) relations, while the second is made throughout life by "participation in one another's existence" (Sahlins 2013, 18). Ngajakula, which involves the mutual recognition of shared Law through the infrastructure of travelling Dreamings, emphasises both. It promotes a sense of kinship with a wider community than arguably was the case prior to European settlement. As Jupurrurla reflected, "they stuck together with olden time law". The genius of Ngajakula (as with *Jardiwanpa*) is in the way it elaborates metaphorical aspects of localised Dreamings to reinforce shared Law.

Acknowledgements

We thank the late Gordon Japangardi Presley, the late Peter Japanangka Williams, Lucy Nampijinpa and other senior Willowra people for encouraging us to record the Ngajakula ceremony and for providing exegesis for this publication. Thanks also to Lance Lewis and Dwayne Jupurrula Ross for their assistance with interpreting the song texts. We also thank Benjamin Lambert for notating the Ngajakula songs and Dr Graeme Skinner for his assistance with the musical score. We are especially grateful to members of the 2018 Willowra Granites Mines Affected Areas Aboriginal Corporation and Nick Raymond for their support, without which the transcription of the Ngajakula songs would not have happened. Our thanks are also due to Angela Zacharek and *yapa* staff of the Willowra Learning Centre, who provided space and a warm welcome for our Ngajakula workshops. We have benefited from the thoughtful comments of our anonymous reviewers and thank them for their efforts. Thanks also to Brenda Thornley for preparing the map and to the editors of this volume for inviting us to contribute to it.

References

Apted, Meiki E. 2010. "Songs from the Inyjalarrku: The Use of a Nontranslatable Spirit Language in a Song Set from North-West Arnhem Land, Australia". *Australian Journal of Linguistics* 30(1): 93–103.

Campbell, Liam. 2006. *Darby: One Hundred Years of Life in a Changing Culture.* Sydney: Australian Broadcasting Corporation and Warlpiri Media Association.

Curran, Georgia. 2011. "The 'Expanding Domain' of Warlpiri Initiation Rituals". In *Ethnography and the Production of Anthropological Knowledge: Essays in Honour of Nicolas Peterson,* edited by Yasmine Musharbash and Marcus Barber, 39–50. Canberra: ANU E Press.

Curran, Georgia. 2019. "'Waiting for Jardiwanpa': History and Mediation in Warlpiri Fire Ceremonies". *Oceania* 89(1): 20–35.

Davidson, Alan A. and C. Winnecke. 1905. *Mr Davidson's Explorations in the Northern Territory of South Australia.* Adelaide: Government Printer.

Dixon, R.M.W., W.S. Ramson and Mandy Thomas. 1990. *Australian Aboriginal Words in English: Their Origin and Meaning.* Melbourne: Oxford University Press.

Dussart, Françoise. 2000. *The Politics of Ritual in an Aboriginal Settlement: Kinship, Gender, and the Currency of Knowledge.* Washington: Smithsonian Institution Press.

Gallagher, Coral, Peggy Brown, Georgia Curran and Barbara Martin. 2014. *Jardiwanpa Yawulyu: Warlpiri Women's Songs from Yuendumu* (including CD). Batchelor: Batchelor Institute Press.

Green, Rebecca, Jennifer Green, Amanda Hamilton-Holloway, Felicity Meakins and David Osgarby. 2019. *Mudburra to English Dictionary*. Canberra: Aboriginal Studies Press.

Handelman, Don. 1988. "Inside-Out, Outside-In: Concealment and Revelation in Newfoundland Christmas Mumming". In *Text, Play, and Story: The Construction and Reconstruction of Self and Society*, edited by Edward M. Bruner, 247–77. Prospect Heights, Illinois: Waveland Press.

Langton, Marcia. 1993. *"Well, I Heard It on the Radio and I Saw It on the Television …": An Essay for the Australian Film Commission on the Politics and Aesthetics of Filmmaking by and about Aboriginal People and Things*. Woolloomooloo: Australian Film Commission.

Laughren, Mary, Kenneth Hale, Jeannie Nungarrayi Egan, Patrick Marlurrku, Paddy Jangala, Robert Hoogenraad, David Nash and Jane Simpson. 2022. *Warlpiri Encyclopaedic Dictionary*. Canberra, ACT: Aboriginal Studies Press.

Laughren, Mary, Georgia Curran, Myfany Turpin and Nicolas Peterson. 2016. "Women's Yawulyu Songs as Evidence of Connections to and Knowledge of Land: The Jardiwanpa". In *Language, Land and Song: Studies in Honour of Luise Hercus*, edited by Peter K. Austin, Harold Koch and Jane Simpson, 419–449. London: EL Publishing.

Meakins, Felicity, Patrick McConvell, Erika Charola, Norm McNair, Helen McNair and Lauren Campbell. 2013. *Gurindji to English Dictionary*. Batchelor: Batchelor Institute Press.

Meggitt, Mervyn. 1962. *Desert People: A Study of the Walbiri Aborigines of Central Australia*. Sydney: Angus & Robertson.

Michaels, Eric. 1986. *The Aboriginal Invention of Television in Central Australia 1982–1986*. Canberra: Australian Institute of Aboriginal Studies.

Morton, John. 2011. "Splitting the Atom of Kinship: Towards an Understanding of the Symbolic Economy of the Warlpiri Fire Ceremony". In *Ethnography and the Production of Anthropological Knowledge: Essays in Honour of Nicolas Peterson,* edited by Yasmine Musharbash and Marcus Barber, 17–38. Canberra: ANU E Press.

Mountford, Charles P. 1968. *Winbaraku and the Myth of Jarapiri*. Adelaide: Rigby.

Nash, David. 1990. "Patrilects of the Warumungu and Warlmanpa and their Neighbours". In *Language and History: Essays in Honour of Luise A. Hercus*, edited by Peter K. Austin, Harold Koch and Jane Simpson, 209–20. Canberra: Pacific Linguistics C-116.

Pensalfini, Rob. 2011. *Jingulu Texts and Dictionary*. Canberra: Pacific Linguistics.

Peterson, Nicolas. 1970. "Buluwandi: A Central Australian Ceremony for the Resolution of Conflict". In *Australian Aboriginal Anthropology: Modern Studies in the Social Anthropology of the Australian Aborigines*, edited by Ronald M. Berndt, 200–15. Nedlands: University of Western Australia Press.

Peterson, Nicolas. 2000. "An Expanding Aboriginal Domain: Mobility and the Initiation Journey". *Oceania* 70(3): 205–18.

Reece, Laurie. 1979. *Dictionary of the Wailbiri (Warlpiri, Walpiri), Language* (Oceania Linguistic Monographs 22). Sydney: University of Sydney Press.

Sahlins, Marshall. 2013. *What Kinship Is – and Is Not*. Chicago: University of Chicago Press.

Sandall, Roger, dir, Nicolas Peterson, narr, and Kim McKenzie, ed. 1977. *A Walbiri Fire Ceremony: Ngatjakula*. Canberra: Australian Institute of Aboriginal Studies.

Spencer, Baldwin and F.J. Gillen. 1904. *The Northern Tribes of Central Australia*. London: Macmillan.

Vaarzon-Morel, Petronella and Luke Kelly. 2020. "Enlivening People and Country: The Lander Warlpiri Cultural Mapping Project". In *Archival Returns: Central Australia and Beyond*, edited by Linda Barwick, Jennifer Green and Petronella Vaarzon-Morel, 111–138. Sydney: Sydney University Press.

Wild, Stephen. 1975. Walbiri Music and Dance in Their Social and Cultural Nexus. PhD thesis, Indiana University, Bloomington.

Wild, Stephen. 1977. "Men as Women: Female Dance Symbolism in Walbiri Men's Rituals". *Dance Research Journal* 10(1): 14–22.

Wild, Stephen. 1979. "A Public Song Series of Central Australia". Unpublished paper presented to the *Third National Conference of the Musicological Society of Australia*, Monash University, 18–21 May.

Wild, Stephen. 1984. "Warlbiri Music and Culture: Meaning in a Central Australian Song Series". In *Problems and Solutions: Occasional Essays in Musicology Presented to Alice M. Moyle*, edited by Jamie C. Kassler and Jill Stubington, 186–203. Sydney: Hale & Iremonger.

Wild, Stephen. 1987. "Recreating the *Jukurrpa*: Adaptation and Innovation of Songs and Ceremonies in Warlpiri Society". In *Songs of Aboriginal Australia*, edited by Margaret Clunies Ross, Tamsin Donaldson and Stephen Wild, 97–120. University of Sydney: Oceania Monographs.

Dolly Nampijinpa (Daniels) Granites (1936–2004)

Dolly Nampijinpa (Daniels) Granites was a Warlpiri leader, artist and land rights advocate. Born a decade before her people were forced to settle at the Central Australian ration depot of Yuendumu in 1946, Dolly showed an early and keen interest in promoting Warlpiri culture beyond the confines of the settlement.

Through marriage and family kin ties, Dolly ultimately acquired fluency in languages and rituals that extended beyond Yuendumu. She used this extensive knowledge – which included Pitjantjatjara, Pintupi, Anmatyerre and Gurunji Dreamings from as far away as Darwin and Uluru – to educate not only the Warlpiri but also numerous non-Aboriginal researchers. She helped found and subsequently chaired the Warlulurlangu Artist Association, which continues to thrive at Yuendumu. She was a key participant in the monumental land claims of 1976 and 1984, which ultimately returned large territories to the Ngalia-Warlpiri.

> I am strong and can know about rituals because I hold this strength about knowing from my father's father and my fathers' sisters, my mothers, my mothers' mothers, my mothers' brothers, and my husbands. I hold them all in my heart and people know I can sing Dreaming stories all the way over many countries. (Dolly Nampijinpa Daniels, 2000)

Judy Nampijinpa Granites (1934–2015)

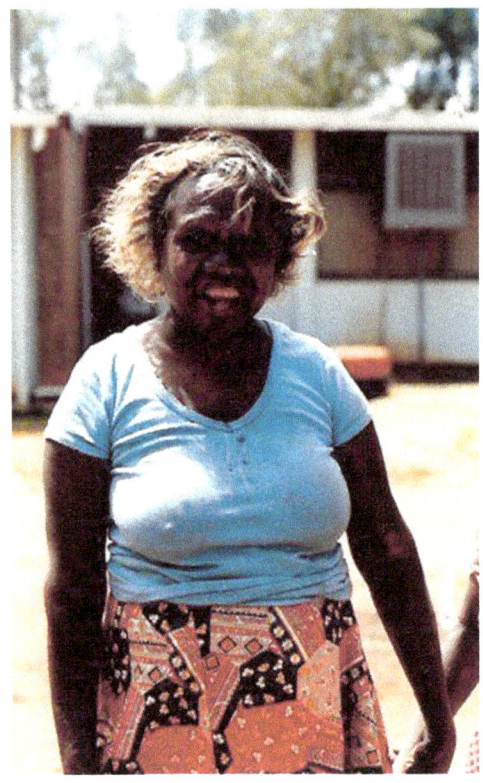

Judy Nampijinpa Granites was an extraordinary Warlpiri leader and land rights advocate. As a child, Judy moved around with her family enjoying their hunting and gathering way of life until her parents came to live near Mount Doreen (where non-Indigenous people mined for copper and tungsten). Along with others, she was relocated to a ration depot called Yuendumu in 1946. Even as an adolescent and young mother of five boys, she showed great interest in ritual and political affairs within and beyond the confines of the settlement of Yuendumu. She encouraged her sons to get educated and involve themselves to better the lives of their people. Judy – through marriages, kin ties and her involvement with missionaries, land rights activists and researchers – visited many Indigenous territories and communities. Judy was an extraordinary teacher and philosopher who promoted the cultural rights of her people with verve and aplomb. She remained curious about other cultures and the plight of other Indigenous peoples worldwide until her tragic death.

Lynette Nampijinpa Granites (c.1945–)

Nampijinpa was born in 1945 at Mount Doreen Station. She grew up and was educated in Yuendumu in the early Baptist Mission. Following on from her older sisters, who were key leaders for ceremonies in Yuendumu for many decades, Nampijinpa is an important senior *yawulyu* singer. She is *kirda* for Warlukurlangu "Belonging to the Fire", Ngapa "Rain/Water" and Pamapardu "Flying Ant" *jukurrpa*. Nampijinpa is also an acclaimed international artist and has exhibited her paintings worldwide. She has also long held an important role on the board of the Aboriginal Areas Protection Authority as well as with the Yuendumu Mediation committee. She worked closely with the Central Land Council alongside her late husband, Harry Nelson Jakamarra.

Chapter 9

To perform or not to perform the Ancestral Fire Dreaming from the Warlukurlangu ranges (Central Australia)

By Françoise Dussart

On 8 August 1983, a few months after my arrival at Yuendumu to conduct original research for my PhD thesis, senior women relaxing on the Women's Museum lawn were talking about an Ancestral Fire Being – ignited by an Ancestral Blue Tongue Lizard that mercilessly chased two ancestral young brothers, his sons. Conversations went on for the next two days and, even with my then-rudimentary understanding of the Warlpiri language, there was no possible mistake – the manifestation of the ancestral beings of the Ancestral Fire Dreaming (*Warlu jukurrpa*) that travelled through the Warlukurlangu ranges (south-west of Yuendumu) would be performed soon in a women's public ceremony (*yawulyu*). A few days later, I was summoned by Lindsay Jampijinpa Turner, who was then president of the Yuendumu Council; he asked me to facilitate a recreational trip to Adelaide for seniors. This was the first of its kind; among the 29 Elders who would come along, only a few had ever visited such a large city. While the dates for the trip were vague, I was tasked with collecting money from the seniors to pay for their return train fares from Alice Springs to Adelaide and their accommodation.

It would take me months before I could understand why the Ancestral Fire Dreaming had been chosen as the centrepiece performance in Adelaide at two local institutions: an Aboriginal college and a local university. This memorable trip would cement, for many years to come, my relationships with two formidable ritual specialists: Judy Nampijinpa Granites (1934–2015) and Dolly Nampijinpa (Daniels) Granites (1936–2004).

In this chapter, I highlight special moments of when, where and why Judy and Dolly orchestrated representations of the Ancestral Fire Dreaming stories over three decades. I show how the performances they led met the pragmatics of their changing world through realignment, diplomacy and advocacy. I explain why, in some instances, Judy and Dolly did not perform the Ancestral Fire Dreaming and chose more inclusive Ancestral Dreaming stories, nurturing their search for greater relatedness and sense of belonging. I conclude with a few reflections on how ceremonial knowledge and reenactments remain mechanisms for withstanding, accommodating and extending other possible ways of what it means to belong in an entangled world (see also Dussart and Poirier 2017; Curran 2020).

Two ritual specialists and the Ancestral Fire Dreaming

Before I begin to chart where and for whom the Ancestral Fire Dreaming that created the Warlukurlangu ranges would be staged over the next 30 years, let me first introduce the two exceptional individuals who, among many others, have celebrated the legacies of their ancestors through incredibly tumultuous decades since they sedentarised in 1946 at a government-run ration depot called Yuendumu. I would be remiss if I did not mention how difficult it has been to celebrate here only two women with ontological connections to the Ancestral Fire Dreaming; however, space is restricted. Both lived relatively long lives and devoted themselves to maintaining what mattered: their kinship relationships and their sense of belonging to their territories crisscrossed by the Dreaming. While they are no longer with us, both would have enjoyed reminiscing about the different performances of their Ancestral Fire Dreaming stories as well as adding to, emending and reflecting on their memories, making what follows so much richer. Thus, what I present here is a truncated version of events anchored in our conversations, observations, recordings, photographs and fieldnotes. Neither of them ever grew bored of telling me about their familial entanglements with one another, with the ancestral beings that crisscrossed the many Countries for which they held patrilineal or matrifilial rights or Countries and associated Dreamings about which they had learned during pan-Indigenous ceremonial meetings. Their patrilineal ties to the Ancestral Fire Dreaming were strong, and both enjoyed singing, telling and performing the stories of the Ancestral Fire Beings.

9 To perform or not to perform the Ancestral Fire Dreaming from the Warlukurlangu ranges (Central Australia)

Judy held rights as an owner (*kirda*) through her father, who was born at Ngarna, a site on the Warlukurlangu ranges. Dolly's father was Judy's father's brother, also born at Ngarna. Dolly and Judy shared the same father's father, the remarkable ritual specialist and leader Wanyu Jampijinpa. Dolly's conception site and place of birth were also located in the Warlukurlangu ranges area, as were those of her father's father. Both Judy and Dolly were very much respected ritual specialists when I arrived at Yuendumu, along with a close brother Jack Jampijinpa Gallagher, a much younger brother Lindsay Jampijinpa Turner (the Yuendumu Council President), two close younger sisters Molly Nampijinpa Langdon and Diana Nampijinpa Marshall, and four close paternal aunts, Rosie Nangala Fleming, Tilo Nangala, Winnie Nangala and Judy-Peggy Nangala. In fact, most owners of the Ancestral Fire Dreaming had resided at Yuendumu since the beginning of the settlement and later at outstations located within a 50-kilometre radius of Yuendumu. The owners of the Ancestral Fire Dreaming from the Warlukurlangu ranges had not been split up between different settlements, as was the case for some other family groups separated in the late 1940s between Yuendumu and Lajamanu, another settlement some 580 kilometres north. Further, the managers of the Ancestral Fire Dreaming, who held their rights and responsibilities through their matriline, also remained at Yuendumu or lived on a nearby cattle station Yuelamu (then called Mount Allan). The reciprocal ties between owners and managers had not been severed – an important element in facilitating the celebration of their Country.

In general, Judy and Dolly were both extremely knowledgeable in all ceremonial matters. As Dolly once remarked, when I marvelled at her extensive knowledge of ritual performances, songlines, designs and experiences, well beyond those she held through her patriline or her matriline and beyond Warlpiri territories.[1]

Dolly, as a younger sister, should have deferred to her older sister Judy for all decisions related to ceremonial performances; however, they always treated each other more as ritual partners recognising each other's strength in the realm of the ontological. Not once did I hear them argue about the correctness of a song or design or ritual choreography or representation of ancestral stories on a canvas for sale. Not once did I witness others challenging their knowledge of a songline, the orchestration of a dance or a ceremonial body design. Under the

---

1 Judy and Dolly as ritual specialists extraordinaire once counted for me how many songlines traversing many Countries and owned by many different Indigenous groups and families they knew: over 30. On average, a senior woman would typically know about 3 or 4.

Figure 9.1. Judy (left) as the older brother, Dolly as the younger brother, both getting ready to perform. Lucy Napaljarri Kennedy as a manager getting ready to join the singers. Photo by Françoise Dussart, 1983.

watchful eyes of their managers, such as the famous Lucy Napaljarri[2] Kennedy and Emma Nungarrayi, their performances for the Ancestral Fire Dreaming enacted the following story.[3]

The Ancestral Fire Dreaming begins at a place called Yampirripanturnu where two handsome Jangala brothers were born from a spearwood tree *(winpiri, Pandora doratoxylon)*. They emerged from this tree, all decorated for ceremonies, with their bodies oiled and red-ochred. Their father, Jampijinpa, was a Lungkarda (Blue Tongue Lizard). All three lived in a place called Panirripanirri near the Warlukurlangu ranges. Since the father was blind, the two Jangala brothers hunted to feed all three (see Figure 9.2). The sons would get up at dawn, straighten their spears and leave.

---

2   Lucy Napaljarri Kennedy was an incredibly active ritual leader who participated in many successful land claims. She was also involved in many initiatives that made the settled lives of people at Yuendumu more interesting and rewarding. She was made a Member of the Order of Australia in 1994 for services to the Yuendumu community. She remains one of the few Indigenous Australians to have received such an honour. Lucy was very proud of having been nominated and for receiving it.

3   See Dussart (2000) for a more detailed account.

9 To perform or not to perform the Ancestral Fire Dreaming from the Warlukurlangu ranges (Central Australia)

Once they were gone, their father would take his spear and his spear thrower and would go hunting for himself – as he was only pretending to be blind. While his sons hunted in the area around Ngarna and in the Warlukurlangu ranges, he would cook his meat and erase all traces of his walking around, eating and cooking before they came home. After spearing many kangaroos, including a special joey, they partially cooked the meat, returned to their camp and offered food to their father, who they believed was hungry. At night, the father was accustomed to wakening and listening to a special joey calling out to his mother – "ts, ts, ts". That night, he did not hear the joey and soon began to suspect that his sons had killed it and given it to him to eat. He was furious and, to punish his sons for having killed his joey, which to him was like a human being, he sang a magical Ancestral Fire Being verse (see Figure 9.3).

The next day, the two sons went hunting and saw a big black cloud of smoke coming from their father's camp; they feared he might get burned, so they decided to return home. The fire starts to surround them, forcing them further south (see Figures 9.4 and 9.5).

But the magical Ancestral Fire Being was soon behind them, at times propelling them into the air as in an explosion of kerosene. In vain, they tried to extinguish it; in vain did they try to return home to their father. The long and fluffy hair of the two Jangalas, as well as their skin, started to burn (see Figure 9.6).

Their bodies were charred, and they could barely walk, continuously pursued by the Ancestral Fire Being. The older brother helped his injured younger brother to enter a men's secret cave located in the Warlukurlangu ranges (see Figure 9.7).

Deploying public representations of the Ancestral Fire Beings' stories as a means of cross-cultural advocacy

At this stage, readers might wonder why I privileged the Ancestral Fire Dreaming story and its reenactments. To my knowledge, a 1971 public performance of this story was the first deployed as a means of cross-cultural advocacy by Yuendumu owners and managers of the Ancestral Fire Dreaming. Following the ceremonial representations of this Dreaming itinerary provides a window into how Yuendumu residents have maintained their intimate relationships with their original territories and, in turn, how they have differently deployed ritual performances to renegotiate relations with one another and other Indigenous Australian groups, as well as illuminate our understanding of how realignments with ceremonial knowledge and performances are entangled with other Indigenous groups and the settler society at large.

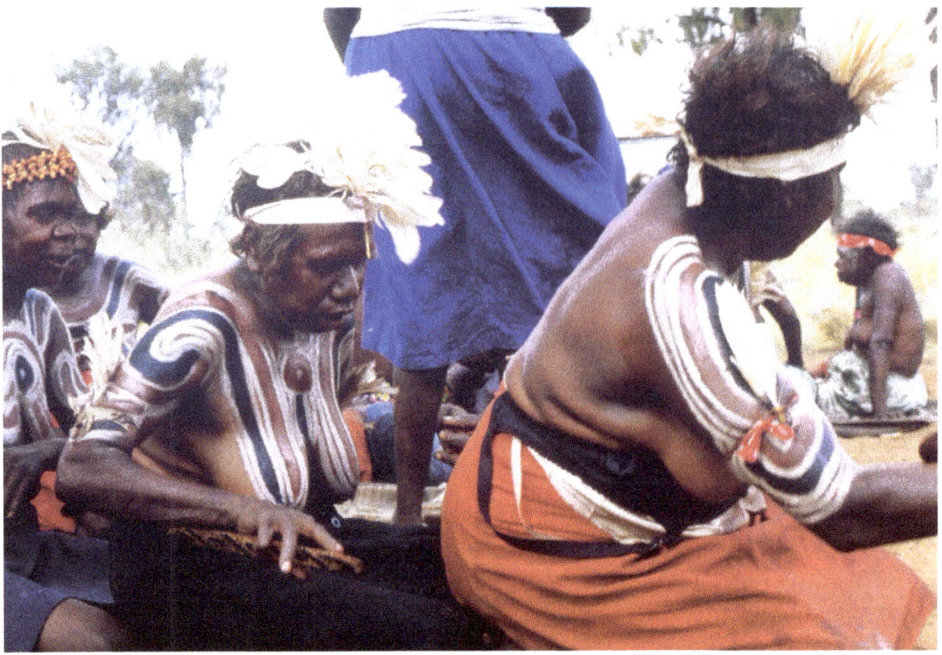

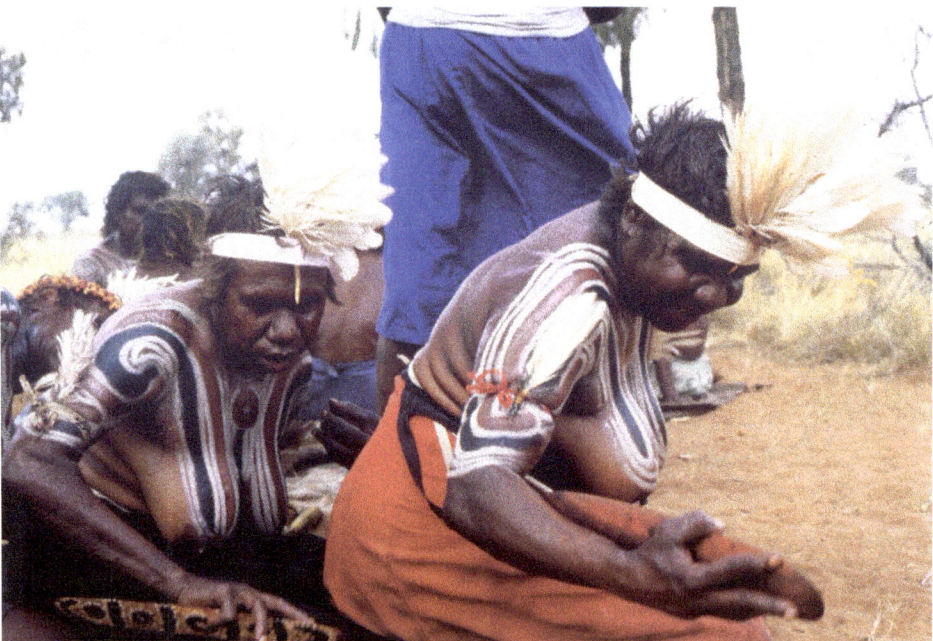

Figure 9.2. (Top) Judy and Dolly going hunting while their father (represented here by Judy-Peggy Nangala) starts singing the magical fire. (Bottom) Judy and Dolly hunting for kangaroos. Photos by Françoise Dussart, 1983.

9 To perform or not to perform the Ancestral Fire Dreaming from the Warlukurlangu ranges (Central Australia)

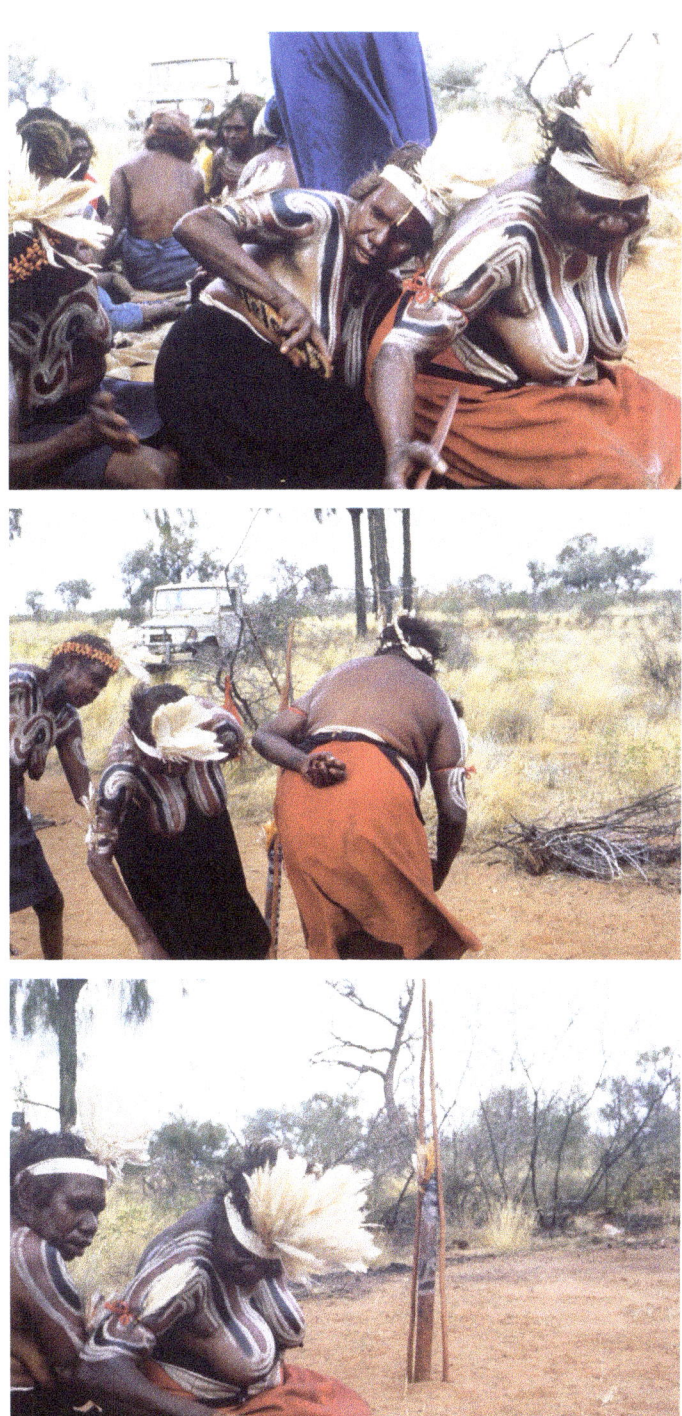

Figure 9.3. (Top) While they hunt, the father redoubles his effort to send the magical fire to destroy his sons. (Middle) The brothers are hunting and finding many kangaroos. (Bottom) The father sees his sons in the distance and can see that the fire is closing in on them. Photos by Françoise Dussart, 1983.

Figure 9.4. (Top) The father relentlessly sings the magical fire. (Bottom) The brothers see black smoke coming from the area where they live and worry about their father and try to run back to him. Photos by Françoise Dussart, 1983.

9 To perform or not to perform the Ancestral Fire Dreaming from the Warlukurlangu ranges (Central Australia)

Figure 9.5. (Top) Soon, the fire is enveloping them and forces them to travel a long way south to Kaltukatjara. (Bottom) They try to push the fire away unsuccessfully and they worry for their father under the watchful eye of a manager Emma Nungarrayi, a sister of Dolly's mother. Photos by Françoise Dussart, 1983.

Vitality and Change in Warlpiri Songs

Figure 9.6. (Top) The fire burns their hair, their ears, their skin off – it burns them inside out. Now they are very worried about their father. (Bottom) They managed to return towards their home camp while the Ancestral fire burns them. Photos by Françoise Dussart, 1983.

9 To perform or not to perform the Ancestral Fire Dreaming from the Warlukurlangu ranges (Central Australia)

Figure 9.7. (Top) They can barely walk, continuously pursued by the magical Ancestral Fire Being. (Middle) The older brother is helping his younger brother. (Bottom) Exhausted and charred, they both enter a men's secret cave. Photos by Françoise Dussart, 1983.

In 1971, Yuendumu was threatened with possible uranium mining in the Warlukurlangu ranges (Dussart 2000). In 1983, both George Japangardi Marshall, a manager for the Ancestral Fire Dreaming married to Diane Nampijinpa, and Jack Jampijinpa Gallagher remembered these trying times well. They both recalled how the traditional owners led by the famous Wanyu Jampijinpa decided to respond to the further desecration of their Country by deploying a ritual performance (see also Glowczewski and Gibson, Chapter 4, this volume). They decided to perform a *purlapa* (men's public ceremony) for the non-Indigenous miners to declare their ownership of the Ancestral Fire Dreaming Country at the time unrecognised by the Commonwealth. That performative answer became quite a significant event. While the miners ceased further exploration as the first test results were disappointing, the traditional owners and managers could only praise their decision to play power diplomacy by singing and dancing the Ancestral Fire Dreaming. From their perspective, the miners had seen the light, so to speak, and understood the powers of the Ancestral Fire Beings whose Country should be kept intact. As related to me a decade later by Jack and George, all believed that their ownership declaration – a men's public representation, or *purlapa* – had been a persuasive mode of land repossession.[4] Their decision to perform a public ceremony usually reserved for Indigenous eyes only would soon be understood by the Yuendumu Warlpiri as one of the rituals that could be performed during land claim reclamations after the passing of the *Aboriginal Land Rights (Northern Territory) Act* of 1976. Following the first land claim hearing, the Warlukurlangu ranges were included in the area recognised as Warlpiri land.

Something else happened after the successful land claim – a remarkable gender rebalancing act – senior female ritual specialists became the ritual spokespersons, so to speak, and took over the performances of all public rituals created for diplomatic and advocacy purposes. Judy and Dolly became experts at deploying their intimate knowledge of the Ancestral Fire Dreaming, among others, for inter- and intracultural audiences. Combined with their early success with the miners ending their search in the Warlukurlangu ranges and their experiences of land claims allowing their ritual knowledge to be used as a tool for legitimating Indigenous claims to vacant crown lands, the public performances of the land-based Ancestral Fire Dreaming became a mode of reference for Warlpiri ritual specialists who saw the importance of keeping the dynamism of Warlpiri people's cultural legacy (see also Dussart 1997), as well

---

4 Morphy noted also in his work with the Yolngu that, progressively, they came to make a connection between performance of Dreaming stories (bark-paintings for the Yolngu) and "political" advocacy in a Western sense (1991, 17).

as reaffirming their ownership of the land to non-Warlpiri and non-Indigenous audiences. While the public performances of the Ancestral Fire Dreaming thus far had been held at Yuendumu or onsite in the Warlukurlangu ranges, in 1983, a new opportunity presented itself that would force on-the-spot performers to reassess their authority (see also Peterson, Chapter 3, this volume) and to realign their power diplomacy strategies.

Bringing the Ancestral Fire Dreaming to a "big city"!

Now back to our four-day recreational trip to Adelaide in late October 1983, some 2,000 kilometres south of Yuendumu. At the time, still very few Yuendumu residents had visited cities unless they were flown into a larger hospital. The Elders wanted to visit Adelaide, go to the zoo, buy clothes at second-hand shops and visit Woollies.[5] To offset some of their expenses, they would be performing public ceremonies for institutions they believed would be keen – that is, willing to compensate them for showing their sacred patrimony – to witness Warlpiri ritual performances. So, as the seniors saved money for their Adelaide excursion, they were also busy negotiating what public representations could be performed. What transpired over several visits to important sacred sites associated with the Ancestral Fire Dreaming during a period of three months prior to the Adelaide visit was that the Ancestral Fire Dreaming would be featured, as well as other Dreamings that crossed the paths of the Ancestral Fire Beings from the Warlukurlangu ranges. A rehearsal of the Ancestral Fire Dreaming at the site of Ngarnka took place, augmented by reenactments of other intersecting Dreaming beings' stories.

As we sat for many hours on a train between Alice Springs and Adelaide, the women checked several times that they had packed everything necessary to perform the Dreaming for their new city audiences. Once in Adelaide, most of the 29 women who travelled to the city led by Judy and Dolly gave two main *yawulyu* performances, first at a local Aboriginal college and then at a university. However, nothing went as originally planned. When we arrived at the local college, only about a third of the women prepared themselves to dance while others would sing. Judy and Dolly decided it would be best to first dance briefly for the Dreaming stories associated with the joint ritual cycle Jardiwanpa, which was about to be performed at Yuendumu, because it involved – in one performance – most of the group painted up. Then, Judy, Dolly, Rosie and Tilo would perform a truncated version of the Ancestral Fire Dreaming. Unlike the rehearsals at Yuendumu and at Ngarna, which featured elaborated performances of different Dreaming stories

---

5   Woolworths – colloquially "Woollies" – is an Australian chain of supermarkets.

owned by different groups one after the other, it became clear early on that payment may not be offered to the performers by the local college, so the representations would be much shorter, revealing as little as possible of their stories. The women reluctantly began to dance and, as they rapidly finished the first reenactment of the Jardiwanpa under Dolly's lead, Judy mumbled under her breath to her fellow performers that "we cannot show the *jukurrpa* and get nothing, they are being disrespectful". The performance dramatically stopped, and Dolly called out to her brother Lindsay, asking him to declare loud and clear in English to their Indigenous audience that "we cannot show our women's painted breasts for nothing!" (see Curran and Dussart, 2023). The audience seemed stunned, and all the school officials could offer were cheese and ham sandwiches after the performances – a very inadequate payment from the performers' perspectives. Thus, they decided to perform an even more condensed version of the Ancestral Fire Dreaming for the second half of their presentation, which lasted barely more than four minutes. The performers were annoyed that the local Indigenous people did not seem to understand that no matter the audience and the circumstances, acceptable payments such as blankets, money and drums of flour should always be offered for performances celebrating Indigenous elemental forces – the Dreaming stories. That evening after dinner, Judy and Dolly were categorical: the women would not perform at the next venue for a university audience without "proper" payment. The selection of the performance sites had been mainly led by contacts that Warlpiri people had in Adelaide, but the question of payments had apparently never been discussed. So, that evening, the pressure was on, and I was tasked to make sure that since university was "my" world, I should demand payment for all the performers! Two days later, we were gathered in a large room with an audience of about 50 or so predominantly non-Indigenous people sitting on the floor, ready to witness the women's *yawulyu*. As about 14 women got ready and painted up, a fellow anthropologist (to whom I had explained our conundrum prior to our arrival over the phone and who had made the event at all possible) scrambled to organise a last-minute payment. I was able to reassure the performers that they would be compensated with a small dollar amount, which seemed to them barely reasonable but reasonable enough to go on with their performances. While disappointed, the performers danced with pride for a very enthusiastic and honoured audience, and their performance of the Ancestral Fire Dreaming was more robust than at the Aboriginal college event. That evening, back at our accommodation, both men and women discussed how the strength of the women's performances made the university audience "happy"[6] and aware of the performers'

---

6   Literally, making one's stomach feel good due to seeing the powers of the marvellous ancestral beings.

9 To perform or not to perform the Ancestral Fire Dreaming from the Warlukurlangu ranges (Central Australia)

knowledge of their Dreamings and their responsibilities towards and ownership of the land. What was performed in Adelaide was a modified version of what they had rehearsed and planned to perform prior to their trip; it bore the mark of creative, historical and political processes of the moment. However, a land-based *yawulyu* for the Ancestral Fire Dreaming had been officially performed for cross-cultural consumption beyond the confines of Warlpiri territories. To some extent, what transpired in Adelaide was that performers expected non-Warlpiri audiences beyond the confines of the settlement to provide travel support and payments, as well as venues to promote Warlpiri performances as a whole. We could add another factor – governmental and non-governmental supports – onto Catherine Grant's 2014 typology measuring musical vitality, as highlighted by the editors of this volume in Chapter 1.

From 1984 until 1989, Judy and Dolly performed the Ancestral Fire Beings from Warlukurlangu at museum openings, such as the opening of the first major Warlpiri exhibition at the South Australian Museum in Adelaide, titled *Yuendumu Paintings: Out of the Desert* in 1988 (Dussart 2014). The Ancestral Fire Dreaming was one of the six large songlines painted on canvas with acrylics featured in the exhibition. At the opening, Dolly, Judy, Rosie and Tilo performed brief *yawulyu* sequences reenacting the stories of the Ancestral Blue Tongue Lizard and his two sons. These sequences were chosen to highlight the personal connection to the stories and the performers. They began by showing the two brothers straightening and picking up their spears each morning to go hunting – a sequence for which Dolly dreamed songs and designs – while the father wiped away his footprints and made his fire look like an old one – a sequence dreamed by Judy's father. As in Adelaide, public representations of specific Dreaming stories never worked out as originally planned but rather became defined by the politics of relatedness in situ.

To perform or not to perform the Ancestral Fire Dreaming stories

A year after the public *yawulyu* for the Ancestral Fire Dreaming in Adelaide, seven women from Yuendumu travelled 1,600 kilometres to Kaltukatjara (Docker River) to participate in a large initiation ceremonial cycle performed by both men and women separately called Kajirri (see Dussart 2000, 169–176; Glowczewski 2016, 246). Before their departure and following a set of conflicts I have discussed elsewhere (Dussart 2000, 166–168), Judy and Dolly were planning to connect the stories of their Ancestral Fire Dreaming that had travelled to Kaltukatjara with those of women from that region. A couple of days after our arrival for the ceremonies at Kaltukatjara, Dolly and Judy decided not to perform the Ancestral Fire Dreaming as it was not a Dreaming itinerary shared by most women in attendance. Instead, Dolly and Judy decided to dance recently revealed stories about Ancestral Emus who travelled and shaped many territories and sites shared by most (see Dussart 2000). This was not a moment of ritual knowledge exchange but rather a realignment of performative priorities, declaring how the specific stories of the travels of the Ancestral Emus were all connected without the traditional transfer of the performative rights of ritual production from the performers to the viewers. Such ceremonial decisions were aligned at the time with the production of encompassing relatedness among Indigenous people residing in Central and South Australia (see also Myers 1986; Peterson 2000). They are also moments when viewers are witnessing and reaffirming the legitimate right of the performers to perform (see Peterson, Chapter 3, this volume).

Performative choices highlighted at the museum opening in Adelaide or at Kaltukatjara constitute a paradigmatic example of what I have observed until 2004 when women performed public *yawulyu* ceremonies privileging inclusiveness and emphasising relatedness (see also Curran, Martin and Barwick Chapter 5, this volume). Such choices must be understood as the realignment of ownership and relatedness. These rearticulations dialogue with initiatives in other ritual performances that continue to ground Indigenous identity and relatedness, such as initiation cycles. As Nicolas Peterson has shown (2000, 213), initiation cycles seem to be widely known by many Indigenous groups throughout Central Australia rather than being under the control of a few ritual specialists – as was the case with specific Dreaming stories bounded by locality and exclusiveness. Selections of public representations of Dreamings are driven by desires for greater pan-Indigenous relatedness in Central Australia, influenced by political calculation and declaration of ritual competence coinciding with cosmological sanction. These realignments, combined with the death of many ritual specialists (e.g., Judy and Dolly), social change and the constant struggles of living, have affected how Warlpiri systems of knowledge, regimes of care and know-how are transmitted and retrieved, and are ever-changing.

9 To perform or not to perform the Ancestral Fire Dreaming from the Warlukurlangu ranges (Central Australia)

Conclusion

A year prior to Judy's death, I visited her in an aged care home in Alice Springs, some 300 kilometres from Yuendumu, where she had been sent. I had brought many recordings of *yawulyu* ceremonies from the 1980s. As she started to sing along for the Ancestral Fire Dreaming, she began to cry softly. I asked if she was crying because so many of her relatives had passed away and that the Ancestral Fire Dreaming was still under taboo and, thus, no longer celebrated. Judy gave me the look! The one she always gave me when I jumped to somewhat incorrect conclusions! She was simply nostalgic for the times when many would re-enact Dreamings with which they were connected personally and geo-specifically to care for their territories, their ancestral beings, their close kin. She was nostalgic for the times when the reenactment of Dreamings – such as the Ancestral Fire Beings they inherited through their patriline – were vital performances to the social production of persons. She was nostalgic for those exclusive reenactments that had to be led by ritual specialists and leaders geo-specifically tied to the Dreaming itinerary. Judy was also worried about how the younger generations would retrieve the knowledge of the Dreaming and engage with its manifestations. Judy was worried that ceremonial performances as a "polyrhetorical" (Pualani 2007, 134) Indigenous strategy would no longer produce efficient spaces for governing and grounding Warlpiri identity, for inter- and intracultural negotiations and conflict resolutions (see many other examples in this volume, particularly Chapters 1, 3 and 4). Many ritual specialists have shared her concerns. In a 2018 interview, ritual leader and activist Harry Jakamarra Nelson eloquently urged young people to listen to recordings and watch videos of ritual ceremonies performed throughout the 20th century so they could be strong and carry on and not get to the stage when, "if the *jukurrpa* goes astray, you're liable to go about aimlessly"[7] (Curran and Barwick 2018). In short, both Judy and Harry hoped that the new generations could understand how to retrieve the different manifestations of the Dreaming and to shape effective spaces of relatedness, belonging and recognition, as well as revitalisation (see also Vaarzon-Morel et al., Chapter 8, this volume).

---

7   "If the *jukurrpa* goes astray, you're liable to go about aimlessly" is translated from the Warlpiri *jukurrpa ngula kaji ka warntarla kari yani kaji kanpa wapakarra wapami*. I want to thank David Nash for his pointed translation and discussing the issues relating to "loss" and "going astray". While, as I understand it from my Warlpiri teachers, the idea of "cultural loss" has a bounded quality and seems to be primarily rooted in a western way of thought, the idea of the Dreaming going astray emphasises the movement qualities of the Dreaming – the force that contextualises spatial relationships and intentions through time. In other words, the Dreaming can never be lost and can always be retrieved.

As Nicolas Peterson (2000) and Georgia Curran (2011) have shown, in the last two decades, Warlpiri people have reinvested their energy in the performances of inclusive rites of passage involving different Indigenous participants scattered over large distances rather than performing rituals professing ownership rights to specific sites and Ancestral Dreamings. Older generations today seem to fear that too much "inclusiveness" may limit the "biopolitical regime of recognition" (Simpson 2018, 171) deployed by newer generations facing further encroachments by the settler state on their lives.

In the last 15 years, women who are now in their late forties and older, such as Cecily Napanangka Granites – Dolly's daughter – have come to care more deeply for the Dreamings for which they hold rights and responsibilities through their patriline and matriline. When I spoke at length to Cecily in 2017 at Yuendumu, she believed that initiatives led by her generation were the way forward, such as compiling knowledge about Dreaming stories recorded or photographed so everyone could continue to be *yapa* (Indigenous people). When I asked her what she meant by that, she replied:

> I want to know where I come from, and I want others to know where they come from. I want *Yapa* to know so *Kardiya* (non-Indigenous people) know where we come from. I want to know it [Dreaming stories], that it is in my heart and in my soul.[8]

Cecily's interests, shared by many of her contemporaries, revolved around intra- and intercultural forms of recognition. Her parents' and grandparents' understanding of belonging was imbricated in webs of kin relations, with the desire for greater relatedness aligned with ceremonial responsibilities. For Cecily's generation, understanding of belonging has pivoted upon the complexities relating to Indigenous people placing themselves within their own shifting historical context and within a settler nation relentlessly modifying its policies about sovereignty and rights. Her understanding of Indigenous difference engages with the complex political exigencies of forms of relatedness of the past, the present and the future, and her endeavour may well lead to a new deployment of more exclusive forms of knowledge combined with inclusive pan-Indigenous and non-Indigenous forms of recognition.

---

8 Personal communication, 2017.

Acknowledgements

I want to thank Yuendumu Warlpiri people for sharing their knowledge and thoughts. I miss my friends Judy, Dolly, Molly, Rosie, Jack, Harry and George. I wish you were still among us and we could once again reminisce together and enjoy what is to come. My debt to them is beyond words. I am grateful to Georgia Curran, Linda Barwick and Nicolas Peterson for their invitation to contribute to this edited volume. Their comments were invaluable.

References

Curran, Georgia. 2011. "The 'Expanding Domain' of Warlpiri Initiation Rituals". In *Ethnography and the Production of Anthropological Knowledge: Essays in Honour of Nicolas Peterson*, edited by Yasmine Musharbash and Marcus Barber, 39–50. Canberra: ANU E Press.

Curran, Georgia. 2020. *Sustaining Indigenous Songs: Contemporary Warlpiri Ceremonial Life in Central Australia*. New York: Berghahn Books.

Curran, Georgia and Linda Barwick. 2018. Filmed Interview of Harry Jakamarra Nelson and Otto Jungarrayi Sims, interviewed by Valerie Napaljarri Martin (PAW2018_-5_10_01). Yuendumu: Pintubi Anmatjere Warlpiri Media and Communications.

Curran, Georgia and Françoise Dussart. 2023. "'We Don't Show our Women's Breasts for Nothing': Shifting Purposes for Warlpiri Women's Public Rituals—*Yawulyu*—Central Australia 1980s–2020s". *Studies in Religion/Sciences Religieuses*. https://doi.org/10.1177/00084298231154430

Dussart, Françoise. 1997. "A Body Painting in Translation". In *Rethinking Visual Anthropology*, edited by Howard Morphy and Marcus Banks, 186–202. New Haven: Yale University Press.

Dussart, Françoise. 2000. *The Politics of Ritual in an Aboriginal Settlement: Kinship, Gender and the Currency of Knowledge*. Washington: Smithsonian Institution Press.

Dussart, Françoise. 2014. "'Mise en Intrigue': Quelques Réflexions sur les Expositions Muséales de Peintures à l'Acrylique des Aborigènes du Territoire du Nord (Australie)". *Anthropologie et Sociétés* 38(3): 179–206.

Dussart, Françoise and Sylvie Poirier (eds). 2017. *Entangled Territorialities: Negotiating Indigenous Lands in Australia and Canada*. Toronto: University of Toronto Press.

Glowczewski, Barbara. 2016. *Desert Dreamers*. Minneapolis: Minnesota University Press/Univocal.

Morphy, Howard. 1991. Ancestral connections: art and an Aboriginal system of knowledge. Chicago: University of Chicago Press.

Myers, Fred. 1986. *Pintupi Country, Pintupi Self: Sentiment, Place, and Politics among Western Desert Aborigines*. Washington: Smithsonian Institution Press.

Peterson, Nicolas. 2000. "An Expanding Aboriginal Domain: Mobility and the Initiation Journey". *Oceania* 70: 205–18.

Pualani Louis, Renee. 2007. "Can You Hear Us Now? Voices from the Margin: Using Indigenous Methodologies in Geographic Research". *Geographical Research* 45(2): 130–39.

Simpson, Audra. 2018. "Why White People Love Franz Boas; Or, the Grammar of Indigenous Dispossession". In *Indigenous Visions: Recovering the World of Franz Boas*, edited by Ned Blackhawk and Isaiah Lorado Wilner, 166–80. New Haven: Yale University Press.

Jerry Jangala Patrick

Jerry Jangala Patrick is one of the original settlers of Lajamanu in the 1950s. He came to Lajamanu (then Hooker Creek) from the Lander River area (Willowra) via Alice Springs and Yuendemu and spent his earlier adulthood working as a stockman on cattle stations in Northern Australia before settling permanently in Lajamanu. While still steeped in traditional Warlpiri culture, Jangala embraced elements of the dominant Australian culture and became the pastor of the Baptist Church in Lajamanu.

Chapter 10

Milpirri: A revitalisation movement, a *purlapa* or a festival?

By Stephen Wild, Steven Wanta Jampijinpa Patrick and Yukihiro Doi

Introduction

Lajamanu is the site of a northern Warlpiri community with a population of approximately 700 individuals. The people call themselves Warnayaka Warlpiri. The town site and surrounding Country were once part of the Wave Hill cattle station; they were excised for an Aboriginal Reserve in about 1950 when Warlpiri people were forcibly moved from southern concentrations of the Warlpiri nation, especially Yuendumu and the Lander River (now Willowra). Prior to Warlpiri occupation, the land belonged traditionally to Gurindji Aboriginal people, who now primarily occupy the town of Wave Hill/Daguragu, north of Lajamanu. The contradiction between traditional ownership and the contemporary occupation of Lajamanu has been a source of unease for its Warlpiri occupiers and the cause of Warlpiri attempts to legitimise the situation. The Aboriginal status of Lajamanu perhaps partly explains the innovation in ceremonial performance represented by Milpirri.

In 1969–1980, Wild carried out field research on Warlpiri songs and dances in Lajamanu, then called Hooker Creek, after the semi-permanent water course on which the town is based (see Wild 1975). At that time, ceremonial activity occupied a large proportion of the time of both women and men, and the future continuity of singing and dancing seemed assured. This optimism was reinforced by the success of the Warlpiri/Gurindji Land Claim (based on the federal 1976 *Aboriginal Land Rights (Northern Territory) Act*), which rested heavily on the relationship between songs and dances and relationships to land. Warlpiri and Gurindji peoples agreed to present one land claim, thus avoiding the issue of the border between the two (see Central Land Council et al. 1978).

Wild returned to Lajamanu in 2007 under a research grant to return recordings of songs made earlier (1969–1980) and investigate the current situation of song performance. Although the return of the song recordings was politely received, it seemed that the songs had largely disappeared because the ceremonies were no longer performed. This situation had troubled local Warlpiri man Steven Jampijinpa Patrick. Jampijinpa is the son of Jerry Jangala Patrick, one of the original settlers of Lajamanu in the 1950s. While still steeped in traditional Warlpiri culture, Jangala embraced elements of the dominant Australian culture and became the pastor of the Baptist Church in Lajamanu.[1] With this fusion of traditions by his father, Jampijinpa was destined to take cultural fusion in another direction.

In 2005, Jampijinpa was a Community Liaison Officer in the Lajamanu Community School, working with school teacher Alan Box. Box and Jampijinpa devised a plan to revitalise Warlpiri ceremonies in Lajamanu, working together with the Lajamanu Community School and Tracks Dance Company (Darwin). The centrepiece of the plan was an evening performance based on a traditional Warlpiri ceremony that included contemporary songs and dances as well as traditional performance elements. Tracks Dance Company, which had been working with elements of the Lajamanu community on dance projects for some years, was to be the choreographer and designer of the performance in consultation with Jampijinpa, the Artistic Director. The school initially provided logistical support for the project, which included other elements in addition to the evening performance. The project was called Milpirri, a Warlpiri word meaning "Storm Cloud", signifying the coming together of two forces, hot and cold air (or traditional and contemporary; Indigenous and settler cultures), to create rain and new growth (revitalised culture). The first evening performance of Milpirri was held in 2005, and it has been held in most alternate years since then (see Tracks Dance Company 2023).

Wild returned again to Lajamanu in 2008, introducing Yukihiro Doi, a PhD student, to the community. Doi focused his research on Milpirri, which he observed and documented in the following years (2009–2012) during his primary period of fieldwork. Doi and Jampijinpa worked closely together on this research and later jointly presented their work at a World Conference of the

---

1   See documentary film of Jerry Jangala with Henry Cooke (Japanangka and O'Shannessy 2020).

10 Milpirri: A revitalisation movement, a *purlapa* or a festival?

International Council for Traditional Music in Canada in 2011, followed by a second presentation at Tenri University, Japan. The following year Jampijinpa was awarded an Indigenous Discovery Research Fellowship at the Australian National University (ANU) by the Australian Research Council. The purpose of the award was to enable Jampijinpa to explore further records of Warlpiri ceremonies for return to Lajamanu and to inform future Milpirri performances. Thus, the original purposes of Wild's visit to Lajamanu in 2007 were fulfilled by Doi's research on Milpirri and Jampijinpa's Research Fellowship to identify and return further research records relevant to the revival of Warlpiri ceremonies.

The remainder of this chapter will document the ceremonial situation at Lajamanu during Wild's earlier research (1969–1980), the initial years of Milpirri (2005–2012) studied by Doi and assisted by Jampijinpa, a brief account of Tracks Dance Company and its role in relation to Milpirri, and a consideration of the kind of phenomenon that Milpirri represents.

Lajamanu (1969–1980)

Songs and dances in 1969–1980 could be considered "communications of the ancestors" because they all came from the Dreaming (*jukurrpa*). There were some apparent exceptions to this generalisation. First, *purlapa* (public songs and dances performed jointly by women and men) could be received by living people from the spirits of dead relatives (*pirlirrpa*) or by unrelated spirits called *kurruwalpa*. However, it seems that the ultimate source of these new *purlapa* was the Dreaming ancestors, after all. A second apparent exception were the songs sung in the local Baptist Church: mostly English songs translated into Warlpiri. However, some Church songs were composed in the Warlpiri language by Warlpiri people and were called "Jesus *purlapa*". They were like traditional *purlapa* but with Christian words. Only the Warlpiri people who gave the Jesus *purlapa* to the Church could say if they really came from the Dreaming ancestors. Finally, young adults performed songs in the country music style, accompanied by guitars. The first performers who sang in this style in Lajamanu formed a band called the Lajamanu Bushrangers. They were popular among young people. Songs recorded by Wild in 1979 comprised covers of performances by other bands. Beyond 1980, the Lajamanu Bushrangers were succeeded by other popular bands, most notably North Tanami Band and Lajamanu Teenage Band. Both bands performed in what has been dubbed the "Desert Reggae" style and achieved success outside Lajamanu. Their songs were original compositions, with some lyrics in Warlpiri and some in English. North Tanami Band released five albums, and Lajamanu Teenage Band released six albums, through CAAMA

Music.[2] The division in music and dance between younger and older Warlpiri people can already be seen in this period.

For most adults in Lajamanu, performances of ancestral songs and dances occupied a large proportion of time not taken up by paid employment. Performances took place either in ceremonies involving the whole community or outside ceremonies involving groups of different sizes. The performances separate from ceremonies were either by all women's groups or all men's groups. Warlpiri women's group performances (*yawulyu*) have been well described by others (Warlpiri Women from Yuendumu 2017; Dail-Jones [Morais] 1984; Shannon 1971) and were largely inaccessible to Wild. Ceremonies involving men were boys' initiation (Kurdiji); a cult ceremony (Kajirri), which is related to Kunapipi of Arnhem Land; Fire Ceremony (Ngajakula and Jardiwanpa, depending on the Dreaming ancestor being celebrated); and *purlapa*. Love Magic Songs (*yilpinji*) were divided into women's songs and men's songs and were performed separately by each sex. They were mostly performed privately by a few individuals to attract the attention of a member of the opposite sex.[3]

The ceremony that most integrated the community was boys' initiation or Kurdiji, which comprised three parts: 1) performances by both women and men of ancestral Dreamings related to the boys being initiated (*Marnakurrawarnu*), performed over one or two evenings of all-night singing (by men) and dancing (by women) of a Women (Karnta Karnta) Dreaming (Kurdiji); 2) men's ancestral performances leading up to the boys' circumcision (*Kirrirdikirrawarnu*, performances of the several parts of boys' initiation occurred over more than a week); and 3) the *Kajirri* ceremony, which, by comparison, occurred over several months, during which recently initiated boys, or "ritual novices" (Marliyarra), were further introduced to the ancestral performances for which they would become the custodians. A Fire Ceremony (Ngajakula/Jardiwanpa) was performed over several weeks by women and men, culminating in a spectacular ritualised burning of the owners of the Dreaming by their managers. A *purlapa* was performed over one or two evenings by women and men.

Most ceremonial performances were connected to Dreaming tracks located on traditional Warlpiri Country, which was seldom, if ever, visited by people living in Lajamanu. The songs and dances were increasingly unrelated to the lived experience of new generations of Lajamanu Warlpiri. One solution was to receive new *purlapa* that were related to the Country they were now

---

2   See CAAMA Music for lists of their albums: https://caamamusic.com.au
3   See Wild (1975) for a more detailed account of ceremonial contexts in Lajamanu and Curran (2020) and Dussart (2000) for an account of ceremonial contexts in Yuendumu.

occupying; one such *purlapa* was received by a Lajamanu man while he was sick in Darwin Hospital. At the same time, new *purlapa* were received that were about traditional Warlpiri Country (see an account of one such *purlapa* in Wild 1984). During a visit by Wild in 1979, Lajamanu was hit by a new cult ceremony called in English "The New Business" or "The Balgo Business", which was derived from the Kimberley region of northern Western Australia.[4] The "New Business" divided the community; those opposed to it camped in the church grounds for protection against forced participation in the new ceremony being performed on the outskirts of Lajamanu. The "New Business" created ceremonial links with Indigenous communities to the West and formed another response to the separation from traditional Country.

Although most performances at Lajamanu in 1969–1980 were the legacy of ancestral songs and dances brought from the Tanami Desert 20–30 years earlier by the first Warlpiri settlers, their dominance was being challenged from several directions. The Baptist Church asserted its influence through Christian songs in Warlpiri language and Warlpiri musical style (Jesus *purlapa*). New *purlapa* about the newly adopted Country were received from ancestral spirits. A whole new ceremony was adopted from northern Western Australia. Finally, young Warlpiri took the first steps to embrace the music of the universal youth culture. These signs of change in music and dance performance heralded a crisis of identity that only grew stronger over the next few decades. A similar crisis was experienced in other Indigenous communities in Northern Australia. However, due to its unique situation, the response in Lajamanu was also unique.

Tracks Dance Company

Tracks Dance Company, based in Darwin, played a crucial role in the creation of Milpirri. The company began in 1988 when one of its founders, Tim Newth, joined Browns Mart Community Arts organisation. With a background in visual art, theatre and dance, one of Newth's earliest projects in his new role was to work with the Lajamanu community to create a theatrical production using elements of Warlpiri traditional and contemporary performance. Although he also worked with other Northern Territory Indigenous communities, Newth's work in Lajamanu has been a central thread of his community arts work for over 30 years. David McMicken joined him a few years later, and the two became legally independent of Browns Mart in 1999 under the current name.

---

4   See papers by Wild, Young and Laughren (Australian Institute of Aboriginal Studies 1981) for accounts of the adoption of the "New Business" in three different Aboriginal communities.

Newth and McMicken are joint Artistic Directors of the company. Since 1988, Newth and McMicken have developed a close relationship with the Lajamanu community. It was evident in Wild's observation of their easy acceptance by people during the preparations for the 2009 Milpirri, for which he was present. Acceptance and familiarity were earned by family visits between Lajamanu and Melbourne (Newth's and McMicken's home city), gruelling trips in traditional Warlpiri Country and extended stays in Lajamanu. Further, gradually, Tracks' success in mounting multiple iterations of Milpirri has earned them respect. Milpirri's Warlpiri Artistic Director, Steven Wanta Jampijinpa Patrick, is a Life Member of Tracks (Tracks Dance Company 2012–2023).

In comparison with other Indigenous events, including the Garma Festival, Milpirri is not necessarily aimed at being a tourist event. When anthropologist Jennifer Biddle (2005) interviewed Newth and McMicken about Milpirri as a specific community-based event, not intended to tour or be nationally staged, Newth confirmed that they aimed to create a work that celebrates place and people and that it is not important for that work to tour or be more broadly recognised. Tracks believed that it ran side-by-side with this Milpirri concept and is conscious of the Lajamanu community's contribution to the development of the program. It is site specific (Biddle 2019).

Milpirri

In 2008, Yukihiro Doi came from Japan to ANU and first visited Lajamanu with his supervisor Stephen Wild. The student was introduced to Steven Jampijinpa and other community members and then undertook to revisit the community for his fieldwork for Milpirri in 2009. From 2008–2012, he made several field trips to Lajamanu. This section will discuss the outcomes of his research and consider the development of the series of Milpirri, each themed on notable Warlpiri rituals and being interpretations of the original event launched at Lajamanu in 2005.

Milpirri 2005

In preparation for *Milpirri 2009*, Doi commenced his literature research in Canberra by reading the book *Ngurra-Kurlu: A Way of Working with Warlpiri People* (2008), written by Jampijinpa. The Warlpiri expression *ngurra-kurlu* was coined and explained by Jampijinpa as the five elements of a Warlpiri world and life view. Doi's research was complemented by other publications that were the products of ideas and efforts of both Tracks and Jampijinpa (available through the Tracks Dance Company website) on the first Milpirri

10 Milpirri: A revitalisation movement, a *purlapa* or a festival?

in 2005. The series of Milpirri events commenced with the theme of ancestral Jardiwanpa ritual. Those involved in Milpirri insisted that *Jardiwanpa* had been reawakened on the occasion of the first Milpirri after several decades of being absent from community life. Tim Newth, who made Tracks' first contact with the community, said, "Indigenous people respond to stories, the telling of their stories from the past to the present. In this way we can begin to get an understanding of the Milpirri dreaming and how they see their school and the relationship it has to their lives" (Ausdance 2011).

School children's hip-hop and break-dance training by Tracks was also an important element leading to the stage performance with a soundtrack by Elders, Lajamanu community council members, and members of the North Tanami Band and the Lajamanu Teenage Band. The scenario of the stage consisted of a prologue, four acts and a finale. Traditional *Jardiwanpa* was performed as the consistent theme of the whole event since each title of the acts was attributed to an aspect of the ceremony. *Makunta-wangu* (matrimoiety) is explained by Jampijinpa as their own Dreaming name in relation to Emu names in accordance with *Jardiwanpa* songs.

Another major innovation of the event was the establishment of the four-colouring system explaining Warlpiri patricouples (see Figure 10.1). In parallel with Jampijinpa's objective to revitalise ceremonial activities through Milpirri, he also had a co-objective to increase school attendance through the children's participation in Milpirri. Initially, it did not result in increased attendance at Lajamanu School. However, Doi observed in later visits that the colouring system had taken root among the school children throughout the event. This colouring method, through its summary of traditional kinship, had a noticeable impact on schoolchildren and can be considered evidence for the interpretation of Milpirri as a "revitalisation movement". Apart from the interpretation of Milpirri as a "movement", the success of the first show in 2005 resulted in its biennial continuation. Restoring traditional songs and dances, as well as achieving unity, at least at the community level, can be seen as a significant achievement of Milpirri.

Colour group	Patricouples
Blue	Jampijinpa, Jangala / Nampijinpa, Nangala
Yellow	Jungarrayi, Japaljarri / Nungarrayi, Napaljarri
Red	Jupurrurla, Jakamarra / Napurrurla, Nakamarra
Green	Japanangka, Japangardi / Napanangka, Napangardi

Figure 10.1. Warlpiri patricouples and the four colour groups for Milpirri.

Another measure of the success of Milpirri is that, for the first time, the male Elders performed traditional ceremony on the basketball court with lighting and speakers. This can be attributed to Jampijinpa's relationship with them and possibly his father's seniority and respect among other older men, as explained in the documentary *Kaja-Warnu-Jangka* (*From the Bush*, Japanangka and O'Shannessy 2020; see Chapter 1, this volume). In general, Elders did not seem to have expected that the performance would have any merit, but Jampijinpa mentioned that the people involved realised that the idea of Milpirri was "much bigger than just two-way teaching in the school" (Patrick, Holmes and Box 2008).

Milpirri 2007

Several developments and new features of the second Milpirri (with a new source of funds) were the inclusion of participants from Yuendumu, the reintroduction of the traditional initiation ceremony (Kurdiji) and teaching the ideas of *ngurra-kurlu* with the inclusion of the Australian coat of arms. The discovery of the coincidence with the symbols of animals surely delighted local people:

> Unexpectedly, we discovered that the symbols appearing throughout the Warlpiri Kurdiji Ceremony also appear in the Australian coat of arms. This revelation inspired the Old People. For years they had been wanting to find a way to get Kardiya (mainstream people) to understand Warlpiri Law. For the Old People, sharing symbols that appear on Parliament House in Canberra with the symbols of the seat of Warlpiri Law, their ceremony, marked a great hope that there could be mutual understanding. (Patrick, Holmes and Box 2008)

10 Milpirri: A revitalisation movement, a *purlapa* or a festival?

Milpirri aimed to include intercommunity activity from the beginning, with the involvement of the Warlpiri Triangle,[5] through Jampijinpa's school connections in the region. However, the first Milpirri was performed only by Lajamanu community members. A government agency and a major corporate sponsor, the Rio Tinto Aboriginal Fund, provided major support for Milpirri from 2007 to 2010 to hold a larger show, in terms of participants, with the help of other Warlpiri communities.

Jardiwanpa dance was also performed in 2007, but the main theme of that year's Milpirri was Kurdiji. It was the first time that Warnayaka Warlpiri people made the *Kurdiji* ceremony (without men's only sections) open to the public. There was a similarity to the first Milpirri in the movement of ancestral male dancers in the Red group with boomerangs, but the novelty was evident in *yawulyu* female dancers with body painting and a greater number of dancers, partly from Yuendumu. *Witi* ("Leafy Poles") dance was performed by Yellow male dancers, with a tall leafy pole tied to each leg, shaken through vigorous movement of the body. This was a large-scale set of dances that was omitted in the abridged initiation ceremony called *Waruwarta*, which Doi observed at a *Kurdiji* ceremony held inside the "Aboriginal Land" sign at the entrance to Lajamanu during the Christmas holidays of 2010–2011 (see also description of the Warawata ceremony, borrowed from Luritja/Pintupi, in Curran 2020).

Several more dances were incorporated into *Milpirri 2007* to be continued as a series in later Milpirri events. "Milpirri (Storm Cloud) Dance" was the title of the event, which has been performed on each occasion by a dancer from the Blue group. *Wulparri* ("Milky Way") Dance, with its accompanying song *Wantarritarri*, was the last dance by Yellow and Green male dancers. Supervised by their mothers behind them, young initiated male dancers jumped continuously with a long yellow string in their hands. As they passed the string to the mothers behind, several male Elder singers could not stand by any longer and went forward to show them how to conduct the ritual.

The contemporary song "Desert People", sung and recorded by the North Tanami Band in 2005, was danced again by all the young performers. The 2007 program had another *kardiya/yapa* or non-Indigenous/Indigenous fusion song called "*Kurdiji* Song", which was not a part of the traditional daytime song "*Marnakurrawarnu*" in the *Kurdiji* and *Waruwarta* ceremonies. This new gospel-like Warlpiri song was made by Jampijinpa originally for lighting *witi* poles and represented the climax of the *Kurdiji* and *Jardiwanpa*

---

5   See Browne and Gibson (2021) for a discussion of the Triangle in the context of bilingual education.

ceremonies (see relaxing of the strictly traditional and introduced binaries of song in Wild 1975).

The cultural education of Milpirri was not limited to the tradition of Warlpiri people but included non-Aboriginal Australians' heraldic design, the Australian Commonwealth coat of arms. During the show, *Milpirri 2007* featured the Australian constitution with Warlpiri interpretation through their panel display of the Australian coat of arms. One of the large panels prepared by the children for the program featured the Australian coat of arms. The symbolism of the coat of arms – namely, the animals, the star and the shield (or *kurdiji* in Warlpiri) – was noted by the Elders, inspiring a Warlpiri representation of the coat of arms. The Milpirri focusing on *Kurdiji* ceremony appears to have satisfied the two-way educational purpose with the display of both the *ngurra-kurlu* diagram and the Australian coat of arms with respect for both the nation of Australia and its Indigenous people.

Milpirri 2009

After participating in Garma Festival 2009 in Arnhem Land and the Endurance Show by Tracks in Darwin, Doi headed for Lajamanu, followed by Tracks dance members, six weeks before Milpirri in October. Recreation combining warming-up and a game for remembering names started among the Tracks instructors and schoolchildren in a small gymnasium. The school did not have a big gymnasium but cooperated with Tracks for their project. Milpirri rehearsals for children in those days were basically an alternative to daily classes. I learned on later visits that 2009 was the last time that Milpirri had such cooperation from the school. Other Tracks staff from Darwin arrived two weeks before the event to set up a sound system at the basketball court, where children attended rehearsals after school. As many children attended and enjoyed the disco in the Youth Hall every Friday night, Milpirri's employment of similar modern technology helped to attract residents in the remote community to it.

Female Elders sitting in line about ten metres behind male Elders on the ground painted elaborate designs in ochre and oil on their bodies in rehearsals. The atmosphere of the male performers was a little different; the senior male singers painted themselves only partly, and young men who were supposed to perform traditional dances in Milpirri were caught up in football. Due to contact difficulties, most performers did not assemble until two days before the final event.

The theme of the *Milpirri 2009* program was *Jurntu Purlapa*, explained as a piece in the *purlapa* genre. Every participant was given a bracelet, depending on which of the four-coloured patricouple groupings they belonged to, worn

10 Milpirri: A revitalisation movement, a *purlapa* or a festival?

on the left or right wrist depending on their matrimoiety, saying, "speak to the land and the land will speak back". The Milpirri introduction commenced with Jampijinpa's narration with the music of DJ Shadow's "Building Stream with a Grain of Salt". The lightning dance or Milpirri *Jukurrpa* Dance by a Blue male dancer and its song by senior male Elders was consistent with those in 2005 and 2007. Traditional Mangulpa ("Black-Headed Spear") was the first dance by the Red group. The performance signifies "many important areas of law and dance through the spear and kangaroo songs, two very important bodies of legal knowledge" (Tracks Dance Company 2009).

The next scene was of the Yellow group's performance titled "Discipline", starting with DJ Shadow's song, Jampijinpa's narration and submission of a hooked boomerang and a painted stick from a Yellow boy and a Yellow girl to the Song-Men and Song-Women. During this section, traditional male dance expressed the Junma ("Stone Knife"); in the past, this created "the chest scars that are administered ceremonially as a sign that one has demonstrated learning and self-discipline" (Tracks Dance Company 2009). Doi was given a eucalyptus-leaf bunch and was accepted to join his skilled skin brothers and fathers in the snake-shaped queue wearing the Yellow design and clothes. He was regarded as the first non-Aboriginal person who performed their traditional dance in Milpirri. At a specific point, the dancers ritually rubbed the earth with the leaves, and the following women dug with their *witi*. After the act entitled "Respect" was performed by the four student pairs and the Green group, in the four body performances, "Responsibility" was conducted by the Blue group. After the four pairs' action and the theme music provided by DJ Shadow, adult Blue men performed the traditional circle dance, Kurrwa ("Stone Axe"), with female dancers.

Milpirri 2009 contained the first trial of flying lanterns in the finale. This was prepared and performed by *kardiya* people or non-Aboriginal residents and visitors, including Stephen Wild, following Jampijinpa's idea that Milpirri – or cloud made by the hot and cold elements – should be made by both *yapa* and *kardiya*. When the lanterns were launching, the essence of the event was sung in a new original song, *Yungkaju Kurdari* ("Milky Way Song"), written by Jampijinpa and sung by Zac Jakamarra Patterson of the North Tanami Band and Kenneth Jungarrayi Martin of the Lajamanu Teenage Band.

Overall, the performance was successful and well received by the audience. In general, Tracks instructors also praised the boys for dancing well, although in general they were typically younger than the hip-hop dancers of the former shows. Three days after the performance in October, Doi participated in a ritual called Kurapaka ("Blanket Exchange"), where female Elders stepped towards

Figure 10.2. *Mangulpa* by male Red dancers. Photo by Yukihiro Doi.

Figure 10.3. *Witi* by Yellow female dancers. Photo by Yukihiro Doi.

10 Milpirri: A revitalisation movement, a *purlapa* or a festival?

Figure 10.4. *Karli* and *wirlki* by male Green dancers. Photo by Yukihiro Doi.

Figure 10.5. Junior boys dancing with DJ Bacon Mix. Photo by Yukihiro Doi.

Figure 10.6. *Karnanganja* by Yellow and Green dancers. Photo by Yukihiro Doi.

Figure 10.7. Sky Lantern being flown by *kardiya* people with "Yungkaju Kurdari". Photo by Yukihiro Doi.

10 Milpirri: A revitalisation movement, a *purlapa* or a festival?

Figure 10.8. Blanket exchange after *Milpirri 2009*, community area near basketball court. Photo by Yukihiro Doi.

the back of the male Elders' semicircle with brand new blankets in their arms. This marked the Closing Ceremony of Milpirri. This is another phase of the traditional and modern mixed life in the remote community.

In June 2010, the Australian Dance Awards in Melbourne invited Lajamanu boys for their hip-hop dance of "Lesson 3" by DJ Shadow, and they were called "Milpirri dancers". At this point, "Milpirri Dance" was interpreted by Tracks Dance Company as any hip-hop dances performed by Lajamanu children. This usage can be considered popular, and young adults in Milpirri held the same attitude when they used the same expression.

Milpirri 2011 and 2012

Except for 2020 (due to the COVID-19 pandemic), 2011 was the only year that the biennial Milpirri was cancelled. *Milpirri 2011* was expected to be held at the Granites'; however, actually, it was only a workshop on a smaller scale. The reasons were the lack of funding and Sorry Business, with the dismal mood of the community due to successive deaths of several important male Elders in the year. Another factor was a new policy of Lajamanu School, which did not permit Tracks to train students during class time.

A key feature of *Milpirri 2011* performed at a new basketball court without any banners was the inclusion of *kurlumpurrngu* (a wind instrument). During the fieldwork before the show, Doi was able to participate in the revival of the instrument and its performance, and he later found that it could contribute to interpreting the phenomenon of Milpirri. Doi had returned to Lajamanu with a *yidaki* (didgeridoo) bought in Darwin. At the Warnayaka Art Centre in Lajamanu, he showed it to the manager, who suddenly began to tell him that she had heard from Jerry Jangala that *yapa* also had a didgeridoo-like instrument in their tradition. Doi's interview with Jangala was the beginning of their restoration project of the rare instrument called *kurlumpurrngu*. This wind instrument can be classified under "423.121.11 without mouthpiece (Some alphorns)' or '423.121.21.38 without mouthpiece (Asia)" in the system created by von Hornbostel and Sachs (1961, 24–27). Three male Elders remembered the instrument, probably in the 1940s; according to Jangala's childhood memories, the *kurlumpurrngu* was used at a *purlapa* called *Jalurinjirri*. The following is a song of this type performed by Jerry Jangala and Teddy Jupurrurla.

Jalurinjirri Jalurinjirri,
Jalangkurrparnu Jarlangkurrparnu
(Calling all the nation. Come and join in the celebration!)

Kurlumpurrngu-na japipalyina,
Warluna matamatarla
(Let the Law shine out. Prevent the flame of culture from dying out.)
(see Doi 2016)

It was performed on advice by Jangala, who (since our visit to his outstation) had been willing to do the rare male ceremony despite the atmosphere of Sorry Business. While Doi was waiting for the performance with two *kurlumpurrngu*, one of which he had just finished making, Tim Newth and Jangala asked only him to dance with the musical instrument. However, he immediately asked Caleb Japanangka, who was supervising schoolchildren and waiting for his own turn at hip-hop dancing, for the favour of dancing the traditional *purlapa* with him. After the boys' and girls' hip-hop dances finished, there was a performance by three male Tracks instructors: David McMicken, Nick Power and Japanangka. Despite the absence of male Elders apart from Jangala, the audience was pleased by the traditional performance of *yawulyu* dancers with strong connection to Tracks Dance Company.

10 Milpirri: A revitalisation movement, a *purlapa* or a festival?

In October 2012, Doi returned to Lajamanu with several other ANU students to participate in Milpirri. Doi stayed there for a short time to confirm that Milpirri was back. The number of visitors, performers and variety of the program were all much greater than in 2011. The show had a formal theme of *Pulyaranyi* ("Winds of Change"), banners were added, and their designs were fully respected as per tradition. Tracks members stuck to their hip-hop dance, demonstrating more sophisticated fusion with traditional *yawulyu* songs and dances. Doi prepared *witi* for their performance and danced the *Witi* dance as in 2007 with his Yellow group brothers.

Conclusion

The title of this chapter asked what kind of phenomenon Milpirri is. It was motivated by a desire to revive ceremonial life, encourage school attendance, create an entertainment event that would attract visitors to Lajamanu and improve relations with the rest of Australia. In comparison with the lack of concern in the community in the 1970s, the loss of ceremonial activity stands out as the primary motivation for Milpirri today. This leads to the conclusion that Milpirri is a revitalisation movement. This interpretation also connects Milpirri with earlier attempts to revitalise the ceremonial life of the community. For example, the "New Business" introduced from north-western Australia in the late 1970s was intended to replace the old ceremonies transplanted from the Tanami Desert some 20 years earlier. Even the older *Kajirri* ceremony was probably an attempt to make the ceremonies brought from the Tanami more meaningful in the new context (Wild 1972). The revival of the instrument *kulumpurrngu* and the accompanying song and dance is another example thereof.

From the viewpoint of the school community, encouraging school attendance is the most important aspect of Milpirri. This argues for it being envisaged as part of the bilingual education program.[6] From the point of view of Tracks Dance Company and their teaching of hip-hop dances for inclusion in Milpirri, it is primarily for entertainment and engagement, parts of which could be presented outside the community. This suggests that Milpirri is a kind of *purlapa*, the least restricted singing and dancing event in traditional Warlpiri culture. Finally, by comparing it with the Garma Festival in eastern Arnhem Land – in part, the

---

6   For further information on bilingual education in Aboriginal communities in the Northern Territories, see Browne and Gibson (2021), Disbray et al. (2020) and Ross and Baarda (2017).

model for Milpirri – it can be considered a festival.[7] The people of Yirrkala, the hosts of Garma, seek to reach out to other Australians to share their culture and their point of view. Similarly, the people of Lajamanu seek to reach out to share their culture and their point of view with the rest of Australia, symbolised partly by the inclusion of the Australian coat of arms.

If considered a revitalisation movement, Milpirri may lack the extensive cultural reconstruction envisaged by Anthony Wallace (1956), who first formulated the concept, unless other innovations at Lajamanu are included. Thus, when the Lajamanu School was initially involved in Milpirri, school children were decorated and taught *purlapa* on the school grounds, and groups of children were taken on bush camps where they learned traditional dances, songs and stories and were taken on hunting trips for bush foods. These activities also favour the interpretation of Milpirri's part of the bilingual education program. Bilingual education is better conceived as bicultural education (or two-way schooling), which has had intermittent support from the Department of Education. Viewing it as a contemporary *purlapa*, with the performance of both traditional and contemporary songs and dances, is problematic due to its inclusion of elements of other non-*purlapa* elements such as *Jardiwanpa*, *Kurdiji* and *yawulyu*.

If seen as a festival, it must be compared with other Aboriginal festivals in the Northern Territory, including especially the Garma Festival. Having a clear function as a revitaliser in culture and education of the community, most of the aspects of Milpirri were not as successful as those of the prior Garma Festival, including the lack of camping facilities and other activities, including the bushwalking program, engagement with the environment of the festival site and accessibility to the remote community. There were many aspects in common between the two festivals, enough to assume that the metaphor "hot air and cold air" of Milpirri originated in the "salt water and fresh water" of Garma Festival. However, the parallel with the concept of an Aboriginal festival does not capture the distinctive essence of Milpirri.[8]

---

7   For a recent consideration of the implications of hip-hop videos made in Central Australian Aboriginal communities, see Dowsett (2021).

8   Parallels between Milpirri and the Japanese festivals (*matsuri*) might be considered regarding several aspects. The ideal of the Milpirri performance shares certain superficial and conceptual similarities with Japanese *matsuri*. These include the prominent use of fire in the night environment. The use of *matsuri* formats to revitalise song and dance genres through popular styles of music can be seen in modern *matsuri* in the latter's commercially successful dance competition, *Yosakoi-Sōran Matsuri*, which can provide analogues in the history of its creation and the functions of a community revitaliser, with the fusion of hip-hop music and traditional instruments (see Doi 2016 for further information about *matsuri* and its parallels with Milpirri).

10 Milpirri: A revitalisation movement, a *purlapa* or a festival?

Milpirri has had the effect of rekindling the interest of the younger Warlpiri generation in the waning traditions of the community. Another success of Milpirri is the colour system devised to represent semi-moiety affiliation, which teaches the children traditional Warlpiri marriage rules. These two aspects, which are important because they are areas of concern for Warlpiri Elders who see children not adopting them, justify the claim that Milpirri is a revitalisation movement, in addition to being an Aboriginal festival.

References

Ausdance. 2011. "Tracks Dance Company". http://ausdance.org.au/articles/details/tracks-dance-company

Australian Institute of Aboriginal Studies. 1981. *Symposium on Contemporary Aboriginal Religious Movement*. Unpublished papers deposited in Australian Institute of Aboriginal and Torres Strait Islander Studies, Canberra.

Biddle, Jennifer. 2005. "Milpirri: Jennifer Biddle in Discussion with Tracks Dance Company". https://epress.lib.uts.edu.au/journals/index.php/csrj/article/view/4421/4755

Biddle, Jennifer. 2019. "Milpirri: Activating the At-Risk". In *Energies in the Arts*, edited by Douglas Kahn, 351–371. Cambridge, Mass.: MIT Press.

Browne, Emma and Fiona Napaljarri Gibson. 2021. "Communities of Practice in the Warlpiri Triangle: Four Decades of Crafting Ideological and Implementational Spaces for Teaching in and of Warlpiri Language". *Languages* 6: article 68 (24 pages). https://doi.org/10.3390/languages6020068

Central Land Council, Nicolas Peterson, Patrick McConvell, Stephen Wild and Rod Hagen. 1978. *A Claim to Areas of Traditional Land by the Warlpiri and Katangarru-Kurinji*. Alice Springs: Central Land Council.

Curran, Georgia. 2020. *Sustaining Indigenous Songs: Contemporary Warlpiri Ceremonial Life in Central Australia*. New York: Berghahn Books.

Dail-Jones [Morais], Megan. 1984. "A Culture in Motion: A Study of the Interrelationship of Dancing, Sorrowing, Hunting, and Fighting as Performed by the Warlpiri Women of Central Australia". Master's thesis, University of Hawaii, Honolulu.

Doi, Yukihiro. 2016. Milpirri at Lajamanu: As an Intercultural Locus of Warlpiri Discourses with Others. PhD thesis, Australian National University, Canberra.

Disbray, Samantha, Carmel O'Shannessy, Gretel McDonald and Barbara Martin. 2020. "Talking Together: How Language Documentation and Teaching Practice Support Oral Language Development in Bilingual Education Programs". *International Journal of Bilingual Education and Bilingualism* 25(4): 1451–66.

Dowsett, Sudiipta Shamalii. 2021. "Sampling Ceremony: Hip-Hop Workshops and Intergenerational Cultural Production in the Central Australian Desert". *The Asia Pacific Journal of Anthropology* 22(2–3): 184–202.

Dussart, Françoise. 2000. *The Politics of Ritual in an Aboriginal Settlement: Kinship, Gender, and the Currency of Knowledge.* Washington: Smithsonian Institution Press.

Japanangka, Maxwell Walma Tasman, dir, and Carmel O'Shannessy, dir. 2020. *Kaja-Warnu-Jangka: From the Bush.* Yuendumu: Pintubi Anmatjere Warlpiri Media and Communications. https://vimeo.com/417511570

Patrick, Stephen Jampijinpa, Miles Holmes and L.A. Box. 2008. *Ngurra-Kurlu: A Way of Working with Warlpiri People.* Alice Springs: Desert Knowledge CRC.

Ross, Tess and Wendy Baarda. 2017. "Starting Out at Yuendumu School: Teaching in our Own Language". In *History of Bilingual Education in the Northern Territory*, edited by Brian C. Devlin, Samantha Disbray and Nancy R.F. Devlin, 247–257. Singapore: Springer.

Shannon, Cynthia. 1971. "Walpiri Women's Music: A Preliminary Study". Bachelor of Arts thesis, Monash University, Clayton.

Tracks Dance Company. 2009. "Milpirri 09 (Jurntu)". http://tracksdance.com.au/milpirri-1

Tracks Dance Company. 2012–2023. "Tracks". https://tracksdance.com.au/

Tracks Dance Company. 2023 "Story Behind Milpirri". https://tracksdance.com.au/landing/story-behind-milpirri.

von Hornbostel, Erich M. and Curt Sachs. 1961. "Classification of Musical Instruments". Translated by Anthony Baines and Klaus P. Wachsmann. *The Galpin Society Journal* 14: 3–29.

Wallace, Anthony F.C. 1956. "Revitalization Movements". *American Anthropologist* 58: 264–81.

Warlpiri Women from Yuendumu and Georgia Curran. 2017. *Yurntumu-Wardingki Juju-Ngaliya-Kurlangu Yawulyu: Warlpiri Women's Songs from Yuendumu* [including DVD]. Batchelor: Batchelor Institute Press.

Wild, Stephen. 1972. "The Role of the Katjirri (GADJARI) among the Walpiri in Transition". *Seminars 1971*, 110–134. Clayton: Centre for Research in Aboriginal Affairs, Monash University.

Wild, Stephen. 1975. Walbiri Music and Dance in Their Social and Cultural Nexus. PhD thesis, Indiana University, Bloomington, Indiana.

Wild, Stephen. 1984. "Warlbiri Music and Culture: Meaning in a Central Australian Song Series". In *Problems and Solutions: Occasional Essays in Musicology Presented to Alice M. Moyle*, edited by Jamie C. Kassler and Jill Stubington, 186–203. Sydney: Hale & Iremonger.

Index

Aboriginal Tent Embassy, Canberra 116, 118, 119
Adelaide trip 299–301
Alekarenge (Ali Curung) xxii, 42, 88, 142, 145, 149, 150, 165, 269
Alice Springs (Mparntwe) xxiii, 7, 56, 88
Alyawarr 7, 232, 233
ancestral beings 21, 262, 264, 287, 299
Ancestral Dancing Women 269
Ancestral Fire Dreaming 287–305, 312
Anmatyerr 7, 65, 101, 148, 207, 218, 219, 258
Ara Irititja 40
Arandic languages, 10, 180, 196, 207, 208
    Warnajarra using words from 209, 218–21, 238
archival engagement 18
archiving documentation 31–50
    digital platforms 33, 40, 41, 46–8
    film 33, 45, 46, 72, 113, 264
    future generations, for 48–50
    on-Country 19, 31–50
    photographs 40, 42, 46, 47, 49
    recordings 38, 42, 45 *see also* recordings
    videoconferencing 37

Warlpiri Media Archive 19, 33, 38–41, 44
Australian Institute for Aboriginal and Torres Strait Islander Studies (AIATSIS)
    archives 33, 38, 41–5, 72, 113, 211, 264
    research 37

"Balgo Business" 313
Barr, Grace 47
barriers to intergenerational transmission 15–16
Barwick, Linda 25, 31, 33, 39, 41, 42, 53, 112, 142–6, 149, 150, 152, 154, 166, 171–89, 305
Barrett, Murray 33, 41
Batty, David 37
Bell, Diane 34
Benesh movement notation 215–16, 251
Betz, David 74
Biddle, Jennifer 33, 34, 41
Black Plum (Yawakiyi) 85, 86, 89
body decorations
    Minamina 65, 115, 121, 129–31, 137–41
    recording of painting 115
    relationship with dance and song text 211–15

body decorations (*continued*)
    Warnajarra 211–15
    Wulpararri 64, 65, 66
Booker, Lauren 46
Box, Alan 310
Broadcasting for Remote Aboriginal Communities Scheme (BRACS) 36
Brown, Jean Napanangka 116
Brown, Joyce Napangardi 130, 141
Brown Nampijinpa, Marjorie 211
Brown Nungarrayi, Edna 151, 152
Brown, Peggy Nampijinpa 6, 25, 103, 104–6, 115, 141
Bush Mechanics 37

Cadden, Anna 113, 114
Campbell, Liam 278
Carrell, Victor 45
Carrumbo (film) 45
Central Australia Aboriginal Media Association (CAAMA) 33
Central Land Council 17, 20, 26, 79, 83, 255, 274, 285
ceremonies 1–10
    passing on knowledge of 6, 15–16
changes in musical settings 126
Charles, Denis 53
Christian songs 311, 313
Cockatoo Creek 33, 39, 45, 201
community engagement 18–19
community-led revitalisation ideas 16–19
    archival resources 18
    documentation of songs and ceremonies 18
    performance spaces and occasions 17
    promoting to wider audience 18–19
    supporting existing ceremonial contexts 17
Coniston Johnny 78
constitutional referendum (1967) 87
Cooke, Henry 310
Country xxv, 4, 15
cross-cultural advocacy 291–9
Curran, Georgia 25, 31, 33, 34, 41, 53, 60, 79, 83, 85, 103, 112, 113, 265, 266, 268, 304, 305

dance camps 17, 46, 47, 115, 119, 124, 125, 126, 199, 201, 252
Daniels, Dolly Nampijinpa 21, 45, 137, 138, 283, 288–305
Desert Reggae style 311
Dickenson Napurrurla, Ada 151, 152
digging sticks 107, 109, 130, 141, 225
digital platforms 33, 40, 41, 46–8
Dixon Japaljarri (Jalyirri), Pharlap 271
DJ Bacon Mix 321
DJ Shadow 319, 323
documentation 18
    archiving 19, 31–50
    history of Warlpiri songs and ceremonies 33–4
Doi, Yukihiro 33, 309, 310, 314–19, 324, 325
Dreaming *see jukurrpa*
dreaming "new" songs 6, 20
Driver Nakamarra, Elaine 152
Driver Nungarrayi, Irene 151, 152
Dussart, Françoise 6, 34, 41, 265–6, 287

Edible Seeds *see* Ngurlu (Edible Seeds)
Egan, Jeannie Nungarrayi 83, 112, 113, 123

Index

Elders xxv
  control of dissemination of knowledge 7
  establishing new ceremonies 271
  instructing young generations 6, 17, 49, 104
Elkin, A.P. 42
Ellis, Catherine 21, 237–8
Emu (Yankirri) *jukurrpa* 20, 89–99
Endangered Languages Archive 34
Endurance Show 318
expert knowledge
  ancestral ceremonies and stories 155–6
  edible seeds 155
  Jipiranpa Country and songlines 157–8
  musical knowledge 159–60

Fight Fire with Fire documentary 35
fire ceremonies *see* Jardiwanpa; Ngajakula
First Nations Media 40
Fisher, Connie Nakamarra 112
Fisher, Simon Japangardi 19, 25, 31, 38–41, 43, 45, 48, 63
Fishhook Nakamarra, Maudie 152
Fleming, Rosie Nangala 289, 299, 301

Gallagher, Coral Napangardi 103, 114
Gallagher, Enid Nangala 47, 166
Gallagher, Jack Jampijinpa 289, 298
Garma Festival 318, 325, 326
Gibson, Barbara Nakamarra (Nakakut) 20, 40, 84–99
Gibson, Beryl 84, 89, 91, 95
Gillen, Francis 263, 265, 267
Glowczewski, Barbara 6, 33, 84, 85, 86, 89, 92, 95

grammatical reduplication 225
Granites, Alice Napanangka 115, 116, 117, 141
Granites, Cecily Napanangka 115, 124, 141, 304
Granites, Dolly Nampijinpa *see* Daniels, Dolly Nampijinpa
Granites, Elsie Napanangka 112, 113, 115, 116, 141
Granites, Geraldine Napanangka 112, 113
Granites, Judy Nampijinpa 21, 109, 113, 121, 128, 284, 288–305
Granites, Kurt Japanangka 35, 53
Granites, Lorraine Nungarrayi 5, 25, 113, 114, 130, 141, 252–3
Granites, Lynette Nampijinpa 5, 45, 112, 113, 120, 121, 123, 141, 285
Granites, Rex Japanangka 5, 25, 26, 45
Granites, Valda Napanangka 112, 113
Grant, Catherine 11
  Musical Vitality and Endangerment Framework 11–16, 301
Green, Jennifer 34
Green Nampijinpa, Maggie 151
Gurindji 7

Haasts Bluff 7, 10, 54
Hale, Ken 6, 33, 60, 79
Hall, Basil 57
Harris, Amanda 45
Henwood, Alice Nampijinpa 6, 25, 54–5, 166
hip-hop dancing xli, 22, 315, 319, 323, 324

Holmes Napangardi, Sarah 33, 146, 147, 153, 156, 165–7, 171, 173, 177, 178, 183
Hooker, Beatty Napanangka 90, 91, 97
Hooker Creek *see* Lajamanu

Incite Arts 47, 115
Indigenous Ranger programs 165–6
Initiated Man (Ngarrka) 90
initiation ceremonies xxiv, xli, 8, 9, 16, 312
intergenerational transmission xxii, 7, 12, 15
   barriers to 15–16
intracultural gatherings 272

Jagst, Lothar xxv
Jakamarra, Long Paddy 36, 59, 74, 76, 79
Jampijinpa, Joe 61, 66
Jampijinpa, Wanyu 289, 298
Jangala, Joe Bird 147, 149
Janganpa (Possum) 85, 88–9
Janyingki 65, 78, 123
Japaljarri, Andy 271
Japaljarri, Chicken Jack 271
Japaljarri, Dinny 73
Japaljarri, Engineer Jack 149, 270, 271
Japaljarri, Jimmy Newcastle 271
Japaljarri, Long Paddy 271
Japaljarri, Peter (Karlijangka) 70, 71, 72, 76, 79
Japaljarri, Wally 59, 67, 72, 77
Japanangka, Arthur 73
Japanangka, Caleb 324
Japanangka, Jack 73
Japanangka, Paddy Lewis 73
Japanangka, Pompey 73
Japanangka, Wirtilki 271

Japangardi, Andy 73
Japangardi, George 73
Japangardi, Sammy 60
Jardiwanpa xxiv, xli, 9, 10, 21, 27, 28, 49, 103, 149, 255, 257, 260–8, 279, 299, 317
   fire ceremony 257, 270, 279, 312
   social purpose 267
Jardiwanpa Yawulyu (book) 103
Jesus *purlapa* 311, 313
jilkaja xli, 10
Jipiranpa 21, 142, 145, 147, 150
   Ngurlu *yawulyu* 142, 145–66
Jones Nungarrayi, Nancy 152
juju-ngaliya xli
jukurrpa xxiv, xxv, xli, 1–9, 17, 21, 32, 44
Jungarrayi 255, 263, 264, 272, 316
Jungarrayi, Banjo 64, 71
Jungarrayi, Jimmy 64, 73
Jungarrayi, Long Mick 73, 271
jural public 77
Jurlarda (Sugar Bag) 208, 262, 275, 276, 277
Jurntu Purlapa 318
juyurdu 9

Kaja-Warnu-Jangka (documentary) 316
Kajirri 97, 301, 312, 325
Kankarlu xli, 26, 70, 76
kardiya xli, 39, 322
Karlarlukarri, Fred Japaljarri 254
karli 321
Karlijangka 70, 71, 72, 76, 79
Karnanganja 89, 90, 322
Katakarinja, Elizabeth Napaljarri 31, 38, 39, 43
Kaytetye 7, 21, 146, 150, 207
   language 208, 218, 227, 228, 237

Kell, Jodie 47
Kelly, Francis Jupurrurla 35, 37, 41, 53
Kelly, Luke 257
Kennedy, Lucy Napaljarri 290
kinship 96, 279, 315
    fire and 265, 266, 279
    networks 96, 133, 266
    rights 108
Kintore 270, 271
kirda xxiv, xli, 26, 27, 96, 267, 278
    Minamina 110, 113, 119, 130
    Ngajakula 255, 261, 269
    Ngapa 54, 81, 83, 285
    Ngarlu 101, 151
    Ngunulurru 254
    Ngurlu 85, 149, 159
    Pawu 203, 205
    Warlukurlangu 285, 289
    Wulpararri 56, 61, 64, 69, 73, 77, 252
    Yankirri 104
    Yawakiyi 85
    Yinapaka 254
Kirrirdikirrawanu xli, 8
Kitson, Jimmy Jungarrayi 271
Kitson, Johnny 271
kukulypa 64
Kulpurlunu 93, 94, 97, 145, 146, 154
Kunajarrayi 65, 77
kunkurdakurdaku 125, 126
Kurapaka (blanket exchange) 319, 323
kurdaitcha birds 125–6
Kurdiji xxiv, xli, xlii, 8, 9, 17, 28, 49, 312, 316, 317, 318
kurdungurlu xxiv, xli, 26, 28, 96, 278
    Jariwanpa 103
    Minamina 112, 131
    Ngajakula 261, 269, 271
    Ngatijirri 203, 205
    Ngurlu 151, 159
    Patirlirri 203, 205
    Wulpararri 61, 63, 65, 66, 77
kurlumpurrngu 324
Kurrakurraja 264, 268, 273–4
kurruwalpa 86
kuruwarri xli, 2, 5, 6, 7
kuturu (ceremonial pole) 129

Lajamanu xxii, xxiii, 7, 17, 22, 26, 34, 82, 87, 94, 107, 264, 267, 307, 309
    Baptist Church 307, 310, 311
    Community School 310, 315, 326
    Milpirri xli, 17, 22, 309–27
    songs and dances (1969–1980) 311–13
Lajamanu Bushrangers 311
Lajamanu Teenage Band 311, 315, 319
Lake Mackay 7
Lambert, Benjamin 277, 280
Lander River 257, 258, 269, 307
Lander Warlpiri Cultural Mapping Project 257
Langdon, Molly Nampijinpa 289
Langton, Lucky Nampijinpa 141
Langton, Marcia 37
Laramba 7
Lauder Nungarrayi, Nancy 152
Laughren, Mary 33, 113, 122, 143, 145–7, 150, 153, 154, 165, 166, 171–89, 207, 211, 238, 268
Law of all Warlpiri 21
Lechleitner, Trish 47
lexical reduplication 223–5
Long, Janet Nakamarra 208

Long, Teddy Jupurrurla 257, 260, 261, 268, 271, 278, 279, 324
Luritja 7
Luther, Maurice Jupurrurla xxv

Macdonald, Gretel 147, 165, 167
Majardi (hairstring waistbelt) 211–16
Mangulpa 319, 320
Marlinja 262, 274
Marnakurrawarnu 312, 317
Marshall, Diana Nampijinpa 289, 298
Marshall, George Japangardi 298
Martin, Barbara Napanangka 61, 103, 110, 112–17, 130, 141
Martin, C. Jampijinpa 271
Martin Jampijinpa, Johnny 271
Martin Jangala, Fuzzy 203, 205
Martin, Kenneth Jungarrayi 319
Martin, Lucy Nampijinpa 203, 205, 211, 212
Martin, Peggy Nampijinpa 203, 205, 207, 208, 211–14, 238
Martin, Valerie Napaljarri 4, 19, 25, 31, 38, 42, 48, 53, 61
matrimoiety 315
McMicken, David 313, 314, 324
Meggitt, Mervyn 71, 272
meter 221–3
Michaels, Eric 37
Milky Way ceremony 61–78, 317
Milpirri xli, 17, 22, 309–27
    2005 314–16
    2007 316–18
    2009 318–23
    2011 and 2012 323–5
    children's involvement 315, 321, 323
    hip-hop dancing xli, 22, 315, 319, 323, 324
    revitalisation movement 315, 327
    songs and dances (1969–1980) 311–13
Milwayi (Central Bandy-Bandy) 262, 275, 276
Minamina 78, 107–32
    jukurrpa 26, 110, 123
    kirda 110, 113, 119, 130
    kurdungurlu 112, 131
    men's songs 107
Minamina *yawulyu* 20, 65, 107–32
    body painting 65, 115, 121, 129–31, 137–41
    changes in musical settings 126
    dance camps 115, 118, 119, 124, 125, 126
    kurdaitcha birds and cultural values 125–6
    language and themes 120–3
    place names 123
    recordings 108, 110–20
    ritual power theme 122–3
    sexual content 124, 125
    story of ancestral women 109–10
    swaying movement 120–1
    text-rhythm to melody layout 127–9, 136
Miyikampi 146, 270
Moon Dreaming 222
Morais, Megan 21, 207, 208, 211, 212, 214, 215
Morrison Nakamarra, Amy 152
Morton, Helen Napurrurla 203, 207, 208, 211
Morton, John 265, 279
Mosey, Anne 45, 46
Mount Barkly *see* Pawu
Mount Doreen Station 27, 54, 59, 81, 83, 199, 285
Mount Liebig 7, 270, 271

Mount Theo/Puturlu *jukurrpa* 103, 115, 116
Moyle, Alice 8, 33
Moyle, Richard 108
Mparntwe (Alice Springs) xxiii, 7, 56, 88
Mudburra 70, 85, 267, 272, 273, 278
multimodal nature of songs 16
Munga 65, 66, 70–1, 74, 78, 79
Mungamunga 97
Munn, Nancy 59
Murphy, Brian 142
Musical Vitality and Endangerment Framework (MVEF) 11, 301
   assessment of Warlpiri songs 12–15
musical vitality of song genres 11–15

Nakakut *see* Gibson, Barbara Nakamarra
Nakamarra, Beryl 254
Nakamarra Jackson, Annette 152
Nampijinpa, Judy 138
Nampijinpa, Leah 211
Nampijinpa, Marilyn 211
Nangala, Judy-Peggy 289, 292
Nangala-Napurrurla, Marjorie Limbiari 152
Nangala, Tilo 289, 299, 301
Nangala, Winnie 289
Napanangka, Beatty 90, 91, 97
Napanangka, Helen 137
Napangardi, Judy 137
Napangardi, Lillian 151, 152
Napangardi, Maggie 137
Napangardi, Mary 138
Napangardi, Millie 137
Napangardi, Peggy 152
Napangardi, Polly 138
Napangardi, Rosie 152
Napangardi, Yarraya 115
Napurrurla, Ivy 152
Napurrurla, Jeanie 137, 138
Napurrurla, Lorraine 152
Nash, David 33, 34, 60, 74, 76, 79, 145, 149, 152, 167, 303
Nelson, Harry Jakamarra 17, 25, 27, 31, 41, 45, 49, 53, 267, 278, 303
Nelson, Paddy 36
Nettl, Bruno 7
"New Business" 313, 325
Newcastle Nampijinpa, Suzie 151
Newth, Tim 313, 314, 315, 324
Ngajakula xxiv, xlii, 9, 10, 18, 21, 254, 257–80, 312
   2018 performance 274–7
   anthropological accounts 263–8
   Dreamings 270, 275–7
   early exchanges 271–3
   fire ceremonies 259, 263, 265, 266, 269, 270, 279

Ngajakula (*continued*)
   history in Lander Warlpiri region 268–73
   kirda 255, 261, 269
   kurdungurlu 261, 269, 271
   learning about songs 278–9
   linguistic and musical features 277–8
   north-eastern Ngajakula songline 273–4
   recording 255, 260–2, 274–7
   revitalisation project 254
   sites 258, 260, 274–5
   songs 258, 273–7
   stories 273–4
   widows mourning 267, 269
   written history 263–8

Ngaliya (southern Warlpiri) xxii, 268
Ngapa (Rain/Water) *jukurrpa* 20, 54, 81, 83, 90–9, 104, 115, 145, 149, 199–200, 285
Ngapangarna (Water bird) 262, 275, 276, 277
Ngardilypa (north-western Warlpiri) xxii
Ngarlu (Sugarleaf) *jukurrpa* 101
Ngarnalkurru 270, 271, 273, 274
Ngatijirri (Budgerigar) *jukurrpa* 101, 203, 205, 252, 266
Ngunulurru 254, 263, 270, 273, 274
Ngurlu (Edible Seeds)
    expert knowledge of 155
    jukurrpa 85, 149, 201
    kirda 151, 159, 201
    kurdungurlu 151, 159
Ngurlu *yawulyu* 142, 145–98
    Edible Seed Dreamings 149
    expert knowledge 155–60
    recordings 142, 145, 149–53
    standard features of rhythmic text 160–2
    text-setting features 164–5
    themes of songs 154
    transgression of musical norms 163–4
    verses and rhythms 171–98
Ngurra-kurlarniyarra (home in the south) xxiv
ngurra-kurlu 314, 316, 318
Ngurra-Kurlu: A Way of Working with Warlpiri People (book) 314
Ngurra-yatujumparra (home in the north) xxiv
night Dreaming 63
North Tanami Band 311, 315, 317, 319
Northern Territory Writers Festival 115, 118, 119, 127
Nungarrayi, Emma 295
Nungarrayi, Maudie 203
Nungarrayi, Ruth 205
Nyirrpi xxii, xxiii, 28, 54, 82
nyurnukurlangu (healing songs) 129
O'Keeffe Napurrurla, Mary 151, 152
Oldfield, Nancy Napurrurla 42
Oldfield, Ruth Napaljarri 47, 101–2, 120
on-Country archiving 19, 31–50
O'Shannessy, Carmel 34
Panungkarla (Ramsay's Python) 262, 264, 275–7
Papunya 7, 88
parnpa xlii, 9, 10
partial reduplication 227–37
    from left edge, base after reduplicant 230
    from left edge, base before reduplicant 229
    from right edge 231
    partial line 236–7
    triplication 232–6
Patirlirri 203, 205
Patrick, Jerry Jangala 238, 268, 307, 310, 324
Patrick, Steven Wanta Jampijinpa 17, 22, 309–11, 314, 319
patricouples 65, 107, 315, 316
patrimoieties 64, 208, 263
Patterson, Zac Jakamarra 319
Pawu 94, 97, 203, 205, 207, 209, 237
Pawurrinji 21, 142, 146, 149, 150, 153, 270
performance 77

choosing whether to perform 301–2
payment for 300
spaces and occasions 17
Peterson, Nicolas 33, 39, 59, 63, 70, 85, 108, 112, 113, 263–7, 268, 274, 302, 304, 305
Peterson, Rosalind 79, 108, 112, 119, 129
Phillip Creek 42
Pintubi Anmatjere Warlpiri Media and Communications (PAW Media) 19, 29, 32
   formation as Warlpiri Media Association 20, 34–7
   Warlpiri Media Archive 19, 33, 38–41
Pintupi 7, 8, 270
Plum (Yawakiyi) 85, 86, 89
poetic reduplication 226–7
Possum (Janganpa) 85, 88–9
Power, Nick 324
Presley, Gordon Japangardi 280
promoting to wider audience 18–19
Purdujurru (Brush-Tailed Bettong) 262, 275, 276–7
purlapa xlii, 9, 17, 22, 42, 61, 63, 116, 238, 298, 312, 318, 325
   Christian words 311, 313
Purluwanti 262–8, 271, 273–4, 276, 277

Rain *jukurrpa see* Ngapa (Rain/Water) *jukurrpa*
recordings
   archives, for 38, 42, 45, 46
   Minamina *yawulya* 108, 110–20
   Ngajakula songlines 255, 260–2, 274–7

Ngurlu *yawulyu* 142, 145, 149–53
Warnajarra *yawulyu* 210–11
reduplication 223–37
   grammatical 225
   lexical 223–5
   partial 227–37
   poetic 226–7
   triplication 232–6
   word repetition 225–6
Reece, Laurie 263
rhythmic texts xxv
Rice Nungarrayi, Jessie 152
Rice, Thomas Jangala 83, 112, 113, 123
rilyi 64
Rio Tinto Aboriginal Fund 317
Robertson Napangardi, Judith 146, 153, 167
Ross, Dwayne Jupurrula 260, 280
Ross, Theresa Napurrurla 19, 146, 153, 158, 167, 171, 177,
Ryder, "Cowboy" George Jungarrayi 254–62, 268, 274, 279

Sahlins, Marshall 279
Sandall, Roger 72, 263
Satellite Dreaming documentary 35, 36
senior singers xxix
Simpson, Jane 145, 149, 167
Simpson Napangardi, Jessie 146, 147, 153, 165, 166, 167
Sims, Bessie Nakamarra 29
Sims, Otto Jungarrayi 25, 29, 32, 45, 53, 60, 61
Sims, Paddy Japaljarri 20, 29, 36, 56–7, 60, 61, 63, 64, 71–4, 77–9
Singing the Milky Way (film) 74
skin names xxiii, xxiv, 96

snake vine 124
song genres 9
song item xxv
song set xxv
songline xxv, 21
Sorry Business 267, 323, 324
Southern Ngaliya dance camps 17, 47, 115, 119, 124, 125, 126, 199, 201, 252
Spencer Baldwin 263, 265, 267
spirit-child (*kurruwalpa*) 86
spirit language 217, 278
Spotted Nightjar 125, 126
Stewart, Paddy Japaljarri 36, 57
Sutton, Peter 6
Sydney University 40, 41
    Archive 42, 43
    Power Gallery 56

Tanami Desert xxii, 3, 7, 17, 45, 47, 85, 87, 150, 274, 313
Tennant Creek xxii, 10, 42, 263, 269
Ti-Tree 7, 34, 82, 201
Tindale, Norman 33, 39
Tracks Dance Company 17, 22, 310, 313–15, 318, 319, 324, 325
travels of initiated men *jukurrpa* 70–1
triplication 232–6
Turner, Lindsay Jampijinpa 289, 300
Turpin, Myfany 34, 147, 154, 159, 167, 182, 188, 207, 208, 211, 212
Two Snakes *see* Warnajarra (Two Snakes) *yawulyu*

verse xxv
Vaarzon-Morel, Petronella 257, 260, 268–71
Vitality and Change in Warlpiri Songs project 41

Wafer, Jim 257, 277
Wakirti (Hansen River Warlpiri) xxii, 42
Walker Napurrurla, Fanny 21, 142–58, 164–7, 171–89
Wallace, Anthony 326
walrajarra 109
Wampana (Wallaby) 85
Wantarri-tarri 317
Warawata xlii, 8
Warlpiri art movement 56
Warlpiri Encyclopaedic Dictionary xxv, 64, 158, 262, 278
Warlpiri interpretive system 94–9
Warlpiri land claim 20, 78, 87, 298, 309
Warlpiri language xxii
Warlpiri Media Archive 19, 33, 38–41, 44
Warlpiri Media Association (now PAW) 20, 32, 34–8
Warlpiri Media Committee 36
Warlpiri orthography xxv, 60
Warlpiri people xxii
Warlpiri regions 4, 7, 8, 209
Warlpiri skin names xxiii, xxiv, 96
Warlpiri social and musical context 7–10
Warlpiri Songlines project 83, 113
Warlpiri Triangle 317
Warlpiri Women from Yuendumu 18, 33, 34, 109, 110, 113, 124, 252
Warlpiri Women's Law and Culture meetings 45–6
Warlpiri Youth Development Aboriginal Corporation 83, 104, 115
Warlu (Ancestral Fire) *jukurrpa* 287
Warlukurlangu Art Centre 83

Warlukurlangu Artists Aboriginal
    Corporation 29, 56, 283
Warlukurlangu (Fire) *jukurrpa* 21,
    104, 287–305
    Adelaide trip 299–301
    cross-cultural advocacy, means of
        291–9
    Kaltukatjara trip 301–2
    kirda 285, 289
    performance 299–302
    ritual specialists 288–91
Warlukurlangu ranges 287, 288, 291,
    298
Warnajarra (Two Snakes) *yawulyu*
    207–51
    Benesh movement notation
        215–16, 251
    body decorations 211–15
    dance not related to text meaning
        216–17
    dance related to text meaning
        215–16
    identifying words in songs 217–
        18
    kirda 203, 205
    meter 221–3
    recordings 210–11
    reduplication 223–37
    relationship between design,
        dance and text 211–15
    verses 242–50
    vocabulary from neighbouring
        languages 218–21, 238
Warnayaka (central-northern
    Warlpiri) xxii, 309
Warrkakurrku (Mala Bore) 110
Warrmala (western Warlpiri) xxii
Warumungu 10, 263
Waruwarta 317
watirirririrri xlii, 27

Watson, Tommy Jangala 81–2
Wawulya (south-western Warlpiri)
    xxii
Wayne, Maisie Napurrurla 201–2
Wayne, Nellie Nangala 199–200
widows mourning 267, 269
Wild, Stephen 6, 33, 34, 45, 113,
    309–14, 319
Williams, Audrey Napanangka 115,
    116
Williams, Peter Japanangka 280
Williams, Selina Napanangka 212,
    214
Willowra xxii, 7, 18, 21, 82, 88, 203,
    205, 208, 211, 261, 268, 270,
    279
    Learning Centre 274, 280
winter solstice ceremony 20, 59–79,
    269
    body decorations 64, 65, 66
    pattern of daily activity 64–70
    performance and jural public 77
winter solstice ceremony (*continued*)
    right to hold 72–3
    songs 74–6
    succession 77
    travels of initiated men 70–1
    Wulpararri (Milky Way) 59–78
wirlki 321
Wirrimanu (Balgo) xxiii, 88, 108
witi poles 70, 224, 317, 319, 320,
    325
women's ceremonies *see yawulyu*
Women's Law and Culture meetings
    17, 45–6
Wood, Murray 36
wooden eggs 95, 96, 98
word repetition 225–6
Wulpararri (Milky Way) ceremony
    59–78, 252, 317

Yakiriya 89, 90, 91, 95, 97, 98
Yankirri (Emu) *jukurrpa* 20, 89–99, 104
yapa xlii
Yarlpiri (Lander River Warlpiri) xxii
Yarlpurru-rlangu (Two Age-Brothers) *yawulyu* 115, 117
Yarripiri (Inland Taipan) 85, 266
Yarripiri's Journey 27
Yawakiyi (Black Plum) 85, 86, 89
yawulyu xlii, 10, 15–18, 21, 22, 312
    decline in women-only subject matter 123–4
    decorations/designs 61, 65
    documentation 203, 205, 215
    Minamina 20, 65, 107–32
    Ngurlu 142, 145–66
    songs 101–2
    videos for learning 46
    Warnajarra 207–51
yidaki (didgeridoo) 324
yilpinji xlii, 10, 124, 312
Yinapaka 254, 262, 270, 274
yinkardakurdaku 125
Yuelamu 7
Yuendumu xxii, xxiii, 18, 19, 21, 26, 27, 28, 34, 35, 54, 56, 59, 107
    Council 287
    Mediation Committee 285
    Men's Museum 27, 83
    Men's Night Patrol 83
    Old People's Program 46, 199, 252
    Sports Weekends 38
    Women's Centre 45, 46, 201
Yuendumu Doors 56, 57
Yuendumu School 27, 38, 47, 56, 81, 83
    Country visits 47
yukurrukurru (dancing board) 129

Yumurrpa (white yam) 201
Yurntumu-Wardingki Juju-Ngaliya-Kurlangu Yawulyu
    book 113, 115, 199, 200
    DVD 113–14, 118, 119, 200, 252

www.ingramcontent.com/pod-product-compliance
Lightning Source LLC
Chambersburg PA
CBHW061123010526
44114CB00029B/2991